What Smart Trainers Know

The Secrets of Success
from the World's Foremost Experts

Lorraine L. Ukens

Editor

JOSSEY-BASS/PFEIFFER
A Wiley Company
San Francisco

Published by

JOSSEY-BASS/PFEIFFER
A Wiley Company
San Francisco

350 Sansome Street, 5th Floor
San Francisco, California 94104-1342
(415) 433-1740; Fax (415) 433-0499
(800) 274-4434; Fax (800) 569-0443

www.pfeiffer.com

Library of Congress Cataloging-in-Publication Data

What smart trainers know : the secrets of success from the world's foremost experts/
      Lorraine L. Ukens, editor.
            p. cm.
      Includes bibliographical references and index.
      ISBN 0-7879-5386-5 (alk. paper)
      1. Employees—Training of. 2. Employee training personnel.
   3. Training. 4. Learning. I. Ukens, Lorraine L.
      HF5549.5.T7 W478 2001
      658.3'124—dc21   2001000183

Printed in the United States of America

We at Jossey-Bass strive to use the most environmentally sensitive paper stocks available to us. Our publications are printed on acid-free recycled stock whenever possible, and our paper always meets or exceeds
minimum GPO and EPA requirements.

Acquiring Editor: Matthew Holt
Director of Development: Kathleen Dolan Davies
Editor: Rebecca Taff
Production Editor: Dawn Walker
Manufacturing Supervisor: Becky Carreño
Cover Design: Jennifer Hines
Illustrations: Lotus Art

Printing   10   9   8   7   6   5   4   3   2   1

CONTENTS

iii

INTRODUCTION

So, what DO smart trainers know?

Lots! In this one-stop compilation of some of the topics that are most important to training and development professionals, you, the reader, can easily tap into a wealth of knowledge and the expertise, insights, and suggestions from many of the leaders in the human resource development (HRD) field.

Because the HRD field is multidisciplinary, it requires practitioners to have a working knowledge of a variety of topics. However, many professionals in the field at this time do not have formal preparation in some of these critical areas. Often, trainers are chosen simply because they are subject-matter experts. They must find many resources, such as books, magazines, and workshops, to obtain the necessary background to help them perform the many functions of their new role effectively. Those practitioners who do attend academic programs may find that there is so much information to be covered that there is time only for a cursory look at many of the topics, especially in regard to training and development issues.

This book provides a comprehensive look at the topics most pertinent to human resource development. It is an aid for new practitioners who want to develop a working knowledge of the field, as well as an opportunity for long-time practitioners to examine various experts' views in one convenient package. All of the authors in this collection are highly regarded experts in their fields, and thus the collection represents some of the best knowledge available.

The thirty-five topics that were chosen do not cover every issue of concern to the HRD professional. Rather, they were selected because they are critical as a basic foundation. The authors present important theoretical research that has been translated into practical applications for the workplace. A list of recommended readings is provided after each chapter to assist the reader in locating additional information. The chapters are categorized into the following five sections.

Strategic Training and Development. This section introduces the reader to how training and development practices are aligned with all aspects of the organization, as well as to the emerging trends that will drive the future of HRD. The authors examine performance improvement, HRD trends, professional roles, learning organizations, change management, organizational culture, and legal issues.

Assessment and Evaluation. This section addresses the importance of examining organization and individual needs, identifying appropriate interventions, then determining whether the desired performance outcomes have been realized. Topics include: conducting a needs assessment, identifying performance interventions, analyzing worker performance, competency models, Kirkpatrick's evaluation model, return on investment, transfer of learning, and performance appraisals.

Training and Development Design. Program design and learning theory are emphasized in this section, including instructional design, learning styles, adult learning, design of training programs, presentation skills, and the role of motivation in the learning environment.

Training and Development Methods. In this section, authors address the issue of how to conduct effective training and development interventions using a variety of delivery methods. Some of the topics covered are active learning, coaching skills, facilitation, games and activities, self-directed learning, multimedia and online training, and distance learning.

Employee and Organizational Development. The final section is focused on special issues of importance to the development of the individual worker as well as to that of the organization as a whole. Here the reader can explore the issues of diversity, leadership development, teamwork, employee development planning, new employee orientation, mentoring, and rewards and recognition.

◌

To the contributors,

I would like to personally thank each of you for giving of your time and effort so that others could share your knowledge and expertise. Without your commitment, this project would never have been possible.

To the reader,

This book attempts to synthesize theory with practical application for all levels of practitioners. I hope that what you read helps you to grow as an HRD professional and fans your enthusiasm about this dynamic field.

Lorraine L. Ukens
Editor

PART ONE

STRATEGIC TRAINING AND DEVELOPMENT

CHAPTER ONE

Shifting from Training to Performance

James C. Robinson
Chairman, Partners in Change, Inc.

Dana Gaines Robinson
President, Partners in Change, Inc.

In the 1990s, many training functions shifted from a focus on training to one on performance improvement. This shift required some trainers to partner with line managers for the purpose of improving on-the-job performance in support of business goals. For trainers to make this transition, they had to reallocate their time and become proficient at conducting performance analyses and implementing solutions. At the same time, training departments were (1) redesigning the process that they used when supporting line managers; (2) clarifying roles of performance consultants and others in the department; (3) providing tools and techniques required for performance improvement; and (4) developing the skills required of those in the departments. Thoughtful planning and commitment to the transition enables the performance consultant and the performance department to be viewed as a strategic business partner to management.

INTRODUCTION

Smart trainers know that they must continuously be alert to the winds of change that are blowing within their field of expertise and the organizations that they support. They are quick to identify:

- The forces that impact their profession;
- The trends initiated by those forces;

- The future state toward which they must transition; and
- The road to travel to reach that future state.

Let us now take a look at how smart trainers manage the journey from training to performance improvement. First, we must clarify that this journey is really a shift from providing primarily training as the solution to problems in the organization to providing a carefully selected set of appropriate solutions that address the performance problem. The rationale for this new way of thinking is the realization that no single solution, whether in the area of training, human resources, process redesign, or any other area, will produce a significant improvement in a performance problem, because rarely is a performance problem the result of a single cause. Therefore, single solutions are woefully inadequate.

THE SHIFT

As early as the 1960s, Tom Gilbert, author of *Human Competence: Engineering Worthy Performance* (1978), recognized the inadequacy of single solutions. While some within training were involved in performance improvement activities in the 1970s and 1980s, it was not until the 1990s that the shift picked up momentum. Two somewhat different, but parallel, forces propelled this shift, which continues today.

Change in Business

One of these forces is the dramatic change taking place in the business community. The globalization of business generates intense competition and results in organizations utilizing their human resources much more effectively to compete. Thus management is more willing to examine various avenues for unleashing the potential of the organization's workforce. In other words, people are becoming the competitive edge in many organizations (Robinson & Robinson, 1998).

In addition, the skill requirements of the workforce are increasing in response to rapid technological changes. More sophisticated equipment and more complicated work processes require more competent workers. In the period between 1981 and 1993, the number of workers receiving formal training increased 45 percent (Bassi, Benson, & Cheney, 1996).

Dissatisfaction with Training

The other main force driving change in the field today is the growing dissatisfaction with training activities and the lack of results from training. Several factors drive this growing dissatisfaction.

First, management's interest in workforce development results in considerably more financial resources being expended. In the United States alone, over sixty billion dollars in direct costs were being spent each year by business organizations at the end of the 1990s. If the costs associated with employees' time off the job to attend training courses were added to this figure, the amount would grow to over two hundred billion dollars per year (Robinson & Robinson, 1998).

Second, while training costs continue to rise, there has been little or no discernible improvement in the results from training. Most of the investment in organizational training and development has been wasted because much of the knowledge and many of the skills gained in training (well over 80 percent by some estimates) is not being fully applied by those employees on the job (Broad & Newstrom, 1992).

Finally, line managers in most organizations see the training function as an expense rather than added value. In addition, those in the training community have been unable to demonstrate clear value because the results of training activities have had little impact on job behavior.

These major forces have prompted the innovators within the training community to shift to a focus on performance improvement. This shift goes far beyond improvement in the technology of training (for example, improvement in needs assessments, gap and cause analysis, and the selection of solutions). Instead, a shift in how the training function works with line managers is required. The elements of this shift are described in Table 1.1.

Partnership with Management

The most dramatic change associated with the shift to performance has been the manner in which trainers—now often called performance consultants—work with line managers.

Previously, trainers had operated either as "experts," or as "pairs of hands." The "expert" approach resulted in training functions determining what courses they would offer, the content of those courses, and how the courses would be delivered. As "pairs of hands," trainers implemented requests from management for specific topics and courses, whether or not training was really needed.

Now, however, trainers operate as performance consultants. They initiate and develop relationships with the key managers within the organization over a period of time. The consultants become knowledgeable about the "business of the business" and, when interfacing with management, use business language. Performance consultants are quick to respond to requests, and they alert management when training alone is not appropriate. In fact, research by Partners in Change, Inc., indicates that effective performance consultants spend 18 percent of their time forming, building, and maintaining relationships with key managers within their organizations.

Previously, both the training function and line managers saw training as a "nice to have." For example, managers might feel that interpersonal communications training would enhance the way people worked together, but they would

Table 1.1. Elements Required to Shift from a Traditional Training Approach to a Performance Approach

Traditional Approach	Performance Approach
Focuses on the solution that is implemented; the solution (training) is the end	Focuses on what people need to do; the solution is a means to an end
Can work independently of client partnerships	Must be partnered to a client (that is, owner of the business need)
Linked to *training* need	Linked to *business* need
Event-oriented	Process-oriented
Reactive	Proactive and reactive
Biased to a solution	Bias-free of solutions
Relies on single solution (generally the consultant's specialty)	Relies on multiple solutions
Front-end assessment is optional; identifying work environment barriers to desired performance rarely done	Front-end assessment is mandatory; performance gaps and causes for gaps are identified
Evaluation of solution typically occurs	Evaluation of the performance and operational results is done

expect little or no impact on business results. However, performance consultants use a performance improvement approach. They first clarify the business need and how management measures the achievement of that need. Once this business goal has been defined, the performance consultants work with line management to answer the question, "What must people do more, better, or differently if this business goal is to be achieved?" This ensures that the performance improvement effort is linked specifically to the achievement of identified business goals.

MAKING THE TRANSITION

Once trainers determine that a shift is required and clarify what a performance approach would look like, then the question becomes how to make the transition. Within the training and development field, there are two parallel, but separate, paths for making the shift—one as an individual contributor and the other as a performance department. As an individual contributor, the consultant reports directly to line management and usually operates independently of a training department.

The Performance Consultant As an Individual Contributor

Some situations are ideal for moving experienced training practitioners into roles of individual performance consultants. The situations that we most frequently observe include:

- A line manager knowledgeable of some of the benefits of performance improvement discusses these possibilities with training practitioners and is receptive to supporting a performance consultant on his/her team;
- The concept of performance improvement excites an individual trainer, who initiates discussions with a line manager; or
- Training leadership, comfortable with a traditional approach, hesitates to move the entire function toward a performance improvement focus, but is supportive of the individual moving to a performance improvement approach.

This change is iterative, rather than occurring overnight. Fred Nickols of The Distance Consulting Company described it as follows: "The transition from trainer to performance consultant isn't a sudden state change (even if you change your job title, unit or employer). Instead, the transition is a matter of extending your reach over time. It boils down to being able to successfully tackle a broader array of problems in the workplace and, based on that success, building your credibility in ways that extends your reach even farther" (Nickols, 2000).

Over a period of time, the performance consultant works with the line manager on increasingly more complex performance problems. It requires more and more of the performance consultant's time. Research by Partners in Change, Inc., indicates that competent, full-time performance consultants spend approximately 78 percent of their time focused on performance improvement activities. See Table 1.2 for a description of those activities.

Often, the line manager has the performance consultant move to the business unit and report directly to the leadership team. Business unit management is usually happy to fund the position when it can have the performance consultant on a full-time basis.

Individual performance consultants find themselves engaged in a variety of activities, ranging from performance improvement projects to coaching business unit managers on workplace performance and issues. It is an open-ended job in which the performance consultant cannot predict what will be the next challenge. Individuals who thrive in this environment are comfortable with ambiguity and are stimulated by problems with solutions that are not initially apparent. Not only do the consultants work effectively with management, but they also form a network of specialists who can be called on to provide specific solutions and work collaboratively with others to improve performance.

Table 1.2. How Performance Consultants Spend Their Time

	Percent of Performance Consultant's Time Spent on Job Output/Accountability
Form and Build Partnerships with Clients Identify and develop relationships with key individuals in the organization independent of any project work	18 percent
Complete Performance Analyses Identify and report performance requirements, performance gaps, and causes of gaps through the use of reliable data collection methods and sources	25 percent
Manage Performance Change Projects Plan, organize, and monitor work done by others in support of projects that have performance improvement within the organization as their purpose	30 percent
Measure Impact of Change Initiatives Evaluate the change in business results, job performance, and work environment factors resulting from the interventions	5 percent

The most successful performance consultants are those who can sense the organizational dynamics and the forces impacting the implementation of performance improvement projects. There is a saying that, "Good pilots fly fifteen minutes ahead of their aircraft." In the same way, "Good performance consultants see problems thirty days before they occur."

Transitioning the Training Department to a Performance Focus

Often, the needs of the organization and the vision of training leadership call for a transition of the training function to one of performance improvement. This typically occurs when training leadership is dissatisfied with the manner by which it works with line management, perhaps working as pairs of hands or as experts. Thus the training department manager, training director, or corporate university president initiates the move toward performance improvement.

Those training leaders who have been successful in shifting their focus to performance improvement realize that they must use performance consulting to transition their own departments. There are documented cases in which the training manager has sponsored a consulting skills workshop for key trainers, only to find that successful transition requires more than a workshop. As we indicated earlier, a single solution to performance change rarely produces the desired results. Therefore, the effective training director realizes that there must be an alignment between the performance improvement process, the organizational structure, and the performance consultant's job design.

Process Alignment

The shift to performance brings about many changes in the way trainers work. Not only are they partnering with line managers, but they also are conducting different types of front-end assessments, implementing multiple solutions, and measuring on-the-job performance and business results. Therefore, the manager of a newly created performance department must rethink how the work will be done. In other words, the manager works with the performance consultant to engineer the workflow. Performance consultants indicate the steps that they will use when partnering with line managers, such as completing performance analysis, managing performance change projects, and measuring the impact of the change initiatives. The very effective performance department managers outline the flow of work in the form of a process model that describes each phase of performance improvement. In many instances, the process model consists of the following phases:

Partnering Phase. In this phase, consultants form strategic business relationships with line managers. This requires a knowledgeable, business-savvy person who consults with line managers without being biased toward a single solution. This person becomes intimately familiar with the goals, strategies, and challenges of the business unit. As a consultant, this person helps the business unit leadership see the performance implications of decisions that it makes. Each consultant supports specific line managers, building sustained relationships— even when a project is not being implemented. Once a project has been identified, the activities move into the next phase of the process.

Assessment Phase. This is a data-collection phase in which the consultant or a project team collects data so they can diagnose the situation and eventually report on the business and performance requirements, gaps, and causes of those gaps. During this phase, the consultant and project team members collect a variety of information regarding the problem and causes of the problem. They must have sufficient technical expertise to analyze the information being collected, so in many instances, the Assessment Phase is handled by a small group of consultants with expertise in the areas being studied. It is this group that provides feedback to the client and helps the client arrive at a combination of appropriate solutions.

Implementation Phase. Because the solutions could require an almost limitless number of specialties, depending on the nature of the causes, this phase requires a variety of individuals with unique technical expertise. The performance consultant often helps to select the individuals who will work on the various solutions. The consultant works with the intervention specialists, who design and implement the change while maintaining contact and communication with the clients.

Measurement Phase. In most projects, results to be measured are determined during the Assessment Phase. In this phase, the data-collection strategy and data-collection tools are formed. Often a specialist in measurement and evaluation becomes part of the team to provide the objectivity and rigor needed. The performance consultant provides the link to the business need and access to the client.

Organizational Alignment

Once the process has been identified, the performance department manager faces the challenge of organizing the function in a manner that supports that process. No one person should do all phases of the process. Most frequently, some consultants are responsible for the Partnership Phase and for being the primary advisor to line management during the other phases. Other specialists are accountable for conducting performance assessments, completing gap and cause analyses, and implementing solutions. Still others have responsibility for designing learning activities and creating learning materials. The manager organizes the department in a manner that meets the needs of the line managers and optimizes the capabilities of the people in the department. In addition, the manager networks with other internal departments and external resources to ensure that a broad array of intervention specialists will be available as needed during the Implementation Phase.

Performer Alignment

Now that the process has been defined and roles within the department have been clarified, the department manager designs jobs that ensure the process can be implemented effectively and projects can be managed successfully. Intervention specialists within the training department and other functions have technical skills that are unique to their areas of expertise. In addition, there are skills that are common for all who interface with clients. Tools, job aids, and templates have to be created for these common situations, such as partnering with line managers and identifying performance improvement projects. Workshops have to be created and facilitated to bring skills to a proficient level. A coaching system has to be established so that consultants and specialists have someone to rely on for whatever situation occurs. The challenge here is to bring everyone in the department to a proficient skill level so that the performance consulting process will operate effectively and efficiently.

Making It Happen

For this transition to be successful, the department manager must keep the big picture in mind and be an advocate of the performance improvement process. Implementation of this process often consists of the following steps, as outlined by Tom LaBonte and Jim Robinson (1999, p. 37):

Step 1: Getting Started. First, a client who has a business need and strong credibility in the organization is sought to sponsor a performance improvement project. This first initiative becomes a learning laboratory for the process.

Step 2: Orchestrating the Transition. The amount of time, energy, and expense required to make a successful transition to the performance improvement process cannot be underestimated. It is important to be sensitive to the individual efforts required of each department in handling the day-to-day training requirements, while also learning and implementing the new process.

Step 3: Building Department Commitment. The department manager must model a commitment to the performance consulting process and the new roles by actively embracing the change. The manager must also anticipate and prepare for resistance. Not everyone will want to go along. The leader can overcome some resistance by clarifying the vision and reinforcing it through supportive actions.

Step 4: Gaining Senior Management Support. It is crucial to position the transition as an important product or service start-up. Identifying critical clients and communicating the benefits help to manage expectations early in the process; this is vital to later success. The consultant under-promises and over-delivers with timely support that delights the client.

Step 5: Measuring Impact. When implementing the transition, a variety of performance and process improvement metrics appropriate for measuring the full impact of performance interventions must be examined. Experienced measurement practitioners should be identified and assigned the role of evaluators. These evaluators become internal consultants, building the measurement model and establishing a baseline of skills required for measurement.

Smart trainers know that a shift to performance is essential if they are to add value to the organization. Although this journey from training to performance improvement is challenging, it is achievable. Many trainers have already made the transition; others are involved in the process, which requires thoughtful consideration and a commitment to execute the plan over time. A successful transition, however, enables the performance consultant to be viewed as a strategic business partner to management and the performance department and as a true asset to the entire organization.

References

Bassi, L.J., Benson, G., & Cheney, S. (1996). *Position yourself for the future.* Alexandria, VA: ASTD.

Broad, M.L., & Newstrom, J.W. (1992). *Transfer of training.* Reading, MA: Addison-Wesley.

Gilbert, T. (1978). *Human competence: Engineering worthy performance.* Alexandria, VA: International Society for Performance Improvement.

LaBonte, T., & Robinson, J. (1999, August). Performance consulting: One organization, one process. *Training & Development, 32–37.*

Nickols, F. (2000, February 24). *More on the transition from trainer to performance consultant.* listserv@lists.psu.edu.

Robinson, D.G., & Robinson, J.C. (1998). *Moving from training to performance.* San Francisco: Berrett-Koehler.

Recommended Reading

Block, P. (2000). *Flawless consulting: A guide to getting your expertise used* (2nd ed.). San Francisco: Jossey-Bass/Pfeiffer.

Fuller, J. (1999). *From training to performance improvement: Navigating the transition.* Washington, DC: International Society for Performance Improvement.

Robinson, D.G., & Robinson, J.C. (1995). *Performance consulting: Moving beyond training.* San Francisco: Berrett-Koehler.

Robinson, D.G., & Robinson, J.C. (1989). *Training for impact: How to link training to business needs and measure the results.* San Francisco: Jossey-Bass.

About the Authors

James C. and *Dana Gaines Robinson* are recognized leaders in the area of performance consulting, assisting organizations in defining performance as it needs to be for the organization to attain its business goals. Additionally, they assist HR and HRD functions in transitioning from a traditional focus to a performance focus. They have consulted with numerous Fortune 500 organizations, including Bank One, Bell South, First Union Corporation, Duracell Inc., Steelcase, and Eli Lilly and Company. Both Jim and Dana are frequent speakers at national conferences, including ASTD (formerly American Society for Training and Development), and International Society for Performance Improvement (ISPI) conferences.

Together the Robinsons have co-authored the books Training for Impact: How to Link Training to Business Needs and Measure the Results *(1989) and* Performance Consulting: Moving Beyond Training *(1995). They co-edited a third book,* Moving from Training to Performance: A Practical Guidebook *(1998), which contains the contributions of more than fifteen authors who share information regarding their own experience in transitioning to a performance focus.*

In May 1999, ASTD presented the Robinsons with the 1998 Distinguished Contribution Award for Workplace Learning and Performance. This award recognizes their landmark work in performance improvement and the sustained impact they have had in the training and human resource industry.

CHAPTER TWO

Trends and the Profession

Joe Willmore
President, Willmore Consulting Group

Most organizations and professionals do not plan well for the future. Yet an understanding of key trends and emerging issues is essential for an effective HRD practitioner. A wide range of social, organizational, content, format, and skill trends are of concern for trainers. This chapter highlights these key trends, as well as methods for identifying and understanding future developments.

FAILURE TO SEE EMERGING ISSUES

Most organizations typically do a poor job preparing for the future and understanding which trends and forces are particularly important to the way they do business. Research by the corporate planning staff at Royal Dutch/Shell found that one third of the companies listed in the 1970 Fortune 500 had disappeared by 1983 (De Geus, 1988, p. 70). Despite planning and forecasting efforts, a significant number of highly successful companies proved to be unprepared for the future. Since 1983, organizational life has become even more turbulent as changes within industries have come at a faster pace and bigger scale. Organizational stability has diminished as the rate of change and organizational dynamics have accelerated and the ways we structure and define our work have changed (Wheatley, 1994).

Training and HRD professionals have, for the most part, failed to anticipate evolving needs and major changes. At an individual level, this has resulted in decreased job security and missed professional opportunities for many trainers. At an organizational level, it has meant minimization or less strategic involvement.

It is not particularly surprising that most trainers and HRD professionals haven't been especially good at identifying emerging issues. For starters, HRD professionals are often not very strategically focused and are often positioned poorly to drive strategic issues within organizations (Bellman, 1994). The combination of increasing work demands, staff shortages, and the degree of change within organizations and industries has often resulted in trainers running faster just to keep up. Who has time to plan and think about the future in such a world?

Additionally, most people (and organizations, for that matter) do a poor job of forecasting. Our mental models (deeply held beliefs and assumptions about a system or how it works) dramatically affect our ability to perceive what is going on. Our mental models often mean we fail to see key developments and new trends (Senge, 1990). History is replete with examples of smart people, organizations, and governments that all failed to perceive warning signs of new developments (Wack, 1985). We tend to plan as if the future will be pretty similar to today, when the reality is that tomorrow will see the emergence and development of new dynamics that radically alter how we do business.

It is essential that trainers and HRD professionals focus on the future. Only by understanding where organizations are headed can we play a strategic role as we proactively prepare for what is to come. Having a better grasp of developments to come allows us to do our jobs better, have more impact in the work we do, and decrease the personal and organizational trauma of many significant changes.

EMERGING ISSUES

What major changes and trends can trainers expect to see? First, trends relevant to HRD professionals will vary somewhat on the basis of role (such as type of training), client (organization or industry served) and location (where you reside). For example, outsourcing of training needs is much more common in Europe than it is in the United States (ASTD, 1999). Additionally, as author William Gibson (personal communication, November 1999) likes to say, "The future is already here; it's just unevenly distributed." Thus, a possible future trend for one person is a part of the status quo for another.

Social and Demographic Trends

A wide range of emerging social and demographic trends are relevant to trainers (Bassi, 1999). In the United States, there is an emerging hourglass generational demographic with the combination of an aging population (comparatively affluent and also willing to extend careers with consulting/subbing/telecommuting roles) and a birth boomlet of younger workers. The combination of population mobility, a brain drain of technology workers from developing nations, and changing immigration patterns will result in increasingly diverse workforces and communities. In North America, for instance, Hispanics are the fastest growing segment of the population, along with growing immigration from Asia and Africa. With the development of the Internet and the wealth of resources online, the gap between information "haves" and information "have nots" continues to widen.

The consequence of all these trends is that HRD professionals will face increasingly diverse training populations that will render previously successful training designs or content obsolete. Trainers won't be able to expect the training approaches that were so successful with Baby Boomers a decade ago to be equally successful with the learning styles and technological sophistication of the "Gen-Next-ers." Traditional stand-up classroom trainers will face the challenge of working with a group of workers unable to get in the same room at the same time because of telecommuting or work demands and who may not speak the same language, thus forcing them to use new approaches.

Market developments and standards (such as mass customization, JIT production, high expectations for service delivery, and individual access to sophisticated software) will raise the bar for expectations on training delivery. Class attendees whose children can produce homework on color printers will be much less tolerant of training materials without graphics and in black & white. Consumers who have become used to individualized products will be far less accepting of corporate courses in which content and cases are the same for participants from both marketing and operations. Individuals, who have become used to overnight mail delivery, personal shoppers, one-hour eye glasses, fifteen-minute oil changes, and fast-food places where they can "have it your way" will be much less understanding of training departments that insist they cannot enroll in a course until next quarter (or that the design takes a month to complete).

Organizational Trends

A series of developments within organizations has had massive impact on trainers and their impact will continue to grow in the future. Organizations have become more global and flatter, as well as much more team-based. These developments will set agendas and course needs.

Most organizations have pushed responsibility for development onto the individual, creating the phenomenon of "Free Agent Learners" (Caudron, 1999). The consequence of this is decreased loyalty to the organization itself and greater turnover. Higher turnover means that trainers may spend a greater percentage of their time focused on orientation and technical training issues.

The combination of accelerated change rates, 24/7 work patterns (especially for global, telco, or IT work), and decreased loyalty have made retention, corporate memory, and subject-matter expertise even bigger issues for organizations. In almost all fields (and certainly within training vendors and consulting firms), there has been industry consolidation as small firms are bought up by larger ones (Galagan, 1998). The difficulty of filling positions (as well as the need to keep key performers) has forced organizations to increasingly accept flexible work arrangements, telecommuting, and unique work structures.

Time pressure and the increased speed of work will continue to exert pressure on trainers. (Some firms have responded by scheduling training at night, on weekends, or in small blocks to reduce conflicts around billable hours.) Increased competition in all industries has also led to a demand for quicker responsiveness and demonstrated effectiveness. Thus, trainers face greater pressure to act quickly and measure results, especially with regard to business objectives or return on investment (ROI).

Content Trends

It is always difficult to assess new demands in course content. Exactly what is a fad and what is an emerging and persistent need? However, several content issues appear to be strong needs for future training. Skills and training around virtual work (such as how to function within a virtual team, managing off-site workers, and performance measurement of telecommuters) will become a key need (Nedra Weinstein, Catalyst Consulting Team, personal communication, April 26, 2000). Diversity will continue to be a major developmental focus. However, greater emphasis will have to be put on generational, cultural, and work style issues within diversity. Organizations will continue to rely more on teams. With shorter product development lifecycles (thus meaning more new services/products) and greater turnover, the need for product knowledge training will increase. Organizations will have a greater need for consulting skills at all levels and functions, so training in consulting competencies will increase.

Software will play an increasing role in how all organizations do business, so software training on a wide range of programs will grow. Technology will be ever present in the way we work; it will not be possible to be a successful trainer or facilitator or OD practitioner and be a Luddite or technophobe (Lisa Kimball, Caucus Systems, personal communication, May 2, 2000). Increasingly, teams will meet online (requiring a facilitator who knows groupware); classroom training will rely heavily on technology; and instructional designers will require some degree of programming skills to develop job aids. The technological sophistication of trainers must increase dramatically, not only to utilize those technologies as trainers but also to train their clients as well.

An issue that is especially relevant to HRD professionals is that of knowledge management, a field that continues to develop and is a very hot and important issue for organizations of the future. The functions driving most knowledge management efforts fall within the information technology (IT) departments.

Consequently, it is not surprising that, in many firms, knowledge management has become synonymous with software. HRD must play a much more active and strategic role in this very key trend—from facilitating the culture change necessary to produce real knowledge management to helping to develop corporate initiatives.

FORMAT AND METHODOLOGY

Besides the change in training topics, how trainers train will also change dramatically. Although there will continue to be some form of traditional, stand-up classroom training, a much greater percentage of training will fall into nontraditional means.

Distance learning is becoming a key area of focus in the profession, as firms rush for ways to develop employees in their dispersed and often global organizations. Developmental approaches that are much more individually oriented (job aids, self-paced instruction, and computer-based training [CBT]) will become more popular as organizations attempt to cope with work days and weeks that never end in a global market where the sun never sets. Additionally, key training functions (such as course registration) will be automated, eliminating some roles within training departments.

Different learning styles, especially those driven through cultural and generational diversity, will force trainers to adapt their designs even further. Learning initiatives that capture knowledge (such as online classes that are easily archived) to enhance corporate memory will become increasingly important. Time pressure will force even more compression of content, especially for organizations that typically focus on billable hours. Communities of practice will become a larger form of "training," and the role of the trainer in such formats will be more as a community recruiter and facilitator than content provider.

COMPETENCIES

By looking at trends in content or format, we've provided examples of a number of skills or competencies that trainers will need to add to their repertoire. Training professionals will also change in a number of ways, and their competencies will have to be adapted.

First, the distinctions between a number of areas, such as performance technology, training, instructional design, facilitation, and organization development (OD) will blur and eventually disappear (Lisa Kimball, Caucus Systems, personal communication, May 2, 2000). Increasingly (in part because trainers will be held accountable for results rather than activities and in part because training will evolve into a range of different formats and methodologies), attempts to distinguish between such fields as "facilitation" and "training" or OD and performance technology will be meaningless. As HRD professionals are expected to produce results and measure outcomes, defining oneself by the activity or intervention you do will be pointless.

Second, technological competence will become essential. Flatter organizations and a need for speed make it much harder for a stand-up trainer to count on the graphics department to generate visuals or the instructional designer to make last-minute revisions. More organizational work continues to gravitate to online or electronic interaction. Because dynamics for virtual teams differ from those for face-to-face teams (Jarvenpaa, Knoll, & Leidner, 1998), trainers must become both techno-literate and aware of these differences so that they can adapt approaches and content to the appropriate medium.

Third, measurement and evaluation skills will be vital. As the world becomes increasingly competitive (and even government and nonprofit organizations find themselves forced to justify funding and effectiveness), trainers will face increasingly strong pressure to demonstrate the impact of their work. Consequently, issues like ROI will become commonplace expectations for trainers.

Fourth, consulting is "in." All trainers, including internal practitioners, must develop their consulting skills. There will be fewer professionals who simply teach standard courses on a regular basis. Instead, trainers will have to be proactive, seeking out potential work within their firms. They will have to be able to build trust and unearth information quickly as they do needs assessments and front-end analysis work. They will have to be able to create buy-in and support from people they have no authority over. And they will have to be good problem solvers.

STAYING CURRENT AND AHEAD

There are a number of ways that a trainer can keep aware of emerging issues and major trends in the field.

- Belong to a professional association such as ASTD (formerly the American Society for Training and Development), Society for Human Resource Management (SHRM), International Society for Performance Improvement (ISPI), or Organization Development Network (ODN)—one that provides opportunities for networking outside your own organization or industry. Ideally, this would be an association that also does good benchmarking and trends research.

- Use tools and approaches that challenge mental models and promote new insight. Examples include such techniques as scenario planning, SWOT (strengths, weaknesses, opportunities, threats) or environmental scanning efforts, Team B efforts (a devil's advocate approach to strategy and planning), and systems thinking initiatives (that look at drivers and causes for certain trends).

- Look outside your immediate environment. Take advantage of external benchmarking research. Refresh your thinking by attending institutes and conferences that stretch your perspective. Expose yourself to professional material that falls outside your job needs or duties. Deliberately look at organizations outside of your industry or geographic area to see what they're experiencing—trends do not start uniformly but emerge unevenly in some areas.

At a time of great change and lots of work, it is too tempting to ignore the future because of immediate demands. Examining future possibilities is essential for professional success. If you understand what is coming, you can make the career adjustments necessary to be successful, as well as be a leader for your clients and organization.

References

ASTD. (1999). *Comparing training practices and investments throughout the world.* Alexandria, VA: Author.

Bassi, L. (Ed.). (1999). *ASTD trends watch: Executive summary.* Alexandria, VA: ASTD.

Bellman, G. (1994, May). The future of workplace learning and performance. *Training & Development,* S37-S38.

Caudron, S. (1999, August). Free agent learner. *Training & Development,* 27–30.

De Geus, A. (1988, April). Planning as learning. *Harvard Business Review,* 70–74.

Galagan, P. (1998, May). Roll 'em up! *Training & Development,* 26–31.

Jarvenpaa, S., Knoll, K., & Leidner, D. (1998, Spring). Antecedents of trust in global virtual teams. *Journal of Management Information Systems,* 29–64.

Senge, P. (1990). *The fifth discipline.* New York: Currency-Doubleday.

Wack, P. (1985, November/December). Scenarios: Shooting the rapids. *Harvard Business Review,* 139–150.

Wheatley, M. (1994, May). The future of workplace learning and performance. *Training & Development,* S47.

Recommended Reading

ASTD. *State of the industry report* (published every January). Alexandria, VA: ASTD.

Kurtzman, J. (Ed.). (1998). *Thought leaders: Insights on the future of business.* San Francisco: Jossey-Bass.

Willmore, J. (1999, December). Four HRD scenarios of the future. *Training & Development*, 38–41.

The future of workplace learning and performance. (1994, May). *Training & Development*, S36-S47.

About the Author

Joe Willmore is president of the Willmore Consulting Group, based in Northern Virginia in the United States. As a performance consultant, his particular areas of expertise involve virtual teams and scenario planning. Besides the United States, he also has worked extensively in Jamaica, Saudi Arabia, and Russia. Willmore is a member of ASTD's National Advisors for Chapters (NAC). He has been a presenter at the ASTD, ISPI, ASQ, AQP, and TOC International Conferences.

CHAPTER THREE

HRD in the Internet World

Patricia A. McLagan
Principal, McLagan International, Inc.

The world of learning is changing drastically, resulting in major implications for the HRD profession. In light of these changes, we must ask ourselves: Where are we going? What are we all about? What roles will add value for the enterprises and people we serve? To help answer these questions, this chapter takes a look at some of the projected contributions HRD practitioners will make, the roles they will assume, and the competencies that will be necessary to perform these roles.

INTRODUCTION

Let's make no mistake. The learning world is changing radically with profound implications for the Human Resource Development (HRD) profession. It requires a big shift from industrial to information age practices. It changes our roles. It calls for expanded and very different competencies!

You say, "But the profession has already made the shift—or moved substantially into the information age." Ah, not totally! Classroom training, measuring success in terms of "hours of training," and evaluating reactions rather than impact still dominate a lot of our thinking. Upward mobility, succession planning for management positions, and job-focused thinking are still the centerpieces of career planning. And experts still try to keep objectivity, distance, and control in many organization development and cultural change projects.

All of these have the earmarks of industrial age, closed system assumptions. They assume a domination hierarchy, keep experts and participants at a distance from one another, assume that one size fits all, and are often more bureaucratic than they need to be.

Yes, many organizations are experimenting with new technologies and assumptions. We dabble with ways to make learning and change more user-centered, customized, quicker, and more streamlined. We try to shift the emphasis to performance and results, hoping that by sheer force of analysis and intent, HRD will finally arrive as a clear contributor to saving shrinking profits and dissolving operating fat. We tout the financial, customer, and employee benefits of learning and culture change and of performance consulting.

Just as we think we are making progress, many of us find ourselves facing a cutthroat world of reengineering and downsizing. Investors intensify their demands for high returns from companies not prepared to compete. Anything that isn't mainstream business or marketing (such as HRD) often is bounced from leadership agendas.

Furthermore, people—young and old—are more used to sound-bite politics, ten-minute news shows, low-demand television, and less and less discretionary time. They rebel at lengthy and thorough learning events. They demand shorter and shorter learning segments, losing patience with theory and reflection. And, of course, they are used to finding what they need on the Internet.

New information access! New challenges! New learning! New learners! New roles for the HRD professional.

At first glance, the market's desire for "fast food learning" is frustrating. But it may be an exciting business to be in after all—at least for some meals! In any event, we have to find new ways to draw on traditional skills related to training, needs analysis, design, development, training and facilitation, evaluation, career and performance support, and OD. Some of the basic skills and energies are valuable. But these and other roles are in flux.

Where are HRD professionals going? What are we all about? What roles will add value for the enterprises and people we serve?

WHERE HRD ADDS VALUE

A place to start is with the end. We can begin to *project* the kinds of contributions we must make. For we are dangling at the front end of a new curve—hanging by wisps of emerging technologies, insights, and opportunities. We stand in the place of "initial conditions" that scientists talk about—the place where actions can create the grooves that future professionals will fall into and follow. It is a place of potentially extraordinary influence and innovation.

As I see it, new century HRD professionals have six big challenges:

1. *Democratize learning and performance* (connect learners and resources; develop skills for self-managed performance, learning and enablement; make great resources accessible; shift to circles; and help people optimize technology);

2. Design learning for *easy access and optimal performance impact*;

3. Facilitate the creation and effectiveness of *learning communities* for knowledge sharing, innovation, and development (common language, mechanisms, operating practices, technology, group process skills);

4. Install the *people practices* for high performance and a humanistic culture;

5. Ensure that *structures, processes, systems are optimized* for people performance and attracting/retaining high talent.

6. Help create and/or implement operational and predictive *measures* related to human resource effectiveness and the organization's ability to attract, optimize, develop, and retain people's energy and capacity.

Democratized Learning and Performance

We are in an environment in which individuals will have many more careers than ever before. It's a time when the life span of knowledge and skills is shrinking. Also, many people are on many teams at the same time. And they have to act fast and innovate and respond to customers even though the problems may not be "theirs." More workers are consultants, contractors, free agents—and those in more traditional relationships don't wear the old organization handcuffs.

People have the tools on their desks, at their homes, on the plane, and in their pockets to access information as events and thoughts occur. They don't need the old intermediaries—the layers of management, the teachers, even the mailperson or the phone operator—to connect to each other and to filter information.

At the same time, the facts are in, reported in every business and economic journal: Organizations where people are informed, where they participate, and where they act quickly and without fear are more profitable. They attract the best talent. And that talent stays! Customers of these more participative places are more satisfied. They come back—again and again.

Yet the traditions of authoritarianism and risk-averse bureaucracy continue to dog our institutions. Many people in leadership roles are unprepared to support a high involvement, high performance environment. They are unconscious of their own use of power and unaware of the impact of their rank. Alternatively, the people they lead often defer to authority, expect to be taken care of, and wallow in dependency and blaming.

A lot of this is unconscious—supported by old myths and the experiences of growing up in authoritarian schools, churches, families, and political environments. For many, authoritarian and dependent relationships have been their working style for a lifetime. Their fathers and mothers worked that way. They know little else.

Verbally, at least, most of us all agree that in the 21st Century authoritarianism and dependency are anachronisms. This is not to say that individuals shouldn't make some decisions in an authoritative way: quickly and without consultation. Sometimes that is necessary and a good exercise of responsibility and leadership. It *is* to say that many exclusionary practices and abdications—by leaders and team members—are destructive for the organization and damaging to the human spirit. They destroy the ability to create the performance communities that we need in today's complex world.

HRD professionals have a double job in meeting these challenges. We have to help people develop the skills and mindsets for self-management, supportive leadership, and self-coordinated learning. And we must find ways to support more effective learning.

Alan Tough (1979) investigated how adults learn and discovered some facts that are very useful today. His research showed that 70 percent of what adults learn intentionally, they manage themselves. But that learning is often not very focused and efficient. He found, in fact, that the learning process breaks down in predictable areas:

- People often don't know what the *"best practices"* are—what to strive for in their learning;

- Even when we know what to learn, it isn't always clear *what our needs* are;

- We have trouble *finding the best resources*—often turning to the most available source of help, not necessarily the best;

- We often quit our learning projects *when the going gets tough*—not realizing that there are plateaus and unfreezing times; and

- We don't *recognize when we're done*—acknowledging that we have accomplished what we set out to do, appreciating our success, and formally closing out the effort.

Similar awareness and skill barriers exist for performance. Many individuals don't go after the strategic and customer information they need for aligning day-to-day work. They fail to negotiate expectations with customers and colleagues. They don't seek out and use feedback that might help continually tweak actions, forge breakthrough ideas, or solve problems in their early stages.

And managers/leaders/supervisors often add to the problems by making it unsafe to raise issues and dangerous to question and propose ideas. Some even rush in to solve problems and take over others' jobs. HRD professionals can help transform these personal learning and performance management practices and help reshape people's views of their roles.

We live in times when self-managed learning is more important and possible than ever before. HRD professionals must help develop the skills, systems, and awareness that will enable people to move through their learning processes quickly and with success. This requires some creativity and attention, but we can do it. We must do it.

Designed Learning

There is abundant data available today. But it is meaningless until someone packages it or applies it to a need or a problem. Ultimately, of course, the learner designs his or her own learning experience by paying attention to some ideas and resources and not to others and by deciding where to use and not use what was learned.

For some needs, the HRD professional can and must facilitate this process. How? By using learning theory and knowledge of human and organization development to sort information and package it. We can create learning maps to help individuals move through various career stages. We can create or find databases and resource networks and make them available to the people we support. And, if necessary, it's the HRD professional's job to design and develop new learning modules or customize existing ones.

Really great design is sensitive to learner needs, business requirements, and diversity issues. It uses delivery methods that make cost/benefit sense. And it helps people quickly convert learning into action and results.

To design learning is to create a work of art—one that engages and involves the learner and even the entire organization in an experience that accelerates growth and effectiveness. In addition, the Internet world challenges us to excellence in this important area.

Learning Communities

Organizations today want important knowledge to spread quickly. They want the ability to match competencies to project needs quickly. Some call the attempt to accelerate this spread, "knowledge management." They see it as a competitive advantage and want to set up conditions to amplify and improve it.

Information technology can provide part of the solution to the knowledge management problem. But the real leverage comes from sharing and conversations between and among people. These conversations can happen in the course of work, in chat rooms, e-mail strings, face-to-face meetings, teleconferences, and videoconferences. We can be assured that more options are coming.

The competitive key is contact. When this contact reaches beyond the day-to-day environment to engage people in knowledge sharing, problem solving, and creative thought, phenomenal synergies are possible. These synergies are good for the business, and they are stimulating to individuals.

HRD professionals can seed the process. We can help establish communities of practice and interest. We can help people develop skills of dialogue and inquiry, of meeting management and creative exploration. We can suggest and reinforce organic gatherings—electronically or in other ways. We can publicize and help create identities for knowledge groups.

HRD professionals also contribute to wildfire learning when we, among other things: (1) design learning events that ask people to involve or contact others; (2) design and encourage team learning; (3) do things that encourage cooperation; (4) create ways for people to find others with similar interests or complementary skills; (5) bring people with similar career interests together; or (6) help the organization move to project-focused rather than job-focused work structures (the former develops lots of relationships and networks).

People Practices for High Performance and Involvement

Many HR practices reinforce the old models of business and relationships. They support paternalism, dependency, and bureaucracy. Look at how "boss-focused" many performance management systems are (the "boss" does a lot of the work of setting goals and giving feedback). Selection in many companies is either done by HR or by the person in charge. Training and learning focus on the teacher more than on the learner. People work in a vacuum and often don't really know how or if they are influencing results.

It's time to shift the focus of many HR practices. Whenever possible, the individual or the team should play an active and participative role. The manager's job is to provide context, be a partner, and hold people to high standards of practice. Individuals who understand the strategy and business context can set and negotiate many of their own goals. They can monitor customer feedback and, if they receive timely and useful performance status information, can easily self-correct. Teams can and should help select their colleagues and even their leaders. (At least, they should have a say!)

The difference between actual and ideal practices may seem subtle. But HR practices that are open and that expect individuals to be key players in making them work reduce sabotage and demoralization. They make it more possible for leaders to play the coaching and support role. And putting more responsibility and tools in the hands of individuals and teams frees HRD people to spend more time on strategy implementation, consulting, and design.

The people practices of any business should reflect and stimulate the values of a high performance enterprise for the 21st Century: customer focus, performance orientation, commitment to quality, flexibility and speed, transparency, partnership and respect, and innovation. It's the HRD professional's job to see that HR practices measure up to these values—in design and in implementation.

Synergies Between People and Business Structures, Processes, and Systems

Who's looking out for people when decisions about organization design, processes, and systems occur in your business? Changes in these areas of the business might look good on paper. They might seem rational and logical. But they may cause big problems in human performance and impact.

Some organizational structures make knowledge sharing difficult, for example. Others allocate work in ways that overload or demotivate and bore people. Some attempts to streamline the organization remove so much muscle and capacity that creativity, planning, and reflection are impossible. There is often not enough slack left for risk taking and crisis response. The HRD role is to be a voice for optimal work designs—or for compensating strategies to offset negative effects (for example, frequent breaks for people doing highly concentrated but repetitive work, such as air traffic controllers).

There is no perfect organizational structure, but some are more conducive to high performance than others. In a knowledge-focused economy, the HRD professional plays a key role in ensuring that work develops and uses the competencies of individuals and teams. The most logical and elegant organization chart is often not the best organization and use of talent.

Business processes and systems are also important for the HRD professional to watch and influence. Many big information systems are being installed today—at very great cost. Many will never realize their potential because the people side wasn't considered. Here's a case in point: Technology makes information available to the people who produce products and serve customers. But levels of management and approval requirements make local decisions impossible. In other words, the people process remains the same while the technology changes. The promise of the technology—to speed up important processes—cannot be fully realized.

The HRD professional must partner with system and process designers to be sure that the people side changes, too. This may involve development, changes in performance management focus, new management practices or work structures, different kinds of communication, and new forms of learning support. Whatever is involved, the HRD professional must be ready to complete the picture and partner with technologists, financial people, and others whose focus may be more mechanistic.

Measures and Feedback Loops for the Human Side of Business

It's not a secret that measures related to people either don't exist or are marginalized in many organizations. This is tragic for the business because worker satisfaction and motivation measures are leading indicators of customer loyalty and, ultimately, profits. Also, focusing on matters such as productivity makes more competitive sense than focusing on profit. Profit relates to both price and performance. Raising prices can make profits look good for a while, but eventually this tactic reduces competitiveness. Improving productivity is a more robust strategy, for it is hard for competitors to match. Improving productivity is a people-centered issue.

Ultimately, the success of even the shortest term financial measures rely on how people are developed and managed in an organization. It's one thing to have the financial facts. It's quite another to have the facts drive action.

The HRD professional can contribute in major ways to the bottom line by helping the organization focus on the leading "people" indicators and by doing things to ensure that people throughout the business actually act on the financial facts.

People indicators include unplanned attrition, attraction of people with critical skills, productivity, participation indices, motivation, and satisfaction indices. Ensuring action requires managers to be accountable for communicating financial facts and using them in performance management conversations. HRD people can also help ensure action by being sure that everyone understands the business as a financial entity, knows the industry and customers, and feels accountable for success at the business level—not just in their cubicles.

ROLES FOR THE HRD PROFESSIONAL

All of this implies a fresh view of the HRD professional. It is a view that draws insights from the roles and competencies studies that have described the field since the early 1980s. But it is primarily driven by the vast changes in the nature of work and learning due to the ascendancy of globalization, technology, information systems, and of learning itself.

I see ten key roles and eight important competencies for HRD professionals as we move fully into the 21st Century.

Ten Key Roles

I like the idea of roles within a field. They help organize our view of work in a way that is independent of organization charts and job descriptions. In a way, roles are chunks of responsibility that can be assembled in many ways. In this case, they are key destinations on a map of HRD work, a menu of sorts to use in deciding the focus of a person's job. No one person performs all roles all the time. And most people are only responsible for a few of the roles.

I choose to define roles in terms of their *outputs*—what they deliver. This is a better framework than tasks (what people in the roles *do*) because there are many possible ways to *do* or perform roles in ways that produce the outputs.

So here are the ten roles and some of the outputs that, given the assumptions in the previous section, define the value-adding work of the HRD professional in the early 21st Century.

Role 1: Business/People Link. As businesses and their environments change, their people requirements change. Also, the environment, demographics, and cultural shifts influence what people need, want, and are willing to bring to work. HRD professionals today stay on top of these shifts and help weave the needs into a high productivity whole. Outputs of this role include

- Strategy-based needs analyses at the organization, process, and individual/team levels;
- Projections of talent requirements and areas of vulnerability;
- Plans to ensure availability of needed talent; and
- Mechanisms for translating strategies into on-the-job actions.

Role 2: Learning and Knowledge System Architect. This is a very large system design role. The HRD professional sets up conditions that enable people to have the knowledge, learning, and information resources they need for high performance. This includes work to help spread tacit learning (learning from failures and successes) and to make the information learning networks more effective. It also includes formal organization of information, job aids, and real-time or planned learning/training. Outputs of this role include

- Architectures and processes for fast knowledge access and for connecting with appropriate resources and people; and
- Designs for learning "curricula" and systems that provide individuals and teams with a map for learning with many resources over time (for example, guidance for developing managerial/leadership talent from early to end career).

Role 3: Learning Experience Designer. Like the previous role, this is a very creative one. It relates to those times that the HRD professional actually must create a new learning experience. The experience might include one or many methods: classroom, computer-aided, video or audio-based, self-study, reading, on-job experimenting, journaling and other reflective exercises, instant access problem solving, coaching—online or in person. The list of possible learning formats is very long, indeed! But this role creates the blueprint for achieving a specific set of learning goals. It considers the audience, geographical issues, learning styles, budgets, and the practicalities of business. Throughout, this role keeps the goal of accelerating performance effectiveness in mind. This means making trade-offs between short-term behavioral interventions and interventions for long-term attitudinal and conceptual impact. Outputs of this role include

- Designs and plans for specific learning events or interventions (*Note:* This role focuses on workshop and related application events—like the builder of a house. The learning and knowledge systems architect develops the entire learning system—like the planner of a city); and
- Specifications for developers (media people, writers, programmers, and so forth).

Role 4: Learning Experience Developer. This role does the actual building of the pieces of the learning system (just as, in a house, the plumbers, electricians, carpenters, and painters turn the blueprint into something tangible). The outputs of this role are as varied as the list of possible learning events. They include

- Video-based learning and performance support;
- Audio-based learning and performance support;
- Computer-based support;
- Leaders' guides and course materials;
- Printed or online self-study packages;
- Printed or online guides for action learning; on-the-job learning; job aids; and
- Databases and help structures for problem-focused learning.

Role 5: Business Structure, Process, and System Advisor. This role focuses on achieving the best marriage of people with structures, processes, and systems. The HRD person brings the human factor into decisions about these areas. Then he or she plans how to help people make these decisions work—quickly and with high performance impact. Outputs of this role include

- Recommendations for and critiques of structure, process, and systems decisions;
- Recommendations for involving people in and communicating changes in these areas;
- Plans for fast and successful implementation through people; and
- Personal coaching during implementation.

Role 6: Learning Effectiveness Coach. Learning and human performance are more important than ever today, but few people have the advanced skills or tools to learn or to support each other's learning. The HRD professional can add tremendous value by helping to develop learning skills and awareness. Outputs he or she provides include

- Support and tools for self-managed learning;
- Support and tools for self-managed performance (for example, information age goal planning, feedback, and continuous improvement);
- Support and tools to develop the coaching/teaching skills of anyone with knowledge to share; and
- Assessments of the learning environment and of the effectiveness of learning/performance practices.

Role 7: Learning Community Organizer. Although learning communities can and do (and should!) arise spontaneously, people with similar interests and needs still don't find one another. For the next decade, the HRD professional will be called on to be a catalyst—to help make learning communities more of a habit. Outputs he or she can provide include

- Guidance structures and processes for assembling learning communities;
- Support for developing skills in knowledge sharing and optimization; and
- Tracking systems to help document shared learnings and make them easily available to others.

Role 8: Group Facilitator/Instructor. There continue to be situations in which the HRD professional personally leads or facilitates group learning. This takes very special skill so that the learning and performance responsibility stays with the participants and that their ability to self-facilitate increases with each intervention. Here are the outputs associated with this role:

- Facilitations of structured learning events (cases, role plays, lectures, and so forth);
- Facilitations of group discussions and information sharing;
- Facilitations of conflict resolution situations;
- Facilitations of problem-solving and decision-making sessions; and
- Transference of process facilitation skills and awareness to group members.

Role 9: Action Measurement Specialist. "Action measurement" means that measures lead to action; they are a vital part of the performance and learning system, not just an end in themselves. The role of the HRD professional is to deliver the following outputs:

- Benchmarks for HRD and the people side of the business (drawn from best practices studies, but also from state of the art thinking and innovations);
- Measurement processes showing the link between people practices and performance and short-term, as well as long-term, business success; and
- Support to enable people to understand and act on measurement data.

Role 10: Culture Change Consultant. As relationships change between people and their leaders and among people and teams, everyone is challenged to adopt new mindsets and assumptions about how to work together and for success in the external environment. This is the essence of culture change. It is an enormous problem, because bureaucracy and domination hierarchy are the main traditional ways of dealing with bigness and complexity. So the HRD professional has work to do to deliver these outputs:

- Database identification and predictions of organization development needs;
- Expanded change management and facilitation skills for *all* people in the organization; and
- Progress and status checks regarding the health and effectiveness of relationships and networks.

These roles add up to the critical mass of HRD. Clearly, the field is very important for organization success as we move into the next waves of change due to globalization, technology and information breakthroughs, and discoveries about learning itself.

Competencies for HRD Success

Roles and outputs tell us about the work. Competencies tell us about the people who perform the work—about the knowledge, skills, and personal qualities they need to excel. Competencies *enable* the work.

Many competencies interweave to enable the ten HRD roles. And there is no absolute formula for doing such complex work in changing times. Furthermore, different individuals will combine different competencies for equally positive effects. Psychologists say that behavior is "over determined." This means that there are many paths to similar outcomes.

With this in mind, here are eight key competencies related to high performance in the HRD roles:

Systemic Thinking. This is the skill of seeing interconnections and patterns in complex situations and information. It is also the skill of being able to hold short-term and long-term issues in mind together, while going beyond the obvious to see subtle clues and trends. This is an important mental skill for analyzing needs and designing effective interventions.

Data Reduction and Packaging. This is the skill of identifying key information and translating it into learner-focused/performance-focused language. It is critical for measurement as well as for learning design and development.

Emotional Intelligence. Self-awareness and emotional self-control are key ingredients of this skill. People who help and advise others have an obligation to have developed strength in this area, or else they may mistake their own issues and priorities for the needs and issues of the organization.

Group Process. This is the skill of facilitating groups to conclusions and learning to which they are committed. It involves guiding both the tasks of the group and ensuring that the group's way of working together builds rather than destroys trust. Because a lot of learning and performance is group-related and much of the analytical and organizing part of HRD work is very interactive, this is a key skill area.

Coaching. This is the skill of helping others be the most they can be—through attitudes of optimism and personalized support. There is usually an element of coaching in every situation an HRD professional faces.

Business Economics Understanding. This is knowledge of the business as a financial institution that adds value for customers. It is imperative that HRD people understand this in order to link HR actions to business issues and needs, for both the short term and the long term.

Change Process Understanding. This knowledge area relates to the business as a performing social system. Change in a social system does not follow the rules of logic and finance. It requires understanding of how organizations and groups actually change and grow and of how to use these insights to accelerate needed changes in culture, practice, operations, processes, and so on. Clearly, the HRD professional plays a key role in change process, as much competitive advantage today comes from the people side of any business.

Learning Theory and Practice. This is the knowledge of how people learn, develop, and change and of the key success factors for facilitating and accelerating personal learning and change. It includes an understanding of the methods and tools available to feed and accelerate the learning process and help learning result in improved performance. Armed with this knowledge, the HRD professional can develop designs, help support learning communities, decide how to turn measurement information into action information, and so on.

These eight competencies are not the only ones an individual needs. But they are the high leverage ones and represent areas of continuous and lifetime learning for anyone in the profession.

CONCLUSION

HRD in the Internet world is a very exciting place to be. As learning moves to a more central position in individual and organizational life, HRD becomes more central. At the same time, so much that affects HRD continues to change—the tools, theories, practices, interconnections, technologies. All are in flux.

The emerging picture of HRD takes on new forms under these conditions. HRD professionals find themselves needing to democratize learning and performance, design learning for high performance impact, create and nurture learning communities, install people practices to support a high performance culture, ensure that organization processes and systems optimize people, and install and implement measures that really add value in managing people.

The roles of the HRD professional, therefore, reflect and respond to these challenges. The roles reflect a partnership view of HRD. It goes beyond performance consulting or learning consulting. It goes beyond training or organization development or career development in the traditional sense. In fact, all of these are included—in the new way that reflects the e-commerce environment that is reshaping how industry and organizations work.

Anyone entering or making a career in the HRD field will find him- or herself developing and using competencies like those listed in the last section. It is a challenging assortment of intellectual, personal, and interpersonal skills, as well as specialized and business knowledge. It is an exciting mix for anyone who is adventuresome and courageous, for anyone who really wants to make the world of work both a better and more exciting place and a higher performance enterprise.

References

McLagan, P.A. (1999, December). As the HRD world churns. *Training & Development,* 20–30.

Tough, A. (1979). *The adult's learning projects: A fresh approach to theory and practice in adult learning* (2nd ed.). Austin, TX: Learning Concepts.

Recommended Reading

Abernathy, D.J., Allerton, H.E., Barron, T., Galagan, P.A., & Salopek, J.J. (1999, November). Trendz. *Training & Development*, 22–43.

ASTD. (2000). *The 2000 ASTD state of the industry report.* Alexandria, VA: Author.

Willmore, J. (1999, December). Four HRD scenarios of the future. *Training & Development*, 38–41.

About the Author

Patricia A. McLagan *is chairman of McLagan International, Inc., and is a part-time professor at Rand Afrikaans University in South Africa. She has devoted her life to constructive human and organizational change. Working with ASTD (formerly American Society for Training and Development), she conducted an international study of the competencies needed by people in the HRD field. McLagan is co-author of* On-the-Level: Performance Communication That Works *and* The Age of Participation: New Governance for the Workplace and the World. *She is also author of* Customer Focused Goals, *as well as many articles about people and management practices in corporations. She has served as a member of the ASTD Board of Governors and on the board of the Instructional Systems Association. She is the fifteenth member and the second woman to be inducted into the International HRD Hall of Fame and a member of the International Adult and Continuing Education Hall of Fame. She holds ASTD's highest award, the Gordon Bliss Memorial Award, and the Larry Wilson Leadership Award.*

CHAPTER FOUR

Learning Organizations

Michael J. Marquardt, Ph.D.
President, Global Learning Associates

Becoming a learning organization has become essential for success in the 21st Century. Learning organizations are dramatically different from organizations that focus only on performance. The Systems Linked Learning Organization Model described in this chapter contains five subsystems: (1) learning dynamics, (2) organization transformation, (3) people participation, (4) knowledge management, and (5) technology utilization. Best practices in learning of companies from around the world are presented.

THE LEARNING ORGANIZATION

As we enter the 21st Century, we are entering a new era in the evolution of organizational life and structure. The immense changes in the economic environment caused by globalization and technology have forced organizations from around the world to make significant transformations in order to adapt, survive, and succeed in the next millennium.

The change we are talking about is not just the external elements of the organization—its products, activities, or structures—but rather its intrinsic way of operating—its values, mindset, even its primary *purpose*. Owen (1991) states this message well when he writes, "There was a time when the prime business of business was to make a profit and a product. There is now a prior, prime business, which is to become an effective learning organization. Not that profit and product are no longer important, but without continual learning, profits and products will no longer be possible. Hence the strange thought: the business of business is learning—and all else will follow" (p. 1).

Organizations with brainpower the size of dinosaurs will not survive in the faster, information-thick atmosphere of the new millennium. Making themselves bigger, heavier, and with tougher "hides" will not be a substitute for greater, agile, and creative brainpower. Or to cite another biological metaphor, putting quicker legs on a caterpillar will never enable the caterpillar to match the range and flexibility it achieves when it has been transformed into a butterfly.

Why Organizational Learning Is Critical

The demands put on organizations now require learning to be delivered faster, cheaper, and more effectively to a fluid workplace and mobile workforce more dramatically affected by daily changes in the marketplace than ever before.

Here are some of these critical issues facing today's corporations:

- Reorganization, restructuring, and reengineering for success, if not just survival;
- Increased skills shortages with schools unable to adequately prepare for work in the 21st Century;
- Doubling of knowledge every two to three years;
- Global competition from the world's most powerful companies;
- Overwhelming breakthroughs of new and advanced technologies; and
- Spiraling need for organizations to adapt to change.

Corporate-wide, systems-wide learning offers organizations the best opportunity of not only surviving but also succeeding. To obtain and sustain a competitive advantage in this new environment, organizations will have to learn better and faster from their successes and failures. They will need to transform themselves continuously into a learning organization, to become places where groups and individuals continuously engage in new learning processes (Schwandt & Marquardt, 2000).

Shoshana Zuboff, in her 1988 classic *In the Age of the Smart Machine,* notes how today's organization may indeed have little choice but to become a "learning institution, since one of its principal purposes will have to be the expansion of knowledge. Not knowledge for its own sake (as in academic pursuit), but knowledge that comes to reside at the core of what it means to be productive. Learning is no longer a separate activity that occurs either before one enters the workplace or in remote classroom settings. Nor is it an activity preserved for a managerial group. The behaviors that define learning and the behaviors that define being productive are one and the same. Learning is the heart of productive activity. To put it simply, learning is the new form of labor" (p. 295).

What Is the "New" in Learning Organizations?

There are seven key paradigm shifts that make a learning organization different from the traditional organization.

Traditional Focus	*Learning Organization Focus*
Productivity	Performance
Workplace	Learning environment
Control	Empowerment
Training	Learning
Worker	Continuous learner
Supervisor/manager	Coach and learner
Engagement/activity	Learning opportunity

As a result of these paradigm shifts, there must be a whole new mindset and way of "seeing" organizations and the interplay between "work" and "learning." Learning must take place as an ongoing by-product of people doing their work—in contrast to the traditional approach of acquiring knowledge before performing a particular task or job (Marquardt, 1996).

OVERVIEW OF SYSTEMS LINKED MODEL

A learning organization has the powerful capacity to collect, store, and transfer knowledge and thereby continuously transform itself for corporate success. It empowers people within and outside the company to learn as they work and utilizes technology to optimize both learning and productivity.

Each of these characteristics is part and parcel of the systems model. In the systems learning organization model, there are five subsystems that are closely interrelated and interface and support one another. (See Figure 4.1.) The core subsystem of the learning organization is *learning,* and this dimension permeates the other four subsystems. Each of the other subsystems—*organization, people, knowledge,* and *technology*—is necessary to enhance and augment the quality and impact of the learning. They are the indispensable partners essential for building, maintaining, and sustaining learning and productivity in the learning organization. The five subsystems are dynamically interrelated and complement each other. If any subsystem is weak or absent, the effectiveness of

Figure 4.1. The Learning Organization Model

the other subsystems is significantly weakened. Let us now briefly examine each of the five dimensions of a fully functioning learning organization.

1. Learning Subsystem

The learning subsystem refers to: (a) levels of learning, (b) types of learning crucial for organizational learning, and (c) critical organizational learning skills.

a. Levels of Learning

Individual learning refers to the change of skills, insights, knowledge, attitudes, and values acquired by a person through self-study, technology-based instruction, and observation.

Group or team learning alludes to the increase in knowledge, skills and competency that is accomplished by and within groups.

Organization learning represents the enhanced intellectual and productive capability gained through corporate-wide commitment and opportunity to continuously improve. It differs from individual and group/team learning in two basic respects. First, organizational learning occurs through the shared insights, knowledge, and mental models of members of the organization. Second, organizational learning builds on past knowledge and experience, that is, on organizational memory that depends on institutional mechanisms (for example, policies, strategies, and explicit models) used to retain knowledge.

b. Types of Learning

Adaptive, Anticipatory, and Generative. *Adaptive* learning is learning from the experience and reflection. *Anticipatory* learning is the process of acquiring knowledge from expecting the future (a vision-action-reflection approach), whereas *generative* learning is the learning that is created from reflection, analysis, or creativity.

Single-Loop, Double-Loop, and Deutero Learning. These types of learning are differentiated by the degree of reflection placed on action that has occurred in the organization.

Action Learning. Action learning involves a learning team, questioning, and reflection on real organizational problems, a commitment to action and learning, and learning facilitation (Marquardt, 1999). Several learning companies have made extensive use of action learning sets to learn and achieve organizational success. General Electric, for one, has declared action learning as a vital strategy in transforming GE "into a global-thinking, fast-changing organization" (Marquardt, p. 217).

c. Skills of Organizational Learning

Systems thinking represents a conceptual framework one uses to make full patterns clearer and to help one see how to change them effectively.

Mental models are the deeply ingrained assumptions that influence how we understand the world and how we take action. For example, our mental model or image of learning or work or patriotism impacts how we relate and act in situations in which those concepts are operating.

Personal mastery indicates the high level of proficiency in a subject or skill area. It requires a commitment to lifelong learning so as to develop an expertise or special, enjoyed proficiency in whatever one does in the organization.

Shared vision involves the skill of unearthing shared "pictures" of the future that fosters genuine commitment and enrollment, rather than compliance.

Dialogue denotes the high level of listening and communication between people. It requires the free and creative exploration of subtle issues, a deep listening to one another, and suspension of one's own views. The discipline of dialogue involves learning how to recognize the patterns of interaction in teams that promote or undermine learning. For example, the patterns of defensiveness are often deeply ingrained in how a group of people or an organization operates. If unrecognized or avoided, they undermine learning. If recognized and surfaced creatively, they can actually accelerate learning. Dialogue is the critical medium for connecting, inventing, and coordinating learning and action in the workplace.

No organization has applied the learning subsystem as much or as well as Arthur Andersen Worldwide. The new learning model at Andersen recognizes that "learning the process of getting the right answer" is the most important issue. The critical task is now to make the learning more efficient and effective. This new model of staff development at Andersen centers on the learner who, as a decision maker, chooses from among various available tools and resources to learn what he or she needs for success. The emphasis is on the learning needed by the learner. The former role of instructor/presenter has been shifted to one of coach/mentor/facilitator (Marquardt, 1996).

2. Organization Subsystem

The second subsystem of a learning organization is the organization itself, the setting and body in which the learning itself occurs. The four key dimensions or components of this subsystem are vision, culture, strategy, and structure.

Vision captures a company's hopes, goals, and direction for the future. It is the image of the organization that is transmitted inside and outside the organization. In a learning organization, it depicts and portrays the desired future picture of the company in which learning and learners create the company's continuously new and improving products and services.

Singapore Airlines, the world's most successful airline, exemplifies how a clear vision can create and transfer powerful learning throughout the organization. Corporate philosophy and documents are filled with statements emphasizing the importance of learning for present and ongoing corporate success (Marquardt & Reynolds, 1994).

Culture refers to the values, beliefs, practices, rituals, and customs of an organization. It helps to shape behavior and to fashion perceptions. In a learning organization, the corporate culture is one in which learning is recognized as absolutely critical for business success, where learning has become a habit and an integrated part of all organizational functions. This rich adaptable culture creates integrated relationships and enhances learning by encouraging values such as teamwork, self-management, empowerment, and sharing. It is the opposite of a closed, rigid, bureaucratic architecture.

At Royal Bank of Canada, learning is a committed three-way partnership among the employee, the managers, and the HRD department. Learning opportunities are available at all times inside and outside of the Bank. As James Gannon, vice president of human resources planning and development, notes, "Learning has to become a way of life rather than a once-in-while type of event" (Marquardt & Reynolds, 1994, p. 233).

Strategy relates to the action plans, methodologies, tactics, and steps that are employed to reach a company's vision and goals. In a learning organization, these are strategies that optimize the learning acquired, transferred, and utilized in all company actions and operations.

Structure includes the departments, levels, and configurations of the company. A learning organization is a streamlined, flat, boundaryless structure that maximizes contact, information flow, local responsibility, and collaboration within and outside the organization.

Hewlett-Packard, once a "lumbering dinosaur" in terms of structure and innovation, has become "gazelle-like" with speed of learning a top priority. Learning teams now rethink every process from product development to distribution. Asea Brown Boveri (ABB) and General Electric have taken similar steps to restructure themselves into learning organizations (Marquardt, 1996).

3. People Subsystem

The people subsystem of the learning organization includes employees, managers/ leaders, customers, business partners (suppliers, vendors, and subcontractors), and the community itself. Each of these groups is valuable to the learning organization, and all need to be empowered and enabled to learn.

Employees as learners are empowered and expected to learn, to plan for their future competencies, to take action and risks, and to solve problems.

Honda is an exemplary company in empowering its people. Honda does not just talk empowerment; it permits people to set out and create the new cars. Robert Simcox, a plant manager, says that Honda people are learning together because they have been "given the power to use their own creativity and imagination" (Marquardt, 1996, p. 105).

Managers/Leaders as learners carry out coaching, mentoring, and modeling roles with a primary responsibility of generating and enhancing learning opportunities for people around them.

Customers as learners participate in identifying needs, receiving training, and being linked to the learning of the organization.

Suppliers and vendors as learners can receive and contribute to instructional programs. *Alliance partners* as learners can benefit by sharing competencies and knowledge. *Community groups* as learners include social, educational, and economic agencies that can share in providing and receiving learning.

4. Knowledge Subsystem

The knowledge subsystem of a learning organization refers to the management of acquired and generated knowledge of the organization. It includes the acquisition, creation, storage, transfer, and utilization of knowledge:

- *Acquisition* is the collection of existing data and information from within and outside the organization via benchmarking, conferences, environmental scans, use of Internet and staff suggestions. For example, Xerox and Sony regularly benchmark and systematically participate in information exchange programs.

- *Creation* is new knowledge that is created within the organization through problem solving and insights.

- *Storage* is the coding and preserving of the organization's valued knowledge for easy access by any staff member, at any time, and from anywhere.

- *Transfer* is the mechanical, electronic, and interpersonal movement of information and knowledge, both intentionally and unintentionally, throughout the organization.

- *Application and validation* are the leveraging of new knowledge into new services, products, and processes.

The knowledge elements of organizational learning are ongoing and interactive instead of sequential and independent. The collection and distribution of information occurs through multiple channels, each having different time frames. An example is an online newsletter that systematically gathers, organizes, and disseminates the collective knowledge of the organization's members.

McKinsey & Company uses some of the following knowledge-management strategies:

- A director of knowledge management coordinates company efforts in creating and collecting knowledge;
- Knowledge transfer is a part of everyone's job and is considered as part of the personnel evaluation process;
- Employees must prepare a two-page summary of how and what they have learned from a project before they receive a billing code;
- Every three months, each project manger receives a printout of what he or she has put into the company's information system;
- An online information system called the Practice Development Network is updated weekly and now has over six thousand documents, including the Knowledge Resource Directory and a guide to who knows what in the company; and
- For any of the thirty-one practice areas of McKinsey, an employee can find the list of its expert members and core documents by tapping into the database (Schwandt & Marquardt, 2000, pp. 156–158).

5. Technology Subsystem

The technology subsystem contains the supporting, integrated, and technological networks and information tools that allow access to and exchange of information and learning. It includes technical processes, systems, and structure for collaboration, coaching, coordination, and other knowledge skills. It encompasses electronic tools and advanced methods for learning, such as computer conferencing, simulation, and computer supported collaboration. All these tools work to create knowledge freeways.

The two major components of the technology subsystem are technology-based learning and technology-based management of knowledge.

Technology-based learning involves the utilization of video, audio, and computer-based multimedia training for the purpose of delivering and sharing knowledge and skills.

Technology for managing knowledge refers to the computer-based technology that gathers, codes, stores, and transfers information across organizations and across the world. It includes elements such as data mining and electronic performance support systems (EPSS).

Federal Express is perhaps the leading learning organization in the world in utilizing technology for improving performance. The company recently began a program for 35,000 of its employees that consists of job knowledge tests linked to an interactive video instruction curriculum on workstations in more than seven hundred locations world-wide. The workers at Federal Express receive over 132,000 hours per year of interactive video instruction (Marquardt & Kearsley, 1999).

CONCLUSION

Learning quickly and systematically is critical for surviving in the 21st Century. The organization that makes learning its core value can rapidly leverage its new knowledge into new products, new marketing strategies, and new ways of doing business. Learning organizations will become the only place where global success is possible, where quality is more assured, and where energetic and talented people want to be.

References

Marquardt, M. (1996). *Building the learning organization.* New York: McGraw-Hill.

Marquardt, M. (1999). *Action learning in action: Transforming problems and people for world-class organizational learning.* Palo Alto, CA: Davies-Black.

Marquardt, M., & Kearsley, G. (1999). *Technology-based learning.* Boca Raton, FL: St. Lucie Press.

Marquardt, M., & Reynolds, A. (1994). *The global learning organization: Gaining competitive advantage through continuous learning.* New York: Irwin.

Owen, H. (1991). *The business of learning.* Potomac, MD: Abbott.

Schwandt, D., & Marquardt, M. (2000). *Organizational learning: From world-class theories to global best practices.* Boca Raton, FL: St. Lucie Press.

Zuboff, S. (1988). *In the age of the smart machine.* New York: Basic Books.

Recommended Reading

Chawla, S., & Renesch, J. (Eds.). (1995). *Learning organizations: Developing cultures for tomorrow's workplace.* Portland, OR: Productivity Press.

Davenport, T., & Prusak, L. (1997). *Working knowledge: How organizations manage what they know.* Boston: Harvard Business School Press.

Garvin, D. (2000). *Learning in action: A guide to putting the learning organization to work.* Boston: Harvard Business School Press.

Nonaka, I. (1991). The knowledge-creating company. *Harvard Business Review, 69*(6), 96–104.

Senge, P. (1990). *The fifth discipline.* New York: Doubleday.

Watkins, K., & Marsick, V. (1993). *Sculpting the learning organization.* San Francisco: Jossey-Bass.

About the Author

Michael J. Marquardt is a professor of human resource development and program director of overseas programs at George Washington University. He also serves as president of Global Learning Associates, a premier consulting firm assisting corporations around the world to become successful global learning organizations.

Dr. Marquardt is the author of fourteen books and over sixty professional articles in the fields of leadership, learning, globalization, and organizational change, including Building the Learning Organization *(selected as Book of the Year by the Academy of HRD),* Organizational Learning: From World-Class Theories to Global Best Practices, Action Learning in Action, Global Leaders for the 21st Century, Global Human Resource Development, *and* Technology-Based Learning. *He has been a keynote speaker at international conferences in Australia, Japan, England, the Philippines, Malaysia, South Africa, Sweden, Singapore, and India, as well as throughout North America.*

Dr. Marquardt's achievements and leadership have been recognized though numerous awards, including the International Practitioner of the Year Award from ASTD (formerly the American Society for Training and Development). He presently serves as a senior advisor for the United Nations Staff College in the areas of policy, technology, and learning systems.

CHAPTER FIVE

Change Management

Jay A. Conger, Ph.D.
Professor, London Business School

Training that focuses on change management holds great potential for building highly adaptive organizations. When conducted properly, it can accelerate change efforts and ensure their successful implementation. Critical to their success, however, are several basic factors. These include a well-articulated change agenda, pre-planning by leaders responsible for the change, thorough assessment processes, learning organized around management cohorts, curriculums designed to elicit collective dialogue, trained facilitators, active feedback mechanisms, and reinforcement mechanisms. Without these, programs will have only limited impact.

INTRODUCTION

Training interventions that facilitate change management are among the most powerful of educational experiences. Bringing together different functions, departments, and levels into a single and often ongoing initiative, they hold the promise of building widespread commitment to new directions. More importantly, these types of initiatives can accelerate the implementation of major change by spreading ownership broadly, ensuring well-coordinated change efforts, and building a shared mindset about implementation approaches. At the same time, these educational interventions are among the most demanding. Their multi-functional and multi-level dimensions often require complicated logistics and rigorous facilitation. Because of the evolving nature of most change efforts, many programs require multiple sessions spread over time. In addition, the better programs track whether objectives have been successfully achieved or not. This requires that program designers be savvy about knowing what are the "right" objectives and how these can best be measured.

A TYPICAL DESIGN FOR CHANGE MANAGEMENT INITIATIVES

While there are numerous variations, the more common training designs for change management involve three phases. The first is an *assessment and agenda-setting* stage. During this phase, program designers conduct assessments of the organization's readiness and capacity for change as well as clarify the change agenda that will guide the actual training experience. Typically, designers interview key players to determine the central issues that the education initiative must address. For example, assessments survey the state of knowledge about change management, potential obstacles to the change effort, the level of organizational readiness, the leadership capabilities of the key players, potential benchmarks to measure progress, and the range of possible implementation approaches. In parallel, the senior-most leaders responsible for the change effort should be engaged in discussions to clarify and refine the change agenda that will be presented in upcoming educational workshops.

The second phase consists of one or ongoing *workshops that have both educational and application components.* Typically, intact work groups or cohorts are brought together in these workshops. In the ideal case, they are mixed in levels and functions so that all those concerned with implementing the change effort are together in the educational experience. This is to ensure a multi-functional perspective that in turn can build consensus and ownership into the change effort. With the aim of generating a sense of urgency and garnering the commitment of participants, the educational program begins with an overview of the organization's change effort and its rationale. This is followed by educational content that provides information on the state of knowledge on change management, along with diagnostic and implementation frameworks. The focus then typically shifts to the application of this knowledge to the change situation facing the participants. Facilitated discussions using change management frameworks and diagnostics are employed to build consensus around the key change issues, identify specific action steps, set targets and goals, assign responsibilities, and establish follow-up steps.

The third phase centers around *ongoing reinforcement* designed to maintain the momentum of the change management workshops. For example, programs might be followed by town meetings to further communicate and disseminate the change effort, the implementation of new reward and performance measurements, and changes in organizational structures and reporting relationships.

Critical Design Elements for Change Management Programs

From studying training initiatives designed to facilitate change management, it has been noted that several elements must be in place to ensure success. These include: (1) a well-articulated change agenda, (2) pre-planning by senior leaders, (3) thorough pre-program assessments, (4) learning organized around management cohorts, (5) curriculums designed to elicit collective dialogue, (6) trained facilitators, (7) active feedback mechanisms, and (8) reinforcement mechanisms. Each of these is explored in some depth below.

Program Content Determined by a Clear Change Agenda. Pivotal to the success of any change management program is the issue of whether the organization's change agenda is well-thought-out. Because these programs provide structured experiences that focus participants on new directions and improve their understanding of how organizational changes need to be implemented in local, day-to-day practice, it is imperative that the change agenda be clear and well-articulated. If the rationale and ultimate outcomes of the change agenda are unclear or clouded by competing initiatives, the educational effort will simply surface underlying conflicts, create frustration, and ultimately increase opposition to the change effort. For example, if program sponsors lack a real understanding of and true conviction about the change agenda, they will be unable to represent the rationale for the changes being proposed. As a result, programs may end up generating more questions than answers.

It is important to note, however, that clarity about the change agenda should not be confused with clarity about the *implementation* of that agenda. Although the change objectives should be clear beforehand, the goal of the educational initiative itself is to engage all involved levels of the organization in determining preferred implementation approaches.

Pre-Work by Senior Levels Responsible for the Change Effort. Although change management initiatives are increasingly designed to cascade down levels and across functions, most begin at the senior-most levels responsible for the change. It is crucial that management at this level first build a shared vision of the change effort's objectives and rationale before asking those below them to take actions in support of it. If this vision remains ambiguous or in dispute, subsequent decisions at all levels—such as key appointments, skill requirements, resource allocation, and implementation plans—will be difficult to make because of the larger uncertainties clouding management's intentions. Getting senior leaders to work closely together to agree on and enact a shared vision can be a difficult challenge. For example, senior managers rarely function as true teams, and the day-to-day demands on senior leaders have a way of distracting attention from longer-term thinking. It is particularly difficult in very large or fluid organizations where senior leaders may be distributed across the globe or may move through positions frequently. Carefully planned exercises, well-focused topics, and dedicated facilitators can help the senior leaders surface their underlying assumptions and force differences of opinion to be discussed and resolved, rather than ignored.

Pre-Program Assessment of the Organization's Readiness and Capacity for Change. Although up-front needs assessment is widely recommended in the development of all new training initiatives, it is frequently omitted in the face of day-to-day pressures and deadlines. Needs assessment, however, is a critical design element in any educational program focusing on change. An effective assessment should cover, at the very least, the following topic areas: (1) identification of key players to be involved in the change effort, (2) their views on the change itself, (3) political/cultural roadblocks and other sources of resistance, (4) resource constraints, (5) new skill and organizational requirements, (6) depth of understanding of change management processes, (7) extent of cross-functional teamwork and communications, and (8) identification of potential champions for change initiatives.

Learning Objectives and Delivery Methods Structured Around Management Cohorts. One of the most important design elements of effective change management programs is their use of cohorts—teams of managers—in the learning process. The goal of cohort learning is not only to build widespread consensus about the need for the change effort, but also about the most effective implementation steps. The team-building aspects of cohort learning should not be underestimated. Collaborative learning in actual work teams enhances knowledge transfer and its practical application. Where relationships are good—but perhaps distant or fragmented—focused time together can encourage individuals to learn more about one another's goals, expectations, and perspectives on the change effort. It also fosters among individuals a better understanding of the problems or obstacles they each face in attempting to achieve their individual goals. A further byproduct of team building is that it often enhances a group's ability to communicate effectively, to discuss issues openly, to lead as a collective, and to consider a broader range of potential solutions.

Curriculums Designed to Elicit Collective Dialogue Between Units and Across Levels. A *multi-level* and *multi-functional* approach is necessary in change management programs. It ensures that all levels and functions of the firm have a consistent understanding of the change agenda, the needs for multi-level coordination, and the implementation steps essential to moving the organization forward. Cascading helps to build consensus about what the change initiative means to individual leaders at different levels of the organization. It ensures that participants make strategically consistent decisions when acting independently.

In addition, cascading initiatives build in forums for managers at more senior levels to convey the organization's change agenda to levels directly below them. Each successive level typically plays a role in helping those below them translate the vision at their level. This works nicely because each level of management is helped by the level above it to understand the change agenda in its own terms and context. Because the initiative cascades downward, higher-level managers have already struggled through the process in earlier sessions and have formed a collective understanding of the implications for what they must accomplish. This makes them ideal coaches for guiding the process at the next level, as they understand the initiative, have wrestled with the concepts, and are familiar with the next level's responsibilities and how they must contribute.

Finally, there is a *symbolic* importance to the downward cascade. Senior management depends on those below them to think critically about the organization's practices and to make significant process improvements at each level. By discussing the change agenda, encouraging comments, answering questions, and incorporating feedback, company leaders demonstrate their conviction to the agenda and their desire to involve other levels in its shaping. Moreover, by practicing open communication and encouraging interaction, these leaders then become role models for others to emulate in their interactions with employees down the line.

Trained Facilitators. It is important to have facilitators in change management programs due to the need to build consensus and to challenge existing worldviews. Because change issues tend to be complex and are often charged, facilitators are critical to keeping working groups focused by ensuring that discussions do not become sidetracked on unproductive tangents. Ideally, these individuals should be from outside the organization itself. Outsider status allows facilitators to question existing assumptions more openly, challenge traditional practices, and remain free from political influence and the potential ramifications of threatening the status quo.

Active Feedback Mechanisms. By active feedback mechanisms, we are referring to specific ways for program designers and sponsors to monitor the views of program participants and to track the program's progress in meeting objectives. One of the most important feedback mechanisms can be the direct interaction between program participants and the program's main sponsors. This can take the form of discussion forums with the senior leaders responsible for the change effort. Open two-way communication between leader-participants and the senior officials sponsoring the initiative can provide each with a feel for the other's goals and concerns. It signals the program's importance, enhances its credibility, and conveys important information. In addition, facilitators can play an important feedback role by relaying general impressions of common problem areas facing working groups or by identifying the best practices of individual working groups that might be widely shared. Finally, follow-up meetings that update participants on implementation progress, new developments, and mid-course corrections are another important feedback mechanism.

Reinforcement Following Programs. One of the greatest risks an initiative built around change management can face is that it will be seen as simply "an event," rather than as part of an ongoing change process. Moreover, these programs raise expectations. Employees leave with a sense of hope and momentum that places an onus on the program's sponsors and designers to maintain its energy and focus. Instead, early successes may rob the initiative of its sense of urgency. Shifts in the firm's environment may lead senior leaders to plan additional initiatives that all too quickly supplant the first. A subsequent radical change in strategy may ultimately undermine the entire effort. These are but a few of the challenges that program designers and corporate leaders must face in the wake of these very demanding interventions.

For the above reasons, periodic reviews are critically important. In addition, changes across a number of organizational dimensions are ultimately required to ensure successful implementation of any change effort. These may include changes in incentive systems, performance measures, job assignments, organizational structures and reporting relationships, selection and promotion criteria, and skills training and development.

CONCLUSION

Training can play a significant role in change management. It must, however, go significantly beyond simply teaching participants about the process of change management and providing diagnostics and frameworks. Instead, it must center on the change effort itself. The knowledge and tools that are learned must be applied immediately to the challenge at hand. By following some of the basic guidelines outlined in this chapter, change leaders can be sure that educational interventions not only help participants become better leaders of change but also ensure that the change process itself is implemented effectively and has long-lasting impact.

Recommended Reading

Conger, J.A., & Benjamin, B. (1999). *Building leaders.* San Francisco: Jossey-Bass.

Conger, J.A., & Xin, K. (1998). Executive education: A lever for organizational change. In J.R. Galbraith, S.A. Mohrman, & E.E. Lawler (Eds.), *Tomorrow's organization.* (pp. 264–285). San Francisco: Jossey-Bass.

Dotlich, D.L., & Noel, J.L. (1998). *Action learning.* San Francisco: Jossey-Bass.

Kanter, R.M., Stein, B.A., & Jick, T.D. (1992). *The challenge of organizational change.* New York: Free Press.

Vicere, A., & Fulmer, R.M. (1997). *Leadership by design.* Boston: Harvard Business School Press.

About the Author

Jay A. Conger is professor of organizational behavior at the London Business School and senior research scientist at the Center for Effective Organizations at the University of Southern California in Los Angeles. Formerly the executive director of the Leadership Institute at the University of Southern California, Conger is one of the world's experts on leadership. An outstanding teacher, he has been selected by Business Week *as the best business school professor to teach leadership to executives. Author of over seventy articles and book chapters and nine books, he researches leadership, boards of directors, organizational change, and the training and development of leaders and managers. His articles have appeared in the* Harvard Business Review, Organizational Dynamics, Business & Strategy, *the* Leadership Quarterly, *the* Academy of Management Review, *and the* Journal of Organizational Behavior. *He is currently the associate editor of the* Leadership Quarterly. *One of his books,* Learning to Lead *(Jossey-Bass, 1992), has been described by* Fortune *magazine as "the source" for understanding leadership development.*

CHAPTER SIX

What Smart Trainers Should Know About Organizational Culture

Edgar H. Schein, Ph.D.
Sloan Fellows Professor of Management Emeritus and Senior Lecturer,
MIT Sloan School of Management

This paper defines what culture is, what the components of any given culture are, how to assess these various components, when an assessment needs to be done as part of any given change program, and how cultural evolution and change have to be tied to the developmental stage of the organization. The role of leadership and the role of the trainer are described.

WHAT CULTURE IS AND WHY IT IS IMPORTANT

Culture is for the group what character or personality is for the individual. It is the invisible but palpable force that determines behavior. Does every group or organization have a culture in this sense? Yes, if the group has shared some significant experiences that allowed the members to learn how to survive in its external environment and to integrate its internal working.

Culture is both the strength from which the group operates and a set of constraints in that what the group has learned will not be given up easily. Once a group has some common learning and experience, that experience will be formulated as a set of shared, tacit assumptions about how to view the world, how to think about it, and how to feel about things. In that sense, culture defines for the members of a group both its external and internal reality.

Culture forms wherever there has been common group experience and learning. Therefore, any unit in an organization that has a common history, including the organization as a whole, will have a culture. The strength and degree of articulation of that culture will depend on the length of time the group has shared experiences, the degree of imposition of values and beliefs on the part of leaders during that history, and the intensity of the emotional learning. If a group has constantly changing leaders and members, it will have a weak culture or no culture at all.

If culture defines how to perceive, think about, and feel about internal and external reality, there will be a communication problem whenever two or more cultures have to work together. This can be observed when the different functional, geographic, product, or market groups of an organization have to work together. It can be observed in the conflicts between field units and headquarters. It is most obvious in acquisitions, mergers, and various types of partnerships and joint ventures.

The Components or Dimensions of Culture

There are many dimensions along which culture can be analyzed. If culture is the group's learned solution to external problems of survival and internal problems of integration, it is most useful to analyze cultural assumptions around what those sets of problems are.

Every group must figure out

- Its mission, primary task, strategy, and goals;
- The means it will use to accomplish these goals;
- The measurement systems it will use to determine its progress; and
- The correction systems it will use if it is off course.

One set of cultural elements, then, will be the learned shared assumptions about *mission, means,* and *measurement.* It is especially important to recognize that strategy and organizational structures and processes become part of a group's culture. They are not independent elements.

Every group must also figure out

- A common language and communication system;
- Its boundaries, identity, and rules for entry and exit;
- How to define authority and other relationships; and
- How to allocate rewards and status.

A second set of cultural elements, then, will be the learned solutions to these internal problems. These dimensions are often more obvious to the culture analyst, but it should not be forgotten that the culture includes the elements of mission, means, and measurement as well.

Every group is embedded in larger groups and larger cultures. When one looks at nations, religions, ethnic groups, and other larger cultural units, one can also define a set of dimensions that anthropologists have used in comparing such larger units. These dimensions reflect the basic human problems of survival and integration. Thus every culture will have embedded in it assumptions about the following fundamental issues:

- How humans relate to nature;
- How reality and truth are defined;
- What human nature is;
- What the basics of human relationships are; and
- The nature of time and space.

Whether and How to "Assess" or "Measure" Culture

Just as there are many approaches to measuring personality, ranging from quantitative surveys to complex projective tests, so there are many approaches to describing and assessing culture. The decision on what methods to use depends largely on the purpose of the assessment and the validity of the theory on which a particular assessment approach is based.

For example, if one were trying to compare large cultural units, one would probably use the more general dimensions, whereas if one were trying to assess how to make two functional units work together better, one would use the three M's and the internal integration dimensions.

For those trainers who want to do general cultural analysis, I have provided some references to books that would give them tools. However, it is my belief that most organizational issues require an intervention approach based on process consultation, and that, in turn, requires cultural *self-assessment* rather than measurement by outsiders. Such self-assessment involves some variant of the following steps:

1. Bring together a diagonal slice of the organization or group being studied (size 15 to 25).

2. Give the group a model of how to think about culture in terms of three levels: the visible artifacts, the espoused values, and the shared tacit assumptions.

3. Have the group brainstorm all the artifacts of their culture they can think of and write them all down on flip charts.

4. As values are articulated, put them on different flip charts and begin to assess with the group whether the observed artifacts, that is, how things are actually done in the organization, match the espoused values.

5. Look for discrepancies between the espoused values and the observed artifacts. Ask what is really driving the observed behavior and probe for the shared assumptions that are taken for granted.

6. Assess the assumptions identified in terms of the degree to which they would aid or hinder making the changes that motivated the assessment in the first place (see below).

7. Encourage building on the existing assumptions, because changing assumptions is much more difficult.

When to Do a Cultural Self-Assessment

Assessing culture for its own sake is a waste of time and energy. A cultural assessment is only relevant in relation to some change agenda having to do with the performance of the organization. If there is a need to improve something or correct something, then it may be relevant to determine whether present cultural dimensions will aid or hinder this effort.

One should always start with the concept of defining the new way of working that is desired. Only when this has been specifically identified and clearly stated should one examine the culture. For example, saying that the organization should become more "team oriented" is not sufficiently specific. Which people on which projects are supposed to do what with each other? Only when this has been clearly articulated should one ask, "Will our culture help us or hinder us in getting to this new way of working?"

If some elements of the culture are a hindrance, then a culture change program may be required, but only then. If an element of the culture needs to be changed, a change team must be formed to design, plan, and implement the change process within the existing culture. The details of that process will depend on the existing culture and what has to be changed (Schein, 1999a, 1999b).

LEADERSHIP AND DEVELOPMENT STAGE

Culture evolves initially from the values and assumptions of founders and leaders. With shared experiences of success, the individual values and assumptions of the leader gradually become shared assumptions. With age and growth, the organization evolves into subgroups and units that develop their own subcultures. Those subcultures will reflect elements of the larger culture, but will also be the product of learning in their own particular environments and thus will differ in varying degrees.

As organizations mature, new leaders will evolve from the existing culture. Thus, in the early stages of an organization, leaders create culture; but at mature stages, culture creates leaders in defining the criteria by which people get ahead.

Cultural evolution then takes place through maverick leaders or leaders from the outside who change some behavior and show that the new behavior is more successful than the old. If the new behavior is not more successful, the leader will lose credibility and be ejected.

Once organizations are at a mature stage with diverse subcultures, they evolve through the differential selection of leaders from the different subcultures. Thus, for example, if an organization faces the need to become more marketing-oriented, it can promote to senior executive positions people from those divisions that are already the most marketing-oriented or experienced. Most culture change occurs through this evolutionary process.

It is the unique responsibility of top leadership to manage this process of cultural evolution, which requires top leaders to have sufficient cultural perspective to perceive what is needed. Top leaders, therefore, need to become culturally "marginal" in their own organization, enabling them to perceive their own organization's culture objectively.

THE TRAINER'S ROLE

Most of all, the trainer must understand culture and cultural dynamics in order to educate members of the organization to the realities of culture. The trainer must develop educational interventions that help people to understand what culture is and does. These interventions must be culturally specific to the organization in which he or she is working; hence, there is no easy formula for what to do.

The best approach is to work around existing change agendas. Identify things that the organization wants to do differently and better. Bring together appropriate groups based on what the issue is to examine the change agenda, to develop specific concepts of "the new way of working," and then help the group to assess the cultural elements that will aid or hinder.

SUMMARY PRINCIPLES

In summary, remember the following principles about culture change:

1. Culture is the most stable part of any given organization. Culture change should, therefore, only be undertaken with full knowledge of how difficult, expensive, and time-consuming that will be.

2. Culture should not be analyzed or changed for its own sake. Like personality, culture is simply part of the ongoing social structure. You only do something about it when the person or organization is dissatisfied with some aspect of their functioning and discovers that the culture can be either an aid or a constraint to making those desired changes.

3. Culture assessment for its own sake does not work because culture is simply too complex. If some changes are desired in how the organization performs, then assessing the culture in relation to those goals makes sense.

4. Culture is a group phenomenon, *a shared set of tacit assumptions.* Therefore, it cannot be assessed with individual questionnaires. It is more effective to get groups together and elicit cultural artifacts, values, and shared tacit assumptions through a focus group process.

5. Culture forms around common experience. Any group or organization that has shared sufficient common experience will have evolved a culture in the sense of shared language, norms of behavior, common values, and assumptions about how things are and should be. If an organization has subgroups such as functional or geographical units, and if those subgroups have shared experience, they will develop cultures of their own that will function as subcultures in the larger organizational culture.

6. Culture and climate are different. Climate is the "feel" of the place and is palpable; culture is largely invisible but is manifested in overt behavior and in climate.

7. The important parts of culture are the shared assumptions about deep, basic issues such as *identity, mission, truth, the nature of relationships, time, space,* and *relationship to nature.* Changes at this level usually require changes of people, in that it is hard for an individual to change assumptions of this sort.

8. It is the fundamental role of *top leadership* to manage cultural evolution. If the leaders do nothing, the culture will evolve by its own dynamics in response to environmental and internal forces.

9. It is the specific role of *trainers* to educate the organization on the realities of culture and to show how culture relates to various change agendas that the organization may be struggling with.

References

Schein, E.H. (1999a). *The corporate culture survival guide.* San Francisco: Jossey-Bass.

Schein, E.H. (1999b). Cultural change. In D. Langdon, K.S. Whiteside, & M.M. McKenna (Eds.), *Intervention resource guide.* San Francisco: Jossey-Bass.

Recommended Reading

Cameron, K.S., & Quinn, R.E. (1999). *Diagnosing and changing organizational culture.* Reading, MA: Addison-Wesley.

Goffee, R., & Jones, G. (1998). *The character of a corporation.* New York: Harper-Collins.

Hofstede, G. (1991). *Cultures and organizations.* London: McGraw-Hill.

Schein, E.H. (1997). *Organizational culture and leadership* (2nd ed.). San Francisco: Jossey-Bass.

About the Author

Edgar H. Schein is the Sloan Fellows Professor of Management Emeritus and senior lecturer at the MIT Sloan School of Management, where he has taught since 1956. He received his Ph.D. in social psychology from Harvard in 1952. His most recent books are The Corporate Culture Survival Guide *(Jossey-Bass, 1999) and* Process Consultation Revisited *(Prentice-Hall, 1999). Dr. Schein is currently the founding editor of* Reflections—The Journal of the Society for Organizational Learning.

CHAPTER SEVEN

Legal Issues for Training and Development

Linda Byars Swindling, Esq.
Attorney-Mediator and Professional Speaker, The Peacemaker

With litigation on the rise, a trainer must know where the major legal pitfalls lie. Many trainers are infringing on others' copyrighted material during training, subjecting themselves to tough penalties. Others are unknowingly excluding or discriminating against participants, risking employment-based lawsuits against employers and clients. Some are facing liability in high-risk training situations. Others unknowingly are revealing confidential information that may result in an economic loss to the organization they train. Smart trainers know how to prevent potential legal problems and how to ask for help when they need it.

OVERVIEW OF THE ISSUES

Mention the words *legal issues* and automatically most trainers' minds jump to one of the following places. First, "I work in the training department. There is no way I need to know the legal aspects of this company, unless I am asked to present them as training material. Also, if something does go wrong, the company will defend me" or "I run my own training and development company. People are not going to waste their time coming after a small operation like mine. I have no money if a judgment were taken against me anyway." Other trainers are aware of legal issues surrounding copyright infringement, but have not been exposed to potential risks elsewhere. Some are intimidated by litigation for numerous reasons and do not know where to obtain information that actually relates to their profession.

This chapter will cover some potential legal risks in training. If you work for an organization, you may want to run certain training practices by your human resources department and by the company's legal representative as well. Usually, minor changes are all that are needed to avoid major risks. The training rule that the only dumb question is the one not asked is especially true when dealing with potential legal risks. Your job is to develop or present training. Whether you are independent or employed, the training field presents some unique legal issues.

PROTECTED INFORMATION

As copyright violations seem to be the issue most people think of when training, we'll begin with protected works.

Copyrighted Information

One of the most common mistakes trainers, experienced and new alike, make is the use of material that is not their own. It is difficult not to base a training program around a book that illuminates the issues so well or to not use a cartoon that sums up hours of training in one overhead or to ignore a song that seems written for the presentation.

What comes as a surprise is the justification seasoned trainers will use when presenting the material. Some trainers will explain that because they purchased and still have custody of the publication in which a cartoon was published, they have the rights to reproduce it. Others state that their application of the copyrighted material falls under the fair use doctrine because the training is a form of teaching or that the training is nonprofit because no additional money is being expended. Others state that because a film clip is only a few minutes or seconds that it is free to be used.

All of these "justifications" lead the way to copyright infringement lawsuits. Materials are copyrighted as protection from people who try to use the work of another as their own. Works can be dramatic, musical, artistic, or literary. Some examples are advertisements, performances, books, music, computer programs, drawings, and other forms of intellectual expression. The ownership interests of a copyright holder are broad, as shown in Exhibit 7.1.

Also protected is information copied electronically from a website. Many think that because the artwork or text has been placed on the Internet that it can be copied freely. Those materials are also subject to copyright laws.

Exhibit 7.1. Interests of Copyright Ownership

The owner of a copyright owns and controls the rights

- To reproduce the work;

- To prepare derivative works based on the work;

- To distribute copies or phonograph records of the work to the public, either by sale or by renting, leasing, or lending;

- To perform the work publicly, as in the case of musical or dramatic presentations or motion pictures;

- To display the work publicly; and

- To perform the work publicly by means of a digital audio transmission, in the case of sound recordings.

The Doctrine of Fair Use

Fair use was created to provide a balance between owners' rights and the public's need to have a free exchange of ideas. Fair use allows one to use a limited portion of another author's work without seeking permission first, if both the author and the place to find the copyrighted material are clearly acknowledged. The legal issue arises with exactly what constitutes a *limited portion*. Information obtained from the copyright office and a talk with an attorney may help shed light on where fair use leaves off and infringement begins. For instance, it would be difficult to use only a limited portion of a cartoon.

In addition, the fair use doctrine provides an exception for nonprofit educational purposes and for criticism, comment, and news reporting. Training is usually related to a commercial enterprise, so fair use will usually *not* protect a trainer against a copyright infringement suit.

Copyright Protection for Your Own Materials

With the protections afforded copyright owners, it makes sense to copyright your own materials. It is a relatively easy and painless procedure. Request an application form from the U.S. Copyright Office. Best of all, both the forms and the circulars describing the copyright process are free. See Exhibit 7.2, which gives contact information. The filing fee is relatively inexpensive ($30 at the date of writing).

The next question is whether you "own" the work you created. If you are employed at the time you create the material, there is a good chance that the copyright ownership belongs to the employer who paid you to create it. The term *work for hire* means that you created the work for someone else. Even if

Exhibit 7.2. Copyright Contact Information

There are numerous ways to receive copyright information, including a twenty-four hour telephone hotline at the Copyright Office [(202)707–9100] and a website [http://www.loc.gov/copyright] or by writing to the following address:

Library of Congress
Copyright Office
Publications Section, LM-455
101 Independence Avenue, S.E.
Washington, DC 20559–6000

---

you are an independent trainer, you may have agreed that any ownership interest in the work you created would go to your client. Be careful before signing away your ownership interest. Charge more if you must give up your ownership interest and the ability to resell the material to future clients.

When you do copyright your materials as an independent trainer, be certain to make this explicit in your dealings with clients. Explain in your agreement that your materials are copyrighted and explain what the client is authorized to do with the material. Many stories are told of trainers who developed their own work only to find their client incorporating the materials after telling them their services were no longer needed.

How to Use Protected Property

The general rule is, if it is not yours and you do not have permission, do not use it. So how do you request permission to use something? The biggest problem is usually finding the owner of the copyright. Generally, cartoons have a distributor and music is licensed from organizations such as the American Society of Composers, Authors, and Publishers (ASCAP) and Broadcast Music, Inc. (BMI). For a sample letter requesting permission, see Exhibit 7.3.

Once you obtain permission to use something, keep clear records of how you used it, including dates, places, and number of attendees. Also, make sure that you acknowledge the copyright holder's ownership on the material. For example, if you are using transparencies or PowerPoint® slides of a cartoon, each slide should state the date of the copyright, the name of the owner or owners, and that permission has been granted to use the materials, for example: "Copyright © 1999 United Media International. All rights reserved. Used with permission of the copyright holder."

Some trainers choose to avoid copyrighted materials entirely. They have custom cartoons created for them, use their own quotes in their own materials, and use royalty free music, which can be of an excellent quality.

Exhibit 7.3. Sample Letter Requesting Reprint Rights

Natasha Cooper
Reprints Rights Manager
United Media
200 Madison Avenue, 4th Floor
New York, NY 10016

Re: Reprint Permission for Dilbert Cartoons

Dear Ms. Cooper:

It is my understanding that United Media controls reprint rights for Scott Adams's cartoon "Dilbert." I am a consultant who presents training seminars on the legal aspects of consulting. Mr. Adams captures the essence of the ethical problems faced by consultants in the two cartoons enclosed. Please consider this my request to use both of these cartoons in future training seminars.

Over the next eighteen months, I will present this topic at approximately twenty functions at locations in the states of Texas, Florida, Georgia, and Virginia. It is anticipated that the attendance will range from fifty to four hundred participants at each session.

Of course, the proper acknowledgement will be placed at the bottom of each transparency.

Please let me know what fees are associated with this use and advise whether the original artwork can be sent to me on a computer disk.

Please contact me at (972)416-3652 if additional information is needed or another action should be taken on my part. Thank you for your help.

Very truly yours,

Linda Swinding, Esq.
The Peacemaker
1120 Metrocrest Drive, Suite 200
Carrollton, TX 75006

Enclosures

E. Biech & L.B. Swindling (2000). *The Consultant's Legal Guide.* San Francisco: Jossey-Bass, p. 211.

Penalties for Using Protected Works

Copyright infringement is taken seriously. More and more people in the music, film, and publishing industries have taken a tougher stance on unauthorized use of their materials. It is not uncommon for licensing companies to send representatives to conferences to determine whether any speaker is using material without permission.

By copyrighting their material, owners have enhanced rights in court cases and can ask for damages, including lost profits, possible statutory damages, court costs, and attorneys' fees. In serious cases, a federal court can enforce criminal sanctions on the infringer, including large fines and even imprisonment. Usually, however, an infringer will be restrained from continuing use of the material and face the possibility of civil damages.

PARTICIPANTS' RIGHTS

It is always important to present material in a way that participants can relate to, so you may be tempted to use actual incidents to make a point. By the very nature of the training profession, you are in contact with many people and hear many stories. Depending on your training topics, you also may deal with very personal issues that if not presented correctly could subject you or the organization to some serious legal claims.

Most employers also are subject to laws that protect their workers from unfair treatment and discrimination on the basis of age, race, gender, national origin, religion, color, disability, and military status. States may have laws that give even stronger protection to certain groups to prevent unfair treatment based on privacy issues, including life style choices.

As an employee of the company or an organization's agent, you must be especially sensitive to these issues. Telling inappropriate jokes regarding someone's gender or age or national origin, for instance, does nothing to enhance a program. Instead it separates some participants from others due to characteristics that cannot be changed. Further, you may have helped to build a case for discrimination against the company. This is especially true if employees are told that the training program is mandatory.

Be prepared to make reasonable accommodations for those with disabilities. Also, always give participants the ability to opt out of any exercises if they do not feel comfortable. You do not want to have others "bully" a teammate to perform a ropes exercise if the participant is pregnant, nor do you want to decide that an employee should not participate in an activity because of age or disability. It is much safer to have an environment in which people feel comfortable stating they do or do not want to participate.

Breach of Confidentiality

Whether you are an employee or an independent trainer, you may be given access to confidential information. Be clear what should remain confidential, as revealing this information could result in economic and other injuries to your company or to your client.

Employees or participants also may feel comfortable telling you private information about themselves. This poses a risk for you, especially if your company or client would want to know. For example, if an employee reveals an incident of sexual harassment in confidence and the trainer does not report the allegation, the organization may be held liable for sexual harassment that was reported but not resolved.

Injuries During Training

A trainer is expected to analyze possible physical dangers and determine whether the learning objectives can be met in a safer or better way. If the risk is greater than the training need, then a different method is needed or the liability issues must be addressed in some way. Some activities have higher risks involved, as shown in Exhibit 7.4.

HOW TO AVOID LIABILITY OR INJURY

In high-risk training activities, one of the best ways to limit your exposure is to conduct a comprehensive safety review of the activity and the proposed facility. If you have no experience with the training activity, you will want to hire an expert or a trainer certified in the proposed activity to identify any risks and to be on hand when the training is conducted. Even if you are an expert or are certified (in rock climbing, for example), hiring another expert to double-check your basic safety measures or to co-facilitate the training may be well worth the investment. You also may want to consider requiring performance bonds from vendors and contractors for adventure-based offerings.

A general rule of thumb is to make sure that everyone knows the basic guidelines and how the training will occur. Participants must feel comfortable raising their concerns and asking questions whenever they are unclear or need additional information.

Insurance

The type of insurance you might need depends on the possible liability due to injuries to a participant, a third person, others' property, or your own property. Many organizations and facilities have insurance to protect against injuries to participants or employees, so first determine whether injuries or accidents are

Exhibit 7.4. Activities That Involve Risk

- Sport climbing;
- Wilderness camping;
- Boating;
- Any activity involving extreme temperatures (hot or cold);
- Skiing or snowboarding;
- Traveling by bus or auto during bad weather or late at night;
- Any access to alcohol;
- Any involvement by children under the age of eighteen;
- Any physical activity that could trigger a heart attack or stroke;
- Any physical activity where a head injury, serious bodily injury, or a broken bone could occur;
- Any travel by auto or truck that occurs on a daily basis (for example, delivery service, trucking, or outside sales);
- Scuba diving, parasailing, or other activities often offered at resorts as part of a business meeting or incentive package you may have put together;
- Medical procedures or medication;
- Food service or preparation;
- Handling of any dangerous chemicals, explosives, or flammable substance;
- Any event involving traffic or crowd control; or
- Any event where personal security for participants is at risk.

E. Biech & L.B. Swindling (2000). *The Consultant's Legal Guide.* San Francisco: Jossey-Bass, p. 221.

covered by an existing policy. If not, obtain additional insurance if appropriate. If the insurance will be an expense for your own training business, factor that expense into your fee structure.

Documentation to Limit Liability

Most people are familiar with releases, the adult version of the permission slip. Releases are signed before surgery, before purchasing a car or household appliance, and before entering into a service agreement. Releases can also be used before training in an attempt to shift some of the responsibility to the participant. Releases explain the potential hazards of an activity, including personal risks associated with it, and then ask the participant to accept those risks. Good releases also explain the rules for the activities and what is expected from the participants.

Usually, a release will not give all the legal protection desired under law, as most states still allow the participant to file a lawsuit or do not excuse the trainer from liability if something happens. However, a well-written release does show that the risks were clearly explained, the participant acknowledged the risks involved, and that he or she was warned to be careful.

The general rule of thumb for avoiding legal liability is to document, document, document! Give written instructions about the training and information about any potential risks to your client. Document incidents that occur during training, especially injuries. Make sure you record any out-of-the-ordinary situations, such as a participant's inappropriate comments or failure to follow instructions. You may also want to keep records regarding instructional objectives, activities, and materials used.

References

Biech, E., & Swindling, L.B. (2000). *The consultant's legal guide.* San Francisco: Jossey-Bass/Pfeiffer.

Recommended Reading

Eyres, P. (1998). *The legal handbook for trainers, speakers, and consultants.* New York: McGraw-Hill.

Managing without the legal hassle. (2000). Video Training for Managers. [Videotape]. Carrollton, TX: Peacemaker Productions.

Sample, J. (1997). *Training programs: How to avoid legal liability* (Publication No. FEP/TP/072597, 1–24). Washington, DC: Bureau of Business Practice.

About the Author

A consultant and professional speaker, **Linda Byars Swindling** *helps managers, business owners, and professionals increase their negotiation skills while avoiding legal disputes. She is a sought-after attorney-mediator who helps judges resolve cases on their dockets and serves Of Counsel to a Texas law firm.*

Swindling is co-author of The Consultant's Legal Guide *and creator of Peacemaker Productions, offering multimedia training programs for managers. Organizations that have benefited from her presentations include The Associates, Tandy Corporation, Dallas Convention and Visitors Bureau, American Heart Association, ASTD, Comdata, Inc., Meeting Professionals International, Food Services Consultants International, M.A.D.D., and Karlee International.*

Swindling is recognized by Who's Who in American Law *and was chosen the Outstanding Speaker of the Year by the Hospitality Sales and Marketing Association International, Dallas. She is a member of the National Speakers Association, ASTD (formerly the American Society for Training and Development), and MPI. She can be reached at www.lindaswindling.com or toll free at (877) 800-5023.*

ASSESSMENT AND EVALUATION

CHAPTER EIGHT

How to Conduct a Needs Assessment That Gets Results

Seth N. Leibler, Ed.D.
President and CEO, The Center for Effective Performance

Ann W. Parkman
Executive Vice President, The Center for Effective Performance

Karen VanKampen
Director, Performance Consulting, The Center for Effective Performance

N eeds assessments can be valuable tools, if they are done correctly. Not only can they pinpoint training and other performance improvement needs, but they also can help you determine practical and realistic solutions that can help your organization achieve the bottom-line business results it requires. This chapter outlines some common misconceptions about needs assessments and offers a high-level overview of how you can effectively utilize needs assessments to help you maximize the benefits of this potentially powerful tool.

WHY CONDUCT A NEEDS ASSESSMENT

Needs assessments can serve as a valuable tool to help manage the rapid changes taking place within organizations today—including mergers and acquisitions, corporate restructuring, downsizing, globalization, and technological advances, just to name a few. Needs assessments are appropriate when:

- You have been asked to implement a training solution;
- You have been asked to help with a performance issue; or
- Your organization is implementing a change that will have a large impact on one or more areas.

Many needs assessments are developed by generating a list of competencies required to perform a job well. To develop this list, the needs assessor typically asks the person whose job is being assessed (and/or his or her supervisor) what skills and knowledge are required to adequately perform this job. The list of competencies is then compared to the training content to determine whether the appropriate skills and knowledge are covered.

Although this form of needs assessment is expeditious, especially when time is of the essence, there are a number of inherent traps that can prevent you from reaching the bottom-line business results the needs assessment was intended to achieve.

Trap 1: Training Isn't Always the Answer

Frequently, needs assessments presuppose that training is the solution to a performance issue (in fact, it is often referred to as a "training needs assessment"). But this isn't always the case. For example, let's say your vice president of operations comes to you and says, "We need time management training. Our managers and supervisors just can't seem to get things done, so we need to teach them how to manage their time." Certainly you can implement the time management training program, but are you absolutely sure this training will solve the problem? Unfortunately, no. You may feel confident that the managers and supervisors will gain some knowledge about time management, but there's no way to be sure that they will be able to "get things done" once they've undergone time management training.

Solution. Before assuming that training is the answer to a performance problem, first make sure that the problem isn't the result of something other than a skill or knowledge deficiency. Other common causes of performance issues include

- Unclear expectations or lack of expectations altogether;
- Improper consequences or incentives;
- Inadequate tools, materials, or work space; and
- Lack of feedback.

Trap 2: People Don't Know What They Don't Know

Relying on job performers to provide you with a detailed description of the skills and knowledge required to be proficient at their jobs creates a risky foundation on which to base a needs assessment. For one thing, it's hard for anyone to articulate what, for many of us, is an internalized and almost unconscious understanding of our job tasks and skills. For another, job performers frequently cannot identify the skills or knowledge they lack to perform their jobs adequately—in other words, they don't know what they don't know.

Solution. It is imperative that you interview the correct people in order to maximize the quality of information you are attempting to retrieve. Table 8.1 gives some guidelines for you to keep in mind.

Trap 3: Performance vs. Competencies

For many, this is the biggest trap of all. While focusing on generating a list of competencies, it's easy to lose focus on the reason you are conducting the needs assessment in the first place—to overcome a specific performance problem or to realize an opportunity for performance improvement. At the same time, competency-based lists tend to be imprecise and vague, using fuzzy terms such as "strong leadership skills," "good facilitator," or "a supportive coach or mentor." Because these descriptions are not behaviorally based, and because they often reflect generic qualities that could apply to a wide range of people, it's difficult to teach these skills in a manner that will result in a positive behavioral change.

Table 8.1. Interview Guidelines

To Assess the Performance of	Do the Following
New hires	• Interview managers/supervisors to determine expectations of new hires; and • Interview and observe exemplary performers to determine what they do on the job to meet expectations.
Those currently performing the job	• In addition to the groups mentioned above, also interview average performers to determine what is getting in the way of desired performance.
A new job position	• Interview the people who created the position; • Interview the people who are affected by the outputs of the position's job tasks; • Interview the people to whom this position reports; and • Interview those who will work closely with the people in this new job.

Solution. Rather than focusing on competencies, focus your needs assessment on the performance issue—the difference between what people are (or are not) doing versus what they should be doing—so that you can identify what the performance level should be and can pinpoint relevant solutions. Here are some examples of interview questions that can help you keep your information-gathering efforts as focused as possible.

- What should the target audience be doing?
- What does the target audience need to know or be able to do to obtain the organizational results?
- What does the target audience need to know or be able to do to meet management and/or customer needs and expectations?
- What does the target audience know now and what can it do now to help meet needs and expectations?
- What is getting in the way of performance in terms of motivation and incentives?
- What is getting in the way of performance in terms of environment (lack of tools, information, resources, time, and so forth)?

HOW TO CONDUCT A NEEDS ASSESSMENT THAT GETS RESULTS

There are several different ways to conduct a needs assessment. Many times, the situation will determine which way to proceed. The situational conditions that can determine your approach include

- Time available;
- People who can or cannot be involved;
- Politics and other sensitivities; and
- Budget.

The following five high-level steps can help you in conducting a successful needs assessment:

1. *Identify and clearly state the issue or opportunity for improvement and the organizational outcomes or needs related to the performance.* It's important that you understand from the beginning exactly what performance issue is being addressed and that everyone (stakeholders, per-

formers, and so on) has the same understanding of this issue. If the issue is not clear, conduct a goal analysis. For example, if you have been told "the customer support staff needs to be more professional when dealing with customers," you must dig deeper to define what being "more professional" means, because this can mean many different things to many different people and to many different organizations. Once you have clearly defined the issue, be sure your client agrees with this definition. Next, determine how solving this issue will make a difference (that is, Is the problem worth solving?). Assuming it will, then recommend ways of attacking the issue through a needs assessment. Discuss data-collection methods and the resources you might require to conduct the assessment. Also determine a timeframe for conducting the assessment.

By clarifying these matters up-front, you will have all of the information you need to stay focused on the true intent of the assessment. You will also be able to link solutions to what is important to your organization.

2. *Decide how you will collect the performance data.* There are a number of ways to collect performance data, including interviews, observations, surveys, and source documents. Select the combination of data-collection methods that best fits your situation. Whenever possible, consider conducting face-to-face interviews. Interviews allow you to ask follow-up questions or to restate your questions as needed to find the information you're looking for. You can also interpret nonverbal cues. Although this method of data collection can be very time-consuming and resource intensive, you will be sure to gather accurate data the first time around.

3. *Analyze the data.* Keeping in mind the clearly stated performance issue and how it affects the organization, document the data you have gathered by identifying consistencies and inconsistencies within the data. Be careful not to jump to conclusions at this point. Just document your findings and the facts within those findings. Once these are documented, identify performance gaps by comparing what the target audience is doing to what they should be doing.

4. *Conduct a cause analysis.* Before deciding on possible solutions to close the performance gap, first identify the causes for the gap. Is the gap due to a lack of skill or knowledge? Are there motivational or environmental barriers to desired performance? Have job expectations and necessary information been adequately communicated to the job performers? If you are unsure of the causes (that is, you do not have the

data to support your cause analysis), ask more questions to determine the true causes of the performance gap. A great tool for analyzing data and figuring out the causes of performance gaps is Mager and Pipe's (1997) Performance Analysis Worksheet. This tool leads you through a series of questions that will help you identify the cause(s) of a performance gap. It will also help you identify possible solutions.

5. *Identify possible performance improvement solutions.* Based on the cause(s) of the performance gap, determine the best solution(s) to close the gap. Keep in mind how the performance issue links to organizational results and needs to ensure that your proposed solution(s) are acceptable and relevant. Also keep in mind your audience's sensitivities and predispositions. For example, if the vice president of human resources has publicly announced that the solution will entail training, make sure that your recommendations include a training solution that is adequately supported by the data. Most likely, you will identify more than one solution, especially if there are multiple causes for the performance gap.

HELPFUL TIPS

No Time for a Needs Assessment?

If time is of the essence, do the best you can with the time and resources you have so that you at least do the following:

- Clearly define the issue and how it affects the organization;
- Identify what the target audience is doing compared to what they should be doing;
- Determine the causes of the performance gap; and
- Identify solutions that will close the gap.

Even an hour of fact finding with your client can uncover some of the performance gaps and the causes of these gaps.

Access the Right People

Be specific regarding the type of people you want to interview, and don't settle for less. There may be times when you are asked to talk with certain people for political reasons. While it may be smart to include these people in the assessment, make sure you understand why they were asked to participate.

Align All Vested Parties

Because a needs assessment can be very revealing, tactfully ensure that all vested parties agree that a needs assessment must be done and that your approach to conducting this assessment is acceptable. By taking into account their sensitivities and any organizational politics, you will be more likely to secure agreement from each party.

Explain Why You Are Gathering Data

When gathering information from people during the assessment, be sure to explain clearly the reason for the interview or data gathering, as well as the goals of the assessment. Be sensitive, factual, and diplomatic in your explanation.

Sort Fact from Opinion

When analyzing the data you have collected, try to ensure that you have mostly facts, rather than opinions or perceptions. To help clarify which is which, consider tactful ways to gain clarification (for example, "Can you give me some examples of what makes you say that?").

Don't Jump to Conclusions

Be careful not to jump from the problem immediately to the solution. To ensure that your recommendations will work the first time around, first complete a cause analysis to uncover the real causes for performance gaps.

Don't Gather Too Much or Too Little Data

Be sure to prioritize your questions so that you obtain essential information first. Focus on the performance gap and the cause(s) of the gap.

SUMMARY

Keep in mind that the information in this chapter is only an overview of how to conduct a needs assessment that generates results. Use this information as a foundation for your approach, and be sure to adjust as necessary based on the situation you are facing.

Reference

Mager, R.F., & Pipe, P. (1997). *Analyzing performance problems.* Atlanta, GA: The Center for Effective Performance.

Recommended Reading

Brethower, D.M., & Smalley, K.A. (1998). *Performance based instruction: Linking training to business results.* San Francisco: Jossey-Bass/Pfeiffer.

Gilbert, T.F. (1978). *Human competence: Engineering worthy performance.* New York: McGraw-Hill.

Kaufman, R., Thiagarajan, S., & MacGillis, P. (1997). *The guidebook for performance improvement.* San Francisco: Jossey-Bass/Pfeiffer.

Mager, R.F. (1997). *Goal analysis.* Atlanta, GA: The Center for Effective Performance.

Robinson, D., & Robinson, J.C. (1995). *Performance consulting: Moving beyond training.* San Francisco: Berrett-Koehler.

Robinson, D., & Robinson, J.C. (1998). *Moving from training to performance: A practical guidebook.* San Francisco: Berrett-Koehler.

Stolovitch, H.D., & Keeps, E.J. (1999*). Handbook of human performance technology: Improving individual and organizational performance worldwide.* San Francisco: Jossey-Bass/Pfeiffer.

Watkins, R., Leigh, D., Platt, W., & Kaufman, R. (1998, September). *Needs assessment—A digest, review and comparison of needs assessment literature.* Washington, DC: International Society for Performance Improvement.

Zemke, R. (1998, March). How to do a needs assessment when you think you don't have time. *Training,* 38–44.

Zemke, R., & Kramlinger, T. (1985). *Figuring things out: A trainer's guide to needs and task analysis.* Reading, MA: Addison-Wesley.

About the Authors

Seth N. Leibler is president and CEO of The Center for Effective Performance (CEP), an Atlanta-based company that supports organizations throughout the world in engineering job performance to meet management's standards. Leibler has served as an executive and consultant in the business of improving human performance for over twenty-five years. For eight years, he managed the Center for Professional Development and Training within the Centers for Disease Control. He has published widely on different aspects of the field of performance technology, including chapters (with Ann Parkman) published in The Guidebook for Performance Improvement, The Handbook of Human Performance Technology, *and* Introduction to Performance Technology. *He has a doctorate in educational psychology from the University of Rochester. He is a past president of ISPI.*

Ann W. Parkman is executive vice president, managing partner, and co-founder of The Center for Effective Performance (CEP). Parkman and her staff have been awarded over twenty national and international professional association awards for the quality of their work. She has more than twenty-five years' experience working with organizations worldwide to improve workforce performance. Prior to founding CEP, she was director of the Centers for Disease Control's Instructional Systems Division. Her writing credits include chapters (with Seth Leibler) published in The Guidebook for Performance Improvement, The Handbook of Human Performance Technology, *and* Introduction to Performance Technology. *She also has written a chapter for* Getting Results: Case Studies in Performance Improvement, *published extensively in* Workforce Training News, *and is a contributing editor to* Corporate University Review. *She is a past president of ISPI.*

Karen VanKampen *has over ten years of experience in developing custom training and performance tools. As director of the Performance Consulting Division for The Center for Effective Performance (CEP), VanKampen oversees the management and quality of CEP's performance improvement projects. She has presented at a number of ISPI conferences and is a certified course manager for the world-renowned Mager Workshops. VanKampen has twelve years of experience in the field of improving workforce performance and standards. Prior to joining CEP, she worked at Marriott International and served as project manager on several successful training projects. She worked as a project manager, analyst, and developer on various projects for small and Fortune 500 companies before joining CEP.*

CHAPTER NINE

The Intervention Questionnaire

Judith A. Hale, Ph.D.
Hale Associates

The Intervention Questionnaire was developed on the premise that interventions work best in combination; that is, usually more than one solution is required to improve the productivity and results of individuals and groups. The successful implementation of a single initiative, such as deploying new technology or solving a problem (for example, production errors or customer complaints), requires the right combination of interventions. Thus, the primary purpose of the Intervention Questionnaire is to help trainers and performance consultants identify whether action is required and, if so, what combination of interventions is necessary to fully support the initiative or to solve a performance problem. The Intervention Questionnaire also serves as an effective tool for helping clients understand what must be done to increase the chances of success. The Questionnaire can help trainers and performance consultants conduct more thorough needs assessments and educate clients on what is required to support, change, or improve people's job performance.

INTRODUCTION

Interventions are purposeful, planned actions intended to influence people's behavior in positive ways that improve organizational results. Large-scale interventions may be labeled as initiatives or company-wide programs. Examples include a change in culture, the reorganization of business units, the deployment of a new technology, an introduction of a management development curriculum, and the certification of specific work groups such as field technicians or customer service representatives. Smaller scale interventions tend to focus on individuals and contained work groups. They might include changing hiring criteria, implementing formal job training, and providing online help systems. Organizations commission initiatives and programs to solve problems and to take advantage of new opportunities. They use the initiative and other programs to help them increase market share, reduce the cycle time for bringing an idea to market, improve customer service, change customer and employee behavior, improve productivity, and increase profits. Exhibit 9.1 shows some examples of the kinds of things organizations do to improve business results and shape people's behavior.

Whenever an organization implements an initiative or program, it expects some degree of improvement or change. Unfortunately, not all of the people who are responsible for launching initiatives understand what people in the workforce require to benefit fully from the initiative. Therefore, it is helpful to think about what the intervention is intended to do and why. Interventions almost always can be put into one of five categories, depending on objectives.

1. Acts that deal with *information,* such as defining what people must know or find out to do the job well, actually communicating that information, and making it accessible through better documentation.

2. Acts that have *consequences,* such as rewarding the accomplishment of goals, measuring actions and outcomes, and enforcing policies.

3. Acts that change the *structure* of work and work relationships or the physical *design* of tools, equipment, and work space, such as reorganizing into cross-functional teams, redesigned forms and data fields on computer screens, and restructuring jobs so that people can telecommute.

4. Acts that increase the *capacity* and *capability* of people, such as providing training, creating job aids, developing online support systems, and so forth.

5. Acts that *align* parts of the organization in order to minimize dissonance or distractions, such as making organizational goals, customer expectations, work design, people's capabilities, and rewards or incentives congruent.

Exhibit 9.2 has more comprehensive definitions and examples of these.

Knowing what organizations *typically* do to improve organizational performance is not enough. Trainers and performance consultants also should know

Exhibit 9.1. Examples of Small-Scale to Large-Scale Interventions

Interventions designed to improve individuals' work performance include

- Redesigning a job or work station to accommodate physical limitations;
- Allowing a flextime work schedule;
- Permitting job sharing;
- Providing personal financial or family counseling through an employee assistance program; and
- Installing an electronic performance support system (EPSS).

Interventions designed to shape or improve work group and team performance include

- Adopting agile manufacturing practices;
- Making cross-training available;
- Implementing self-directed work teams;
- Conducting diversity training;
- Holding competitions; and
- Building identity through department slogans or uniforms.

Interventions designed to improve the performance of whole departments and divisions include

- Adopting uniform standards;
- Replacing traditional compensation structures with job banding;
- Creating vision and mission statements;
- Installing intranet and e-mail systems; and
- Holding business units accountable for profit and loss.

Interventions designed to improve the performance of major divisions, subsidiaries, and whole companies include

- Selling off a product line, plant, or division;
- Buying or merging with another division or company;
- Decentralizing and/or centralizing staff functions;
- Consolidating functions;
- Reengineering major cross-functional processes, such as taking an order from a customer to shipping the finished product; and
- Adopting a new logo, corporate name, or brand image

Exhibit 9.2. Five Styles of Intervention

Interventions are any purposeful act designed to solve a problem, change behavior, increase outputs, or improve outcomes. They can be classified under one or more of thirteen families:

Acts Related to *Information*

The intent is to facilitate agreement, clarify meaning, and make information available when it is needed and in a format that is useful.

1. *Define,* that is, specify the purpose, intent, and desired outcomes, and clarify roles, relationships, and responsibilities to assure agreement on and commitment to what is expected of people, the goal, and the measures of success.

2. *Inform,* that is, actually communicate information so people know what is expected of them and what constitutes adequacy, proficiency, and goal accomplishment.

3. *Document,* that is, put the information in a form so it can be retrieved when required and in a format that is useful.

Acts Related to *Consequences*

The intent is to encourage and reward desired behaviors and results, yet discourage and not inadvertently reward undesirable behaviors and results.

4. *Measure,* that is, give people the metrics and benchmarks they require to monitor and compare their own productivity and results to some standard or expectation.

5. *Reward behavior and results,* that is, overtly recognize and bestow awards to people who demonstrate the preferred behaviors and accomplish the desired outcomes.

6. *Enforce,* that is, review work and results and expend consequences to those whose behavior or outcomes are not what is desired.

Acts Related to the *Structure* and *Design* of Work, Relationships, and Things

The intent is to improve the efficiency of work structures and the design of the workplace, equipment, tools, and systems.

7. *Organize or reorganize,* that is, change the structure of roles, jobs, duties, tasks, and reporting relationships to eliminate redundancy and waste and improve cycle time, accountability, and efficiency.

8. *Standardize or automate,* that is, adopt common processes, procedures, tasks, equipment, tools, materials, components, and work practices to eliminate waste, leverage economies of scale, and facilitate the interchange of people and equipment to increase efficiency and reduce costs.

9. *Design or redesign,* that is, change the physical work environment, workplace, equipment, and tools to improve safety, facilitate ease of use, reduce errors, and reduce costs.

Acts Related to Increasing *Capacity* and *Capability*

The intent is to enable people to perform useful work.

10. *Reframe,* that is, redefine the current situation or dilemma in ways that create a different mental model so people can see new possibilities, challenge assumptions, and come up with workable solutions.

11. *Counsel,* that is, provide advice and guidance to help people deal with work, personal, family, and financial issues so they spend more time on task and experience fewer distractions.

12. *Instruct,* that is, train people so they acquire and maintain the skills and knowledge required to perform their work.

Acts Related to the *Alignment* of Policy, Structure, Practice, and Rewards

The intent is to make organizational systems congruent.

13. *Align,* that is, strive to make work goals, structure, actual practice, and what is rewarded congruent versus conflicting, synergistic versus suboptimal.

---

which interventions to apply to affect people's performance and why. They should have a better understanding of what they want the intervention or combination of interventions to accomplish. The Intervention Questionnaire has been designed to help trainers, consultants, and managers identify the full scope of actions required to support a large initiative, change people's behavior, solve a problem, and improve performance.

DESCRIPTION OF THE INSTRUMENT

The Intervention Questionnaire is designed around The Hierarchy and the Family of Interventions (Hale, 1998), a performance model that confirms that people have the information, measures, structure, standards, tools, equipment, and capacity required to do new work or to do work differently.

The Intervention Questionnaire has a number of uses. For example, it can be used to train people in how to do a needs assessment. It can help managers identify barriers to people's performance and to plan the implementation of a new structure, technology, product, or policy. It can also help trainers, consultants, and managers set baselines measures to evaluate the effectiveness of an initiative or program.

The Intervention Questionnaire is different from other instruments in that there are no "right" or "wrong" answers and you do not keep score. The first part of the instrument (Exhibit 9.3) contains a series of questions designed to guide you through a needs assessment. The answers help you identify opportunities to improve your results. The second part (Exhibit 9.4) contains descriptions of possible performance problems and directs you to a set of actions more likely to resolve the problem.

Your goal in filling out the Questionnaire is to find corroborating evidence that your answers accurately reflect the situation. You can obtain the answers through interviews, observations, and document reviews. The results will help you to decide what limits people's ability to be effective in specific jobs or as members of a larger work effort. The answers can also serve as a baseline against which to measure what and how much change occurred after taking action.

Part Two then directs you to the actions that will help people be more effective, linking problems to corrective actions. Read the problem descriptions in the first column and find those that best reflect your situation. Look in the next column for recommended solutions.

HOW TO ADMINISTER THE QUESTIONNAIRE

The Intervention Questionnaire can be administered in either of two ways. The more obvious way is to answer as many questions in Part One as you can on your own. When you don't know an answer, you can decide whether knowing it would be of value, and if so, find a way to get the answer. For Part Two, you can simply review the descriptions and recommended actions, then, based on your understanding of the situation, build a plan or business case for future action.

Another way to use the Questionnaire is to meet with your client and answer the questions in Part One together. The benefit is that you will gain from one another's understanding of the issue, identify those areas in which you want to confirm the accuracy of your understanding, discuss the value of taking action, and agree on how to proceed. Then review the descriptions in Part Two with your client and mutually develop a course of action.

However it is used, the Intervention Questionnaire is designed to help you identify what is true, what is suspected, and what should be further validated. It will help you develop a plan of action to support a new initiative or solve a performance problem most effectively.

Exhibit 9.3. The Intervention Questionnaire, Part One

Instructions: Mark each question either yes or no where indicated. There is space after each question for any comments you wish to make or to make notes for yourself if you need corroborating evidence or where there is a conflict in the information you have received.

1. **Information**

   1.1. Do the people doing the work know what they are expected to accomplish?   Y   N

   Comments:

   1.2. Do the people who supervise the work, manage the team, and rely on the products produced by the workers share the same understanding of what and how much is expected, why, and how the work should be accomplished as the people doing the work?   Y   N

   Comments:

   1.3. Do the people doing the work have ready access to the information they need?   Y   N

   Comments:

   1.4. Is the information accurate and complete?   Y   N

   Comments:

   1.5. Is the information in an easily retrievable form?   Y   N

   Comments:

2. **Consequences**

   2.1. What is rewarded and celebrated, for example, activity, accomplishment, compliance, maintenance of relationships, innovation, and so forth?

   Comments:

   2.2. Does that which is rewarded support the goals of the job, task, or work unit?   Y   N

   Comments:

   2.3. What is measured, for example, activity, accomplishments, compliance, innovation, or other things?

   Comments:

   2.4. Is what is measured known and agreed to by management and workers?   Y   N

   Comments:

2.5. Does that which is measured support the goals of the job, task, or work
unit?   Y   N
Comments:

2.6. Are there consequences for noncompliance with policy?   Y   N
Comments:

2.7. Do people receive the feedback they require to learn or improve?
Y   N
Comments:

2.8. Are job procedures documented, current, and used?   Y   N
Comments:

3. Structure and Design

3.1. Are jobs, duties, tasks, roles, and responsibilities well-defined?
Y   N
Comments:

3.2. Does the current organizational structure of jobs and tasks support
communication, decision making, and accountability?   Y   N
Comments:

3.3. Are tasks grouped efficiently?   Y   N
Comments:

3.4. Do procedures exist and are they followed?   Y   N
Comments:

3.5. Are processes well-defined, measured, and followed?   Y   N
Comments:

3.6. Do workers have to use nonstandard equipment, materials, or tools?
Y   N
Comments:

3.7. Should any tasks be automated?   Y   N
Comments:

3.8. Does the work space support communication, cooperation, and the goals
of the job or task?   Y   N
Comments:

Exhibit 9.3. (*cont.*)

___

3.9. Does the work environment (light, heat, noise, and so forth) support communication, cooperation, and the goals of the job or task?
Y   N
Comments:

4. Capacity and Capability

4.1. Are there job aids, signs, labels, or other cues to support people doing the job?   Y   N
Comments:

4.2. Are people resistant to change?   Y   N
Comments:

4.3. Are people preoccupied with personal or professional issues not related to the job?   Y   N
Comments:

4.4. Are people's skills kept current?   Y   N
Comments:

4.5. Are people cross trained sufficiently to support growth, redeployment, or multi-tasking?   Y   N
Comments:

4.6. Are support systems available, such as EPSS, mentoring, job sharing, online help screens, and so forth, so that people can work faster, more accurately, or solve difficult problems?   Y   N
Comments:

4.7. Are developmental opportunities readily available and encouraged?
Y   N
Comments:

5. Alignment

5.1. Do management practices match the values of the organization?
Y   N
Comments:

5.2. Do work practices support the organization's goals?   Y   N
Comments:

___

Exhibit 9.4. The Intervention Questionnaire, Part Two

Information

If you have evidence that

- People are unclear, disagree, or have different expectations of others or the work to be accomplished; OR
- There are conflicting objectives; OR
- People are not in consensus about what they mean, expect, require, hope to accomplish, and so forth:

Then meet with the client to decide

- How agreement and clarity will be achieved;
- Who needs to be involved, how, and when;
- Who will present the problem and explain why resolution is important;
- Who will facilitate gaining clarity and agreement; and
- How to measure success.

If you have evidence that

- Information required for the work has changed or people have changed; OR
- People are uninformed about the consequence of poor performance; OR
- People do not receive the information they require:

Then meet with the client to

- Identify the information people should have and the amount of detail the information should contain;
- Decide how best to distribute the information that people require;
- Decide who will do it and when;
- Identify the required resources; and
- Decide how to measure success.

If you have evidence that

- Information is not accessible over time, or the information is complex; AND
- Job aids, manuals, help screens, and so forth are lacking or inadequate, inaccurate, or hard to get to; AND
- Variance in behavior is undesirable and can be reduced with more accessible information:

Then meet with the client to

- Gain the client's commitment to documenting information in a form that makes it easily accessible and facilitates consistent interpretation or compliance;
- Decide how to best codify the information so it is available in a form people can use;
- Decide who should be involved and who will arrange for their involvement and when; and
- Decide how you will measure the effectiveness of the documentation.

Consequences

If you have evidence that

- Current incentives either reinforce the wrong behaviors or ignore the desired behaviors; OR

Then meet with the client to

- Identify behaviors or outcomes to reinforce *and* behaviors or results to stop rewarding;

Exhibit 9.4. (*cont.*)

- There are few incentives for people to do more or better work:

- Decide how to stop the use of incentives that undermine the desired behaviors or send contradictory messages;
- Come up with appropriate incentives and the procedures and criteria for receiving the incentive or reward;
- Identify whom to involve, how, and when; and
- Decide how to measure success.

If you have evidence that
- People do not know what criteria are being used to judge productivity, results, value, and so on; AND
- People could better control their own performance if they knew what the criteria were; OR
- Measures of proficiency are lacking or inappropriate; OR
- Consequences for poor or unacceptable performance are hidden or not enforced; OR
- Someone's private agenda is being met by not actualizing consequences:

Then meet with the client to
- Gain agreement on the importance of making public what is being measured, what metrics are being used, who is doing the measuring, and why;
- Identify ways people can do their own measuring;
- Decide what to measure and what metrics to use;
- Decide who should be involved;
- Decide who will arrange for their involvement and when; and
- Decide how to measure success.

Structure

If you have evidence that the current structure
- Is inefficient, results in redundancy, adds unnecessary cost, overly burdens cycle time; OR
- Hides accountability; OR
- Interferes with service:

Then meet with the client to
- Gain commitment to restructure work or to set up a task force to redesign the way work gets done;
- Decide what changes to make and how;
- Decide who should be involved, why, and when; and
- Decide how to measure results or improvement.

If you have evidence that the variance or lack of standards or standardization

Then meet with the client to
- Gain commitment for doing a

in equipment, materials, specifications, procedures, and common practice
- Adds unnecessary cost; OR
- Negatively affects yield or the quality of work:

feasibility study or cost/benefit analysis to determine whether standards or standardization is appropriate;
- Decide what should be standardized;
- Decide whom to involve, why, when, and how;
- Decide how to facilitate the development, testing, and implementation of the new standards or standardization; and
- Decide how to measure success.

If you have evidence that the current work space, equipment, tools, and materials
- Encumber work; OR
- Result in non-value-added activity; OR
- Put health or safety at risk; OR
- Add time, cost, and errors:

Then meet with the client to
- Gain commitment to a feasibility study or cost/benefit analysis of redesigning the space, equipment, tools, or materials;
- Decide whom to involve, why, when, and how;
- Decide who will own the project and facilitate change; and
- Decide how to measure success.

Capacity and Capability

If you have evidence that
- Old attitudes about work are preventing innovation or growth; OR
- There is a need for tactics that facilitate breaking old models, letting go of the past, and coming up with new possibilities; OR
- People are stuck or keep applying the same solution with no results; OR
- There is a lot of resistance to change:

Then meet with the client to decide
- What opportunities are available to get people to let go;
- What the approach might be;
- Whom to involve;
- How to do it and when; and
- How to measure success.

If you have evidence that people are preoccupied with or distracted by personal or career issues; AND this
- Limits productivity; OR
- Adds unnecessary costs; OR

Then meet with the client to
- Identify what resources are available that are designed to help people take action and feel more in control;
- Decide whom to involve and when; and

Exhibit 9.4. (*cont.*)

- Interferes with others' work; OR
- Calls into question their effectiveness:

- Decide how to measure success.

If you have evidence that indicates
- Current performance is suffering or future performance will suffer because of lack of skills and knowledge; OR
- People's skills are out of date; OR
- People need cross training so they can be re-deployed; OR
- There is a need to develop people for the future:

Then meet with the client to
- Gain commitment to building and reinforcing skills and knowledge;
- Decide who requires development, why, and by when;
- Decide how best to fulfill the needs;
- Decide how to best develop and deliver the program; and
- Decide how to measure whether or not the development achieves the desired results.

Alignment

If you have evidence that
- Current messages, behaviors, systems, structures, or environment do not support the organization's goals; OR
- What people say is not what they do; OR
- What people do is not what the organization wants; OR
- How people do the work is not in keeping with the organization's values or public image:

Then, meet with the client to
- Identify what is out of alignment and recommend ways to bring it into alignment;
- Decide who should be involved, how to involve them, and by when; and
- Decide how to measure success.

Reference

Hale, J.A. (1998). *Performance consultant's fieldbook: Tools and techniques for improving organizations and people.* San Francisco: Jossey-Bass/Pfeiffer.

Recommended Reading

Langdon, D.G. (2000). *Aligning performance: Improving people, systems, and organizations.* San Francisco: Jossey-Bass.

Langdon, D.G., Whiteside, K., & McKenna, M. (1999). *Instruction resource guide: 50 performance improvement tools.* San Francisco: Jossey-Bass.

About the Author

Judith A. Hale *is the author of* The Performance Consultant's Fieldbook *(Jossey-Bass/Pfeiffer, 1998),* Performance-Based Certification *(Jossey-Bass/Pfeiffer, 2000),* The Training Manager's Competencies *(ibstpi, 1989), and co-author of* Achieving a Leadership Role for Training *(Quality Resources, 1995). She has been a consultant to management since 1974 and has worked with a variety of profit and nonprofit organizations from all industries. Her services include consultation on needs assessment, certification, implementation strategies, and performance management.*

CHAPTER TEN

Performance Analysis: Testing the Waters

Allison Rossett, Ph.D.
Professor of Educational Technology, San Diego State University

Catherine Tobias
Lieutenant Commander, U.S. Coast Guard

This chapter provides an overview for performance analysis, a systematic and systemic approach to engaging with the client and other key sources to tailor cross-functional solution systems to the opportunity or problem. Performance analysis shakes you out of your shoes and into those of others in the organization. It enables you to see things in fresh and complex ways and to provide a more vivid view to customers (Rossett, 1999). Particularly important to trainers, performance analysis tempers the excitement about training with the recognition that its key messages do not readily or automatically transfer to the workplace. The chapter, predicated on earlier work by Rossett (1987, 1999), is spiced with many examples, including several from the U.S. Coast Guard.

THE FIRST WAVE

Performance analysis is *the study we do in order to figure out what to do.* It is taking some time at the start of a project to test the water, that is, gather opinions, facts, and data in order to get to what Robert Mager called "the heart of the matter." Performance analysis allows us to make diligent recommendations based on many points of view. For example, during the diagnosis stage, doctors consult with their colleagues, review medical literature, order tests, and study patient statistics. Similarly, during performance analysis, professionals go beyond the initial request to gain insight into an organization, workplace, job, and individual.

Performance analysis is the initial step, but it's not the only analysis that should occur. Think of analysis as happening continuously and in waves. The first wave is performance analysis. Engineering companies call it "scoping." Why do we do performance analysis? Because excitement about training must be tempered with the recognition that its key messages do not readily or automatically transfer to the workplace. A broad and systemic approach to training that involves key players and policies is critical for improved performance (Foxon, 1997; Hale, 1998; Rossett, 1996).

The U.S. Coast Guard takes this type of broad and systemic approach to determine which initiatives hold the most promise for the problem or opportunity at hand. For example, in the late 1990s, Coast Guard headquarters received a request for a Spanish language training program to improve law enforcement efforts in the Caribbean, Gulf of Mexico, and Central America. Coast Guard performance consultants met with internal and external experts from law enforcement, international affairs, training, and the Defense Language Institute. After reviewing opinions and documentation, the Coast Guard believed that "the heart of the matter" suggested more than a Spanish training course could deliver. Significant resources were then dedicated to an extensive needs assessment that resulted in the development of a service-wide foreign language program that addresses all relevant language training (not just Spanish), as well as translation technologies, personnel tracking, job assignments, and incentives.

This first wave of analysis, performance analysis (PA), directs the kinds of waves that must follow. A focused training needs assessment (TNA) should occur after a performance analysis to assure that skills, knowledge, and motivation are considered. Training needs analysis leads to the design and development of appropriate instructional and informational programs and materials (Rossett, 1999). It might involve in-depth study of subject matter, audience analysis, determination of prerequisite skills and attitudes, establishment of consensus approaches and standards, and determination of the details that underpin learning, information, and even knowledge management programs.

The Defense Language Institute in Monterey, CA, conducts a type of focused TNA for all branches of the military. From time to time, numerous subject-matter experts and model performers come together to discuss job tasks that require foreign language skills. This assessment is used to determine the degree of language proficiency required in speaking, listening, reading, and/or writing for an array of job tasks. Service decision makers then establish or revise foreign language requirements and learning programs. Remember that each service first tests the waters with a performance analysis to confirm that skills and knowledge are lacking. Table 10.1 and Figure 10.1 represent performance analysis and training needs assessment.

Note from the table that performance analysis results in a plan, an approach, and broad involvement. Training needs assessment follows later when we know

Table 10.1. Performance Analysis and Training Needs Assessment

Performance Analysis	Training Needs Assessment
Scoping to figure out what to do	Gathers detail sufficient for a training or information solution
Results in a data-driven description of what is needed and why	Results in classes, job aids, online reference and training, documentation
Is the initial response to the request for assistance from the customer	Directs attention to those needs that are linked to gaps in skills, knowledge, and motivation
Results in a plan and probably a report	Results in tangible learning and support products
Defines the problem or opportunity	Provides details regarding the right way or ways to do it
Defines cross-functional solution systems and points to the people in the organization who must collaborate	Identifies the details of exemplary performance and perspectives so that they can be authenticated, communicated, and taught

that training is indeed going to be appropriate and we require details that will cement the training. Remember the Defense Language Institute example. The performance analysis defined many training needs that transcended the original request. Training needs assessment then generated the solutions, such as classes, online learning, job aids, documentation, an online help system, or some combination of those.

A VAST SEA

Performance analysis is required because there are numerous ways to achieve higher performance, not just training. In another example, the Coast Guard wanted to figure out why recruiters weren't meeting their goals and what to do about it. A revision to the recruiter training curriculum seemed like an obvious solution, but performance analysis revealed a vast sea of other significant recruiting issues, such as personnel selection procedures, recruiting office locations, and medical entry standards for recruits. In this situation, revised training for recruiters would be a worthy but not sufficient solution. The Coast Guard realized that it had to bring numerous players, not just training professionals, to the table to address the problem.

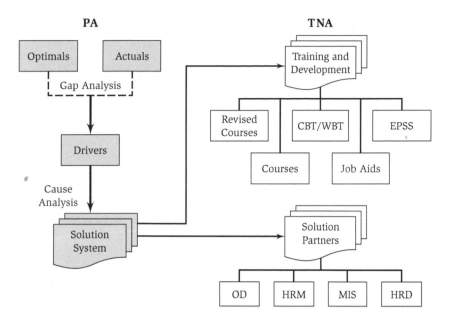

Figure 10.1. Performance Analysis and Training Needs Assessment

As you can see, not only does performance analysis define what the need or opportunity is, but it also helps to identify how to move the people and the organization in the right direction. It allows people up and down the organization, and outside it, such as suppliers and customers, to have input. The result is a better and more palatable effort.

CASTING YOUR NET

The purpose of performance analysis is to cast a wide net for needs and possible solutions. Some of the core kinds of information to look for are described in the following paragraphs.

Define the Desired State

You can capture the desired state by interviewing the client or sponsor; reviewing the literature; examining specifications and policies; talking to experts; and watching successful performers. To define the desired state for the foreign language example, Coast Guard performance consultants asked the sponsor questions such as

- As you look at the other services and their efforts in this area, what are they doing that you'd most like to see done in the Coast Guard?

- What other options have you read or heard about that might have the potential to solve this problem?

- What are you hoping to accomplish by implementing those practices?

In addition, the consultants reviewed existing policies, consulted with external agencies, reviewed the literature, and solicited input from the field. The result was a series of statements about the desired state. This desired state served as the foundation for subsequent planning, shown below.

> All Coast Guard missions requiring foreign language skills are executed effectively and efficiently.

- Foreign language requirements are identified.

- Foreign language skills are tracked.

- Coast Guard units have appropriate translation services and/or technologies.

- Foreign language training, certification, and education meet the Coast Guard's skill and knowledge needs.

- Units have the right mix of linguists to accomplish their missions.

- Linguists are compensated for additional duty.

Defining the desired state set the direction for the rest of this study. As Lewis Carroll wrote in *Alice in Wonderland,* "If you don't know where you're going, any place will do."

Focus on Problem Areas

While spring boarding from a desired state can be useful, sometimes you may want to begin questioning by focusing on the problems at hand. Safety training provides a vivid example. Would you want to focus on *generic* safety, or would you target injuries and insurance claims? The latter, typically.

When the Coast Guard was experiencing problems meeting its recruiting goals, performance consultants asked recruiters questions such as

- Which areas of the recruiting process do you find challenging?

- What reasons do people give for deciding not to join the Coast Guard?

- Why are so many applicants rejected?

Answers to these questions revealed, among other things, that recruiters had difficulty with sales and marketing, that the booming economy was attracting more and more young people away from the military, and that an inordinately high number of applicants were being medically disqualified. Finding out what was really happening allowed the Coast Guard to focus its energies where the needs were greatest, rather than revising and spawning a vanilla recruiter training program.

Describe Performance Drivers

Here the professional seeks to find what it will take to move toward the desired state, after gaining a sense of *why,* from many perspectives, including the literature, the experts, and those closest to the work.

Table 10.2 summarizes possible drivers for performance. Also known as barriers and constraints, this model owes a debt to prior work by Mager and Pipe (1984), Harless (1975), and Gilbert (1978).

During performance analysis, Coast Guard performance consultants asked questions about what had been getting in the way of recruitment, what it would take to make changes happen, and what would encourage higher performance. The answers revealed that recruiters did not market the service because they didn't know how to market, that no one ever held them accountable for their numbers, and that they were using antiquated computer systems. Identifying these drivers—skills and knowledge, motivation, and environment—helped point performance consultants to the appropriate next waves, in this instance, TNA and root cause analysis.

Match Solutions to Drivers

At this point, after the analysis, we have a sense of what it will take to get the desired performance and a much better perspective from which to plan the project. As you can see from Table 10.3, possible solutions go far beyond training and development. That is because performance analysis is predicated on assumptions about the power of systems and alignment to improve performance. Training is only one aspect of a system.

The Coast Guard's work on recruiting provides an example. Giving recruiters the right training was just one part of the solution. For the system to address the problem, it also had to find the right people for the job and put them in the right places. In addition to a completely revamped recruiter training curriculum, this project resulted in revised personnel selection procedures to ensure that those best qualified received assignments as recruiters. The Coast Guard also relocated many of its offices to cities with a high population density of minorities and youth with a propensity for military service. The study also resulted in a review of medical entry standards to determine whether they were unnecessarily stringent. And recruiters received new computer laptops. All of these recommendations *together,* presented in Table 10.4, proved to be a more powerful solution than training alone would have been.

Table 10.2. Performance Drivers and Some Examples

Drivers	Examples
Focus on Individuals	
Skills, Knowledge, Expectations, Information	• Nurses avoid the new software for drug record keeping because they don't know how to use it • Teachers fail to contact parents because they don't know they are expected to, that it's part of their job • Engineers create new code rather than reusing libraries of existing code because they don't know what's available and where to find it
Motivation	• Financial analysts don't see the value in the new software and continue to use old methods • Many salespeople resist using computers, noting that they're "people people," not techies
Focus on Culture	
Environment	• Operators must enter a nine-digit number three times during the order process • The HMO makes the process of contacting a doctor onerous, involving many gatekeepers, so that it will discourage patients from attempting to contact doctor
Incentives	• Supervisors who rate employees as other than stellar are expected to fill out forms and attend meetings to justify their ratings • The most work and the most difficult work goes to the people who are the most effective

DEALING WITH CURRENTS

As shown in Table 10.4, performance analyses require an array of aligned efforts, where colleagues across an organization must come together to improve safety, sales, processes, or strategic uses of technology. Such collaborations cannot be taken for granted. Some strategies to encourage collaboration to achieve performance improvement include

• Make certain that a high-level sponsor is ready to play an active role in encouraging cross-functional collaboration on the project;

Table 10.3. Drivers and Solutions

Driver	Description	Solutions
Lack of skill, clarity about expectations, knowledge or information	People don't because they don't know how, or they've forgotten, or there's just too much to know	• Education/training • Information support (job aids) • Documentation • Coaching and mentoring • Clarity re: standards • Communications initiatives • Knowledge bases
Weak or absent motivation	People don't because they don't care, don't see the benefits, or don't believe they can	• Education/training • Information support (job aids) • Documentation • Coaching, mentoring • Participatory goal setting • Communications initiatives
Ineffective environment, tools, processes	People don't because processes or jobs are poorly designed, or because necessary tools are unavailable	• Reengineered work processes • New or improved tools or technologies or work spaces • Job design or redesign • Job enrichment • Participatory decision making • Knowledge bases
Ineffective or absent incentives	People don't because doing it isn't recognized, doing it is a hassle, or not doing it is ignored	• Improved appraisal/ recognition programs • Management development • New policies

Table 10.4. Coast Guard Solution System Defined by Drivers

Problem	Drivers	Solutions
Recruiters don't spend much time marketing the Coast Guard	Don't know how	Provide marketing training, job aids
		Distribute best marketing plans to other recruiters
	Not the job they think they're supposed to do	Set policy for marketing standards and clarify job descriptions
	No motivation	Provide education on value of marketing
	Ineffective tools	Provide recruiters with new computers and cellular phones
	Too much other paperwork to do	Streamline reporting requirements
		Supply each recruiting office with an administrative assistant
	No incentive	Enforce marketing plan deadlines
		Publicly praise effective marketers

- Solicit assistance to make certain that the people who need to participate are ready, willing, and able;
- Work to redefine positions so that cross-functionality is a priority, rather than an oddity;
- Share findings with resonance for colleagues across the organization when those findings emerge, rather than waiting to deliver the final report; and
- Find a way to form informal relationships across the organization, because those enhance other collaborations.

At times you may find that the sponsor is focused on a pre-determined solution and reluctant to devote time to performance analysis. In these situations, focus on the questions that need to be asked and the value of a fresh look at the situation. Invite colleagues to participate in countering cross-currents. When the sponsor for the Coast Guard's foreign language needs assessment was hesitant to devote time to collect data from the field, internal performance consultants solicited support from the East Coast and West Coast staff, who stated that hard data would be worth the wait. Data analysis later revealed that the most significant problems were not related to Spanish, but to Asian languages in the

Pacific and Gulf of Mexico. Sharing these findings across the organization garnered much needed support for a collaborative effort.

SUMMARY

Performance analysis sets the stage for further analyses and a substantively and politically robust solution system. When smart trainers use performance analysis to take stakeholders to "the heart of the matter" at the start of a project, rather than clinging to habits or history, the rest of the voyage becomes far more certain.

References

Foxon, M.J. (1997). The influence of motivation to transfer, action planning and manager support on the transfer process. *Performance Improvement Quarterly, 10*(2), 42–63.

Gilbert, T. (1978). *Human competence: Engineering worthy performance.* New York: McGraw-Hill.

Hale, J. (1998). *Performance consultant's fieldbook.* San Francisco: Jossey-Bass.

Harless, J.H. (1975). *An ounce of analysis is worth a pound of objectives.* Newnan, GA: Harless Performance Guild.

Mager, R.M., & Pipe, P. (1984). *Analyzing performance problems.* Belmont, CA: Pitman Learning.

Rossett, A. (1987). *Training needs assessment.* Englewood Cliffs, NJ: Educational Technology Publications.

Rossett, A. (1996, March). Training and organizational development: Siblings separated at birth. *Training, 33*(4), 53–59.

Rossett, A. (1999). *First things fast: A handbook of performance analysis.* San Francisco: Jossey-Bass/Pfeiffer.

Recommended Reading

Argyris, C. (1993). *Knowledge for action: A guide to overcoming barriers to organizational change.* San Francisco: Jossey-Bass.

Robinson, D.G., & Robinson, J.C. (1995). *Performance consulting.* San Francisco: Berrett-Koehler.

Rossett, A. (1997, July). That was a great class, but. . . *Training & Development, 51*(7), 18–24. http://www.astd.org/CMS/templates/index.html?template_id = 1& articleid = 10988

Rossett, A. (1999). Buffy's global fitness: Automation and perspiration for a better you. [Online.] http://edweb.sdsu.edu/courses/EDTEC540/Syllabus/Buffy/index.html

Rossett, A. (1999, May). Knowledge management meets analysis. *Training & Development, 53*(5), 62–68.

Rummler, G., & Brache, A.P. (1990). *Improving performance: How to manage the white space on the organization chart.* San Francisco: Jossey-Bass.

Zemke, R., & Kramlinger, T. (1982). *Figuring things out: A trainer's guide to needs and task analysis.* Reading, MA: Addison-Wesley.

About the Authors

Allison Rossett is a professor of educational technology at San Diego State University and consultant in performance and training systems. She is the author of First Things Fast: A Handbook for Performance Analysis *and the associated free Web tool, www.jbp.com/rossett.html, both winners of ISPI's (International Society for Performance Improvement) Instructional Communications Award for 1999.*

Lieutenant Commander Catherine Tobias is an internal performance consultant at U.S. Coast Guard Headquarters in Washington, DC. A graduate of the Educational Technology master's degree program at San Diego State University, she analyzes organizational level issues and engineers cross-programmatic solutions systems. She has published research on the journey from training to performance in Performance Improvement Quarterly *and has presented at several international conferences. Previously, she served as a navigator aboard the Barque EAGLE, America's Tall Ship, a training vessel for entry-level Coast Guard personnel.*

CHAPTER ELEVEN

The Art and Science of Competency Modeling

Richard Lepsinger
Managing Vice President, Right Manus

Anntoinette Lucia
Managing Vice President, Right Manus

Competency models help organizations align employee behavior with the organization's strategy and culture. In this chapter, real-life examples illustrate how to implement competency models, including how to address strategic business issues and enhance human resource management (HRM) systems. Tips for implementing competency-based selection, training and development, appraisal, and succession planning systems and descriptions of key implementation steps are provided. The authors also explain how to develop competency models.

COMPETENCY MODELS

Competency models that identify the capabilities needed to perform a job have been in use for more than three decades. In the last five years, interest in them and their potential to help staffing and development efforts has increased dramatically. As issues of globalization, competition, and leadership dominate the strategic agenda, organizations have begun to recognize the need to articulate the skills, knowledge, and personal characteristics its people must have to perform successfully. Competency models provide a precise definition of the capabilities needed to meet critical business challenges, creating alignment among the business strategy, organizational culture, and employee behavior.

Let's look at how one company used a competency model to address its business needs. A mortgage banking company's successful launch of its paperless mortgage product (with little or no documentation needed to apply for a mortgage) was met aggressively by the competition. To respond, the company realized it had to develop its sales force. It had to increase the number of salespeople in the field, address the high rate of turnover, and improve the wide variance of sales effectiveness. The company determined that the sales managers, who hired people and managed the sales force day-to-day, did not have a clear picture of what was required to do the job. The company's solution was to develop a sales competency model (Table 11.1) that was used in two ways. First, it was integrated into the company's selection system to make sure that everyone involved in the hiring process was working from the same criteria. Second, the model was incorporated into the performance management system to ensure that salespeople would receive coaching and feedback on the behaviors and skills that had the strongest correlation to success on the job.

The term "competency" has been used to describe the capability of both organizations and individuals. Because our focus is on the individual, we will use the widely accepted definition of competency among human resource specialists: "A cluster of related knowledge, skills, and attitudes that affects a major part of one's job (a role or responsibility), that correlates with performance on the job, that can be measured against well-accepted standards, and that can be improved via training and development" (Parry, 1996, p. 50). It is essentially a pyramid (see Figure 11.1) built on the foundation of inherent talents and incorporating the types of skills and knowledge that can be acquired through learning, effort, and experience. At the top of the pyramid is a specific set of behaviors that are the manifestation of all the innate and acquired abilities.

Expressing the capabilities in behavioral terms is important for two reasons. First, for a competency model to be useful as a human resource tool, it must not only define the competencies but also provide examples to illustrate when a particular competency is being demonstrated in a job. Second, although innate *characteristics* are fixed in a person, for the most part, *behaviors* can be modified and taught. In other words, it might be difficult (some would say impossible) for a person lacking in empathy to develop that trait, but empathetic behaviors, such as listening to customers' needs and addressing their concerns, can be fostered through training and development.

BUSINESS NEEDS ADDRESSED BY COMPETENCY MODELS

Clarifying Job and Work Expectations

A competency model answers two questions: "What skills, knowledge, and characteristics are required to do the job?" and "What behaviors have the most direct impact on performance and success in the job?" In *selection* systems, a

Table 11.1. Competency Model for a Sales Position

Ability

Mental Agility	Ability to deal with multiple issues and details; alertness; learning capacity
Quantitative Reasoning	Ability to reason with, analyze, and draw conclusions from numbers; feeling comfortable with quantitative data
Divergent Thinking	Ability to see and think beyond the obvious and formulate original solutions

Personality

High Emotional Stamina	Ability to maintain focus and effectiveness under stressful and frustrating situations
Assertiveness	Ability to take command of face-to-face situations while displaying appropriate tact and diplomacy
Self-Sufficiency	Ability to maintain one's motivation and work independently for extended periods of time with minimal support and approval
Sociability	Desire to interact with others; project warmth; relate to a wide variety of people
Competitiveness	Desire to win and to achieve and surpass goals; persistence in the face of obstacles
High Energy Level	Ability to establish and maintain a fast pace and tempo

Skills

Basic Selling Skills	Establishing rapport; determining customer needs; relating benefits to product features; handling objectives; closing
Problem Solving	Anticipating problems; inviting ideas; distinguishing symptoms from causes; modifying proposals; implementing solutions
Presentation Skills	Ability to communicate to large and small groups and establish rapport with the group; articulate delivery of ideas; read group cues; effectively use visual aids and maintain a commanding presence
Coaching/Training Skills	Assessing learning needs and closing knowledge gaps; simplifying information; ensuring understanding; reinforcing desired behavior; motivating the learner

Table 11.1. (*cont.*)

Knowledge

Financial Analysis	Understanding the financial impact of decisions on the customer, the customer's customer, and the organization
Computer Literacy	Basic computer skills for application to marketing programs, including prospect lists, customer contacts, and relevant economic data
Product Knowledge	Expertise related to the organization's product and services, as well as other crucial aspects of the business
Competitive Environment	Knowledge of competitive forces and how the organization and its products stack up against competitors and their products

competency model ensures that all interviewers are looking for the same set of abilities and characteristics. In *training and development* and *appraisal* systems, a competency model provides a list of the behaviors and skills that must be developed to maintain satisfactory levels of performance. For *succession planning,* competency models ensure that decision makers are focused on the same set of attributes and skills and that these attributes and skills are important and relevant to success in the position(s) under consideration.

By clarifying performance expectations, competency models also serve the interests of the individual. Specific job requirements provide people with a clear understanding of what is expected of them. Training and development targeted to relevant skills and behaviors for effective job performance can enhance an individual's personal development. Appraisal systems focused on the use of specific behaviors and practices that directly contribute to effective organizational performance offer people a road map for recognition, reward, and possible advancement. A shared understanding between an organization's leaders and its employees about how to perform the work and what it takes to succeed helps retention rates, job satisfaction, and the achievement of strategic goals.

Hiring the Best Available People

By clarifying the specific behaviors and practices that enable employee effectiveness, competency models increase the likelihood that the right people will be found and placed in the right jobs. Costs associated with hiring (such as re-

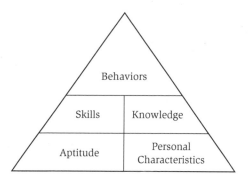

Figure 11.1. Pyramid Competency Model

Lucia and Lepsinger, 1999.

cruitment firm fees and signing bonuses) can be targeted more precisely. By providing performance-based criteria for recruitment, assessment, and development, a well-developed competency model accelerates the development of a capable, diversified workforce. A competency-based approach to selection demands that managers and others involved use effective assessment techniques and make decisions based on data rather than on impressions, feelings, or biases.

Maximizing Productivity

By identifying relevant skill gaps, competency models help to ensure that training and development dollars will be spent wisely, that is, on programs and developmental experiences that teach crucial skills and behaviors. Competency models also allow for the development of appraisal systems that evaluate people on their use of the specific behaviors and practices that directly contribute to organizational competitiveness. This encourages both the business and the individual to stay focused on what will have the greatest impact on success.

Enhancing the 360-Degree Feedback Process

A 360-degree feedback process involves collecting perceptions about a person's behavior and the impact of that behavior from the person's bosses, direct reports, colleagues, fellow members of project teams, internal and external customers, and suppliers. The result is a comprehensive portrait of a person's behavior on the job. The "reality check" offered by the process makes it a popular training and evaluation tool in many organizations.

Although the 360-degree feedback process is useful for describing how people actually carry out their work, it can be made more meaningful by focusing on the behaviors necessary to perform the job most effectively. Competency models help to ensure that the 360-degree feedback relates specifically to the competencies critical to the individual's and the organization's success. Survey items that are job specific, relevant, and representative of current performance requirements are likely to lead to greater acceptance of feedback by the population assessed. Additionally, a competency-based survey ensures that feedback is concrete and can be easily discussed, which enables those being assessed to pinpoint key action steps they can take to address skill gaps or other developmental areas. Finally, it enables an organization to compare aggregate data on performance across different regions, locations, and business units.

Adapting to Change

In this era of rapid change, the nature of people's jobs is often in flux and they may require new skills to take on changing roles in the organization. Competency models provide a tool for determining exactly what skills are required to meet both today's needs and probable future needs. By using a competency model, an organization can begin to adjust its selection criteria to reflect the new demands of the role and to identify skill gaps and decide which ones ought to be addressed immediately.

Aligning Behavior with Organizational Strategies and Values

A competency model can be an effective way to communicate the values of senior management and the performance goals that management expects people to focus on. Competency-based appraisal systems can be used to distinguish individuals who possess the characteristics required to build and maintain an organization's values (for example, working as a team, respecting individuals, being innovative, or taking initiative) and who exhibit the behaviors that will support these values on a day-to-day basis. In this way, competency models can reinforce and clarify messages about changing strategy and culture.

HOW COMPETENCY MODELS CAN ENHANCE HRM SYSTEMS

Understanding the value of competency models for various HRM systems will help you decide how to apply them to your organization. Table 11.2 summarizes the benefits of using competency models for each HRM system discussed here.

Implementing a Competency-Based Selection System

Many organizations find that they encounter less resistance to using competency models for selection than for other HRM processes. Enhancing or modifying the selection system may seem more benign and less risky to some stakeholders

Table 11.2. Benefits of Using Competency Models with Various HRM Systems

Use	Benefit
Selection	• Provides a complete picture of job requirements • Increases the likelihood of hiring people who will succeed in the job • Minimizes the investment (both time and money) in people who may not meet the company's expectations • Ensures a more systematic interview process • Helps distinguish between competencies that are trainable and those that are more difficult to develop
Training and Development	• Enables people to focus on the skills, knowledge, and characteristics that have the most impact on effectiveness • Ensures that training and development opportunities are aligned with organizational values and strategies • Makes the most effective use of training and development time and dollars • Provides a framework for ongoing coaching and feedback
Performance Appraisal	• Provides a shared understanding of what will be monitored and measured • Focuses and facilitates the performance appraisal discussion • Provides a focus for gaining information about a person's behavior on the job
Succession Planning	• Clarifies the skills, knowledge, and characteristics for the job or role in question • Provides a method to assess a candidate's readiness for the role • Focuses training and development plans to address missing competencies • Allows an organization to measure (number of high-potential perform

than attempting to apply the model to appraisal and succession planning. In addition, the impact of competency-based selection on the quality of hiring decisions is relatively easy to measure.

For these reasons, we recommend starting with selection when implementing competency models. An early win and good word of mouth will make it much easier to start using competency models in other HRM systems. If your overall objective is to link all HRM systems through the use of competency models, the hiring process is the logical place to start.

To implement a competency-based selection system, an organization must have the following:

- A validated competency model that is predictive of success on the job;
- A set of interview questions that helps interviewers determine whether a candidate has the required competencies or the potential to develop them;
- Interviewers with the necessary training and experience to evaluate the extent to which a candidate has the competencies or the potential required for the job; and
- Forms to record results and help compare and evaluate candidates.

A validated competency model helps ensure that hiring decisions are based on criteria that specifically predict success on the job, rather than whatever might seem relevant to a particular interviewer. Given the costs associated with making poor selection decisions—training, recruitment, and lowered productivity—hiring that is based on criteria proven relevant to performance offers great value.

Once the competencies for effective performance have been identified, an interviewer must be able to determine whether a job candidate possesses or is able to develop them. Therefore, the interviewer must ask the right questions and conduct an effective interview. He or she must be able to use interview questions to probe for specifics, then interpret responses in terms of competencies. In addition, a standard format for collecting information about the interviewee increases the likelihood that facts and impressions are not forgotten or misrepresented with the passage of time.

Implementing a Competency-Based Training and Development System

Generally, there is not much resistance to using competency models to enhance the relevance and effectiveness of training and development programs. Increasingly, 360-degree feedback and competency modeling are becoming closely ned (especially in their application to training and development systems). many organizations have already begun introducing competencies through feedback questionnaires.

Such questionnaires contain a list of the relevant behaviors for effectively performing a job or function. Many organizations use these to create awareness of the need for change, focus people on their strengths and developmental needs, identify organizational development needs, and monitor improvement on the job.

Four requirements exist to implement a competency-based training and development system:

- A set of behavioral examples that describe the competencies on the job;
- A process to identify the extent to which people are currently using these competencies effectively;
- An awareness of training and development opportunities that will help people learn and develop certain competencies; and
- A support and follow-up mechanism to ensure that skill and knowledge gaps are closed.

Skills, knowledge, and characteristics do not necessarily lend themselves to direct observation. Competencies such as "teamwork" or "self-sufficiency" can be interpreted differently by different people. Thus, definitions of competencies must include observable behaviors.

Let's use consulting as an illustration. One definition of "consulting" is checking with people before making decisions that affect them, encouraging participation in decision making, and allowing others to influence decisions. This is helpful but leaves room for interpretation, provides little guidance about behaviors required for effective consulting, and makes it difficult to measure the frequency and effectiveness with which a person demonstrates the competency. Examples of good consulting behaviors could include the following:

- Asking people to help plan efforts and activities that require support and commitment;
- Soliciting input on proposals;
- Encouraging people to express concerns or doubts about a proposal;
- Listening to concerns or doubts about plans or strategies without becoming defensive; and
- Modifying plans and strategies to deal with concerns and incorporate suggestions.

The process of identifying developmental needs, whether you use 360-degree feedback or a more traditional boss-coach/direct report method, should include two components: a means to collect data about the use of competencies and a method for providing a person with results in a way that is easily understood and action oriented. To address weaknesses identified during the feedback process requires that one know what training and development options are available. These may include onsite training, university programs, working with a coach, and on-the-job experiences.

Implementing a Competency-Based Appraisal System

Surprisingly, a competency-based appraisal system is no more difficult to implement than a system that does not use competency models. All appraisal systems should include guidelines by which employees' capabilities can be reviewed and evaluated during the performance discussion. In reality, the quality of these guidelines varies to a great degree. One client we worked with used only main headings, such as leadership, management, and teamwork. Another client wanted a flexible system that allowed the manager to focus the discussion on areas that he or she felt were most relevant at the time. This system's guidelines included questions such as, "What are this person's strengths?" "What has he/she done particularly well?" "What are this person's weaknesses?" and "What does he/she need to do differently?" Such vague or overly broad criteria can create problems, as there may be a lack of focus, difficulty reaching agreement, and/or the direct report may not see the relevance of the criteria during the appraisal.

The key requirements for implementing a sound appraisal system include

- A description of relevant behaviors that everyone agrees are critical to job performance;
- A method to collect data on the behavior of the person being evaluated; and
- The ability to have a constructive discussion.

A competency-based appraisal system helps increase the likelihood that discussions will be clear, address issues that directly relate to job performance, and achieve a balance between business objectives and how those objectives were achieved.

Many appraisal systems lack sufficient information for appraisers to monitor and evaluate performance effectively and accurately. Appraisers tend to emphasize *what* has been accomplished, with little attention to *how* it was accomplished. A competency-based appraisal provides specific behavioral examples against which to measure performance, ensuring that both the *what* and the *how* are evaluated.

A competency model can also help with data collection, first, by providing managers with a specific list of behaviors to observe and monitor during the evaluation period and, second, if additional perspectives are sought, by enabling the appraiser to conduct more efficient, focused conversations with the colleagues and customers of the person being reviewed.

Three factors are necessary to have a constructive performance discussion: (1) the appraisal process itself must be perceived as user-friendly rather than threatening or burdensome, (2) both parties must have effective communication and problem-solving skills, and (3) both parties must come prepared for the discussion. Simply adding a competency model will not ensure that these criteria are met. However, when competencies are seen as relevant and important to job performance, participation in the appraisal tends to improve. A well-constructed model can help the manager focus on the critical behaviors for successful performance. Both the appraiser and the individual under review are more likely to take the discussion seriously and to come up with developmental plans and suggestions for improvement.

Implementing a Competency-Based Succession Planning System

Four elements are required to implement an effective competency-based succession planning system. These elements include

- Competency models for critical jobs and roles;
- A method to evaluate and develop succession candidates;
- An understanding of the methods and opportunities for developing competencies; and
- Alignment of all the HRM systems.

Competency models have two applications in succession planning. First, they may be used as the basis for assessing current employees to identify high-potential ones who have the potential to fill key positions. Second, competency models help to ensure that people being hired have the potential to fill more senior positions in the company in the future.

For example, in our firm, we have competency models for the project coordinator and consultant positions. When we are looking for a project coordinator, we use competency models as the basis for the interview. The project coordinator competency model helps us assess whether the person has the skills, knowledge, and characteristics to do that job. The consultant competency model enables us to determine whether the interviewee has the potential to do the consultant work. In fact, when we are hiring project coordinators, we are already looking at their potential to become consultants.

Succession planning is unique among human resource management processes in that it depends a great deal on the quality of the input from other HRM systems. As the saying goes, you can't make a silk purse out of a sow's ear, so an organization must have a solid pool of people to choose from in order to ensure that its succession planning process can be effective. The best succession planning system in the world cannot succeed unless the selection, training and development, and appraisal systems also are working effectively. These systems must be designed to ensure that people who have the required capability or potential are hired, their abilities are enhanced, and their potential is nurtured through learning experiences, coaching, and feedback. We strongly believe that the use of competency models across all HRM systems will provide the necessary consistency and continuity to ensure that an organization has the talent required to outperform the competition today and in the future.

HOW COMPETENCY MODELS ARE DEVELOPED

There are two ways to develop a competency model: (1) start from scratch or (2) start with a validated, generic model. The key steps of each approach are summarized in Table 11.3.

Starting from Scratch

This method calls for developing a competency model using data collected from interviews with incumbents and informed observers, focus groups, and on-the-job observations. The data are also analyzed to identify the competencies significant to effective performance. The "starting from scratch" method is appropriate for developing a competency model for any job, function, or role in the organization. Although this method is the most time-consuming, it also yields the best results.

Starting with a Validated Competency Model

The second approach uses a validated competency model as the starting point instead of extensive interviews and observations of incumbents on the job. This approach may save time in terms of data collection, analysis, and validation, but because a generic competency model was not developed with a specific job or position in mind, it may not highlight the technical skills and knowledge required for success in the job or position under consideration. This method is best suited for leadership and management roles that cut across several functions and for positions that require a limited amount of technical skills and knowledge.

CONCLUSION

Much of the success of a competency model project hinges on the ability to translate the model into useful tools and formats for application in HRM systems. After all, the information gathered while developing the model will be of little

Table 11.3. Two Approaches to Developing a Competency Model

Starting from Scratch	Starting with a Validated Competency Model
1. Identify performance criteria for individuals and work units	1. Identify performance criteria for individuals and work units
2. Identify individuals and work units that meet, exceed, and fall below these performance criteria	2. Identify individuals and work units that meet, exceed, and fall below these performance criteria
3. Interview job incumbents and informed observers	
4. Observe job incumbents directly— "a day in the life"	
5. Develop interim competency model—analyze data for themes and patterns, look for differences between exceptional and standard performers	
6. Administer survey and/or conduct focus groups to include a wider population and test degree of relevance and importance of competency to the job	3. Administer survey and/or conduct focus groups to include a wider population and test degree of relevance and importance of competency to the job
7. Analyze survey or focus group data and refine model	4. Analyze survey or focus group data and refine model
8. Validate model—administer 360-degree questionnaire to identify competencies that correlate with exceptional performers	5. Validate model—administer 360-degree questionnaire to identify competencies that correlate with exceptional performers
9. Finalize model	6. Finalize model

value to people unless they have a means of applying it. If they are not sure how to translate insights into action, the model is likely to sit on a shelf. To avoid such an outcome, we offer the following suggestions:

- Make sure that the purpose and importance of the competency model are understood, both by people who are responsible for using it in human resource practices and by the individuals who will be measured against it.
- Include specific behavioral examples in the competency definition that are applicable to the job or role under consideration.
- Solicit feedback about the usefulness of the model's application and hold discussions with managers and incumbents to assess how well the model is being applied.
- Remember that the model is not set in stone—as the needs and landscape of a business shift, you will want to revisit it to determine whether it is still valid as a predictor of successful performance.

Keep these tips in mind as you develop and use competency models in your organization. They should go a long way to ensuring your success.

References

Lucia, A., & Lepsinger, R. (1999). *The art and science of competency models: Pinpointing critical success factors in organizations.* San Francisco: Jossey-Bass/Pfeiffer.

Parry, S.R. (1996, July). The quest for competencies. *Training,* 48–56.

Recommended Reading

Lepsinger, R., & Lucia, A. (1997). *The art and science of 360° feedback.* San Francisco: Jossey-Bass/Pfeiffer.

About the Authors

Richard Lepsinger is managing vice president of Right Manus, a global organization that specializes in helping businesses implement their strategies successfully. He has been a consultant in the areas of management and organization development for over twenty years. Lepsinger has extensive experience in formulating and implementing strategic plans and in developing and using feedback-based technology to help organizations and managers identify their strengths and weaknesses. He has addressed executive conferences and made presentations on the topics of strategic leadership, strategy formulation and implementation, 360-

degree feedback and its uses, and developing and using competency models to en-hance organizational effectiveness. He has worked with large-scale management simulations as part of assessment and training interventions since 1979.

Anntoinette Lucia *is managing vice president of Right Manus, a global organi-zation specializing in helping businesses implement their strategies successfully. Her consulting work has included facilitating strategic organizational change; team building for senior management teams; linking human resource plans to strategic plans; ensuring the successful integration of teams following mergers; designing, conducting, and evaluating executive and management development programs; and using feedback systems to help individual executives improve their effectiveness. Lucia designed a program for the Center for Creative Leadership that focuses on career and professional development planning for high-potential managers.*

CHAPTER TWELVE

The Four-Level Evaluation Process

Donald L. Kirkpatrick, Ph.D.
Professor Emeritus, University of Wisconsin

T he four levels help clarify the elusive term "evaluation." Some training and development professionals believe that evaluation means measuring changes in behavior that occur as a result of training programs. Others maintain that the only real evaluation lies in determining final results that occurred because of training programs. Still others think of evaluation only in terms of the comment sheets that participants complete at the end of a program. Others are concerned with the learning that takes place, as measured by increased knowledge, improved skills, and changes in attitude. They are all right. This chapter presents four levels of the evaluation process and explains how to use them to evaluate training programs effectively.

PROCESS OF EVALUATION

There are three reasons for evaluating training programs. The most common is to improve future programs. The second is to determine whether a program should be continued or dropped. The third is to justify the existence of the training department by demonstrating to top management that training has tangible, positive results. By doing such evaluations, trainers will find that their jobs are secure, even if and when downsizing occurs. Management's impressions can be greatly influenced by trainers who evaluate at all levels and communicate the results.

In most organizations, large and small, there is little pressure from top management to prove that the benefits of training outweigh the cost. Managers at high levels are too busy worrying about profits, return on investment, stock prices, and other matters of concern to the board of directors, stockholders, and customers. They pay little or no attention to training unless they hear bad things about it. As long as trainees are happy and do not complain, trainers feel comfortable, relaxed, and secure. If trainees react negatively to programs, trainers begin to worry, because the word might get to high-level managers that the program is a waste of time.

Recently, however, upper-level managers in a few organizations are putting pressure on trainers to justify their existence. Some have even demanded to see tangible results as measured by improvements in sales, productivity, quality, morale, turnover, safety records, profits, or even return on investment. In these situations, training professionals must evaluate their programs at four separate levels and may need some guidelines for doing so.

What about trainers who do not feel pressure from above to justify their existence? I suggest that they operate as if there were going to be pressure and be ready to evaluate their programs. Even if the pressure for results never comes, trainers will benefit by becoming accepted and respected by others and satisfied about their own results.

The four levels represent a sequence of ways to evaluate programs. Each level is important. As you move from one level to the next, the process of evaluation becomes more difficult and time-consuming, but it also provides more valuable information. None of the levels should be bypassed. The four levels are listed below:

- Level 1—Reaction;
- Level 2—Learning;
- Level 3—Behavior; and
- Level 4—Results

We will take a look at each level in more depth.

Level 1—Reaction

This level measures how those who participate in the program react to it—basically a measure of customer satisfaction. It is important not only to get such a reaction, but to get a positive reaction, as the future of a program may depend on it. In addition, if participants do not react favorably, they probably will not be motivated to learn the material. Positive reactions may not ensure learning, but negative reactions almost certainly reduce the possibility of its occurring.

Measuring participant reactions is important for several reasons. First, reactions give us valuable feedback that helps us to evaluate the program, as well as comments and suggestions for improving future programs. Second, soliciting reactions lets trainees know that the trainers are there to help them do their jobs better and that they need feedback to do so. Third, reaction sheets can provide quantitative information that you can give to managers and others. Finally, reaction sheets can provide trainers with quantitative information that can be used to establish standards of performance for future programs.

Reactions are not only important but also easy to collect and to evaluate. Most trainers use some type of reaction sheets. There are dozens of forms and various ways of using them. Some are effective, some are not. Here are some guidelines that will help trainers receive maximum benefit from the use of reaction sheets:

1. Determine what you want to find out. In every program, it is imperative to obtain reactions about both the subject and the trainer, and it is important to separate these two. Trainers may also want to obtain trainees' reactions to one or more of the following: facilities, schedule, meals, case studies, exercises, audiovisual aids, handouts, and the value that participants place on individual aspects of the program.

2. Design a form that will quantify reactions. The ideal form provides the maximum amount of information and requires the minimum amount of time to complete. When a program is over, most trainees are anxious to leave and don't want to spend a lot of time completing evaluation forms. Some even think that no one really will consider their comments, so they don't see the point.

3. Encourage written comments and suggestions. The numerical ratings that you tabulate provide only part of the participants' reactions. You also want the *reasons* for the reactions or suggestions for what can be done to improve the program. Typically, because reaction sheets are passed out at the end of a program and participants are anxious to leave, most will not take time to write in their comments. You can obtain comments by making the completion of reaction sheets part of the program or by passing the forms out at the beginning of the program and stressing the importance of comments and suggestions. Always make sure that you have their reaction sheets before participants leave the room.

4. Obtain honest responses. This may seem to be an unnecessary requirement, but it is important. To ensure honesty, do not ask participants to sign the forms and ask them to put completed forms in a pile on a

table so there is no way to identify the person who completed an individual form.

5. Develop acceptable standards. Ratings can be used to establish a standard of acceptable performance, for example, a particular percentage of "good" responses. This standard can be based on a realistic analysis of what is possible, considering such conditions as budgets, facilities available, skilled instructors available, and so forth.

6. Measure reactions against standards and take appropriate action. If the standards you set are not met, you may need to make a change in some facet of the program, for example, leaders, facilities, subject matter, or whatever. You also can live with the unsatisfactory situation or change the standard.

7. Communicate reactions as appropriate. The trainers may want to see the reactions or at least a summary of them. Other members of the training department should have access to them also. Communicating the reactions to others in the organization depends on two factors: who wants to see them and with whom the training staff wants to communicate. Before sharing, first determine whether the reasons to see the reactions are legitimate.

Measuring reactions is both important and easy to do. The data are important to share with top management for decision-making purposes and also important because the interest, attention, and motivation of participants has much to do with the learning that occurs. Remember that trainees are customers, and customer satisfaction has a lot to do with repeat business.

Level 2—Learning

Learning can be defined as the extent to which participants *change attitudes, improve knowledge,* and/or *increase skills* as a result of attending a program. For example, programs dealing with topics such as diversity in the workplace aim primarily at changing attitudes and technical programs such as computer training aim at improving skills. Programs on topics such as leadership, motivation, and communication can be aimed at all three objectives. In order to evaluate learning at the end of a program, one must determine the specific objectives prior to running it. No change in behavior can be expected unless one or more of your learning objectives have been accomplished. Moreover, if we were to measure behavioral change (Level 3) and we found no change in behavior, the likely conclusion would be that no learning took place. This conclusion may be erroneous, as it may be that the organizational climate prevents or discourages behavioral change.

The measurement of learning is more difficult and time-consuming than simply collecting participant reactions. Here are some guidelines:

1. Use a control group if practical. The control group does not receive the training, while the experimental group does. The purpose is to provide evidence that change has taken place. Any difference between the control and experimental groups can be associated with learning that took place because of the training program. Care must be taken to match the groups in all significant characteristics for a valid comparison.

2. Measure knowledge and/or attitudes before and after the program. The difference indicates what learning has taken place. A pre-test and post-test must be constructed or chosen for this purpose and scores must be compared. If little or no learning has taken place, little or no change in behavior can be expected. Such an evaluation is also important for measuring the effectiveness of the instructor in increasing knowledge and/or changing attitudes.

3. Evaluate any increase in skills. If the objective of the program is to increase participant skills, then a performance test is needed. A pre-test will be necessary, as it is possible that the participants already possess some of the skills being taught. If you are teaching something entirely new to everyone, then the post-test alone will measure the extent to which they have learned the skill.

Evaluating learning is important because, without learning, no change in behavior will occur.

Level 3—Behavior

Level 3 evaluation determines the extent to which changes in behavior occur due to what was learned during the training program. What happens when trainees leave the classroom and return to their jobs? How much transfer of knowledge, skills, and attitudes occurs? In other words, what changes in behavior on the job occurred because people attended the training?

It is obvious that these questions are more complicated and difficult to answer than were the questions at the first two levels. First, trainees cannot change their behavior until they have an opportunity to do so. Second, it is impossible to predict when a change in behavior will occur. Third, the trainee may apply the learning to the job and come to one of the following conclusions: "I like what happened, and I plan to continue to use the new behavior." "I don't like what happened, and I will go back to my old behavior." "I like what happened, but the boss and/or some time restraints prevent me from continuing it."

When you evaluate change in behavior, you have to make some important decisions: When to evaluate, how often to evaluate, and how to evaluate. Below are some guidelines for evaluating behavior change.

1. Use a control group, if practical. This is similar to what was mentioned earlier in the evaluating learning section.

2. Allow time for behavior change to take place. As already indicated, no evaluation should be attempted until trainees have had an opportunity to use the new behavior. Even if a participant has an immediate opportunity to transfer the training to the job, allow some time for this transfer to occur. For some programs, two or three months after training is a good time for evaluation; for others, six months is more realistic. Be sure to give trainees time to get back to the job, consider the new suggested behavior, and try it out.

3. Evaluate both before and after the program, if practical. For example, when planning a supervisory training program, determine the kind of behavior that supervisors should have in order to be most effective. Before the program, measure the behavior of the supervisors. Then after the program, measure the behavior of the supervisors again to see whether any change has taken place in relation to the knowledge, skills, and/or attitudes that the training program taught. By comparing the behaviors before and after the program, you can determine any change that has taken place. Many times it is not practical to measure behavior on a pre-program basis. Then the approach is to ask, "What are you doing differently from what you did before you attended the program?"

4. Survey and/or interview persons who know the behavior well. Four questions must be answered: "Who is best qualified?" "Who is most reliable?" "Who is most available?" "Are there any reasons why one or more of the possible candidates should not be used?"

5. Obtain either 100 percent response or a sampling.

6. Repeat the behavioral evaluation at the appropriate times. What an appropriate time is is different from one organization to another and from one situation to another, but it is important to know whether behavior has truly changed, so follow up.

7. Consider cost versus benefits.

No final results can be expected unless a positive change in behavior occurs. Therefore, it is important to see whether the knowledge, skills, and/or attitudes learned in the program transfer to the job. The process of evaluating behavior is complicated and often difficult. Decide whether to use interviews, survey questionnaires, or both. You must also decide whom to contact for the evaluation.

Two other difficult decisions you must make are when and how often to conduct the evaluation. Whether to use a control group is still another important consideration. These factors discourage most trainers from even making an attempt to evaluate at Level 3. But something beats nothing, and I encourage trainers to at least do some evaluation of behavior, even if it isn't elaborate or scientific. Simply ask a few people: "Are you doing anything different on the job because you attended the training program?" If the answer is yes, ask, "Can you briefly describe what you are doing and how it is working out? If you are not doing anything different, can you tell me why? Did you learn anything that you can use on the job? Does your boss encourage you to try out new things, or does your boss discourage any change in your behavior?" Also ask: "Do you plan to change some of your behavior on the job in the future?" If the answer is yes, then ask, "What do you plan to do differently?" Questions like these can be asked on a questionnaire or in an interview. A tabulation of the responses can provide a good indication of changes in behavior. If the program is going to be offered a number of times in the future and the potential results of behavior changes would be significant, then a more systematic and extensive approach should be used.

Level 4—Results

Results can be defined as the final results that occurred because the participants attended the program. Results can include such things as increased production, improved quality, decreased costs, reduced frequency and/or severity of accidents, increased sales, reduced turnover, and higher profits and return on investment. It is important to recognize that results like these are the reason for having some training programs. Therefore, the final objectives of the training program need to be stated in these terms. Some guidelines for evaluating results include

1. Use a control group if practical.
2. Allow time for results to be achieved.
3. Measure both before and after the program if practical.
4. Repeat the measurement at appropriate times.
5. Consider cost versus benefits.
6. Be satisfied with evidence if proof is not possible.

Evaluating results (Level 4) provides the greatest challenge to training professionals. But that is why we train, and we ought to be able to show tangible results that more than pay off the cost of training. In some cases, such evaluation can be done—and quite easily. Programs that aim at increasing sales, reducing accidents, reducing turnover, and reducing scrap rates can often be evaluated in terms of results. And the cost of the program is not too difficult to determine. A comparison between the dollar value of the change in results and the cost of the training can readily show that training pays off.

Most of the programs that I teach have results as a focus. When I conduct a management workshop on how to manage change, I certainly hope that those who attend will make better changes in the future and that the changes will be accepted and implemented enthusiastically. The results will be such things as better quality of work, more productivity, more job satisfaction, fewer mistakes, improved rapport between supervisors and subordinates, and other positive things. When I teach leadership, motivation, and decision making, I expect participants to understand what I teach, accept my ideas, and use them on the job. This will, of course, lead to tangible results. But how can I tell? Can I prove or even find evidence beyond a reasonable doubt that the final results show improvement? The answer is a resounding no. There are too many other factors that affect results.

So what should a trainer do when top management asks for tangible evidence that training programs are paying off? Sometimes, you can find evidence that positive results have occurred. In other situations, you will have to go back a level or two and evaluate changes in behavior, learning, or both. In many cases, positive reaction sheets from supervisors and managers can be used to convince top management. After all, if top management has any confidence in the management team, it may be enough to know that the supervisors and managers feel that the training was worthwhile.

If your programs aim for tangible results rather than just teaching management concepts, theories, and principles, then of course it is desirable to evaluate in terms of results. Most importantly, be satisfied with evidence, because proof is usually impossible to find.

IMPLEMENTING AN EVALUATION PROCESS

How can you implement an evaluation process that covers the four levels? Where do you start? What do you do first? These are typical questions from trainers who are convinced that evaluation is important but have done little about it. I suggest that you start at Level 1 and proceed through the other levels as time and opportunity allow. Some trainers are anxious to get to Level 3 or 4 right away because they think the first two aren't important. Don't do that. Suppose, for example, that you evaluate at Level 3 and discover that little or no change in behavior has occurred. What conclusions can you draw? The first conclusion you might come to is that the training program was no good, and you might decide to discontinue it or at least modify it. This conclusion may be entirely wrong. The reason that there was no change in job behavior may be that the climate prevents it. Supervisors may have gone back to the job with the necessary knowledge, skills, and attitudes, but the boss wouldn't allow change to take place. Therefore, it is important to evaluate at Level 2 so you can determine whether there was learning.

The first step in implementing the evaluation concepts, theories, and techniques described earlier is to understand the guidelines of Level 1 and apply them in every program. Use a philosophy that states, "If my customers are unhappy, it is my fault, and my challenge is to please them." If you don't think this way, your entire training program is in trouble. It is probably true that you seldom please *everyone*. It is a rare occasion when everyone in my training classes grades me as excellent. Nearly always, some participants are critical of my sense of humor, some content that I presented, or the quality of the audiovisual aids. I often find myself justifying what I did and ignoring their comments, but I shouldn't do that. My style of humor, for example, is to embarrass participants—I hope in a pleasant way so that they don't resent it. That happens to be my style, and most people enjoy and appreciate it. If I get only one critical comment from a group of twenty-five, I will ignore it and continue as I did in the past. However, if the reaction is fairly common because I have overdone it, then I will take the comment seriously and change my approach.

I used to tell a funny story in class. It was neither dirty nor ethnic. Nearly everyone else thought it was funny, too, and I had heard no objections to it. One day, I conducted a training class with social workers. I told the story at the beginning of the class and proceeded to do the training. After forty minutes, I asked whether anyone had a comment or question. One woman raised her hand and said, "I was offended by the joke you told at the beginning of the session, and I didn't listen to anything you said after that." I couldn't believe it! I was sure she was the only one who felt that way, so I asked, "Did any others feel the same way?" Seven other women raised their hands. There were about forty-five people in the class, so the percentage was very much in my favor. But I decided that that particular joke had no place in future meetings. If she had been the only one, I probably would still be telling it.

The point is this: Look over all the reaction sheets, and read the comments. Consider each one. Is there a suggestion that will improve future programs? If yes, use it. If it is an isolated comment that will not improve future programs, appreciate it, but ignore it.

Evaluating at Level 2 isn't that difficult either. All you need to do is to decide what knowledge, skills, and attitudes you want participants to have at the end of the program. If there is a possibility that one or more of these three already exists, then a pre-test is necessary. If you are presenting something entirely new, then no pre-test is necessary. You can use a standardized test if you can find one that covers the things you are teaching. Or you can develop your own test to cover the knowledge and attitudes that you are teaching.

Levels 3 and 4 are not as easy. A lot of time will be required to decide on an evaluation design. Knowledge of statistics may be desirable to determine the level of significance. Check with the research people in your organization for help in the design. If necessary, you may have to call in an outside consultant to help you or even do the evaluation for you. Remember the principle that the possible benefits from an evaluation should exceed the cost of doing the evaluation, and be satisfied with evidence if proof is not possible.

There is another important principle that applies to all four levels: You can borrow evaluation forms, designs, and procedure from others, but you cannot borrow evaluation results. If another organization offers the same program as you do and they evaluate it, you can borrow their evaluation methods and procedures, but you can't say, "They evaluated it and found these results. Therefore, we don't have to do it, because we know the results we would get." Learn all you can about evaluation. Find out what others have done. Look for forms, methods, techniques, and designs that you can copy or adapt. But ignore the results of these other evaluations, except out of curiosity.

Evaluation is a science and an art. It is a blend of concepts, theory, principles, and techniques. It is up to you to do the application. May you be successful in doing it.

Reference

Kirkpatrick, D.L. (1996). *Evaluating training programs: The four levels* (2nd ed.). San Francisco: Berrett-Koehler.

Recommended Reading

Kirkpatrick, D.L. (Ed.). (1998). *Another look at evaluating training programs.* Alexandria, VA: ASTD.

Parry, S.B. (1997). *Evaluating the impact of training.* Alexandria, VA: ASTD.

Phillips, J.J. (Ed.). (1997). *Handbook of training evaluation and measurement methods.* Houston, TX: Gulf.

Robinson, D.G., & Robinson, J.C. (1989). *Training for impact: How to link training to business needs and measure the results.* San Francisco: Jossey-Bass.

About the Author

Donald L. Kirkpatrick is professor emeritus, University of Wisconsin, and a widely respected teacher, author, and consultant. He has over thirty years of experience as professor of management at the University of Wisconsin and has held professional training and human resource positions with International Mineral and Chemical Corporation and Bendix Corporation. Kirkpatrick is the author of many inventories and books, including How to Manage Change Effectively *and* How to Improve Performance Through Appraisal and Coaching, *which received "Best Book of the Year" awards from the Society for Human Resource Management. He is past president of ASTD (formerly, American Society for Training and Development) and is best known for developing the internationally accepted four-level approach for training programs. He received his B.B.A., M.B.A., and Ph.D. degrees from the University of Wisconsin, Madison.*

CHAPTER THIRTEEN

The Return on Investment (ROI) Process

Jack J. Phillips, Ph.D.
*President, The Jack Phillips Center for Research and Assessment,
A FranklinCovey Company*

Patricia Pulliam Phillips
Chairman and CEO, The Chelsea Group

Measuring the return on investment (ROI) in education, training, human resource development, and performance improvement is a topic of much debate. It is rare for any topic to stir up emotions to the degree the ROI issue does. Return on investment is characterized as flawed and inappropriate by some, while others describe it as the only answer to their accountability concerns. The truth probably lies somewhere between. Understanding the drivers for the ROI process and the inherent weaknesses and advantages of ROI makes it possible to take a rational approach to the issue and implement an appropriate mix of evaluation strategies that includes ROI. This chapter presents the basic issues and trends concerning ROI measurement.

KEY ROI ISSUES

A Comprehensive Process[1]

The ROI Process™ is a comprehensive process that provides a scorecard of six measures. These measures represent input from various sources during different time frames. The measures include: (1) Reaction and satisfaction, (2) Learning; (3) Application and implementation, (4) Business impact, (5) Return on

---

[1]The ROI Process™ and the Jack Phillips Center for Research™ are trademarks owned by the FranklinCovey Company.

investment, and (6) Intangible benefits. In addition, the ROI Process utilizes at least one technique to isolate the effects of the program from other influences. This comprehensive measurement system requires success with many issues and must become a routine part of the learning development cycle.

ROI Is Here to Stay

One thing is certain in the ROI debate—it is not a fad. As long as there is a need for accountability of education and training expenditures and the concept of an investment payoff is desired, ROI will be utilized to evaluate major investments in education and training.

A "fad" is a new idea or approach or a new spin on an old approach. The concept of ROI has been used for centuries. The 75th anniversary issue of *Harvard Business Review* (HBR) traced the tools used to measure results in organizations (Sibbet, 1997). In the early issues of HBR, during the 1920s, ROI was the emerging tool to place a value on the payoff of investments. In recent years, the application of the concept has been expanded to all types of investments, including training and education, change initiatives, and technology (Phillips, 2000).

With increased adoption and use, it appears that ROI is here to stay. Today, hundreds of organizations are routinely developing ROI calculations for education and training programs. The ROI Network™, a professional society with over five hundred members, allows practitioners an opportunity to share information and tools around ROI (roinetwk@aol.com). Other listservs and networks have been formed within organizations to focus on ROI and the accountability issue. Nearly one thousand individuals have been certified to implement the process within their organizations. Three casebooks have been developed to show specific applications of ROI (Phillips, 1994, 1997a,b; Phillips & Phillips, 2000), and a fourth casebook describes successful implementation of the ROI process (Phillips, 1998). This level of interest and activity is more evidence that the ROI process is here to stay.

Why ROI?

There are good reasons why return on investment is such a hot topic. Although the viewpoints and explanations may vary, some things are very clear. First, in most organizations education and training budgets have continued to grow year after year (Industry Report, 1999). As expenditures grow, accountability becomes a more critical issue. A growing budget creates a larger target for internal critics, often prompting the development of an ROI process.

Second, Total Quality Management and Continuous Process Improvement have brought increased attention to measurement issues. Today, organizations measure processes and outputs that were not previously measured, monitored, and reported. This focus has placed increased pressure on the education and training function to develop measures of program success.

Third, the proliferation of new hardware and software has created a need for accountability. For years, the implementers of new technology have not been held accountable for its return on investment. Organizations have been willing to buy new technology, not knowing whether the application would actually generate an appropriate return on investment. Project sponsors have been burned by inappropriate and improperly designed technology implementations. Today, that situation is changing, particularly in education and training. Administrators and executives who fund new projects are asking for demonstrated accountability, with a commitment to measure the return on investment after initial implementation.

Fourth, restructuring and reengineering initiatives and the threat of outsourcing have caused education and training executives to focus more directly on bottom-line issues. Many education and training processes have been reengineered so that programs are more closely aligned with business needs, and maximum efficiencies are required in the training cycle. These change processes have brought increased attention to evaluation issues and have resulted in measuring the contribution of specific programs.

Fifth, the business management mindset of many current education and training managers causes them to place more emphasis on economic issues within the function. Today's education and training manager is more aware of bottom-line issues in the organization and more knowledgeable of operational and financial concerns. This new "enlightened" manager often takes a business approach to education and training, and ROI is a part of the strategy.

Sixth, there has been a persistent trend of accountability in organizations all over the globe. Every support function is attempting to show its worth by capturing the value that it adds to the organization. From the accountability perspective, the education and training function should be no different from the other functions—it must show its contribution to the organization.

Seventh, top executives are now demanding return on investment calculations from departments and functions where they were not previously required. For years, training and education managers convinced top executives that training cannot be measured, at least at the monetary contribution level. Yet, many of the executives are now aware that it can and is being measured in many organizations, thanks in part to articles in publications aimed at top executives (Corporate Training: Does It Pay Off?, 1995). Due to this increased awareness, top executives are subsequently demanding the same accountability from their training and education functions. In some extremes, these functions are being asked to show the return on investment or face significant budget cuts (Geber, 1994). Others are just being asked for results. The CEO for a global telecommunications company recently described it this way: "For years we have evaluated training with measures such as number of participants, number of programs, length of programs, cost of programs, and content of programs. These are input focused measures. Now, we must show what these programs are doing for our company and speak in terms that we can understand. We need output focused measures" (personal communication). These no-nonsense comments are being repeated throughout major organizations.

Concerns with ROI

Although much progress has been made, the ROI process is not without its share of problems and drawbacks. The mere presence of the process creates a dilemma for many organizations. When an organization embraces the concept and implements the process, the management team is usually anxiously waiting for results, only to be disappointed when they are not quantifiable. For an ROI process to be useful, it must balance many issues, including feasibility, simplicity, credibility, and soundness. More specifically, three major audiences must be pleased with the ROI process to accept and use it.

Practitioners. For years, education and training practitioners have assumed that ROI could not be measured. When examining a typical process, they found long formulas, complicated equations, and complex models that made the ROI process appear to be too confusing. With this perceived complexity, practitioners could visualize the tremendous efforts required for data collection and analysis, and more importantly, the increased cost necessary to make the process work. Because of these concerns, practitioners are seeking an ROI process that is simple and easy to understand so that they can easily implement the steps and strategies. Also, they need a process that will not take an excessive amount of time to implement. Finally, a process is needed that is not too expensive. In summary, from the perspective of the practitioner, the ROI process must be user-friendly, time-saving, and cost-efficient.

Senior Managers/Sponsors/Clients. Managers, who must approve education and training budgets, request programs, or cope with the results of programs, have a strong interest in developing the ROI. They want a process that provides quantifiable results, using a method similar to the ROI formula applied to other types of investments. Senior managers have a never-ending desire to have it all come down to ROI calculations, reflected as a percentage. They, as do practitioners, want a process that is simple and easy to understand. The assumptions made in the calculation and the methodology used in the process must reflect their frame of reference, experience, and level of understanding. They do not want, or need, a string of formulas, charts, and complicated models. Instead, they want a process that, when necessary, they can explain to others. More importantly, they need a process with which they can identify—one that is sound and realistic enough to earn their confidence.

Researchers. Finally, researchers will only support a process that measures up to close examination. Researchers usually insist that models, formulas, assumptions, and theories be sound and based on commonly accepted practices. Also, they want a process that produces accurate values and consistent outcomes. If estimates are necessary, researchers want a process that provides the most accuracy within the constraints of the situation, recognizing that adjustments need to be made when there is uncertainty in the process.

The challenge is to develop acceptable requirements for an ROI process that will satisfy researchers and, at the same time, please practitioners and senior managers. Sound impossible? Maybe not.

Criteria for an Effective ROI Process

To satisfy the needs of the three critical groups described, the ROI process must meet several requirements. Ten essential criteria for an effective ROI process are outlined below (Phillips, 1997a). These criteria were developed with input from hundreds of education and training managers and specialists:

1. The ROI process must be *simple,* devoid of complex formulas, lengthy equations, and complicated methodologies. Most ROI attempts have failed with this requirement. In an attempt to obtain statistical perfection, several models and processes have become too complex to understand and use. Consequently, they are not being implemented.

2. The ROI process must be *economical,* with the ability to be easily implemented. The process should have the capability to become a routine part of education and training without requiring significant additional resources. Sampling for ROI calculations and early planning for ROI are often necessary to make progress without adding new staff.

3. The assumptions, methodology, and outcomes must be *credible.* Logical, methodical steps are needed to earn the respect of practitioners, senior managers, and researchers. This requires a very practical approach for the process.

4. From a research perspective, the ROI process must be *theoretically sound* and based on generally accepted practices. Unfortunately, this requirement can lead to an extensive, complicated process. Ideally, the process must strike a balance between maintaining a practical and sensible approach and a sound and theoretical basis for the procedures. This is perhaps one of the greatest challenges to those who have developed models for the ROI process.

5. An ROI process must *account for other factors* that have influenced output variables. One of the most often overlooked issues, isolating the

influence of an education program, is necessary to build credibility and accuracy within the process. The ROI process should pinpoint the contribution of the program when compared to the other influences.

6. The ROI process must be appropriate with a *variety of programs.* Some models apply to only a small number of programs, such as productivity training. Ideally, the process must be applicable to all types of education and training and other programs, such as career development, organization development, and major change initiatives.

7. The ROI process must have the *flexibility* to be applied on a pre-program basis as well as a post-program basis. In some situations, an estimate of the ROI is required before the actual program is developed. Ideally, the process should be able to adjust to a range of potential time frames for calculating the ROI.

8. The ROI process must be *applicable with all types of data, including hard data,* which is typically represented as output, quality, costs, and time; and *soft data,* which includes job satisfaction, customer satisfaction, absenteeism, turnover, grievances, and complaints.

9. The ROI process must *include the costs* of the program. The ultimate level of evaluation compares the benefits with costs. Although the term ROI has been loosely used to express any benefit of education or training, an acceptable ROI formula must include costs. Omitting or understating costs will only destroy the credibility of the ROI values.

10. Finally, the ROI process must have a successful *track record* in a variety of applications. In far too many situations, models are created but never successfully applied. An effective ROI process should withstand the wear and tear of implementation and prove valuable to users.

Because these criteria are considered essential, an ROI process should meet the vast majority, if not all criteria. The bad news is that most ROI processes do not meet these criteria. The good news is that the process presented below meets all of the criteria.

BUILDING THE PROCESS

Building a comprehensive measurement and evaluation process is best represented as a puzzle where the pieces are developed and put in place over time. Figure 13.1 depicts this puzzle and the pieces necessary to build a comprehensive measurement and evaluation process. The first piece of the puzzle is the selection of *an evaluation framework,* which is a categorization of data. The

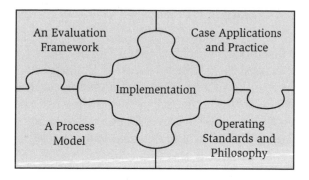

Figure 13.1. ROI: The Pieces of the Puzzle

balanced scorecard process (Kaplan & Norton, 1996) or the four levels of evaluation developed by Kirkpatrick (1975) offer the beginning points for such a framework. The framework selected for the process presented here is a modification of Kirkpatrick's four levels to include a fifth level: return on investment.

Next, an ROI *process model* must be developed showing how data is collected, processed, analyzed, and reported to various target audiences. This process model ensures that appropriate techniques and procedures are consistently utilized to address almost any situation. Also, there must be consistency as the process is implemented.

The third piece of the puzzle is the development of *operating standards.* These standards help ensure the results of the study are stable and not influenced by the individual conducting the study. Replication is critical for the credibility of an evaluation process. Operating standards and guiding principles allow for replication, so that if more than one individual evaluates a specific program, the results are the same.

Next, appropriate attention must be given to *implementation* issues as the ROI process becomes a routine part of the education and training function. Several issues must be addressed involving skills, communication, roles, responsibilities, plans, and strategies.

Finally, there must be successful *case applications and practice* describing the implementation of the process within the organization, the value a comprehensive measurement and evaluation process brings to the organization, and the impact the specific program evaluated has on the organization. While it is helpful to refer to case studies developed by other organizations, it is more useful and convincing to have studies developed directly within the organization.

The remainder of this chapter focuses on the individual pieces of the evaluation puzzle: developing a comprehensive ROI process.

AN EVALUATION FRAMEWORK

The ROI process described in this chapter adds a fifth level to the four levels of evaluation developed by Kirkpatrick (1975) to measure the success of training. The concept of different levels of evaluation is both helpful and instructive to understanding how the return on investment is calculated. Table 13.1 shows the five-level framework used in the ROI Process.

Level 1, *Reaction, Satisfaction, and Planned Action,* measures satisfaction of program participants, along with their plans to apply what they have learned. Almost all organizations evaluate at Level 1, usually with a generic, end-of-program questionnaire. While this level of evaluation is important as a customer-satisfaction measure, a favorable reaction does not ensure that participants have learned new skills or knowledge.

Level 2, *Learning,* focuses on what participants learned during the program, using tests, skill practices, role plays, simulations, group evaluations, and other assessment tools. A learning check is helpful to ensure that participants have absorbed the program material and know how to use it properly. However, a positive measure at this level is no guarantee that what is learned will be applied on the job. The literature is laced with studies showing the failure of learning to be transferred to the job (for example, Broad, 1997).

At Level 3, *Application and Implementation,* a variety of follow-up methods are used to determine whether participants applied on the job what they learned. The frequency and use of skills are important measures at Level 3. While Level 3 evaluation is important to gauge the success of the application of a program, it still does not guarantee that there will be a positive business impact in the organization.

Table 13.1. Five Levels of Evaluation

Level	Measurement Focus
1: Reaction, Satisfaction, & Planned Action	Measures participants' reaction to and satisfaction with the program and captures planned actions
2: Learning	Measures changes in knowledge, skills, and attitudes
3: Application & Implementation	Measures changes in on-the-job behavior and progress with planned actions
4: Business Impact	Measures changes in business impact variables
5: Return on Investment	Compares program monetary benefits to the costs of the program

The Level 4, *Business Impact,* measure focuses on the actual results achieved by program participants as they successfully apply what they have learned. Typical Level 4 measures include output, quality, costs, time, and customer satisfaction. Although the program may produce a measurable business impact, there is still a concern that the program may cost too much.

Level 5, *Return on Investment,* the ultimate level of evaluation, compares the monetary benefits from the program with the program costs. Although the ROI can be expressed in several ways, it is usually presented as a percentage or cost/benefit ratio. The evaluation chain is not complete until the Level 5 evaluation is conducted.

While almost all education and training organizations conduct evaluations to measure satisfaction, very few actually conduct evaluations at the ROI level. Perhaps the best explanation for this situation is that ROI evaluation is often characterized as a difficult and expensive process. When business results and ROI are desired, it is also very important to evaluate the other levels. A chain of impact should occur through the levels as the skills and knowledge learned (Level 2) are applied on the job (Level 3) to produce business results (Level 4). If measurements are not taken at each level, it is difficult to conclude that the results achieved were actually caused by the program. Because of this, it is recommended that evaluation be conducted at all levels when a Level 5 evaluation is planned. This is consistent with the practices of benchmarking forum members of ASTD (formerly, American Society for Training and Development) (Kimmerling, 1993) and best-practice corporate universities as identified in a study conducted by the American Quality and Productivity Center (AQPC, 2000).

THE ROI PROCESS MODEL

The calculations of the return on investment in education and training begins with the model shown in Figure 13.2, where a potentially complicated process can be simplified with sequential steps. The ROI process model provides a systematic approach to ROI calculations. A step-by-step approach helps keep the process manageable so users can address one issue at a time. The model also emphasizes the fact that this is a logical, systematic process that flows from one step to another. Applying the model provides consistency between ROI calculations. Each step of the model is briefly described below.

Evaluation Planning

One of the most important and cost-saving steps in the ROI process is planning the evaluation. By considering key issues, time, money, and frustration can be

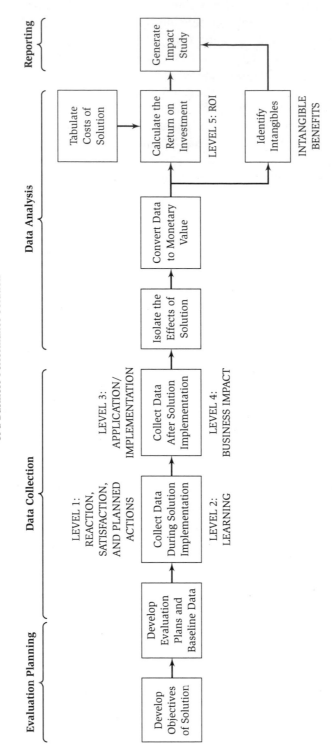

THE ROI PROCESS™

Calculating the Return on Investment
of a Business Performance Solution

Evaluation Planning

Develop Objectives of Solution

Develop Evaluation Plans and Baseline Data

Data Collection

Collect Data During Solution Implementation

LEVEL 1: REACTION, SATISFACTION, AND PLANNED ACTIONS

LEVEL 2: LEARNING

Collect Data After Solution Implementation

LEVEL 3: APPLICATION/ IMPLEMENTATION

LEVEL 4: BUSINESS IMPACT

Data Analysis

Isolate the Effects of Solution

Convert Data to Monetary Value

Tabulate Costs of Solution

Calculate the Return on Investment

LEVEL 5: ROI

Identify Intangibles

INTANGIBLE BENEFITS

Reporting

Generate Impact Study

Figure 13.2. The ROI Process Model

significantly reduced. There are four specific elements that should be considered during the initial stages of the planning process.

1. Evaluation purposes are considered prior to developing the evaluation plan. The purposes will often determine the scope of the evaluation, the types of instruments used, and the type of data collected. For example, when an ROI calculation is planned, one of the purposes is to compare the cost and benefits of the program. This purpose has implications for the type of data collected (hard data), type of data collection method (performance monitoring), the type of analysis (thorough), and the communication medium for results (formal evaluation report). For most programs, multiple evaluation purposes are pursued.

2. A variety of instruments are used to collect data. The appropriate instruments are determined in the early stages of developing the ROI. Questionnaires, interviews, and focus groups are common instruments. When deciding which instruments to use, those most fitting to the culture of the organization and most appropriate for the setting and evaluation requirements should be considered.

3. Training programs are evaluated at five different levels as illustrated in Table 13.1. Data should be collected at Levels 1, 2, 3, and 4, if an ROI analysis is planned. This helps ensure that the chain of impact occurs as participants learn the skills, apply them on the job, and obtain business results.

4. A final element in planning evaluation is the timing of the data collection. Sometimes, pre-program measurements are taken to compare with post-program measures. In some cases, multiple measures are taken at different times throughout the process. In other situations, pre-program measures are unavailable and specific follow-ups are taken after the program. The important issue is to determine the timing for the follow-up evaluation. For most education and training programs, a follow-up is usually conducted from three to six months after the program.

These four elements—evaluation purposes, instruments, levels, and timing—are all considerations in selecting the data collection methods and developing the data collection plan. Once this preliminary information is gathered, the data collection plan and ROI analysis plan are developed.

The Data Collection Plan. After the above elements have been considered and determined, the data collection plan is developed. The plan outlines in detail the steps to be taken to collect data for a comprehensive evaluation, and usually includes the following items:

- Broad areas for objectives are developed for evaluation planning; more specific program objectives are developed later;
- Specific measures or data descriptions are indicated when they are necessary to explain the measures linked to the objectives;
- Specific data collection methodologies for each objective are listed;
- Sources of data such as participants, team leaders, and company records are identified;
- The time frame in which to collect the data is noted for each data collection method; and
- Responsibility for collecting data is assigned.

The ROI Analysis Plan. The ROI analysis plan is a continuation of the data collection plan. This planning document captures information on several key issues necessary to develop the actual ROI calculation. These issues include:

- Significant data items, usually Level 4, business impact measures, but in some cases could include Level 3 data;
- The method for isolating the effects of the training and education program;
- The method for converting data to monetary values;
- The cost categories, noting how certain costs should be prorated;
- The anticipated intangible benefits;
- The communication targets—those to receive the information; and
- Other issues or events that might influence program implementation.

These two planning documents are necessary to successfully implement and manage the ROI process.

Collect Data

Following the planning process, implementation begins. Data collection is central to the ROI process. Both hard data and soft data are collected. Data are usually collected during two time frames. During the training process, Level 1 and Level 2 data are collected. Following the training, Level 3 and Level 4 data are collected. A variety of methods are used to collect the post-program data to be used in the ROI evaluation.

- Follow-up *surveys* are taken to determine the degree to which participants have utilized various aspects of the program. Survey responses are often developed on a sliding scale and usually represent attitudinal data. Surveys are useful in collecting Level 3 data.

- Follow-up *questionnaires* are administered to uncover specific applications of education and training. Participants provide responses to a variety of open-ended and forced-response questions. Questionnaires can be used to capture both Level 3 and 4 data.

- On-the-job *observation* captures actual skill application and use. Observations are particularly useful in customer-service training and are more effective when the observer is either invisible or transparent. Observations are appropriate for Level 3 data.

- Post-program *interviews* are conducted with participants to determine the extent to which learning has been utilized on the job. Interviews allow for probing to uncover specific applications and are appropriate with Level 3 data.

- *Focus groups* are conducted to determine the degree to which a group of participants has applied the training to job situations. Focus groups are appropriate with Level 3 data.

- *Program assignments* are useful for simple, short-term projects. Participants complete the assignment on the job, utilizing skills or knowledge learned in the program. Completed assignments can often contain both Level 3 or 4 data.

- *Action plans* are developed in programs and are implemented on the job after the program is completed. A follow-up of the plans provides evidence of program success. Level 3 and 4 data can be collected with action plans.

- *Performance contracts* are developed where the participant, the supervisor, and the instructor all agree on specific outcomes from education and training. Performance contracts are appropriate for both Level 3 and 4 data.

- Programs are designed with a *follow-up session,* which is utilized to capture evaluation data as well as present additional learning material. In this session, participants discuss their successes with the program. Follow-up sessions are appropriate for both Level 3 or 4 data.

- *Performance monitoring* is useful where various performance records and operational data are examined for improvement. This method is particularly useful for Level 4 data.

The important challenge is to select the data collection method or methods appropriate for the setting and the specific program, within the time and budget constraints of the organization.

Isolate the Effects of the Program

An often overlooked issue in most evaluations is the process used to isolate the effects of education and training. In this step of the ROI process, specific strategies are explored that determine the amount of output performance directly related to the program. This step is essential because there are many factors that will influence performance data after education and training programs are conducted. The specific techniques utilized at this step will pinpoint the amount of improvement directly related to the program. The result is increased accuracy and credibility of the ROI calculation. The following techniques have been utilized by organizations to address this important issue (Phillips, 1996a):

- *A control group* arrangement may be used to isolate impact. With this technique, one group participates in the program while another, similar group does not. The difference in the performance of the two groups is attributed to the program. When properly set up and implemented, the control group arrangement is the most effective way to isolate the effects of education and training.

- *Trend lines* are used to project the value of specific output variables if the program had not been undertaken. The projection is compared to the actual data after the program, and the difference represents the estimate of the impact. Under certain conditions, this strategy can be an accurate way to isolate the impact of education and training.

- When mathematical relationships between input and output variables are known, a *forecasting model* is used to isolate the effects of a program. With this approach, the output variable is predicted using the model with the assumption that the program is not conducted. The actual performance of the variable after the program is then compared with the forecasted value to estimate the impact of education and training.

- *Participants estimate* the amount of improvement related to education and training. Here, participants are provided with the total amount of improvement, on a pre- and post-program basis, and are asked to indicate the percent of the improvement that is actually related to the program.

- *Supervisors of participants estimate* the impact of education and training on the output variables. The supervisors are presented with the total amount of improvement and are asked to indicate the percent related to the program.

- *Senior managers estimate* the impact of education and training. In these cases, managers provide an estimate or "adjustment" to reflect the portion of the improvement related to the program. While these are perhaps inaccurate, there are some advantages to having senior management involved in this process, such as senior management ownership of the program.

- *Experts provide estimates* of the impact of education and training on the performance variable. Because the estimates are based on previous experience, the experts must be familiar with the type of training and the specific situation.

- In supervisory and management training, the *subordinates of participants identify changes in the work climate* that could influence the output variables. With this approach, the subordinates of the supervisors receiving training determine whether other variables changed in the work climate that could have influenced output performance.

- When feasible, *other influencing factors are identified and the impact estimated or calculated,* leaving the remaining unexplained improvement attributed to education and training. In this case, the influence of all other factors is developed and the program remains the one variable not accounted for in the analysis. The unexplained portion of the output is then attributed to the program.

- In some situations, *customers provide input* on the extent to which training has influenced their decision to use a product or service. Although this strategy has limited applications, it can be quite useful in customer service and sales training.

Collectively, these ten techniques provide a comprehensive set of tools to isolate the effects of education and training.

Convert Data to Monetary Values

To calculate the return on investment, data collected at Level 4 is converted to monetary values to compare with program costs. This requires a value to be placed on each unit of data connected with the program. Ten approaches are available to convert data to monetary values where the specific technique selected usually depends on the type of data and the situation (Phillips, 1996b):

- *Output data is converted to profit contribution or cost savings.* With this approach, output increases are converted to monetary value based on their unit of contribution to profit or the unit of cost reduction. These values are standard values, readily available in most organizations.

- The *cost of quality is calculated* and quality improvements are directly converted to cost savings. These values are standard values, available in many organizations.

- For programs where employee time is saved, the participant *wages and benefits are used for the value of time.* Because a variety of programs focus on improving the time required to complete projects, processes, or daily activities, the value of time becomes an important and necessary issue.

- *Historical costs and current records* are used when they are available for a specific variable. In this case, organizational cost data are utilized to establish the specific value of an improvement.

- When available, *internal and external experts* may be used to estimate a value for an improvement. In this situation, the credibility of the estimate hinges on the expertise and reputation of the individual.

- *External databases* are sometimes available to estimate the value or cost of data items. Research, government, and industry databases can provide important information for these values. The difficulty lies in finding a specific database related to the situation.

- *Participants estimate* the value of the data item. For this approach to be effective, participants must be capable of providing a value for the improvement.

- *Soft measures are linked, mathematically, to other measures* that are easier to measure and value. This approach is particularly helpful when establishing values for measures that are very difficult to convert to monetary values, such as data often considered intangible, like customer satisfaction, employee satisfaction, grievances, and employee complaints.

- *Supervisors and managers* provide estimates when they are both willing and capable of assigning values to the improvement. This approach is especially useful when participants are not fully capable of providing the input or in situations in which supervisors need to confirm or adjust the participant's estimate.

- *Education and training staff estimates* may be used to determine a value of an output data item. In these cases, it is essential for the estimates to be provided on an unbiased basis.

This step in the ROI model is very important and is absolutely necessary to determine the monetary benefits from education and training programs. The process is challenging, particularly with soft data, but can be methodically accomplished using one or more of the above techniques.

Tabulate Costs of Program

The next step in the process is tabulating the costs of the program. Tabulating the costs involves monitoring or developing all of the related costs of the program targeted for the ROI calculation. Among the components that should be included are

- The cost to design and develop the program, possibly prorated over the expected life of the program;
- The cost of all program materials provided to each participant;
- The cost of the instructor/facilitator, including preparation times as well as delivery time;
- The cost of the facilities for the program;
- Travel, lodging, and meal cost for the participants, if applicable;
- Salaries plus employee benefits of the participants for the time they attend the program; and
- Administrative and overhead costs of the education and training function allocated in some convenient way to the training program.

In addition, specific costs related to the needs assessment and evaluation should be included, if appropriate. The conservative approach is to include all of these costs so that the total is fully loaded.

Calculate the ROI

The return on investment is calculated using the program benefits and costs. The cost/benefit ratio is the program benefits divided by cost. In formula form it is

$$BCR = \frac{\text{Program Benefits}}{\text{Program Costs}}$$

The return on investment uses the net benefits divided by program costs. The net benefits are the program benefits minus the costs. In formula form, the ROI becomes

$$ROI\ (\%) = \frac{\text{Net Program Benefits}}{\text{Program Costs}} \times 100$$

This is the same basic formula used in evaluating other investments where the ROI is traditionally reported as earnings divided by investment. The ROI from some programs is high. For example, in sales, supervisory, leadership, and managerial training, the ROI can be quite large, frequently over 100 percent, while the ROI value for technical and operator training may be lower.

Identify Intangibles

In addition to tangible monetary benefits, most education and training programs will have intangible nonmonetary benefits. Data items identified that are not converted to monetary values are considered intangible benefits. While many of these items can be converted to monetary values, for various reasons they often are not, for example, because the process used for conversion is too subjective and the resulting values lose credibility in the process.

These intangible benefits may include: Increased job satisfaction; increased organizational commitment; improved teamwork; improved customer service; reduced complaints; and reduced conflicts. For some programs, these intangible nonmonetary benefits are extremely valuable, often carrying as much influence as the hard data items.

OPERATING STANDARDS AND PHILOSOPHY

To ensure consistency and replication of studies, operating standards must be developed and applied as the process model is utilized to develop ROI studies. It is extremely important for the results of a study to stand alone and not vary depending on the individual conducting the study. The operating standards detail how each step and issue of the process will be handled. Exhibit 13.1 shows the ten guiding principles that form the basis for the operating standards.

The guiding principles not only serve as a way to consistently address each step, but also provide a much needed conservative approach to the analysis. A conservative approach may lower the actual ROI calculation, but it will also build credibility with the target audience. For additional information on operating standards see other resources (Phillips, 1997).

ROI IMPLEMENTATION

Although progress has been made in the implementation of ROI, significant barriers can inhibit the process. Some of these barriers are realistic; others are actually myths based on false perceptions. The key implementation issues are briefly discussed in this section.

Discipline and Planning

A successful ROI implementation requires much planning and a disciplined approach to keep the process on track. Implementation schedules, evaluation targets, data collection plans, ROI analysis plans, measurement and evaluation policies, and follow-up schedules are required. Only a carefully planned implementation will be successful.

Responsibilities

There are two areas of responsibility when implementing ROI. First, the entire training and education staff is responsible for measurement and evaluation.

Exhibit 13.1. Ten Guiding Principles

1. When a higher level evaluation is conducted, data must be collected at lower levels.

2. When an evaluation is planned for a higher level, the previous level of evaluation does not have to be comprehensive.

3. When collecting and analyzing data, use only the most credible source.

4. When analyzing data, choose the most conservative among alternatives.

5. At least one method must be used to isolate the effects of the solution.

6. If no improvement data are available for a population or from a specific source, it is assumed that little or no improvement has occurred.

7. Estimates of improvements should be adjusted for the potential error of the estimate.

8. Extreme data items and unsupported claims should not be used in ROI calculations.

9. Only the first year of benefits (annual) should be used in the ROI analysis of short-term solutions.

10. Costs of the solution should be fully loaded for ROI analysis.

Whether they are involved in designing, developing, or delivering programs, these responsibilities typically include

- Ensuring that the needs assessment includes specific business impact measures;

- Developing specific application objectives (Level 3) and business impact objectives (Level 4) for each program;

- Focusing the content of the program on performance improvement, ensuring that exercises, case studies, and skill practices relate to the desired objectives;

- Keeping participants focused on application and impact objectives;

- Communicating rationale and reasons for evaluation;

- Assisting in follow-up activities to capture application and business impact data;

- Providing technical assistance for data collection, data analysis, and reporting;

- Designing instruments and plans for data collection and analysis; and
- Presenting evaluation data to a variety of groups.

The second area of responsibility regards details for those involved directly in measurement and evaluation, either on a full-time basis or as a primary duty. The responsibilities around this group involve six key areas:

1. Designing data collection instruments;
2. Providing assistance for developing an evaluation strategy;
3. Analyzing data, including specialized statistical analyses;
4. Interpreting results and making specific recommendations;
5. Developing an evaluation report or case study to communicate overall results; and
6. Providing technical support in any phase of the ROI process.

Staff Skills Development

Many training staff members neither understand ROI nor have the basic skills necessary to apply the process. The typical training and development program does not focus on business results; it focuses more on learning outcomes. Consequently, staff skills must be developed to utilize the results based approach. The following ten skill sets have been identified as necessary for the implementation of the ROI:

1. Planning for ROI calculations;
2. Collecting evaluation data;
3. Isolating the effects of training;
4. Converting data to monetary values;
5. Monitoring program costs;
6. Analyzing data, including calculating the ROI;
7. Presenting evaluation data;
8. Implementing the ROI process;
9. Providing internal consulting on ROI; and
10. Teaching others the ROI process.

Needs Assessment and Performance Analysis

Many education and training departments do not conduct adequate needs assessment prior to implementing a training program. When this occurs, programs are often implemented for the wrong reasons (such as an effort to chase a popular fad or trend in the industry). If the program is not needed, there will probably be insufficient economic benefit from the program to offset the costs, yielding a negative ROI.

The ROI process is often undertaken to improve the evaluation of existing programs. This process often uncovers inadequate front-end analysis. By improving the front-end analysis, only programs actually needed and properly aligned with business needs will be implemented, resulting in positive contribution to the organization's bottom line. Consequently, the implementation of the ROI Process will cause many organizations to improve the front-end analysis to ensure that there is proper alignment with business needs.

Communication

To communicate the progress with ROI requires two key strategies. The first strategy involves a routine reporting of impact studies. In this case, impact evaluation reports are generated and communicated to a variety of target audiences. Streamlined versions are available, including executive summaries and a one-page presentation of six PowerPoint® slides. The important point is to tailor the communication of an impact study directly to the target audiences, minimizing their time to review results, while building respect for the process.

The second issue involves a progress report of all evaluation. Here, a scorecard is developed to show the six types of data rolled up for the entire training and development function. Data collected from different programs are combined and integrated in a typical reporting format. Exhibit 13.2 shows the scorecard for a major training and education function.

Costs and Time Savings Approaches

The ROI process will add costs and time to measurement and evaluation, although the amount will not be excessive. A comprehensive ROI process will probably cost no more than 4 to 5 percent of the overall education and training budget. The additional investment in ROI will be offset by the additional results achieved from these programs and the elimination of unproductive or unprofitable programs. The challenge is to find ways to save time and costs as the ROI process is implemented. Some of the most valuable approaches are

- Plan for evaluation early in the process;
- Build evaluation into the training process;
- Share the responsibilities for evaluation;
- Require participants to conduct major steps;
- Use short-cut methods for major steps;
- Use sampling to select the most appropriate programs for ROI analysis;
- Use estimates in the collection and analysis of data;

Exhibit 13.2. Sample Corporate University Scorecard

Corporate University Scorecard

0. Indicators

    1. Number of Employees Trained

    2. Training Hours Per Employee

    3. Training Investment as a Percentage of Payroll Costs

    4. Percentage of Alternative Delivery

I. Reaction and Planned Action

    1. Percentage of Programs Evaluated at This Level

    2. Ratings on Seven Items vs. Targets

    3. Percentage with Action Plans

    4. Average Projected ROI, with Adjustment

II. Learning

    1. Percentage of Programs Evaluated at This Level

    2. Types of Measurements

    3. Self-Assessment Ratings on Three Items vs. Targets

    4. Pre/Post–Differences

    5. Standard Test Scores

III. Application

    1. Percentage of Programs Evaluated at This Level

    2. Ratings on Three Items vs. Targets

    3. Percentage of Action Plans Complete

    4. Barriers (List of Top Ten)

    5. Enablers

    6. Management Support

IV. Business Impact

    1. Percentage of Programs Evaluated at This Level

    2. Linkage with Measures (List of Top Ten)

    3. Types of Measurement Techniques

    4. Types of Methods to Isolate the Effects of Programs

    5. Investment Perception

V. ROI

    1. Percentage of Programs Evaluated at This Level

    2. ROI Summary for Each Study

3. Methods of Converting Data to Monetary Values
4. Cost Per Participant
VI. Intangibles
  1. List of Intangibles (Top Ten)
  2. How Intangibles Were Captured

- Develop internal capability to implement the ROI process;
- Utilize Web-based software to reduce time; and
- Streamline the reporting process.

Additional information on these approaches is found in other sources (Phillips & Burkett, 2000).

Fear and Misconceptions

Education and training departments often do not pursue ROI because of fear of failure or fear of the unknown. A concern may exist about the consequence of a negative ROI, and staff members may feel threatened. The ROI process also stirs up the traditional fear of change. This fear is often based on unrealistic assumptions and a lack of knowledge of the process and is so strong that it becomes a realistic barrier to many ROI implementations.

The false assumptions about the process will keep training and education staff members from attempting ROI. Following are typical faulty assumptions:

- *Managers do not want to see the results of education and training expressed in monetary values.* In many cases, managers *do* want to see the results of education and training expressed in monetary terms; but for years, they were told it could not be done. As mentioned earlier, there is a greater awareness now among executives that education and training can be measured like other business practices. This awareness is increasing interest and requests for these measures.

- *If the CEO does not ask for the ROI, he or she is not expecting it.* As CEOs become more aware of the process to calculate the ROI in training, they want to begin seeing results immediately. The ROI process is not a quick fix and takes time to learn and fully integrate into a training organization. With this in mind, many organizations are developing ROI impact studies long before senior management asks for them.

- *"As the manager of education and training, I have a professional, competent staff; therefore, I do not have to justify the effectiveness of our programs."* This may be true for some organizations—at least at present. But with the ongoing changes in the business community, it is becoming less and less common to see any function not required to show its bottom-line impact. When budget allocations take place, the functions with a "place at the table" are usually the ones that prove their contribution.

- *The training and development process is a complex, but necessary, activity; consequently, it should not be subjected to an accountability process.* The training and development process is complex and, like other complex processes, can be quite costly to the organization. With this in mind, many organizations are holding the training and education function to the same standard of accountability as other processes.

These false assumptions and others must be addressed and analyzed so they do not impede the progress of ROI implementation (Phillips & Pulliam, 1999).

CASE EXAMPLES AND PRACTICE

It is extremely important for the ROI process to be utilized in organizations with a history of actual application. The ROI process described is rich in tradition, with application in a variety of settings with over one hundred published case studies. In addition, thousands of case studies will soon be deposited in a website/database for future use as a research and application tool. However, it is more important to obtain success with the ROI process within the organization and to document the results as impact studies. Consequently, the training and education staff is encouraged to develop their own impact studies and compare with others. Impact studies within the organization provide the most convincing data to senior management teams that the training and education function is adding significant value and that the six types of data reported form the basis for actions for improvement. Case studies also provide information needed to improve processes in the different areas of the training function, as part of the continuous improvement process.

CONCLUSION

ROI calculations are being developed by hundreds of organizations to meet the demands of influential stakeholders. The result is a process that shows the value-added contribution of education and training in a format desired by many senior administrators and executives. However, this chapter demonstrates that the ROI process represents a significant and challenging dilemma for most organizations. While there are many drivers for the tremendous interest in, and need for, the ROI process, some question its appropriateness, accuracy, and necessity. To counter this perception, the process must be based on a sound framework, using a process model that provides step-by-step procedures and credible methodologies. Through careful planning, methodical procedures, and logical and practical analysis, ROI calculations can be developed reliably and accurately for any type of education and training program.

References

AQPC. (2000). *The corporate university: Measuring the impact of learning.* Houston, TX: American Quality and Productivity Center.

Broad, M.L. (Ed.). (1997). *In action: Transferring learning to the workplace.* Alexandria, VA: ASTD.

Corporate training: Does it pay off? (1995). *William and Mary Business Review.* Supplement.

Geber, B. (1994, February). A clean break for education at IBM. *Training,* 33–36.

Industry Report 1999. (1999, October). *Training, 34*(10), 33–75.

Kaplan, R.S., & Norton, D.P. (1996). *Balanced scorecard.* Boston: Harvard Business School Press.

Kimmerling, G. (1993, September). Gathering best practices. *Training & Development, 47*(3), 28–36.

Kirkpatrick, D.L. (1975). Techniques for evaluating training programs. In D.L. Kirkpatrick (Ed.), *Evaluating training programs* (1–17). Alexandria, VA: ASTD.

Phillips, J.J. (Ed.). (1994). *In action: Measuring return on investment* (Vol. 1). Alexandria, VA: ASTD.

Phillips, J.J. (1996a, March). Was it the training? *Training & Development, 50*(3), 28–32.

Phillips, J.J. (1996b, April). How much is the training worth? *Training & Development, 50*(4), 20–24.

Phillips, J.J. (1997a). *Return on investment in training and performance improvement programs.* Houston, TX: Gulf.

Phillips, J.J. (Ed.). (1997b). *In action: Measuring return on investment* (Vol. 2). Alexandria, VA: ASTD.

Phillips, J.J. (Ed.). (1998). *In action: Implementing evaluation systems and processes.* Alexandria, VA. ASTD.

Phillips, J.J. (2000). *The consultant's scorecard.* New York: McGraw-Hill.

Phillips, J.J., & Phillips, P.P. (2000). *In action: Measuring return on investment* (Vol. 3). Alexandria, VA: ASTD.

Phillips, J.J., & Pulliam, P.P. (1999, May/June). Dispelling the ROI myths. *Corporate University Review,* 32–36.

Phillips, P.P., & Burkett, H. (2000). *ROI on a shoestring,* ASTD InfoLine Series. Alexandria, VA: ASTD.

Sibbet, D. (1997). 75 years of management ideas and practice, 1922–1997. *Harvard Business Review.* Supplement.

Recommended Reading

Fisher, S.G., & Ruffino, B.S. (1996). *Establishing the value of training.* Amherst, MA: HRD Press.

Kirkpatrick, D.L. (1998). *Evaluating training programs* (2nd ed.). San Francisco: Berrett-Koehler.

Parry, S.B. (1997). *Evaluating the impact of training.* Alexandria, VA: ASTD.

Phillips, J.J. (1996). *Accountability in human resource management.* Houston, TX: Gulf.

Phillips, J.J. (1997). *Handbook of training and evaluation and measurement methods* (3rd ed.). Houston, TX: Gulf.

Phillips, J.J. (Ed.). (1999). InfoLine Series on Evaluation. Alexandria, VA: ASTD.

    Volume 1—Level 1 Evaluation: Reaction and Planned Action (Issue #9813)

    Volume 2—Level 2 Evaluation: Learning (Issue #9814)

    Volume 3—Level 3 Evaluation: Application (Issue #9815)

    Volume 4—Level 4 Evaluation: Business Results (Issue #9816)

    Volume 5—Level 5 Evaluation: ROI (Issue #9805)

Phillips, J.J., Phillips, P.P., & Zuniga, L. (2000). Evaluating the effectiveness and the return on investment of e-learning. In *What works online: 2000,* Alexandria, VA: ASTD.

Phillips, J.J., Stone, R.D., & Phillips, P.P. (2000). *The human resources scorecard.* Houston, TX: Gulf.

About the Authors

A world-renowned expert on measurement and evaluation, **Dr. Jack J. Phillips** *provides consulting services for Fortune 500 companies and workshops for major conference providers. He is the author or editor of more than thirty books—ten about measurement and evaluation—and more than one hundred articles. His expertise in measurement and evaluation is based on extensive research and more than twenty-seven years of corporate experience. In 1992, Phillips founded Performance Resources Organization (PRO), an international consulting firm providing comprehensive assessment, measurement, and evaluation services. In 1999, PRO was acquired by the FranklinCovey Company and is now known as The Jack Phillips Center for Research. He may be reached at roiresearch@mind spring.com.*

Patricia Pulliam Phillips is chairman and CEO of The Chelsea Group, a research and publishing company focused on accountability issues in training, HR, and performance improvement. She has an M.A. in public and private management from Birmingham-Southern College. She is certified in ROI evaluation, serves as co-author on the subject in several publications, and contributed to Evaluating Training Programs, 2nd ed., by Donald L. Kirkpatrick, and HRD Trends Worldwide, by Jack J. Phillips. Phillips is co-author of Measuring Return on Investment in Human Resources: The Process and Case Applications, and ROI on a Shoestring, ASTD InfoLine Series. She may be reached at pattifaye@aol.com.

CHAPTER FOURTEEN

Transfer of Learning to Performance

Mary L. Broad, Ed.D.
Principal Consultant, Performance Excellence

This chapter summarizes evidence of low levels of performance in many organizations, describes factors that affect performance, and presents recent research and best practices that can help ensure transfer of learning to full performance. Next, a suggested process for performance consultants describes how to use transfer concepts in work with internal and external clients, to achieve full return on training investments. This includes identifying performance goals and gaps, involving key stakeholders, and developing collaborative transfer strategies to support full transfer of learning to performance. Finally, a case study at a transportation company illustrates transfer strategies in action.

THE PERFORMANCE GAP

Recent advances in the development and delivery of learning experiences bring us significantly more options and resources to support learning than ever before. Unfortunately, we also have evidence that effective learning often does not result in effective performance. Evaluation of outcomes of many learning and other interventions shows that new knowledge, skills, and behavior may be learned but are seldom fully applied on the job. Some evidence of this lack of full performance:

- In a survey of leading U.S. and European companies, 98 percent of one hundred sixty-six responding companies reported problems (55 percent) or serious problems (43 percent) in gaining more productivity and higher performance from their work force (Figure 14.1; Csoka, 1994).

- Noted performance consulting experts warn, "Typically, less than 30 percent of what people learn is ever actually used on the job" (Robinson & Robinson, 1998, p. 5).

- When organizations try to increase their capabilities in "soft" areas (for example, ability to move faster in the marketplace), "Most surveys show that efforts to implement these soft organizational capabilities have a 75 percent failure rate" (Ulrich, 1997, p. 10).

Today, learning professionals must demonstrate direct and measurable support in achieving full performance by

- Collaborating with managers and other organizational stakeholders to specify performance goals;

- Developing effective instruction—and other interventions—to help workers reach those goals; and

- Gaining stakeholder agreement to use transfer strategies to support full application of learning to work performance.

FACTORS AFFECTING PERFORMANCE

Why is it so difficult to obtain high levels of performance in today's organizations? The answer: There are complex factors, beyond the learning intervention itself, that combine to encourage or discourage effective performance. Table 14.1 presents a model of these organizational factors at the performer level.

All of these factors should be present in the organizational system to ensure effective workforce performance. As these experts say, "If you pit a good performer against a bad system, the system will win almost every time" (Rummler & Brache, 1995, p. 13, 64).

To help improve performance, training professionals should partner with key stakeholders in the organization—executives, managers, human resource professionals, and employees at all levels—to help them recognize these factors (or their absence) in work settings. Then, stakeholders have a basis on which to analyze, develop, and ensure effective performance.

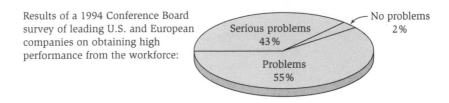

Results of a 1994 Conference Board survey of leading U.S. and European companies on obtaining high performance from the workforce:

Serious problems
43%

No problems
2%

Problems
55%

Figure 14.1. Problems Reported in Obtaining High Workforce Performance

L. Csoka, *Closing the Human Performance Gap.* Research Report No. 1065-94-RR. New York: Conference Board, 1994.

RESEARCH AND BEST PRACTICES IN TRANSFER OF LEARNING

We now have impressive research and best practices on achieving transfer of learning into performance. Many training professionals have successfully partnered with stakeholders to promote the value of strategies that support transfer. Important findings are reported below. (For more research, see Baldwin & Ford, 1988; Broad, 1997a, b; Broad, in press; Broad & Newstrom, 1992.) Guidelines for supporting transfer can be applied in any organizational setting.

Research, Best Practices, and Guidelines

Table 14.2 presents a summary of selected research and best practice highlights in several important areas.

We can derive important transfer guidelines from the work of Rummler and Brache and of other researchers (Baldwin & Magjuka, 1991; Brinkerhoff & Montesino, 1995; Feldstein & Boothman, 1997; Newstrom, 1986; Seitz, 1997). These guidelines follow:

- Experienced trainers estimate very low levels of transfer for typical, unsupported training activities. (Managers almost invariably say that actual transfer levels are even lower than these estimates by trainers.)

- Primary stakeholders in transfer are managers (at various levels), trainers (including performance consultants and other learning specialists), and learners (performers). Stakeholders may also include internal/external customers, suppliers, unions, co-workers, and others.

- Typical barriers to transfer occur in many organizations. (Common barriers are listed in Table 14.2, Newstrom, 1986.)

- Managers are most powerful in supporting transfer. They should
  - Communicate directly with learners before and after the learning

activity to emphasize the learning's need and importance to the organization, and their expectations for performance;

- Demonstrate their personal involvement before, during, and after the learning activity;

- Consider making the learning mandatory for specific learners;

- Consider having learners (and their sponsoring organizations) apply for training by describing transfer support to be provided by the organization, before, during, and after the learning experience;

- Provide learners the opportunity to explore content before the learning activity;

- Make learners accountable for applying the new knowledge and skills to their jobs;

- Provide learners with any equipment and other resources that are necessary for applying new knowledge and skills; and

- Ensure sufficient practice opportunities immediately following the learning activity.

Table 14.1. Factors Affecting Performance

Factors Related to Work Environment and Training

Clear performance specifications (expected outputs, standards)

Necessary support (resources, priorities, responsibility, authority, time)

Clear consequences (reinforcement, incentives, rewards)

Prompt feedback (how well performance matches expectations)

Individual capability (physical, mental, emotional capacity, experience)

Necessary skills and knowledge (training, learning to perform)

Adapted from Rummler & Brache, *Improving Performance.* San Francisco: Jossey-Bass, 1995.

TRANSFER STRATEGIES

How can we apply transfer research and best practices to improve performance? The following procedure shows how performance consultants can work with clients to incorporate these ideas into the organization's practice and culture.

Step 1. Enhance and maintain knowledge and skills as a performance consultant:

Table 14.2. Research on Transfer

Researcher	Research Focus	Conclusions	Reference
Newstrom	Perceptions of HRD professionals	*Estimates of Typical Levels of Transfer* Immediately following training: 41 percent Six months after training: 24 percent One year after training: 15 percent *Stakeholders:* Managers (most powerful, least active on transfer), trainers, learners *Barriers:* Lack of reinforcement on the job Impediments in the work environment Nonsupportive organizational climate Learners: new skills are impractical Learners: discomfort with change Separation from instructional source Poor instructional design, delivery Negative peer pressure	"Leveraging Management Development through the Management of Transfer." *Journal of Management Development*, 1986, 33–44.
Baldwin & Magjuka	Signals from managers to learners on transfer importance	*Management Signals of Transfer Importance:* Learners are accountable for using skills. Learning programs are mandatory. Managers give prior information on learning's need, importance. Managers' presence demonstrates involvement, investment of own time and effort.	With Broad: *Transfer of Training: Action-Packed Strategies to Ensure High Payoff from Training Investments,*1992. Reading, MA: Addison-Wesley. Organizational Training and Signals of Importance: Linking Pre-Training Perceptions to Intentions to Transfer. *HRD Quarterly,* Spring 1991, 25–36.

Source	Focus	Findings	Reference
Brinkerhoff & Montesino	Pre/post discussions with boss	Learners who had pre/post-course discussions with boss (on new skills, applications, etc.) reported significantly higher skill levels, support.	Partnerships for Training Transfer. *HRD Quarterly*, Fall 1995, 263–274.
Feldstein & Boothman	Differences between learners who rated selves as high or low performers after training	*High performance learners had* Explored content (software) before training Pre/post discussions with boss Clear idea on how to apply new skills Frequent practice after training *Their managers/supervisors had* Reasonable expectations for behavioral change Commented on behavior changes *Low performance learners and their supervisors* Had none of the above factors supporting use of new skills	Success Factors in Technology Training. Ch. 2 in Broad (Ed.), *In Action: Transferring Learning to the Workplace*, 1997, ASTD.
Seitz	Learners bid for training based on strong transfer support from their organizations	*Learner's Situation Analysis:* Application for training requires potential learners, and their sponsoring organizations, to identify: Potential impact on improved organizational results due to new skills Planned transfer strategies to support successful application of skills by learner Success measures (Level 3, 4) by which behavior and results will be measured	Transfer Strategies for Communities: Substance Abuse Prevention. Ch. 9 in Broad (Ed.), *In Action: Transferring Learning to the Workplace*, 1997, ASTD.

- View organizations as complex systems (Senge, 1990; Wheatley & Kellner-Rogers, 1996);

- Develop knowledge of the organization and industry;

- Become adept at performance analysis and performance improvement; and

- Enhance partnering and consulting skills (Block, 1999).

Step 2. Identify projects, clients, and stakeholders:

- Seek situations and clients with needs for improved performance; and

- Identify stakeholders (employees, co-workers, internal/external customers, and suppliers).

Step 3. Meet with clients and stakeholders to discuss performance requirements:

- Agree on need and priority for performance improvement;

- Identify gaps between desired and actual performance;

- Determine which performance factors (Table 14.1) are present or missing;

- Identify learning requirements and other performance interventions;

- Identify workplace barriers to performance (Table 14.2) and plan to remove or reduce them; and

- Identify measures of success (learner reaction, learning, performance, results) and develop baseline data.

Step 4. Plan transfer strategies with stakeholders:

- Develop transfer support strategies by all stakeholders before, during, and after learning activities and other interventions; and

- Integrate strategies among all stakeholders and form into a transfer strategies matrix (see ACBL matrix, Table 14.3).

Step 5. Implement transfer strategies together with project implementation:

- Coordinate and track implementation of transfer strategies among all stakeholders; and

- Observe and measure impact of strategies.

Step 6. Report to stakeholders on transfer strategies and outcomes:

- Document effective strategies for repeated use;

- Measure project outcomes (reaction, learning, performance, results); and

- Calculate return on investment (ROI) for entire project (Phillips, 1996).

Step 7. Market transfer support to other potential clients:

- Seek other organizations and clients with needs for performance improvement;

- Emphasize return on investment (ROI) from earlier projects;

- Describe transfer strategies and present transfer matrix examples; and

- Publicize endorsements and illustrative anecdotes from satisfied clients.

TRANSFER AT ACBL

American Commercial Barge Lines (ACBL) is one of the largest inland barge and towing companies in the world. Headquartered in Jeffersonville, Indiana, ACBL employs 3,200 people throughout the United States and South America. Cargoes include steel, grains, coal, and chemicals. Operating conditions include every kind of weather, day and night, seven days a week on the inland river system from the Mississippi River to the Atlantic coast and from the equator to the Canadian border. In an industry in which injury and loss of life have long been considered "a cost of doing business," ACBL since 1994 has created a powerful participative safety culture with transfer of learning at its core. For this organization, the ability to effect changes in employee attitude and behavior through effective transfer strategies is literally a question of life and death.

ACBL's safety successes over this six-year period include

- A 43 percent decrease in personal injuries—with a 67 percent increase in employee hours due to rapid growth and new markets;

- A 45 percent decrease in cost of claims related to personal injuries;

- An average annual deck crew turnover rate that has stabilized at 50 percent of the industry average; and

- New hires (most vulnerable) at 50 percent of deck work force but only 10 percent of total injuries.

Key Stakeholders in Building a Participative Safety Culture

Important stakeholders in this dramatic change process include

- Glenn Hotz, ACBL's assistant vice president of corporate safety;
- Andy Cannava, marine superintendent, safety;
- Julie Hile, principal of the Hile Group, performance consultants with eleven years of transportation industry experience focusing on safety and transfer (Julie had partnered with Glenn in previous projects.);
- Associates across ACBL at all levels who contributed to:
  - An early precedent-setting meeting of vessel safety representatives;
  - Collaborative projects building on that meeting's outcomes; and
  - An innovative course, "Five Minutes or Five Days," which used transfer strategies to spread participative approaches throughout ACBL.

Interventions

From 1994 to 1996, Glenn and Andy collaborated with colleagues from other departments on projects to lay the groundwork for a shift from standard hierarchical leadership to a participative model. For example, ACBL's Safety and Fleet Operations functions became full partners in promoting this culture shift.

In 1994, Glenn and Andy organized a landmark safety representatives meeting to jump-start the shift. Julie facilitated this meeting that—for the first time—encouraged vessel crew members to voice their concerns and insights about fleet operations directly to top managers.

Based on the meeting's outcomes, functional managers and crew members—supported by Julie and her partners—worked together on important changes:

- Vessel safety standards raised to world class;
- Shared vision and goal setting across ACBL and on individual vessels;
- Collaborative revision of the fleet's safety rule book with supporting facilitation guides for safety reps; and
- Decentralization of responsibility for the safety function out to involve every employee, to make safety "everybody's business."

By 1996, Glenn believed the time was right for development of a strategic network of ACBL associates, many involved in earlier projects, who would energize and spread the participative ACBL culture as facilitators, learners, and collaborators. Glenn requested Julie's "Five Minutes or Five Days: Strategies for

Leading, Learning, and Collaboration," a three-day course that prepares participants for effective leadership roles at all levels across the organization.

"Five Minutes or Five Days" taught the benefits of participative leadership with concrete actions for each participant to adopt, practice, and establish in the workplace. Concepts of transfer of learning supported the shift in behavior at the work site:

- Identifying *stakeholders* in any desired behavioral change: employee learners, their managers, co-workers, trainers, internal/external suppliers and customers, and others;
- Working with stakeholders to determine *strategies by all*—before, during, and after learning activities—to eliminate barriers and support effective performance changes back on the job;
- Monitoring and encouraging all stakeholders to maintain *support* for transfer; and
- Evaluating and reporting *outcomes* to show performance changes and bottom-line results.

The course also showed managers, staff associates, and crew members dramatically trying out new leadership strategies together and reconfigured corporate's role so top stakeholders joined the session to meet participants' needs. Finally, it explicitly taught transfer of learning and helped participants apply transfer strategies to their own initiatives. As an example, they developed a transfer matrix (called a "scaffold" in their construction lingo) to make the most of frequent, unplanned five-minute hallway conversations, with transfer strategies before, during, and after such a meeting.

Before the course, Glenn and Andy invited "key" stakeholders to identify the best participants from their functions. Criteria for selection included

- High leadership potential and credibility among ACBL colleagues;
- Willingness to think "outside the box";
- Inclination toward continuous learning; and
- Representation of a work group/function that could influence safe work practices.

The short list of invitees also included "crackerjack" ACBL personalities who had not yet shifted toward participative practices.

Glenn, Andy, and Julie listed transfer strategies by stakeholders—before, during, and after the course (Table 14.3)—and leveraged long-standing stakeholder

Table 14.3. Transfer Strategies Matrix for ACBL

	Before	During	After
Corporate and Fleet Safety (CFS) Glenn Hotz and Andy Cannava	Meet with facilitator to set course goals Collaborate with leaders of other departments in selecting participants Meet with facilitator and select participants to agree on course goals, agenda, design Review with facilitator other project work by participants Champion course with executive leaders to ensure their participation as requested Ensure ACBL vice president-operations knowledge of and visit to meeting Distribute and collect completed pre-work questionnaires, forward to facilitator	Attend course Listen actively to participant concerns and insights Demonstrate own learning in course Seek participant contact and relationship building opportunities Call on corporate system "owners" to join course to respond to participant questions Take notes Acknowledge individual participant contributions and questions in side conversations	Act as agreed on issues raised during course Match participant insights and key skills with assignment to career-building project teams Interface with facilitator and leaders of other departments on plans for transfer support Act on notes taken Review facilitator letters to participants Write follow-up cover letter for facilitator's individual letters
Facilitator Julie Hile	Meet with CFS and select participants to agree on course goals, agenda, design Design interactive/dialogic course Design course pre-work questionnaire Review completed pre-work questionnaires	Facilitate interactively Ensure multi-sensory learning strategies Draw on learners' experiences and stories Listen through Embed research and expertise into learners' perspectives and contributions Integrate learnings from pre-work questionnaires into meeting Capture participant ideas, concerns, and questions on flip charts	Transcribe meeting flip charts and distribute to all participants Write individualized letters of acknowledgement to participants (copies to CFS and leaders of other departments) Consult with CFS and leaders of other departments on follow-up actions and agreed-on deliverables

Participants	Complete and return pre-work questionnaire to CFS Advise facilitator and CFS on course goals, agenda, design	Attend course Link ideas from pre-work to course activities Test new leadership skills against personal experience Speak up: Ask questions, offer suggestions, raise concerns Network with CFS, other participants, facilitator, and SMEs Set goals for applications after course Communicate interest in special projects to CFS, leader of department, other participants, and facilitator	Review facilitator flip chart/letter packets Review insights and new skills with leader or manager of department Begin special projects as assigned and appropriate Continue networking with CFS, leader or manager of department, other participants, and SMEs Model changed behaviors on the job
Leaders of Other Departments	Collaborate with CFS in selecting participants Meet with participant direct reports to discuss course relevance to their work Review other project work done by participants with facilitator	Support participants' work coverage during course Visit course, as invited Note other participants with whom direct report is networking Continue shaping follow-on opportunities	Review insights and new skills with participant direct reports Act as agreed on plans, opportunities, and support raised in pre-course meeting Interface with CFS on recommendations for transfer support Review facilitator letters to participants and flip chart packet
Other Corporate SMEs	Network with CFS on course format Prepare for on-the-spot response to participants' questions/concerns	Attend course as invited Listen through participant questions and concerns Respond candidly and as fully as possible to questions and concerns	Act as agreed on issues raised during visit to course Review participant insights with CSF and leaders of departments and consider special projects within own area of influence Interface with CFS on transfer support Act on notes taken Review course flip charts

relationships to urge active performance of transfer tasks. Each item in the matrix is a carefully engineered transfer strategy that reflects application of transfer research and best practices in the ACBL setting. (This can be a model for a similar transfer strategies matrix in another organizational setting.)

Following the course, participants—supported by Glenn and Andy—generated high-potential interventions, with their constituents and with major stakeholder support, to address improvement opportunities. Participants stayed in touch, compared notes, and coached one another through rocky spots. Spinoff interventions included

- A new mates' and captains' training curriculum (how to treat and teach people);
- Deep redesign of recruiting and new-hire orientation, including participative approaches and improved communications with prospective associates' families;
- New steersman and tankerman development processes;
- Revision of the fleet's boat operations manual;
- New yawl training;
- More associate-generated content in ACBL's safety newsletter; and
- ACBL mate participation in industry-wide work with professional associations.

Of the spinoffs, Andy observes, "Once people saw our enthusiasm, the possibility of sharing the vision increased many fold. Our main work on the process was to get more and more people involved." Glenn, Andy, and other stakeholders coached project teams toward shared vision and involvement of stakeholders and learners.

Long-Range Impacts of Transfer at ACBL

Due to three ACBL sessions of "Five Minutes or Five Days" over time, transfer principles have become a widespread way of doing business. For any change process, those involved routinely identify stakeholders and develop a transfer strategy matrix. Stakeholders at all levels have new involvement and responsibilities in designing, planning, and implementing programs, so those who know the work best contribute ideas, participate, and gain full satisfaction at achieving goals.

Qualitative examples of this impact from course participation follow:

- Senior managers no longer accept decisions from direct reports without input from employees at all levels;

- ACBL captains who came through "Five Minutes or Five Days" have been promoted to new levels of responsibility;
- ACBL associates now use transfer concepts: "Wait a minute. We are in the 'before' phase here . . ."
- Mates work closely with vendors to design simulator training, in a complete break with past practices of isolated vendor design; and
- Transfer strategies are routinely used by associates in various functions, such as mate/facilitators Rick Embry and Mike Nadicksbernd (designing performance processes), mate Ron Matne (recruiting low-turnover new hires), and mate Rick Smith (writing policy for ACBL's liquid division).

Quantitative measures resulting from training and other interventions include

- Yawl incidents reduced from one per twenty boats annually to zero incidents in the last year;
- Automobile incidents to and from boats were one per twenty boats; now reduced by 84 percent; vessel incidents (collisions, groundings) reduced by 38 percent;
- Overall 70 percent reduction in personal injuries over seven quarters in two of ACBL's newest subsidiaries; and
- A 50 percent reduction in injuries and a complete turnaround in one ACBL associate company's operating performance in one year.

ACBL now mobilizes people in performance goal-setting and transfer strategies system-wide. Glenn observes, "This work is change process in action. It has less to do with specific content being conveyed in particular ways and more to do with management's commitment to results."

Julie adds, "The core purpose of ACBL's use of transfer concepts is clarification for *all* associates of how to catalyze desired performance at all levels."

References

Baldwin, T.T., & Ford, J.K. (1988). Transfer of training: A review and directions for future research. *Personnel Psychology, 41,* 63–105.

Baldwin, T.T., & Magjuka, R. (1991, Spring). Organizational training and signals of importance: Linking pre-training perceptions to intentions to transfer. *Human Resource Development Quarterly,* 25–36.

Block, P. (1999). *Flawless consulting: A guide to getting your expertise used* (2nd ed.). San Francisco: Jossey-Bass/Pfeiffer.

Brinkerhoff, R.O., & Montesino, M.U. (1995, Fall). Partnerships for training transfer. *Human Resource Development Quarterly,* 263–274.

Broad, M.L. (1997a). Overview of transfer of training: From learning to performance. *Performance Improvement Quarterly, 10*(2), 7–21.

Broad, M.L. (Ed.). (1997b). *In action: Transferring learning to the workplace.* Alexandria, VA: ASTD.

Broad, M.L. (In press). Managing the organizational learning transfer system: A model and case study. In E.F. Holton & T.T. Baldwin (Eds.), *Managing and changing learning transfer systems in organizations.* Baton Rouge, LA: Academy of Human Resource Development, and San Francisco: Berrett-Koehler.

Broad, M.L., & Newstrom, J.W. (1992). *Transfer of training: Action-packed strategies to ensure high payoff from training investments.* Reading, MA: Addison-Wesley.

Csoka, L. (1994). *Closing the human performance gap.* New York: The Conference Board.

Feldstein, H.D., & Boothman, T. (1997). Success factors in technology training. In M.L. Broad (Ed.), *In action: Transferring learning to the workplace* (pp. 19–33). Alexandria, VA: ASTD.

Newstrom, J.W. (1986). Leveraging management development through the management of transfer. *Journal of Management Development,* (5), 33–45.

Phillips, J.L. (1996). ROI: The search for best practices (February, 42–47); Was it the training? (March, 28–32); How much is the training worth? (April, 20–24). *Training & Development, 50.*

Robinson, D.G., & Robinson, J.C. (1998). *Moving from training to performance: A practical guidebook.* San Francisco: Berrett-Koehler, and Alexandria, VA: ASTD.

Rummler, G.A., & Brache, A.P. (1995). *Improving performance: How to manage the white space on the organization chart* (2nd ed.). San Francisco: Jossey-Bass.

Seitz, S. (1997). Transfer strategies for communities: Substance abuse prevention. In M.L. Broad (Ed.), *In action: Transferring learning to the workplace* (pp. 145–164). Alexandria, VA: ASTD.

Senge, P.M. (1990). *The fifth discipline: The art & practice of the learning organization.* New York: Currency-Doubleday.

Ulrich, D. (1997). *Human resource champions: The new agenda for adding value and delivering results.* Boston: Harvard Business School Press.

Wheatley, M.J., & Kellner-Rogers, M. (1996). *A simpler way.* San Francisco: Berrett-Koehler.

Recommended Reading

Holton, E.F., & Baldwin, T.T. (Eds.). (In press). *Managing and changing learning transfer systems in organizations.* Baton Rouge, LA: Academy of Human Resource Development, and San Francisco: Berrett-Koehler.

Stolovitch, H.D. (Ed.). (1997). Special issue on transfer of training—transfer of learning. *Performance Improvement Quarterly, 10* (2).

About the Author

Dr. Mary L. Broad, *with Performance Excellence, helps organizations improve human performance systems through strategic planning, performance technology, and transfer of learning. Recent clients include L.G. Electronics (South Korea), U.S. Department of Defense (Office of Family Policy), U.S. Marshals Service, National Academy of Public Administration, Food and Drug Administration, Georgia State Department of Human Resources, Groupe INSEP (France), Lexis-Nexis, Vitro Comercial (Mexico), and National Safety Council. She is co-author of* Transfer of Training: Action-Packed Strategies to Ensure High Payoff from Training Investments *(Addison-Wesley, 1992) and editor of the casebook* In Action: Transferring Learning to the Workplace *(ASTD, 1997).*

She has presented internationally for professional groups in the United States and in El Salvador, Indonesia, Ireland, Kuwait, Mexico, Panama, South Korea, and Singapore. Dr. Broad served on ASTD's board of directors for 1993–95, is a Future Search facilitator, and is an instructor for Information Mapping, Inc. She is on the adjunct faculty for the Human Resource Development graduate program at George Washington University. (She can be contacted at 301.657.8638; marybroad@earthlink.net.)

CHAPTER FIFTEEN

Developing and Conducting a Legally Defensible Performance Appraisal

Gary P. Latham, Ph.D.
Secretary of State Professor of Organizational Behavior,
Joseph L. Rotman School of Management, University of Toronto

Deborah L. MacKenzie
Ph.D. Candidate, Joseph L. Rotman School of Management,
University of Toronto

A performance management system is critical to an employee's effectiveness. When implemented properly, it ensures high employee productivity. This chapter explains how to establish a legally defensible performance management system. Specifically, ways to conduct a job analysis, develop a behavioral-based appraisal instrument, select appraisers, and set goals with and provide feedback to employees are described. The chapter concludes with a discussion of the role of a coach in gaining an employee's commitment to goals.

WHAT IS A PERFORMANCE APPRAISAL?

For most people, a performance appraisal is a one-on-one interaction with an employer. Typically, a manager sits down with the employee one to four times a year to provide feedback regarding the employee's performance. Most people dread these appraisals because they often lead to conflict and defensiveness by both parties. Employees often attack the appraisal instrument ("You evaluated me on the wrong things.") as well as the appraiser ("Why did you wait until now to give me this information? You are not even qualified to evaluate me."). The result is a decrease, rather than an increase in the employee's performance. What are the solutions?

Conduct a Job Analysis

To ensure that employees perceive that they are evaluated on the right things, conduct a job analysis to identify the behaviors necessary to achieve optimal performance. To ensure that the person who is conducting the appraisal, as well as the employee who is receiving it, views the instrument as assessing the "right" things, the job analysis should identify behaviors that enable the implementation of the organization's strategy or business plan with excellence. Two components of a legally defensible job analysis are (1) that it be in writing, and (2) that the information is collected from subject-matter experts (SMEs) (Thompson & Thompson, 1982). Subject-matter experts are people who have the opportunity to observe the activities of the person in question frequently, are aware of the objectives of the job, and can discern effective from ineffective performance. They usually include supervisors, employees, subordinates, customers, as well as the employee him- or herself.

Flanagan's (1954) critical incident technique (CIT) is the most widely used method to conduct a job analysis for performance appraisal purposes. The objective of the CIT is to identify the critical behaviors necessary to perform the job effectively.

Typically, SMEs are asked by a trained interviewer to recall five effective and ineffective incidents that they have observed on the job in the last six to twelve months. For example, "Please think of five behaviors an effective . . . [e.g., electrician] does on the job that an ineffective . . . [e.g., electrician] fails to do." Following recall of each incident, SMEs are asked three questions: (1) What were the circumstances surrounding the incident? (2) What did the individual do that that was effective/ineffective? and (3) In what way is this an example of effective/ineffective performance? The most important criteria to remember when conducting the CIT is to prompt, not lead, the SME's responses and to use a friendly, neutral tone throughout the interview.

The information collected in the job analysis interviews is used to construct the appraisal instrument.

Develop the Appraisal Instrument

One method of measuring an individual's performance is to assess outcome measures, such as profits, costs, or turnover. The problem with using outcome measures is that they are often affected by factors beyond the person's control. Consequently, the employee can be rewarded or punished undeservedly. Moreover, outcome measures in themselves do not indicate what the person needs to start doing, stop doing, or consider doing differently. Hence, behaviorally based measures of job performance, such as "behavioral observation scales"

(BOS), are used to make explicit for the appraiser and the employee what the person must do to achieve an outcome or outcomes. (See Exhibit 15.1.)

The advantage of using a BOS is that it facilitates explicit performance feedback by identifying strengths as well as areas in which employees can increase their contribution to the organization. Latham and colleagues (Wiersma & Latham, 1986; Wiersma, van den Berg, & Latham, 1992) found that the BOS was preferred over appraisal instruments because it was perceived as practical by supervisors who used it, as well as lawyers who had to defend it. In addition, the use of BOS is consistent with employment legislation (Feild & Holley, 1982).

Know the Law

North American organizations must be able to provide legally defensible reasons for promotions, demotions, transfers, layoffs, and terminations (Martin, Bartol, & Levine, 1986). Decisions based on a person's age, race, gender, color, religion, marital status, national origin, or physical disability are prohibited.

To minimize legal challenges, organizations should: (1) Conduct a job analysis to identify the critical behaviors of the job in question; (2) Incorporate the

Exhibit 15.1. Sample BOS

Time Management

1. Arrives fifteen minutes prior to starting time
   Almost Never   0   1   2   3   4   Almost Always
2. Plans schedule a week in advance (e.g., call customers to set up meetings)
   Almost Never   0   1   2   3   4   Almost Always

Training and Development

3. Takes additional courses to improve skills
   Almost Never   0   1   2   3   4   Almost Always
4. Seeks help on tasks that are difficult
   Almost Never   0   1   2   3   4   Almost Always

Teamwork

5. Helps train new employee
   Almost Never   0   1   2   3   4   Almost Always
6. Talks positively about other co-workers
   Almost Never   0   1   2   3   4   Almost Always

Total Score = _____

critical behaviors into the appraisal instrument; (3) Train appraisers how to use the appraisal instrument; (4) Document the appraisals; and (5) Give employees the opportunity to appeal those appraisals that they perceive as not fair (Latham & Wexley, 1994).

WHO SHOULD BE THE APPRAISER?

It will not come as a surprise to most readers that how a child behaves with parents is not necessarily the way the child behaves with grandparents or friends in the schoolyard. Similarly, how a person behaves with one's boss is not necessarily the way that the person behaves with peers, subordinates, or customers. So, who should be the appraiser?

Supervisor Appraisals. The manager is in a position of authority to make administrative decisions regarding wage increases, promotion, demotion, and so forth. Unfortunately, supervisor appraisals are often biased and, therefore, lack validity and reliability. This is largely attributed to two factors: (1) The supervisors themselves are often too emotionally involved in the decision (Longnecker, Sims, & Gioia, 1987), and (2) Supervisors often lack the opportunity to observe their subordinates' performance (Komaki, 1986, 1998). Thus, supervisor appraisals should be conducted in conjunction with other sources of appraisal.

Self-Appraisals. Self-appraisals facilitate employee development and growth by enhancing self-regulation to set goals and to monitor progress toward them. Moreover, self-appraisals increase the employee's "voice" in the appraisal process, and hence, enhance perceptions of fairness.

To make self-appraisals effective: (1) Base the appraisal instrument on the job analysis (Campbell & Lee, 1988); (2) Inform employees that the self-appraisal will be verified against other measures (Lane & Herriot, 1990); and (3) Provide the employee with comparative information (Farh & Dobbins, 1989). Self-appraisals improve in accuracy with experience (Somers & Birnbaum, 1991).

Peer Appraisals. Appraisals by co-workers are highly reliable (Gordon & Medland, 1965) and valid (Korman, 1968) predictors of job performance. The courts appreciate peer appraisals because: (1) Peers are usually in a position to observe the job incumbent frequently, and (2) Using a number of peers increases the number of independent judgments.

For peer appraisals to be effective, the peers must: (1) Be assured anonymity; (2) Have the opportunity to observe the employee performing the job frequently; (3) Be aware of the person's work objectives; and (4) Be capable of distinguishing competent from incompetent performance.

Subordinate Appraisals. The benefit of using subordinate appraisals is that they provide valuable feedback on the extent to which a manager is perceived as supportive of people. It pinpoints areas where team building is needed. It encourages reciprocity in that, when subordinates see a manager making changes based on their feedback, they too are likely to make changes based on feedback from the manager. Bernardin and Beatty (1987) found that subordinate appraisals are especially useful when the items to be rated are behaviorally specific. In addition, it was found that subordinate appraisals must be anonymous and that managers should be allowed to keep the results of the appraisal confidential for at least three months, to allow them to correct the situation before the data are shared with their bosses.

Customer Appraisals. Customer appraisals can provide unique information that is not readily available to one's boss, peers, or subordinates. Although there has been minimal research on this source of appraisal, Schneider and Bowen (1995) have written a book that summarizes ways to obtain maximum value from this informative source. Again, the customer should be assured anonymity in the evaluation, and the evaluation should be based on observable behavior identified through job analysis as necessary for ensuring customer loyalty and satisfaction.

360-Degree Performance Measurement

As already mentioned, multiple appraisers can include one's self, subordinates, peers, and boss, as well as customers. An instrument that incorporates these multiple perspectives of an employee's performance is referred to as a 360-degree performance measure. A person may be seen as a star by one's boss, have strong support from one's subordinates, and yet be disliked intensely by peers. A 360-degree appraisal using BOS makes clear the reasons for these outcomes. For example, a person may have increased profits by 22 percent, defended successfully two subordinates who had grievances filed against them by the union, but refused to cooperate with peers on issues that crossed their respective businesses. So who should be the appraiser? The answer is "all of the above." The 360-degree appraisal makes it difficult for an employee to argue that "the wrong person evaluated me."

The benefit of using a 360-degree instrument is that it provides a complete picture of the employee's strengths and areas for needed improvement. Coaches should use this information to facilitate employee development.

Train Appraisers to Be Objective

Errors in judgment result when an appraiser relies on subjective or intuitive information. These errors include first impressions, "similar to me," stereotyping, halo error, and contrast effects. The most effective training programs are ones that give people a frame of reference for making evaluations (Latham & Wexley, 1994). This is done by allowing them to practice rating hypothetical employees shown on a videotape, providing them feedback on their objectivity, and allowing them to practice, practice, practice to increase their objectivity.

PERFORMANCE MANAGEMENT

A key to effective performance management is for supervisors to stay in the role of a coach. A coach helps people discover what they should start doing, continue doing, or consider doing differently. A coach provides feedback to employees on a continual basis regarding progress toward the attainment of goals.

Give Continual Feedback

The once-a-year formal appraisal generally results in minimal improvements in performance (Nathan, Mohrman, & Milliman, 1991). Hence, a metaphor of performance appraisals is that they are, at best, the frosting on the cake. The cake itself is performance management. This change in wording from performance *appraisal* to performance *management* is more than semantics; it is a shift in thinking and behavior from that of an appraiser to that of a coach. The use of the word coach is borrowed deliberately from sports. If a child's soccer coach waited until the end of the game, or worse, until the end of the season to give the child performance feedback, most parents would insist that the coach be terminated. The job of coach is to let people know on an ongoing basis when they are doing well and to engage them in discussion on when, where, and how they can do better. The job of a coach is to instill in people the desire for continuous improvement. To do this, a coach must give ongoing feedback.

Set Goals

Feedback that doesn't lead to the setting of *specific, measurable, attainable, relevant* goals with a *time frame* (SMART) has little or no effect on subsequent behavior. Goal setting theory (Locke & Latham, 1990) and studies at the Weyerhaeuser company (Latham, Mitchell, & Dossett, 1978) showed that SMART goals result in higher performance than easy goals, or urging people to "do your best." The importance of goal setting to performance management is that SMART goals: (1) focus direction, (2) increase effort, as well as (3) increase persistence. Moreover, the attainment of goals provides people with a sense of accomplishment. To the extent that the goals are SMART, they minimize the probability of conflict or disagreement regarding their attainment between employee and coach.

Two variables that a coach must focus on to ensure employee commitment to the goal are an employee's outcome expectancies and self-efficacy (Bandura,

1997). Employees must see the relationship between what they do and the outcomes that they can expect. For example, a coach must help people see the relationship between how one approaches a peer (for example, with sarcasm) and the subsequent behavior of that peer (for example, lack of cooperation).

Self-efficacy refers to one's conviction or lack thereof that one "can cause, bring about, or make happen." People with low self-efficacy look for legitimate reasons to abandon the goal. That is, they interpret setbacks, obstacles, and resulting poor performance as proof that the goal is not attainable by them. People with high self-efficacy perceive the same events as the challenge, the fun, and the excitement inherent in the pursuit of the goal.

There are at least three ways that a coach can work with employees to increase their self-efficacy. The first is enactive mastery, namely, sequencing the assignment of tasks or projects in such a way that they guarantee success. A series of small wins builds one's confidence.

Second, find a model or models with whom the person identifies—a person who has either mastered the task or is in the process of doing so. Models with whom one identifies provide proof that "if we can, so can you."

Third, identify the person's significant other or a person to whom the employee listens. People tend to behave in accordance with the expectations of those who are significant to them. The significant other can be a powerful confidence booster—or the obverse. If the former, invite the significant other to have an informal conversation with the employee as to why the employee can attain the goal. If the latter, explain to the significant other the ways, often unintentionally, that the person's confidence is being undermined. If it is intentional, counsel the employee on the detrimental effect of having this person as a significant other.

The most powerful significant other on behavior is oneself. Therefore, the coach should listen carefully to the employee's self-talk. If it is positive, comment on it positively. If it is negative, listen to the employee's logic and counter it with evidence regarding the person's ability and successful past accomplishments that indicate that the goal is, with effort and persistence, within the person's reach.

THE FORMAL APPRAISAL

The formal appraisal should contain no "surprises" for the employee. On the basis of ongoing dialogue between the coach and the employee, both parties should all but know what each would say. The purpose of the appraisal is to summarize what has been said in the past and to set new goals. Guidelines for a coach in conducting the appraisal are as follows:

- Summarize what the person has done well;
- Focus the conversation on desired rather than undesired behavior;
- In doing so, focus on the future rather than the past; and
- Conclude the appraisal with the setting of three to five SMART goals.

References

Bandura, A. (1997). *Self-efficacy: The exercise of control.* New York: W.H. Freeman.

Bernardin, H.J., & Beatty, R.W. (1987, Summer). Can subordinate appraisals enhance managerial productivity? *Sloan Management Review,* 63–73.

Campbell, D.J., & Lee, C. (1988). Self-appraisal in performance evaluation: Development versus evaluation. *Academy of Management Journal, 13,* 302–314.

Farh, J.L., & Dobbins, G.J. (1989). Effects of self-esteem on leniency bias in self-reports of performance: A structural equation model analysis. *Personnel Psychology, 42,* 835–850.

Feild, H.S., & Holley, W.H. (1982). The relationship of performance appraisal system characteristics to verdicts in selected employment discrimination cases. *Academy of Management Journal, 25,* 392–406.

Flanagan, J.C. (1954). The critical incident technique. *Psychological Bulletin, 51,* 327–358.

Gordon, L.V., & Medland, F.F. (1965). The cross-group stability of peer ratings of leadership potential. *Personnel Psychology, 18,* 173–177.

Komaki, J.L. (1986). Toward effective supervisors: An operant analysis and comparison of managers at work. *Journal of Applied Psychology, 71,* 270–279.

Komaki, J.L. (1998). *Leadership from an operant perspective.* London: Rutledge.

Korman, A.K. (1968). The prediction of managerial performance: A review. *Personnel Psychology, 21,* 295–322.

Lane, J., & Herriot, P. (1990). Self-ratings, supervisor ratings, positions, & performance. *Journal of Occupational Psychology, 63,* 77–88.

Latham, G.P., Mitchell, T.R., & Dossett, D.L. (1978). The importance of participative goal setting and anticipated rewards on goal difficulty and job performance. *Journal of Applied Psychology, 63,* 173–181.

Latham, G.P., & Wexley, K.N. (1994). *Increasing productivity through performance appraisal* (2nd ed.). Reading, MA: Addison-Wesley.

Locke, E.A., & Latham, G.P. (1990). *A theory of goal setting and task performance.* Englewood Cliffs, NJ: Prentice Hall; pp. 1–26. Reprinted in R.H. Steers, L.W. Porter, & G.A. Bigley (1996). *Motivation and leadership at work.* New York: McGraw-Hill.

Longnecker, C.O., Sims, H.R., & Gioia, D.A. (1987). Behind the mask: The politics of employee appraisal. *Academy of Management Executive, 1,* 183–193.

Martin, D.C., Bartol, K.M., & Levine, M.J. (1986). The legal ramifications of performance appraisal. *Employee Relations Law Journal, 12,* 370–395.

Nathan, B.R., Mohrman, A.H., Jr., & Milliman, J. (1991). Interpersonal relations as context for the effects of appraisal interviews on performance and satisfaction: A longitudinal study. *Academy of Management Journal, 34,* 352–369.

Schneider, B., & Bowen, D. (1995). *Winning the service game.* Boston: Harvard Business School Press.

Somers, M.J., & Birnbaum, D. (1991). Assessing self-appraisal of job performance as an evaluation device: Are the poor results a function of method or methodology? *Human Relations, 44,* 1081–1091.

Thompson, D.E., & Thompson, T.A. (1982). Court standards for job analysis test validation. *Personnel Psychology, 35,* 865–874.

Wiersma, U., & Latham, G.P. (1986). The practicality of behavioral observation scales, behavioral expectation scales, and trait scales. *Personnel Psychology, 39,* 619–628.

Wiersma, U., van den Berg, P.T., & Latham, G.P. (1992). Dutch reactions to behavioral observation, behavioral expectation, and trait scales. *Group and Organization Management, 20,* 297–309.

Recommended Reading

Arvey, R.D., & Murphy, K.R. (1998). Performance evaluation in work settings. *Annual Review of Psychology, 49,* 141–168.

Latham, G.P., Skarlicki, D., Irvine, D., & Siegel, J. (1993). The increasing importance of performance appraisals to employee effectiveness in organizational settings in North America. In C. Cooper & I. Robertson (Eds.), *International Review of Industrial and Organizational Psychology* (pp. 87–132). Chichester, England, United Kingdom: Wiley.

Latham, G.P., & Latham, S.D. (2000). Overlooking theory and research in performance appraisal at one's peril: Much done, more to do. In C. Cooper & E.A. Locke (Eds.), *International Review of Industrial and Organizational Psychology.* Chichester, England, United Kingdom: Wiley.

Yammarino, F.J., & Atwater, L.E. (1997). Do managers see themselves as others see them? Implications of self-other rating agreement for human resources management. *Organizational Dynamics, 25,* 35–44.

Gary P. Latham is the secretary of state professor of organizational effectiveness in the faculty of management at the University of Toronto. He has been awarded fellow status by both the American and Canadian Psychological Associations, the American Psychological Society, and the Academy of Management. In 1996, he was made a fellow of the Royal Society of Canada. He is the past president of the Canadian Psychological Association. Dr. Latham's contribution to the field of human resources has been in the areas of performance management, selection, and training and development. He is the co-developer of the Behavioral Observation Scales (with K. Wexley) and the Situational Interview (with L.M. Saari, E.D. Pursell, and M. Campion).

Deborah L. MacKenzie *received her Honors B.S. in psychology from the University of Toronto. She is currently a doctoral student of organizational behavior and human resource management at the University of Toronto. A student member of the Canadian Psychological Association, American Psychological Association, Society for Industrial & Organizational Psychology, and Academy of Management, her primary research focus is on the application of social cognitive theory and goal setting to organizational issues.*

PART THREE

TRAINING AND
DEVELOPMENT DESIGN

CHAPTER SIXTEEN

The Future of Instructional Design

William J. Rothwell, Ph.D., SPHR
Professor, The Pennsylvania State University

To answer the question of the future of instructional design, this chapter offers several predictions: (1) In the future, learners will take more responsibility for their learning than ever before, posing a unique challenge for traditionalist instructional designers, who have thought in terms of organizing experiences for learners; (2) The term "instructional design" is likely to be supplanted entirely by such new terms as performance design, performance consulting, performance enhancement, performance engineering, performance facilitation, or similar terms that recognize the importance of achieving results through performance interventions other than instruction; (3) More attention will be paid to ways to integrate high-tech design and delivery methods with real-time learner support; (4) Instruction will be concurrently engineered more frequently, with designers on one continent working virtually with their counterparts on other continents, and barriers created by differences in language, culture, and technology will be surmounted; (5) Instruction will split into two kinds: (a) instruction focused on the past or present that is designed to communicate information and (b) instruction focused on the future that is designed to create new information; (6) The traditional instructional design model will be supplanted by alternatives; and (7) More attention will be paid to forecasting the financial benefits of instruction, selecting appropriate performance improvement interventions, and clarifying desired payoffs before instructional investment decisions are made.

INTRODUCTION

What is the future of instructional design? The answer to this question is important, as it would help practitioners and academicians alike focus on leading the target and being proactive, rather than on trailing events and reacting to problems. Many people seek answers to the question.

This chapter offers predictions about how to answer that question based on an analysis of books and articles published about instructional design over the last few years. The chapter is organized around answering such related questions as these: (1) *Who* will do instructional design in the future? (2) *What* will be the definition of instructional design? (3) *When* will instruction be designed? (4) *Where* will instruction be designed? (5) *Why* will instruction be designed? (6) *How* will instruction be designed? and (7) *How much* will instruction cost in the future, and how will those costs be compared to its benefits?

WHO WILL DO INSTRUCTIONAL DESIGN IN THE FUTURE?

Trends point toward more learner empowerment in the future. As learners have access to vastly increasing amounts of on-demand information and learning resources at their fingertips from the World Wide Web, they are moving beyond self-directed to empowered learning. That means learners are taking charge of their own learning process. They are becoming *free agent learners* who aggressively manage their own learning—with or without approval from organizational superiors, training departments, HR managers, or others (Caudron, 1999). Much more than self-directed learning, free agent learning places the individual learner at center stage, and heightened learner motivation and increased interactivity are keys to this free agentry (Filipczak, 1996; Spitzer, 1996). Like people who indiscriminately and frequently change television channels using remote controls, learners of the future will increasingly be driven by immediate needs and interests. Even now, learners grow bored with linear instruction, preferring nonlinear instruction that is focused on their problems and interests. That change will only intensify in the future.

Traditionally, learners have had everything done for them by instructional designers, who analyzed performance problems, assessed training needs, examined work settings and learner characteristics, formulated instructional objectives, prepared test items and other metrics by which to measure learning upon completion of instruction, sourced instructional materials to meet the instructional objectives, selected the media by which instruction would be delivered, organized and delivered the content, and evaluated the results. But the role for instructional designers is changing. More learners in the future will take charge of their own learning, driven by the frenetic pace of work in organizations and the easy availability of e-learning resources available at any time or place to meet their work- and life-related needs. In the future, attention will focus more on the role of instructional designer as a facilitator, one who guides others through the process of learning on their own (Rothwell, 1999). That will include individually oriented (and group- or team-oriented) learning experiences that will be prepared according to strict instructional design standards (Beard, 1999). In the meantime, learners will need to learn more about their own learning process (learning how to learn) and more about designing instructions for others. This will help them take maximum advantage of what is known about learning styles and preferences, learning disabilities and problems, and other issues influencing the individual's ability to take charge of his or her own learning process (Rothwell, 1999).

WHAT WILL BE THE DEFINITION OF INSTRUCTIONAL DESIGN?

Traditional definitions of instructional design have emphasized what is done to build instruction. For instance, Gropper and Ross (1987) explain that "the design of consumer goods provides an appropriate, if surprising, model for the design of training. Like an automobile, a typewriter, or a television set, a training program is something to be planned, engineered, developed, tried out, sent back to the drawing board, tried out again, and delivered in final form. If developed in this disciplined fashion, like other products, the training program will do the job it was designed to do" (p. 196). The goal of the instructional designer would then be to create learning experiences in much the same way that an engineer designs a product to be manufactured.

More recent definitions suggest that the goal of instructional design, and by implication of instructional designers, is to achieve results. In that sense, "the field of instructional design is associated with analyzing human performance problems systematically, identifying the root causes of those problems, considering various solutions to address the root causes, and implementing the solutions in ways designed to minimize the unintended consequences of corrective action" (Rothwell & Kazanas, 1998, p. 3). The instructional designer is thus interested in achieving improved outputs or outcomes (performance), rather than merely creating a commodity (training) or carrying out an activity (the design of training).

Increasingly, however, instructional designers realize that instruction—and results—are driven by the internalized mental processes of the learners themselves (Coombs & Smith, 1998). Moreover, instructional design itself is misnamed if the goal is to achieve results, considering that only 10 percent of all performance problems is attributable to deficiencies of individual knowledge, skill, or attitude, but that 90 percent is traceable to organizational or management deficiencies (Rothwell, Hohne, & King, 2000).

As a consequence, in the future, the term *instructional design* is likely to be supplanted entirely by such terms as *performance design, performance consulting, performance enhancement, performance engineering, performance facilitation,* or similar terms that recognize the importance of achieving results.

WHEN WILL INSTRUCTION BE DESIGNED?

Time has become a strategic resource. That accounts for a continuing, and escalating, obsession with high-tech delivery methods (Hamel & Ryan-Jones, 1997). It also accounts for interest in finding a means by which to slash the (often too lengthy) process required to prepare, deliver, and realize the benefits from rigorously designed instruction (Broadbent, 1998; Chapman, 1995; "Five 'rule-of-thumb tips,'" 1996; "How to accelerate," 1997; Klimczak & Wedman, 1997). Instructional designers are, therefore, experimenting with improved development tools to reduce design time (Dills, 1998; Eugenio, 1998; Glade, 1998). They are also experimenting with other efforts to slash cycle times, such as *rapid prototyping* (in which instruction is drafted, tested with learners in real time, and then "fixed"), improved templates, and other ways to speed up the time from the detection of a human performance problem to the delivery of instruction.

In the future, look for more attention to be paid to ways to integrate high-tech design and delivery methods with real-time learner support. The future may thus be with such fast methods as real-time messaging, desktop consulting by video, and sophisticated ways to integrate video, graphics, text, sound, and animation in real time (El-Tigi & Branch, 1997; Rakes, 1996).

WHERE WILL INSTRUCTION BE DESIGNED?

The separation between working life and personal life is gradually diminishing as a direct result of technological advancement. People can now be reached by cell phone or wireless computers in their cars, on airplanes, or even on submarines. The world is a smaller place due to technological innovation.

In a bid to reduce the time needed to design instruction, it is increasingly likely that technology-based instruction will be concurrently engineered. Instructional designers on one continent can toil through their workdays on training design, perhaps from their homes, and then transfer files virtually to designers on other continents, where the workday is just beginning. As in product design, this approach can slash development time, because someone is always working on a 24/7 schedule. The only real barriers to this approach that now exist are language, cultural, and technological differences (Ritchie & Earnest, 1999). Those barriers are not insurmountable. At the same time, this approach can take advantage of sizable wage differences existing between developed and developing economies.

WHY WILL INSTRUCTION BE DESIGNED?

Instruction has traditionally equipped people with the knowledge, skills, and abilities they need to perform. Instruction has tended to be past- or present-focused: It helps learners become versed on the lessons gained by experience and stored in the organization's institutional memory as embodied in policies, procedures, job descriptions, and corporate culture. One example of such past-oriented instruction is new employee orientation, which informs people about the work rules, policies, and procedures established in the past. Another example is upgrading training, which equips workers with what they need to know and do to cope with changing technology, work methods, and working conditions.

In the future, however, instruction may split into two kinds: (1) past- or present-focused; and (2) future-focused. Past- or present-focused instruction will be disseminated most often by asynchronous online and Web-based training methods. Its purpose is to provide the knowledge, build the skills, and shape the attitudes needed to meet current challenges or communicate lessons learned from the past as expressed in an organization's policies, procedures, or work rules. Future-focused instruction will become key to the competitive advantage of many organizations. It will often, though not always, be delivered by synchronous face-to-face group meetings. It will harness the creative, risk-oriented power of small groups. Its goal will be to create new knowledge, pinpoint new skills, and shape new attitudes or beliefs. As such, it will serve as a sort of human-oriented research and development function that will tap into, and build, the organization's intellectual capital.

Also in the future, organizations will move away from thinking of just disseminating knowledge, building skills, and shaping attitudes. All trends point toward an increasing emphasis on building competencies, where the often-misunderstood term *competency* means "an underlying characteristic of an employee (that is, motive, trait, skill, aspects of one's self-image, social role, or a body of knowledge) which results in effective and/or superior performance in a job" (Boyatzis, 1982, pp. 20–21). Despite continued use of task and job analysis (Loughner & Moller, 1998), trends point toward more acceptance of competencies as a foundation for human resource management and instructional design efforts (DuBois & Rothwell, 2000; Rothwell & Lindholm, 1999). A key advantage of competencies is that they encompass a more comprehensive view of what constitutes human performance, and competency models are thus superior to such work-based methods as job or task analysis as a foundation for performance improvement interventions.

HOW WILL INSTRUCTION BE DESIGNED?

Traditionally, instruction has been designed by those skilled in the instructional design process. Indeed, instructional design has emerged as a profession or field of practice in its own right (Rothwell & Kazanas, 1998). But that may change in the future.

There are several reasons why it may change. First, as noted above, learners are becoming more willing and able to structure their own learning experiences. They may need help to do that, as traditional education has focused more on subject matter (content) than on providing instruction on learning how to learn (process). Second, as information dissemination becomes more technologically based—and the love affair with technologically based methods is not likely to diminish, considering how much has been written about that in recent years—one of two scenarios is likely: (1) Technologists (such as MIS specialists, software engineers, and other technology professionals) will supplant instructional designers, or (2) Designing instruction using technologically based methods is likely to emerge most often as a team effort, with instruction designed with a group consisting of instructional designers, hardware and software technologists, subject-matter experts, and representatives of targeted learner groups. If the latter scenario should prove to be the norm, then the traditional instructional design model (as described, for instance, in Rothwell & Kazanas, 1998) will be supplanted by more appropriate alternatives, such as a newly reinvented ISD model or some version of the action learning model (as described by Rothwell, 1999). Key advantages of using the action learning model are that learners and other stakeholders become more involved (and thus assume more ownership) in the design process and can simultaneously build training while also solving a work-related performance problem. Of course, a key disadvantage of using the action learning model is that involvement takes time away from daily work duties for those participating in these projects.

Recently, the traditional instructional design model has come under mounting attack as being inappropriate to deal with contemporary concerns, and the reasons for those attacks are not likely to abate in the future (Braden, 1996; Cohen & Jurkovic, 1997; HerrNacker, 1999; Merrill, 1996; Tennyson, 1999; Willis, 1998).

HOW MUCH WILL INSTRUCTION COST IN THE FUTURE, AND HOW WILL THOSE COSTS BE COMPARED TO ITS BENEFITS?

In recent years, instructional designers have been under the gun to prove the financial and non-financial value of what they do (Rothwell, 1998). Managers and other stakeholders have become less tolerant of instruction that does not yield changes in on-the-job behaviors or work performance or provide demonstrable payoffs in productivity increases or other improvements. As a result, much has been written recently about ways to demonstrate return on training investments (Wagner & Derryberry, 1998), improve the comprehensiveness of training evaluation methods (Sleezer, Gradous, & Maile, 1999), improve the transfer of training from off-the-job instructional settings to on-the-job work settings to increase the impact, and focus attention on change efforts in work settings. This attention is likely to become more pronounced in the future as instructional designers work with stakeholders to avoid building unrealistic expectations that training alone will always yield immediate payoffs and clarify the desired results before training or other performance improvement interventions are implemented (Gayeski, 1998).

It is also likely that, with the advent of more sophisticated decision-support systems (see, for instance, Advisor P.I.™, which at the time of publication could be reviewed in demo form at http:\\www.astd.org), instructional designers will be able to work collaboratively with their stakeholders to compare the relative costs and benefits of various performance improvement interventions before interventions are implemented. That makes the choice of a performance improvement intervention comparable to an investment decision. A shift is also already underway to establish performance objectives (Rothwell, Hohne, & King, 2000) that define changes back on the job, rather than continue to rely on instructional objectives, which merely define what learning mastery has been achieved by learners upon completion of training. Both changes are likely to contribute to focusing attention on desired results rather than on mere activities or processes.

CONCLUSION

So, *What is the future of instructional design?* According to what has been reported here, that question can best be answered by several predictions:

- *Who will do instructional design in the future?* In the future, learners will take more responsibility for their learning, and that will pose a challenge for instructional designers who have traditionally thought in terms of organizing experiences *for* learners.

- *What will be the definition of instructional design?* The term instructional design is likely to be supplanted entirely in the future by such new terms as performance design, performance consulting, performance enhancement, performance engineering, performance facilitation, or similar terms that recognize the importance of achieving results.

- *When will instruction be designed?* Look for more attention to be paid to ways to integrate high-tech design and delivery methods with real-time learner support.

- *Where will instruction be designed?* Instruction in the future will be concurrently engineered. Designers on one continent can toil through their workdays on training design, perhaps from their homes, and then transfer their files virtually to designers on other continents, where the workday is just beginning.

- *Why will instruction be designed?* In the future, instruction will split into two kinds: (1) Instruction focused on the past or present, designed to communicate information; and (2) instruction focused on the future, designed to create new information.

- *How will instruction be designed?* The traditional instructional design model will be supplanted by more appropriate alternatives, such as a newly reinvented ISD model or some version of the action learning model.

- *How much will instruction cost in the future, and how will those costs be compared to its benefits?* In the future, as in the recent past, instructional designers will have to prove the financial value of what they do. More attention will be paid to forecasting the benefits of instruction, selecting appropriate performance improvement interventions, and clarifying desired payoffs before investments are made.

Use the worksheet in Exhibit 16.1 to structure your own and others' thinking in your organizations about what the future of instructional design might mean to your organizations.

Exhibit 16.1. Worksheet on Future of Instructional Design

Directions: For each question posed in Column 1 below and for each prediction based on the question appearing in Column 2 below, write your notes in response to the questions appearing over Columns 3 and 4. Work individually. When you finish, compare notes with others in your organization and use the collective opinions of your group to begin planning for change in your organization.

Column 1	Column 2	Column 3	Column 4
Question	Prediction Based on the Chapter	What do you think will be the effects of this trend in your organization in the future?	How do you believe your organization should plan to react to—or anticipate—the trend and its effects in your organization?
1 *Who will do instructional design in the future?*	In the future learners will take more responsibility for their learning and that will pose a challenge for instructional designers who have traditionally thought in terms of organizing experiences for learners.		
2 *What will be the definition of instructional design?*	The term *instructional design* is likely to be supplanted entirely in the future by such new terms as *performance design, performance consulting, performance enhancement, performance engineering, performance facilitation,* or similar terms that recognize the importance of achieving results.		
3 *When will instruction be designed?*	Look for more attention to be paid to ways to integrate high-tech design and delivery methods with real-time learner suppport.		

Exhibit 16.1. (*cont.*)

4 *Where will instruction be designed?*	Instruction in the future will be concurrently engineered. Designers on one continent can toil through their work days on training design, perhaps from their homes, and then transfer their files virtually to designers on other continents, where the workday is just beginning.
5 *Why will instruction be designed?*	In the future, instruction will split into two kinds: (1) instruction focused on the past or present, designed to communicate information; and (2) instruction focused on the future, designed to create new information.
6 *How will instruction be designed?*	The traditional instructional design model will be supplanted by more appropriate alternatives, such as a newly reinvented ISD model or some version of the action learning model.
7 *How much will instruction cost in the future, and how will those costs be compared to its benefits?*	In the future, as in the recent past, instructional designers will have to prove the financial value of what they do. More attention will be paid to forecasting the benefits of instruction, selecting appropriate performance improvement interventions, and clarifying desired payoffs before investments are made.

References

Beard, M. (1999). Evolution of the ID process at Sprint. *Performance Improvement, 38*(8), 21–25.

Boyatzis, A. (1982). *The competent manager: A model for effective performance.* New York: John Wiley & Sons.

Braden, R. (1996). The case for linear instructional design and development: A commentary on models, challenges, and myths. *Educational Technology, 36*(2), 5–23.

Broadbent, B. (1998). The training formula. *Training & Development, 52*(10), 41–43.

Caudron, S. (1999). Free agent learner. *Training & Development, 52*(8), 26–30.

Chapman, B. (1995). Accelerating the design process: A tool for instructional designers. *Journal of Interactive Instruction Development, 8*(2), 8–15.

Cohen, S., & Jurkovic, J. (1997). Learning from a masterpiece. *Training & Development, 51*(11), 66–70.

Coombs, S., & Smith, I. (1998). Designing a self-organized conversational learning environment. *Educational Technology, 38*(3), 17–28.

Dills, C. (1998). The table of specifications: A tool for instructional design and development. *Educational Technology, 38*(3), 44–51.

DuBois, D., & Rothwell, W. (2000). *The competency toolkit.* (Vols. 1 & 2). Amherst, MA: HRD Press.

El-Tigi, M., & Branch, R. (1997). Designing for interaction, learner control, and feedback during web-based learning. *Educational Technology, 37*(3), 23–29.

Eugenio, V. (1998). Implementing learning technologies? Start with a strategic plan. *Corporate University Review, 6*(2), 33–39.

Filipczak, B. (1996). Engaged! The nature of computer interactivity. *Training, 33*(11), 52–58.

Five "rule-of-thumb" tips for calculating how long it takes to develop training. (1996). *Training Directors' Forum Newsletter, 12*(9), 5.

Gayeski, D. (1998). Out-of-the-box instructional design. *Training & Development, 52*(4), 36–40.

Glade, B. (1998). Synergy simplifies CBT authoring. *Technical Training, 9*(4), 6–7.

Gropper, G., & Ross, P. (1987). Instructional design. In R. Craig (Ed.), *Training and development handbook: A guide to human resource development* (3rd ed.) (pp. 195–216). New York: McGraw-Hill.

Hamel, C., & Ryan-Jones, D. (1997). Using three-dimensional interactive graphics to teach equipment procedures. *Educational Technology Research & Development, 45*(4), 77–87.

HerrNeckar, A. (1999). Instructional design for web-based, post-secondary distance education. *Journal of Instruction Delivery Systems, 13*(2), 6–9.

How to accelerate your instructional-design process—without sacrificing training quality. (1997). *Training Directors' Forum Newsletter, 13*(4), 5.

Klimczak, A., & Wedman, J. (1997). Instructional design project success factors: An empirical basis. *Educational Technology Research & Development, 45*(2), 75–83.

Loughner, P., & Moller, L. (1998). The use of task analysis procedures by instructional designers. *Performance Improvement Quarterly, 11*(3), 79–100.

Merrill, M. (1996). Instructional transaction theory: Instructional design based on knowledge objects. *Educational Technology, 36*(3), 30–37.

Rakes, G. (1996). Visuals in instructional design. *Performance & Instruction, 35*(3), 30–32.

Ritchie, D., & Earnest, J. (1999). The future of instructional design: Results of a delphi study. *Educational Technology, 39*(1), 35–42.

Rothwell, W. (Ed.). (1998). *Creating, measuring & documenting service impact: A capacity building resource: Rationales, models, activities, methods, techniques, instruments.* Columbus, OH: The EnterpriseOhio Network.

Rothwell, W. (1999). *The action learning guidebook: A real-time strategy for problem solving, training design, and employee development.* San Francisco: Jossey-Bass/Pfeiffer.

Rothwell, W., Hohne, C., & King, S. (2000). *Human performance improvement: Building practitioner competence.* Houston, TX: Gulf.

Rothwell, W., & Kazanas, H. (1998). *Mastering the instructional design process: A systematic approach* (2nd ed.). San Francisco: Jossey-Bass.

Rothwell, W., & Lindholm, J. (1999). Competency identification, modeling and assessment in the USA. *International Journal of Training and Development, 3*(2), 90–105.

Sleezer, C., Gradous, D., & Maile, C. (1999). A step beyond univision evaluation: Using a systems model of performance improvement. *Performance Improvement Quarterly, 12*(3), 119–131.

Spitzer, D. (1996). Motivation: The neglected factor in instructional design. *Educational Technology, 36*(3), 45–49.

Tennyson, R. (1999). Instructional development and ISD4 methodology. *Performance Improvement, 38*(6), 19–27.

Wagner, E., & Derryberry, A. (1998). Return on investment (ROI) in action: Techniques for "selling" interactive technologies. *Educational Technology, 38*(4), 22–27.

Willis, J. (1998). Alternative instructional design paradigms: What's worth discussing and what isn't. *Educational Technology, 38*(3), 5–16.

Recommended Reading

Caropreso, E., & Couch, R. (1996). Creativity and innovation in instructional design and development: The individual in the workplace. *Educational Technology, 36*(6), 31–39.

Dean, P., & Ripley, D. (1998). *Peformance improvement interventions instructional design & training: Methods for organizational learning.* Washington, DC: International Society for Performance Improvement.

Jonassen, D. (1997). Instructional design models for well-structured and ill-structured problem-solving learning outcomes. *Educational Technology Research & Development, 45*(1), 65–94.

Layng, J. (1997). Parallels between project management and instructional design. *Performance Improvement, 36*(6), 16–20.

Liang, C., & Schwen, T. (1997). Critical reflections on instructional design in the corporate world. *Performance Improvement, 36*(8), 18–19.

Loughner, P., & Milheim, W. (1999). World wide web sites for instructional design and human performance technology. *Performance Improvement, 38*(1), 32–36.

Silber, K. (1998). The cognitive approach to training development: A practitioner's assessment. *Educational Technology Research & Development, 46*(4), 58–72.

Wake up! (and reclaim instructional design). (1998). *Training, 35*(6), 36–42.

Welsh, T. (1999). Implications of distributed learning for instructional designers: How will the future affect the practice? *Educational Technology, 39*(2), 41–45.

Wilson, B. (1999). Evolution of learning technologies: From instructional design to performance support to network systems. *Educational Technology, 39*(2), 32–35.

About the Author

William J. Rothwell is president of Rothwell and Associates as well as professor of human resource development in the Department of Adult Education, Instructional Systems and Workforce Education and Development on the University Park Campus of The Pennsylvania State University. Before 1993, he was an assistant vice president for a major insurance company and a training director in a state government agency. He has worked full-time in human resource management and employee training and development from 1979 to the present. As a consultant, Dr. Rothwell's client list includes over thirty-five companies from the Fortune 500.

Dr. Rothwell is a prolific author. His latest books include The Role of Analyst *(2000, ASTD),* The Role of Evaluator *(2000, ASTD), and* The Competency Toolkit *(with David DuBois), (2000, HRD Press).*

CHAPTER SEVENTEEN

What Every Smart Trainer Should Know About Learning

Maxine Arnold Dalton, Ph.D.
Director, Global Leadership, Center for Creative Leadership

The term "learning styles" represents a host of dissimilar theories and tools. This chapter reviews many of these, differentiates among them, and addresses when one theory or approach might be preferred over another. The chapter focuses most specifically on the concept of meta-cognition and learning tactics as tools to employ when the trainer's objective is to teach individuals how to learn from the naturally occurring experiences of the workplace after they leave the classroom.

INTRODUCTION

A host of books and surveys is available to help trainers understand how adults learn. This plethora of information is both a blessing and a curse. A mismatch between a tool or theory and a training objective can confound a trainer's intentions.

A trainer must know that each book or offering is likely to be based on a somewhat different theory of learning and that each is appropriate for a somewhat different situation. It is not that the theories and practices of adult learning are in conflict with one another. Rather, researchers on the topic of learning enter the complex arena of adult learning through different doors, so what each notices and seeks to understand is influenced by a different perspective. Trainers need to understand these different perspectives on learning so that they can choose the theoretical point of view that best meets their training objectives. A skilled trainer will be able to understand and use the appropriate theory and tools for the situation at hand.

In this chapter, I will present two frameworks for cataloguing a variety of theories and tools of adult learning. I then will focus on one particular training practice—how to use the process of meta-cognition to teach managers and aspiring managers how to learn. I am indebted to many thinkers and writers in the field.

ADULT LEARNING THEORIES

One useful framework for understanding theories of adult learning has been developed by Curry (1987). Curry suggests that theories of adult learning can be categorized within three concentric circles labeled *personality preference, information processing style,* and *learning behavior* (see Figure 17.1). Personality represents the core of the individual—those basic drives that we bring with us at birth and that influence us throughout our life span. Introversion and extroversion are examples of traits that are relatively stable throughout the course of life and that influence the next ring in the model, information processing style.

Personality also influences how a person feels about learning in general, which means admitting that one "does not know." The poles on the openness scale of the five factor model of personality describes individuals who are intrigued by the unknown versus individuals who are drawn to concrete certainty (Costa &

Figure 17.1. Categorizing the Influences on Learning
Adapted from Curry, 1987.

McCrae, 1991). An example of another tool that illustrates the influence of personality on learning is the Myers-Briggs Type Indicator (Briggs & Myers, 1977).

Information processing style describes the information to which a person pays attention and how he or she processes it. Deduction and induction are examples of information processing style—in one case observing a phenomenon and creating a theory to explain one's observations and, in the other case, creating a theory and searching for the data to confirm or disconfirm the theory. An example of a tool that illustrates the influence of information processing style on learning is the Learning Styles Inventory (Kolb, 1985). Based on work by Margerison and Lewis (1979), extroverts are more likely to engage in active experimentation. Introverts are more likely to engage in reflective observation.

Personality and information processing style both influence the behaviors that an individual uses in order to learn—whether the individual prefers to learn by attending a course, asking a colleague for advice, or going online. An example of a tool that illustrates the variety of learning behaviors that a person might use is the Learning Tactics Inventory (Dalton, 1999). Note that these factors—personality, information processing style, and learning behavior—are all internal to the individual.

A trainer can use Curry's framework to select tools designed to measure "learning style." Tools representing measures of personality give a person information about preferences, along with the knowledge that these preferences are very difficult to change. Tools representing measures of information processing style help a person understand how he or she thinks and may induce him or her to consider a broader cognitive repertoire. Tools representing learning behaviors give a person information about how he or she goes about the business of learning and introduce the person to some new strategies.

Another useful framework for organizing the various theories of adult learning is offered by James and Blank (1993). These authors make the distinction between factors internal to the individual and factors external to the individual, such as teaching methods, media, and curriculum. They then categorize factors internal to the individual as "the manner in which, and the conditions under which, learners most efficiently and most effectively perceive, store, and recall what they are attempting to learn" (p. 47). They sort these internal factors into three categories: *cognitive style*—the learner's typical mode of perceiving, thinking, problem solving, and remembering; *affective style*—the learner's typical model of arousing, directing, and sustaining behavior); and *physiological style,* such as one's health, nutrition, and circadian rhythm (p. 48).

A special circumstance of affective style is the work on perceptual modalities that describes how individuals receive information. James and Galbraith (1985) suggest that there are seven perceptual modalities—visual, aural, print, interactive, haptic, kinesthetic, and olfactory—and that individuals have a dominant or preferred style of receiving information. Trainers who want to ensure that they are presenting material in a way that the participants will find compatible will want to train to the full range of modalities.

A third framework for the trainer to consider is *context*. Where is the learning taking place? Is the trainer most interested in the classroom setting—in employing that optimum combination of internal and external factors such that the material the trainer has to present will be attended to, understood, and used by the greatest number of participants? Or is the trainer most interested in teaching the adult *how to learn* from the naturally occurring experiences of the workplace *after* he or she leaves the classroom? The goal of the first situation is a matching task. The trainer is attempting to modify his or her instructional design to meet the needs of a diverse group of classroom participants. The goal of the second situation is to teach participants the skill of meta-cognition so that each participant can understand his or her preferred learning strategies and intentionally expand these strategies. The second situation teaches classroom participants how to take responsibility for their own learning after the training program is over.

It is to this second strategy that I would like to turn. Research and practice into how managers and executives learn the skills and perspectives that make them effective and successful suggests that these skills are most often learned within the naturally occurring experiences of the workplace. In other words, the work itself is the classroom. Using the language of Knowles (1950) and Marsick and Watkins (1990), what takes place in the classroom is formal learning. What takes place in the workplace is either informal learning or incidental learning. What I am suggesting here is that the role of the trainer represents some combination of the two—using the formal classroom setting to teach managers how to learn more purposefully and effectively from the informal and incidental experiences of the workplace. In this case, the role of the trainer is to teach managers and aspiring managers how managerial skills and perspectives are learned and how best to learn from the opportunities available to them.

Some research suggests that managers who learn the most from the experience are those who have the broadest range of learning tactics available to them. Using the framework introduced early in this chapter, learning tactics are those behaviors (influenced by personality preference and information processing style) that individuals most typically use when they are faced with a developmental learning task. These tactics can be sorted into four categories of behavior:

1. *Action* tactics—learning by doing;

2. *Thinking* tactics—learning by remembering and recalling the past, comparing and contrasting it with the present, and imagining the future;

3. *Accessing* others—learning with others through the use of role models, feedback and advice; and

4. *Feeling* tactics—managing the anxiety associated with uncertainty and not knowing, so as to be willing to engage in developmental opportunities.

Individuals able to use a variety of tactics from each of these four categories are more likely to engage in a wide variety of opportunities and learn in a manner appropriate to the task at hand. Individuals who are governed by their unexamined personality preferences are less likely to possess the broad repertoire of skills necessary to be adaptable and flexible. They have learned only those skills from those situations using those tactics with which they are comfortable. And so, for example, a manager who uses action tactics may be drawn to situations requiring single-minded decisiveness, and this manager may have mastered the skills required to manage emergencies. He or she may not be very effective in situations requiring the use of thinking tactics or tactics predicated on accessing others. This manager would not have learned the skills necessary to excel in management situations requiring asking others for advice or thoroughly considering the pros and cons of a variety of options.

In teaching managers how to take responsibility for their own learning, become more versatile learners, and be more effective managers, the trainer's job is to teach classroom participants to recognize how they learn (the process of meta-cognition), give them concrete examples of how they can expand their learning repertoire, and help them understand that, if one aspires to complex and broad managerial roles, one must possess a broad repertoire of skills learned in a variety of challenging situations using a variety of learning tactics. Acquiring these skills is predicated on having a broad range of learning tactics in one's quiver and an understanding of when to use each one.

USING META-COGNITION TO TEACH MANAGERS HOW TO LEARN FROM EXPERIENCE

There are three steps in teaching managers how to learn from experience.

1. The first step is *multi-source feedback.* Managers who are seeking to become more intentional about learning in the workplace must have a current understanding of their baseline skills so that they may set appropriate developmental goals. This feedback step also might include the administration of a personality measure so that the individual can understand his or her preferences and appreciate why he or she has chosen particular learning tactics over the years.

2. The second step is goal setting. Managers often need assistance in setting clear and behavioral developmental goals—goals of mastery rather than performance. Performance is about demonstrating what you already know how to do. Performance goals are evaluative goals, and managers are likely to become more interested in avoiding a negative evaluation, rather than in learning what they need to learn. Mastery is about acquiring a new skill or perspective. Goals of mastery require an individual to engage in a challenging learning opportunity and practice a new skill as often as necessary, using role models to see how it is done and feedback from others to serve as a mirror to the effort.

3. The third step is teaching the actual process of meta-cognition. Managers need to recognize how they learn—what tactics they use—so that they can intentionally adopt novel learning tactics. For example, managers who typically use the tactic of accessing others for help, support, and advice need to adopt tactics that will move them to learn by direct experimentation. Managers who typically learn in a solitary and inwardly focused manner need to adopt some tactics that call on them to access others. Managers who avoid challenging opportunities so as not to appear "stupid" need to adopt some tactics for managing anxiety. It is very likely that a manager's skill level and a manager's learning tactics are enmeshed. This means that a person with poor interpersonal skills probably never uses learning tactics that involve accessing others. But this person will not be able to acquire interpersonal skill without accessing others.

The trainers' role is to teach managers how they learn and bring other options to their awareness. The learning goal for the trainer is to have the manager leave the training experience conscious of his or her learning tactics, understanding the limits of those tactics, with clear strategies for trying out new tactics. We would want each manager touched by this training experience to be able to enter any novel experience saying to himself or herself, "What can I learn here? How shall I learn it? What am I learning here? How would I do it differently next time?"

SUMMARY

There are a variety of ways for trainers to use theories of adult learning in the work that they do. Different approaches may help a trainer think through curriculum design, the medium of delivery, and the strategy for gaining and maintaining the attention of the participants in the classroom. The skilled trainer needs to understand exactly what he or she means when speaking of "learning style," as the term itself has come to stand for a variety of theories and training interventions. In this chapter, we have reviewed two frameworks for categorizing the various theories of learning and learning style and focused on one particular point of view—how the trainer can use the strategy of meta-cognition to help participants become more effective at learning from the naturally occurring experiences of the workplace after they leave the classroom.

References

Briggs, K.C., & Myers, I.B. (1977). *Myers-Briggs type indicator.* Palo Alto, CA: Consulting Psychologists Press.

Costa, P.T., Jr., & McCrae, R.R. (1991). *Revised NEO personality inventory (NEO PI-R) and NEO five-factor inventory (NEO-FFI) professional manual.* Odessa, FL: Psychological Assessment Resources.

Curry, L. (1987). *Integrating concepts of cognitive or learning style: A review of attention to psychometric standards.* Ottawa, Ontario, Canada: Curry, Adams & Associates.

Dalton, M. (1999). *Facilitator's guide for the learning tactics inventory.* San Francisco: Jossey-Bass/Pfeiffer.

James, W.B., & Blank. W.E. (1993). Review and critique of available learning-style instruments for adults. In R.G. Brockett & A.B. Knox (Series Eds.) & D.D. Flannery (Ed.), *New directions for adult and continuing education: Applying cognitive learning theory to adult learning* (Vol. 59, pp. 47–57). San Francisco: Jossey-Bass.

James, W.B., & Galbraith, M.W. (1985). Perceptual learning styles of adult high school graduates and nongraduates. *Lifelong Learning, 8,* 20–23.

Knowles, M. (1950). *Informal adult education.* New York: Association Press.

Kolb, D.A. (1985). *Learning styles inventory.* Boston: McBer.

Margierson, C.J., & Lewis, R.G. (1979). *How work preferences relate to learning styles.* Cranfield, England, United Kingdom: Cranfield School of Management.

Marsick, V.J., & Watkins, K.E. (1990). *Informal and incidental learning in the workplace.* New York: Routledge.

Recommended Reading

Dalton, M., & Hollenbeck, G.P. (1996). *How to design an effective system for developing managers and executives.* Greensboro, NC: Center for Creative Leadership.

Dalton, M., & Swigert, S. (Under review). *Learning versatility and managerial performance.*

Dweck, C.S. (1986). Motivational processes affecting learning. *American Psychologist, 41,* 1040–1080.

Hollenbeck, G.P., & McCall, M.W., Jr. (1999). Leadership development: Contemporary practice. In A.I. Kraut & A.K. Korman (Eds.), *Evolving practices in human resource management: Responses to a changing world of work* (pp. 172–200). San Francisco: Jossey-Bass.

Kolb, D.A. (1984). *Experiential learning.* Englewood Cliffs, NJ: Prentice Hall.

Lombardo, M.M., Bunker, K., & Webb, A. (1990, April). *Learning to learn.* Paper presented at the Fifth Annual Conference of the Society for Industrial and Organizational Psychology, Miami, FL.

McCall, M.W., Jr., Lombardo, M.M., & Morrison, A.M. (1988). *The lessons of experience: How successful executives develop on the job.* Lexington, MA: Lexington Books.

Mezirow, J. (1991). *Transformative dimensions of adult learning.* San Francisco: Jossey-Bass.

Mirvis, P.H., & Hall, D.T. (1996). Careers as lifelong learning. In A. Howard (Ed.), *The changing nature of work* (pp. 323–361). San Francisco: Jossey-Bass.

Schraw, G., & Dennison, R.S. (1994). Assessing meta-cognition. *Contemporary Educational Psychology, 19,* 460–475.

Seibert, K.W. (1996). Experience is the best teacher, if you can learn from it. In D.T. Hall & Associates (Eds.), *The career is dead—long live the career: A relational approach to careers* (pp. 246–264). San Francisco: Jossey-Bass.

Tesluk, P.E., & Jacobs, R.R. (1998). Toward an integrated model of work experience. *Personnel Psychology, 51,* 321–355.

Wislok, R.F. (1993). What are perceptual modalities and how do they contribute to learning? In R.G. Brockett & A.B Knox (Series Eds.) & D.D. Flannery (Ed.), *New directions for adult and continuing education. Apply cognitive learning theory to adult learning* (Vol. 59; pp. 5–13). San Francisco: Jossey-Bass.

About the Author

Maxine Arnold Dalton is director of global leadership research at the Center for Creative Leadership (CCL) in Greensboro, North Carolina. In this role she manages projects dedicated to understanding how people become effective in global leadership roles. Dr. Dalton has trained, made presentations, and published on a number of topics related to management and executive development. She has co-authored a CCL report, How to Design an Effective System for Developing Managers and Executives. *She has authored book chapters on the use of 360-degree surveys in organizations, on developing people for global assignments, and on introducing 360-degree processes in other cultures. She has written a CCL guidebook on becoming a more versatile learner and co-authored a Center report on success in international assignments. She and her colleagues have developed an instrument designed to assess learning versatility. Her doctorate is in industrial psychology from the University of South Florida in Tampa.*

CHAPTER EIGHTEEN

What We Know About Adult Learning

Ron Zemke
President, Performance Research Associates, Inc.

Susan Zemke
Senior Consultant, Linkage, Inc.

A dult learners are not simply large children. The conditions that motivate and inspire them to engage in learning something new are sharply detailed and pragmatic. Although motivated adults can learn under many circumstances, self-direction, activate participation, and clear progress toward self-selected goals greatly facilitate the process.

ADULT LEARNING

Learning is as natural to human beings as breathing, eating, sleeping, running, jumping, playing, and procreating. And as far as anyone can tell, we maintain that natural capacity as long as any of the others.

For the last thirty plus years, there has been an evolving school of thought or philosophy that adult learners—as opposed to children, adolescents, college sophomores, and lab rats—are a unique and special subgroup in need of its own study, theory, and set of educational practices.

Adult learning stopped being an academic topic in 1973 with the publication of Malcolm Knowles' highly readable, mass appeal book, *The Adult Learner: A Neglected Species*. Knowles and his book were an instant hit with adult educators and trainers. Knowles' contentions and theorization were based on four assumptions:

1. Adults both desire and enact a tendency toward self-directedness as they mature, although they may be dependent in certain situations.

2. Adults' experiences are a rich resource for learning. Adults learn more effectively through experiential techniques of education, such as discussion or problem solving.

3. Adults are aware of specific learning needs generated by real-life tasks or problems. Adult education programs, therefore, should be organized around life application categories and sequenced according to learners' readiness to learn.

4. Adults are competency-based learners in that they wish to apply newly acquired skills or knowledge to their immediate circumstances. Adults are, therefore, "performance centered" in their orientation to learning.

We have twice before visited the vast literature that is adult learning theory and research, looking for the most important nuggets for a working trainer of adults to bear in mind when designing, developing, and delivering training (Zemke & Zemke, 1995, 1981). As in our previous synthesis, we divide what we garnered from our most recent scan into three basic categories:

- Adults' motivation to learn;
- Curriculum design for adults; and
- Adults in the classroom.

MOTIVATION TO LEARN

Adults can be ordered into a classroom and prodded into seats, but they cannot be forced to learn. On the other hand, adults who see a need or have a desire to know something new are quite resourceful—witness the enrollment of gainfully employed adults in continuing education programs at community colleges, vo-techs, and universities across the world, not to mention the success of proprietary self-development seminars, sports skills camps, and self-funding adult study groups in virtually every industrial and post-industrial country. Adults seek out and demand learning experiences—when the conditions are right.

Conditions

Timing Is Important. Several longitudinal studies in corporations have demonstrated that newly promoted supervisors and managers need to receive training as nearly concurrent with promotions and changes in responsibility as possible. The longer such training is delayed, the less impact it appears to have on job performance.

Information technology trainers are beginning to report a similar phenomenon. Training a work group on a new software package or upgraded hardware configuration loses its impact unless the equipment or software is ready to install. The longer the group has to wait for the new equipment or software, the less impact the training has on effective use. There is, it appears, a time and a tide for adults to learn—and a time after which they cannot be enticed to participate with a chateaubriand and a baseball bat.

Adult Learning Is Largely Problem Centered. It has been argued that there are people who learn for the sake of learning. Hobbyists go to conventions and class, retirees take golf and tennis lessons and join book clubs, none of which is job- or "problem-" related. But more often than not, adults seek out learning experiences in order to cope with life change events. Marriage, divorce, a new job, a promotion, being fired, retiring, losing a loved one, and planning a vacation are examples of life change events that bring the need to learn something new to the minds of many.

The learning experiences these adults seek out, and respond best to, are those most directly related to the life change events that triggered their seeking. If 80 percent of the change being experienced is job-related, it is important that the learner perceive the learning event as primarily work-related or job-focused. Adults are generally willing to engage in learning experiences before, after, or even during the actual life-change event. Once convinced that the change is a certainty, adults will engage in any learning that promises to help them cope with the transition, including seminars on coping with change.

Personal Growth or Gain Is Often a Second-Level Motivation That Can Be Appealed To. Although immediate utility is most often the motivation behind adult learning efforts, it need not be the only motivation. There is, for instance, some evidence that job skills training is more readily engaged in by adults, when it is seen as applicable to life skills. Increasing or maintaining one's sense of self-esteem and pleasure are strong secondary motivators for engaging in learning experiences. Having a new skill or extending and enriching current knowledge can be both, depending on the individual's personal perceptions.

Motivation to Learn Can Be Increased. While the aphorism, "The best motivation is self-motivation" is generally true, there is some evidence that adult learners who are with you in body only can be led into participation and learning. If you can stimulate curiosity about the subject matter, demonstrate early on that the learning will in some way be immediately useful and that the risk is low, some of the uncaring and poorly motivated can be converted. Sometimes something as simple as an exploration of positive and negative expectations can clear the air and gain participation.

CURRICULUM DESIGN

Adults, when faced with a classroom and thirty chairs facing forward, know exactly how to act—like bored twelve-year olds. Twelve to eighteen years of pedagogic conditioning can do that to you. The warning is an important one for the designer of adult learning experiences. If you begin your design assuming that thirty adults seated in chairs facing forward is the optimum learning environment and idiom, don't be surprised if what you end up with is bored compliance. There are alternatives.

Adults Are Capable of Designing and Managing Their Own Learning

Adults, according to Knowles and educational researcher Allen Tough (1979), are perfectly capable of acquiring skills, knowledge, and self-insight through educational experiences of their own design and conduct. In the 1970s, Tough found, much to the surprise of most adult learning experts, that adults typically spend five hundred or more hours a year engaged in five "learning projects" of their own design. Although subsequent research has taken issue with Tough's numbers—one highly regarded study put the figures closer to three learning projects and 150 hours a year—the concept of adults as self-directed learners, capable of mastering new skills and knowledge without the help of an instructor, is well accepted today.

Knowles adds one important caveat to this self-directed learning idiom. Self-direction is only appropriate when the learner has some basic level of experience with the content. "Pedagogical methods are appropriate in those cases in which the adult is indeed a dependent learner," he said, adding, "for example, the person may have no experience with a personal computer. The andragogical teacher will have to provide didactic instruction up to the point where the learner has acquired enough information and skill to be able to direct his or her own learning" (personal communication, March 2, 1995).

Adults Can Learn from One Another

Tough's research into self-directed learning found that an adult's learning project was hardly a solitary affair. Self-directed learners tend to be very eclectic in their media/method choices. While adults prefer self-directed learning experiences seven to one over group learning experiences lead by a professional educator, they will attend lectures and short seminars *if* these seem to be the shortest route to their destination. The adult learner is a very efficiency minded individual. Tough suggests that the typical adult learner asks, "What is the cheapest, easiest, fastest way for me to learn to learn to do *that*?" and then proceeds independently along this self-determined route. On average, the self-directed adult enlists 10.6 other people in his or her learning project (Tough, 1979).

Hint: Give them a chance to learn from each other in your designs.

The Learning Experience Should Be Problem Centered

Working adult learners tend to be less interested in, and enthralled by, survey courses than are full-time, professional students. They tend to prefer single-concept, single-theory courses that focus heavily on the application of the concept to relevant problems. This tendency increases with age. In addition, the learning experience should acknowledge, respect, and be relevant to the learner's personal goals for the program.

Pre-Program Assessment Is Important

It is almost unconscionable today to consider designing a program that doesn't take into account the entry-level knowledge and understanding of the participants. This is especially true of same-company, same-department groups. For example, to begin a team-building experience or diversity seminar *without* an assessment of where individuals stand on critical issues, or information on the state of relationships, or the goals of local management for the effort clearly defined is to brook inefficiency and foggy focus bordering on malpractice.

The Learning Design Should Promote Information Integration

Adults need to be able to integrate new ideas with what they already know if they are going to keep—and use—the new information. Information that conflicts sharply with what is already held to be true, and thus forces a re-evaluation of the old material, is integrated more slowly. Information that has little "conceptual overlap" with what is already known is acquired slowly. Fast-paced, complex, or unusual learning tasks interfere with the learning of the concepts or data they are intended to teach or illustrate, when the new is too "foreign" to participants.

Dr. K. Patricia Cross, author of *Adults as Learners* (1981), outlines a four-step summary of design criteria for maximum information integration:

1. The presentation of new information should be meaningful, and it should include aids that help the learner organize it and relate it to previously stored information.

2. It should be presented at a pace that permits mastery.

3. Presentation of one idea at a time and minimization of competing intellectual demands should aid comprehension.

4. Frequent summarization should facilitate retention and recall.

Exercises and Cases Should Have Fidelity

Adults will tolerate, but are not enthusiastic about, farfetched cases and artificial exercises. They prefer activities that are realistic and involving, that stimulate thinking, and that have some—but not too much—challenge. There are, it seems, fine—but clear—lines between exercises and games adults find entertaining and/or useful and those they find just plain "silly." While adults prefer "active" to "passive" learning (they like relevant exercises, cases, games, and simulations), there needs to be a reflective element attached to the activity if learning is to occur. While there is no evaluative data to speak of, there is great enthusiasm in the literature for team-based, computer interactive simulations and games, such as high fidelity (realistic) learning experiences.

Feedback and Recognition Should Be Planned

Adults need to know what they are trying to accomplish and how they are doing. Program design should include time for exploration of participants' goals and expectations—and clear acknowledgment of those that will not be met—and ground rules regarding mutual and separate responsibilities for the learning experience. Adults tend to take errors personally and are more likely to let them affect self-esteem. Therefore, they tend to apply tried-and-true solutions and take fewer risks. There is even evidence that adults will misinterpret feedback and "mistake" errors for positive confirmation. It is important that feedback opportunities be available. If peers are going to be asked to give feedback, time should be spent modeling the feedback process. Modeling feedback, like the modeling of most interpersonal skills, is more effective than giving didactic instruction about feedback.

ADULTS IN THE CLASSROOM

Prior to the modern era of adult learning theory, most of the work in adult education focused on teacher behavior. So it is ironic that we still know so little about effective classroom facilitation technique. Most of what is passed off as "proven" is simply a compost of tricks and tips, philosophy and theory passed on from master performers to their acolytes. Still and all, it is possible to piece together commonalties from all this advice, and suggest some useful guiding principles.

Create a Safe/Comfortable Environment

If you've ever walked into a dark motel function room the morning after a late night party and wondered how in the heck you are going to turn the mess into a learning environment, you know the importance of setting. Think of the seminar room as your "learning living room" and encourage participants to do the same. But to make that imagery into reality, the physical and psychological environment must be carefully managed. The physical room must be conducive to learning. Light, sound, heat and cold, supplies, and amenities must be conducive to thought, focus, and serious discourse. The psychological environment must be under control as well. Participants need the mix of known and unknown, active and passive, serious and whimsical that keeps them involved at an optimum level.

Facilitation Is More Effective than Lecture

There are times when straight lecture is effective: When the trainees have zero grounding in the subject matter, when rules and regulations have to be passed along, and when matters of finance, fact, and law are being discussed. But by and large, facilitation (engaging the learner in objective setting for the learning and tapping the learner's experience and opinions to create important parts of the content) and assisting participants in coming to conclusions through their own arguments tends to work better.

Activity Promotes Understanding and Retention

In some ways, it's as simple as recognizing that most adults aren't used to sitting passively for long stretches. Without activity, they turn into mushrooms before your eyes. But there is more to it than that. Despite—and frequently because of—the presence of an instructor/authority figure, many participants are reluctant to share ideas, feelings, confusions, annoyances—whatever—with the group. Using small, breakout group techniques increases the chance that the reticent will contribute and collaborate.

IN THE END . . .

Helping adults acquire new skills and knowledge is at the same time the most exhilarating and irritating, challenging and frustrating way to make a living we can think of. It takes patience—and forbearance, flexibility, and humor—and a strong belief that what you are doing matters. And if we keep prying and prodding, testing and trying, we might yet turn this art form into a science of sorts.

References

Cross, K.P. (1981). *Adults as learners: Increasing participation and facilitating learning.* San Francisco: Jossey-Bass.

Knowles, M.S. (1984). *The adult learner: A neglected species* (3rd ed.). Houston: Gulf.

Tough, A. (1979). *The adult's learning projects: A fresh approach to theory and practice in adult learning* (2nd ed.). Austin, TX: Learning Concepts.

Zemke, R., & Zemke, S. (1981, June). 30 things we know for sure about adult learning. *Training*, 45–52.

Zemke, R., & Zemke, S. (1995, June). Adult learning: What do we know for sure? *Training*, 31–39.

Recommended Reading

Brookfield, S.D. (1986). *Understanding and facilitating adult learning.* San Francisco: Jossey-Bass.

Knowles, M.S. (1980). *The modern practice of adult education: From pedagogy to andragogy* (2nd ed.). New York: Cambridge Books.

Merriam, S.B. (1993, Spring). An update on adult learning theory. *New Directions for Adult and Continuing Education, 57.* San Francisco: Jossey-Bass.

Zemke, R., & Gunkler, J. (1985, April). 28 techniques for transforming training into performance. *Training*, 48–63.

About the Authors

Ron Zemke is president of Minneapolis-based Performance Research Associates, Inc., a consulting firm specializing in service quality audits, management and front-line service training, and needs assessment, as well as senior editor of Training *magazine. Zemke is the co-author of the 1985 best seller,* Service America!— *a book credited with starting the service quality revolution. He is also the co-author of the best-selling* Knock Your Socks Off Service *book series, as well as the best-selling* Generations at Work *(AMACOM 2000).*

Susan Zemke is a senior consultant for the Central Region of Linkage Incorporated, a Lexington, MA, based consulting firm. She has over twenty years of experience in a variety of human resource positions, including college relations, staffing, compensation, and training and development. Her clients include Ralston Purina, DaimlerChrysler, The Principal Financial Group, and State Farm Insurance.

CHAPTER NINETEEN

Designing Effective Training Programs

Karen Lawson, Ed.D.
President, Lawson Consulting Group

A successful training program is based on a systematic approach to designing effective instruction that benefits both the employees and the organization. The ongoing and cyclical process consists of five parts: Needs assessment, design, development, delivery, and evaluation. This chapter presents an overview of the training design process. It introduces the reader to the training components or the topics within the context of the "systems" approach to training. It also addresses how the training program fits together and how training outcomes are linked to organizational needs and goals.

INTRODUCTION

Training is a process, not an event. This simple, yet fundamental concept should be the driving force in the design and development of all training programs. A successful training program is based on a systematic approach to designing effective instruction with high impact for both the participants and the organization.

ASSESSING NEEDS

The first phase of effective training design is assessing needs. An accurate needs assessment is the core of any training program. It provides the basis for program development and establishes the criteria for measuring the success of the program after its completion.

Needs assessors are much like physicians who ask a series of questions and order a battery of medical tests to uncover and treat the causes rather than the symptoms of an ailment. Needs assessment is the process of determining the cause, extent, and appropriate cure for organizational ills. The process addresses the organizational context and combines organizational analysis, data gathering, and interviewing techniques to identify and shrink the gap between desired and actual knowledge, skills, and performance. It is a careful study of the organizational context, the job itself, and the knowledge, skills, and abilities of the job incumbents.

Simply put, the process identifies both the desired performance and the current performance. The difference, the gap between the actual and desired levels of performance, becomes the training need and provides the basis for training design. Correct problem identification (cause) is the key to developing and implementing corrective measures (cure). Reasons for conducting a needs assessment are as follows:

- To determine whether training is needed;
- To determine causes of poor performance;
- To determine content and scope of training;
- To determine desired training outcomes;
- To provide a basis of measurement; and
- To gain management support.

The needs assessment process can be as detailed and involved as needed or desired. Many factors must be taken into consideration, including time, money, number of people involved, and resources available, to name a few. Table 19.1 (Lawson, 1998) offers a comparison between an in-depth and a mini needs assessment.

Regardless of the depth of the assessment, the process is the same. Exhibit 19.1 (Lawson, 1998) provides an overview of the needs-assessment process.

WRITING INSTRUCTIONAL OBJECTIVES

After the needs assessment has been completed and the data gathered, analyzed, and reported to the appropriate people, the next phase involves the overall design of the training program. And the first step in the design process is to write learning objectives.

Table 19.1. In-Depth vs. Mini Needs Assessment

	In Depth	Mini
Type of Information	Quantitative	Qualitative
Methods	Multi-tiered approach Surveys Observation Interviews Focus groups Document reviews	Interviews Focus groups
Scope	Widespread organizational involvement Broad-ranging objectives	Fewer people involved Short-term focus
Length	Several months to a year	Few days to a week
Cost	Expensive	Inexpensive
Focus	Linked to defined outputs Long-term	Immediate, quick results
Exposure/Visibility	High profile and risk	Lower risk

Source: Lawson, 1998, p. 4.

Learning objectives or outcomes state what the learner will be able to do at the end of the training program or at the end of a phase of training. They describe the planned outcome of the training rather than the training process—results rather than procedure.

Why Set Objectives?

Objectives serve as a type of contract. If participants know the program or session objectives from the beginning, they will know what they will be learning. Objectives give participants a sense of direction. They know what to expect from you and what you expect from them.

Objectives serve as the basis for the design and development of the program, that is, the instructional plan. They help the trainer focus clearly on the desired outcomes and determine what the participants need to know and do in order to meet those objectives. The concept of designing a training program is analogous to planning a trip: The objectives are the destination and the instructional

Exhibit 19.1. Needs Assessment Process

Step One: Identify Problem or Need

- Determine organizational context
- Perform gap analysis
- Set objectives

Step Two: Determine Needs Analysis Design

- Establish method-selection criteria
- Assess advantages and disadvantages of methods

Step Three: Collect Data

- Conduct interviews
- Administer questionnaires
- Administer surveys
- Review documents
- Observe people at work

Step Four: Analyze Data

- Conduct qualitative analysis
- Conduct quantitative analysis
- Determine solutions/recommendations

Step Five: Provide Feedback

- Write report
- Make an oral presentation
- Determine next step

Source: Lawson, 1998, p. 7.

plan is the itinerary. In other words, you first decide where you want to go (objectives) and then decide how you are going to get there—how long the trip will take and what means of transportation you will use (methods and materials).

Objectives should be written from the participant's point of view, not the trainer's. The emphasis should not be on what you want to cover but on what you want the participant to value, understand, or do with the subject, information, or skills after the training program is over.

Objectives are used to measure success. Because they describe what the participant will be able to do at the end of the training, the objectives automatically become the standard against which success is measured.

Finally, objectives are a sales tool. You develop the program objectives based on the needs assessment you conducted earlier. You then can use these objectives to tell the participants' managers exactly what your training will do for their employees. These managers will have a much better understanding of what the training will and won't do.

Types of Objectives

Objectives fall into three categories of skill development: attitude, skill, and knowledge.

Attitude Development. Objectives that address attitude development deal with attitudes, values, or feelings. These objectives are appropriate when you want to change people's attitudes or increase their awareness of certain issues or ideas.

Skill Development. Objectives for skill development deal with behavior. These are much easier to identify and to determine whether they have been met. They focus on a person being able to perform a task or procedure.

Knowledge Development. Knowledge development objectives have to do with content or cognitive learning. They relate to the ability to demonstrate acquired knowledge, to comprehend information, and to analyze concepts.

Essential Characteristics of Objectives

For objectives to be useful, they must meet certain criteria:

- *Be objective and measurable.* Your objectives should describe exactly what the participant will be able to do at the end of the training session, that is, the objective will specify the kind of behavior (if possible) that will be accepted as evidence that the participant has achieved the objective.
- *Be results-oriented, clearly worded, and specific.* Learning outcomes should be written as action-oriented statements outlining specific activities and measurement of performance, including the minimum level of acceptable performance.
- *Be written from participant's perspective.* Objectives must specify what the participants will be able to do, rather than describe the trainer's activities or the experience of the session.
- *Describe the participants' behavior.* Effective objectives describe what the participants must do to demonstrate their understanding, knowledge, or skill.

Components of an Objective

Writing objectives is not an easy task. The first challenge is to think of objectives from the participant's viewpoint, and the second challenge is to write them as performance outcomes. The easiest way to write an objective is to start by examining its three components: performance, conditions, and criteria.

Performance. Ideally, the objective should describe behavior that can be observed, that is, what the participant will be able to do as a result of the training. This is not always possible, particularly when dealing with attitude objectives. When the objective is not observable, you will have to specify the consequences of the learned behavior that can be accepted as evidence of achievement. For example, for a diversity training program, an objective might be to "increase the participant's awareness of and sensitivity to workplace diversity issues."

The objective must use specific action verbs that are not subject to various interpretations. Words such as *understand, know,* and *learn,* for example, are not acceptable. You cannot observe those behaviors. Table 19.2 (Lawson, 1998) offers a few action verbs for each of the desired learning outcomes.

Conditions. The objective should explain the circumstances under which the participant will be performing the activity, as well as describe the equipment, supplies, and job aids that may or may not be used on the job. Furthermore, the work setting and any other pertinent information that is used to direct the action should be included in the objective.

Criteria. Finally, the objective specifies the level or degree of proficiency necessary to perform the task or job successfully. In other words, it indicates the quality of the performance required in achieving the objective. Thus, information in the criteria is used to evaluate acceptable performance. The objective may involve such things as speed, time constraints, maximum number of mistakes permitted, productivity level, or degree of excellence. Keep in mind, however, that not all standards can be quantified and it may be necessary to describe the criteria in terms of reactions, viewpoints, and principles.

WRITING AN INSTRUCTIONAL PLAN

After you have written your learning outcomes or objectives, the third phase in the design process is to develop the instructional plan. As smart trainers know, for training to be effective, participants must be actively involved in the learning process. To that end, the training design should reflect an active, experiential approach, allowing participants to discover ideas, principles, and concepts through

Table 19.2. Action Verbs to Describe Learning Objectives

Learning Type	Related Action Verbs	
Attitude Development	adjust	decide
	analyze	evaluate
	assess	pick
	choose	select
	criticize	
Skill Development	assemble	prepare
	compute	process
	construct	prove
	copy	record
	count	repair
	demonstrate	solve
	design	speak
	develop	transcribe
	draw	type
	measure	write
	operate	
Knowledge Development	cite	identify
	compare	list
	contrast	name
	define	quote
	describe	recite
	detect	recognize
	differentiate	relate
	distinguish	repeat
	enumerate	reproduce
	explain	

Source: Lawson, 1998, p. 68.

a series of well-planned and well-executed structured experiences. Because the adult, in particular, learns by doing and not by being told, the design and development process includes very few didactic elements.

An instructional plan identifies what will be accomplished (learning outcomes), what will be said or presented (content), and how the content will be communicated (methods and media). The content flows naturally from the learning outcomes or objectives. One of the biggest challenges trainers face is determining how much content to include. We have a tendency to want to include everything we know about a topic, resulting in an "information dump" on the participants. This approach is not only boring, but ineffective. Learn to distinguish between "need-to-know" versus "nice-to-know" information. Ask yourself, "What do the participants really *need* to know in order to do their jobs, improve their performance, and so forth?"

Selecting, Designing, and Developing Active Training Methods

After you have decided on the content and the sequence of its delivery, the next step is to determine *how* you are going to communicate the material. In other words, you will decide what methods and materials you are going to use. You then will develop or select specific activities or structured experiences and specific training aids. These methods may include the use of assessment instruments; activities such as role plays, case studies, and simulations; and a host of cooperative learning or active learning techniques. Table 19.3 (Lawson, 1998) provides an overview of various instructional methods, their purpose, and when to use them.

Your selection of methods and materials should reflect adult learning principles and consideration of different learning styles. Based on what we know about adult learning, learning styles, and the characteristics of today's learner, active training is the most effective means of delivering training. Research shows that people understand concepts better, retain information longer, and are more likely to apply the learning when they are actively involved in the learning process.

CREATING A POSITIVE LEARNING ENVIRONMENT

The success or failure of a training session is often determined long before the first participant sets foot in the training room. The trainer's job is to create and maintain an environment conducive to learning and to create opportunities for participants to experience personal growth, a sense of achievement and accomplishment, and recognition and rewards. This consideration of a positive learning environment becomes an integral part of the design process.

It is important that participants come to the training session with a positive mindset. Far too often, trainers find themselves facing participants who do not want to be there or don't even know why they are there. Although it's the manager's job to prepare the participant for the training program, rarely does this happen. This means that you are going to have to do what you can to involve the participants before the training session. You can send a letter and pre-session questionnaire to the participants, welcoming them to the session, providing an outline of the session and logistical information, and explaining anything that they should do prior to the session, such as reading assignments, self-assessment instruments, or the questionnaire.

Table 19.3. Instructional Methods—When to Use

Method	Purpose	When to Use
Role Playing	Help participants practice skills used in interactions	To practice newly acquired skill To experience what a particular situation feels like To provide feedback to participants about their behavior
Games	Provides nonthreatening way to present or review course material	To help grasp total program content To present dry material in an interesting way To add a competitive element to the session
Simulations	Recreates a process, event, or set of circumstances, usually complex, so that participants can experience and manipulate the situation without risk and then analyze what happened	To integrate and apply a complex set of skills To elicit participants' natural tendencies and provide feedback on those tendencies To provide a realistic, job-related experience
Observation	Certain participants act out or demonstrate behaviors, tasks, or situations while others observe and give feedback	To show group how to perform procedure or apply a skill or behavior To increase participants' observation, critiquing, and feedback skills To demonstrate behavior modeling
Instruments	Provide feedback; self-assessment	To identify areas for improvement To establish a baseline for future growth
Mental Imagery	Helps participants increase understanding, gain insight	To address affective learning To stimulate thinking, imagination To replace role playing
Writing Tasks	Help participants reflect on their understanding of concepts, information, ideas	To provide for individual input

Lecturette	Conveys information when interaction or discussion is not desired or is not possible	To convey information quickly within short time period To communicate same information to large numbers of people To provide basic information to a group that is not knowledgeable
Small Group Discussions	Offers opportunity for participants to express opinions, share ideas, solve problems, interact with others	To generate ideas To find out what participants think about a particular subject To increase level of participation To encourage group interaction and build group cohesiveness
Case Study	Allows participants to discover certain learning points themselves	To apply new knowledge to a specific situation To practice problem-solving skills
Task Exercise or Activity	Allows participants to work with the content in small groups	To test participants' understanding of concept or process To promote group collaboration To increase participants' confidence in their ability to apply learning on the job

Source: Lawson, 1998, pp. 91–94.

When designing and developing a training program, pay particular attention to the opening activities. The opening activities are critical to setting the proper positive learning environment. Meaningful, well-planned, and relevant opening activities: (1) Help create a safe learning environment; (2) grab participants' attention and stimulate their thinking; (3) involve them in the learning process from the start; and (4) introduce them to the content.

Experiential and Active Training Activities

It's not enough just to incorporate activities into the training program. How you execute and facilitate the activities often makes the difference between an excellent program and one that is simply satisfactory. Your ability to create a positive and dynamic learning environment relies heavily on your use of active training techniques.

Active training is based on cooperative learning theory and techniques. Cooperative learning is defined as the instructional use of small groups so that students work together to maximize their own and each other's learning (Johnson, Johnson, & Smith, 1991). This means that, for most of the activities, participants will be working in small groups or pairs.

Using Visual Aids

Visual aids play an important part in helping participants learn and retain information; however, they should never take the place of training. The key word here is *aid*. So-called training sessions that consist of a series of PowerPoint® or other computer-generated slides are presentations, not training. True training is an active process on the part of the participants, not the trainer. Here are some specific reasons to use visual aids:

- To capture attention;
- To reinforce points;
- To organize information;
- To promote understanding;
- To support the spoken message; and
- To emphasize key points.

Regardless of which type of visual aid you choose (transparencies, slides, flip charts, etc.), keep in mind the following guidelines:

- Limit their use;
- Keep the visual simple;
- Make it easy to read;

- Use color; and
- Use it, then lose it.

Table 19.4 (Lawson, 1998) provides a summary of the advantages and disadvantages of various visual aids.

LINKING EVALUATION TO THE NEEDS ASSESSMENT

As mentioned at the beginning, training is a process, one that is ongoing and cyclical. This means that the process does not end when the last participant leaves the training room. The process must include evaluation techniques linked to the needs assessment conducted in Phase 1. You must develop evaluation techniques that measure, at a minimum, participant reaction (level 1), participant learning (level 2), and transfer of learning (level 3). To evaluate a training program effectively, you will need to compare results (outcomes, performance) with your preset success criteria to determine the value of the program and how it ties into the organization's goals. Your ability to design an effective training program that incorporates all phases of the instructional design process will result in both tangible and intangible positive results for the participants, the organization, and you, the trainer.

Table 19.4. Using Visual Aids

Aid	Advantages	Disadvantages	When to Use
Chalkboards	Spontaneous Easy to use Inexpensive Erasable Attention getter Breaks lecture monotony	Slow Temporary Poor readability Limited to chalk Turn back to audience Association with school days Messy	Small, informal meetings Spontaneous idea development Brainstorming sessions
Flip Charts	Spontaneous Advance preparation Better contrast Permanent Easy to use Portable Allows you to present ideas in sequence Inexpensive Colorful (depending on range of colors in your set of markers) Dependable	Bulky Limited to writing No flexibility in size or sequence Expensive if prepared professionally Tendency for trainer to write small to get all ideas on one page Paper tears easily	Small groups Lectures with spontaneous highlighting Brainstorming Lists, procedural steps
35 mm Slide	High quality Photographic detail Very portable Easy to operate Can accommodate any size group Voice can be integrated With remote control, trainer can move around	Dark room Usually expensive Can appear "canned" Slides become focal point, not speaker Does not show motion Long sequences encourage mental absenteeism	Repetitive programs where photographic detail and professional look is important Training programs or product displays with sound and music added

	Advantages	Disadvantages	Best Used For
Overhead Projector	Fast, simple preparation of transparencies (any copier) Lights on Speaker faces audience Any size group Spontaneous or advance preparation Very flexible Optional quality Inexpensive Exact illustrations can be portrayed Easily updated	Projector can block view unless positioned carefully Less portable than 35 mm Transparency preparation so simple that people tend to use items that are too "busy" Tendency to overuse Focus on overhead projectors sometimes difficult to control	Financial & technical presentations Group sales presentations Seminars, workshops where speaker wants to maintain rapport
Videos	Professional Good discussion generator Immediate feedback Any size group Effective for demonstrating how *not* to do something Most effective for learner-centered training Both sight and hearing are utilized in learning "Expert" on tape can reinforce what the trainer has been saying	Dark room Expensive Used as substitute for lesson or presentation	Supplement to a training program Visual feedback of trainee performance Create mood or feeling as prelude to speaker's presentation

Source: Lawson, 1998, pp. 162–163.

References

Johnson, D.W., Johnson, R.T., & Smith, K.A. (1991). *Cooperative learning: Increasing college faculty instructional productivity* (ASHE-ERIC Higher Education Report No. 4). Washington, DC: The George Washington University, School of Education and Human Development.

Lawson, K. (1998). *The trainer's handbook.* San Francisco: Jossey-Bass/Pfeiffer.

Recommended Reading

Kirkpatrick, D. (1994). *Evaluating training programs: The four levels.* San Francisco: Berrett-Koehler.

Piskurich, G.M., Beckschi, P., & Hall, B. (Eds.). (2000). *The ASTD handbook of training design and delivery.* New York: McGraw-Hill.

Silberman, M. (1998). *Active training* (2nd ed.). San Francisco: Jossey-Bass/Pfeiffer.

Silberman, M., & Lawson, K. (1995). *101 ways to make training active.* San Francisco: Jossey-Bass/Pfeiffer.

Sugar, S. (1998). *Games that teach: Experiential activities for reinforcing training.* San Francisco: Jossey-Bass/Pfeiffer.

About the Author

Karen Lawson is an international consultant, speaker, and author of several books on management development and training. As founder and president of Lawson Consulting Group, Inc., she has built a successful consulting firm specializing in organization and management development. She has extensive consulting and workshop experience in the areas of management, executive development, team development, and communication across a wide range of industries, including financial services, pharmaceutical, chemical, petroleum, health care, and government.

In her consulting work with Fortune 500 companies as well as small businesses, Lawson uses her experience and knowledge of human relations to help leaders at all levels make a difference in their organizations. She has held many key leadership positions in professional organizations, including ASTD (formerly, American Society for Training and Development) and the National Speakers Association (NSA). She also has received numerous professional awards for her contributions to the training profession. She has presented at many regional and national professional conferences and is on the adjunct faculty of several colleges and universities. Lawson holds a doctorate in adult and organizational development from Temple University.

CHAPTER TWENTY

What I've Learned:
The Picture is Bigger than You Think!

Bob Pike, CSP, CPAE
Chairman and CEO, The Bob Pike Group

It is critically important to recognize that, when there are performance problems, training is not always the answer. However, when we do determine that training is a part of the solution, we need to keep in mind that training is a *process,* not an event. To maximize training's results, we need three people to be committed to the process: the manager, the participant, and the trainer. A CORE (close, opening, review, energize) approach to training events is presented in this chapter. Recognizing that adults need to be actively involved in the learning process, suggestions are made for ways in which trainers can engage participants.

INTRODUCTION

Years ago training was an event. Someone asked you to do it, you did. We were what Peter Block would call "a pair of hands." Then some of us got smart (or at least smarter)! We didn't wait to be asked. We developed things and put them in a catalog. We were proactive.

Neither of these is the smartest way to go.

One of the biggest things I've learned is that when performance is the problem, training isn't necessarily the solution. There could be a variety of factors impacting performance, including systems problems (your equipment doesn't work or isn't available), policy or procedure problems (you are actually punished for performance), recruiting problems (you don't set the right entry standards and hire people who cannot do the job), placement problems (you have good people, but not in the jobs that fit their natural styles, strengths, talents, or abilities), or coaching problems (you don't need training—just help with a little piece of what you do that's slowing everything else down).

However, training may be part of the performance solution. I like to ask three questions to see whether this is true. I call it the AWA formula:

1. Is the person ABLE to do the job?
2. Is the person WILLING to do the job?
3. Is the person ALLOWED to do the job?

If the answer to number one is no, then training may be part of the solution. But no amount of training is going to improve performance if there is no motivation on the employee's part (number 2) or their boss doesn't let the person apply what is already known (number 3).

VIEWING TRAINING AS A PROCESS

Another thing I've learned is that training is a process; it's not an event. The process begins long before the training is ever delivered and doesn't end until we see the knowledge and skills taught in the training being used on the job. This means that a number of people have a significant part to play in seeing to it that the training's purpose is accomplished.

The purpose of training is to get results on the job. In order to maximize those results, we need three people to be committed to the process: The manager who sends the person, the participant himself or herself, and the trainer who is doing the assessment, design, delivery, and follow-up.

The manager plays a significant role in all of this. The manager can do more to create a motivational environment for the employee than the trainer ever can. Just a few of the things (of more than fifty) we've learned to ask managers to do in order to improve the results we get from training are

1. Actively participate in the needs assessment process so that we can accurately identify performance gaps and needs for improvement that really are keeping the manager's team and team members from getting the results the manager would like to see.

2. Meet with participants before they attend training and set mutual goals and expectations for the course. This includes asking the participant to

develop an action plan to be implemented after the formal training with the manager's support.

3. Minimize the need for the participant to be called out of training while the formal training process is going on.

4. Meet with the participant after the formal training is over to approve his or her action plan.

5. Ensure that the participant has the chance to use the skills and apply the knowledge on the job after the training is over.

TRAINING DESIGN AND DELIVERY

Another thing I've learned is that today we literally have shorter attention spans because of media. For that reason, we apply the 90/20/8 rule to all of our training design and delivery. Adults can listen with understanding for ninety minutes. They can listen with retention for only twenty minutes. We need to change the pace every eight minutes.

Commercial television in the United States doesn't go more than eight minutes without a commercial break. The average high school graduate has watched 19,000 hours of television, yet has been in class only 14,000 hours. Students are almost programmed to want a mental break every eight minutes. We chunk our content into twenty-minute modules—and then involve the participants in some way every eight minutes. It could be a question they answer with a partner or a small group. It could be a sixty-second activity the group does. It could be adding to their action idea list. It could be writing something on a Post-it® Note and adding it to a wall chart that we're building. All of these increase attention and retention.

CORE Approach

We also have to get to the CORE (close, opening, review, and energize) of our training. In other words, every training needs a strong *close,* but most trainers don't close—they just run out of time. Every training needs a strong *opening.* Yet often, trainers do nothing to break preoccupation and facilitate networking—they just leap right into the content. You can't teach until people are ready to learn.

We also need to *review* and revisit content. But people are turned off with the word review—so we need to review without them even being aware that we are reviewing. Things as simple as asking people in pairs to come up with two questions class members should be able to answer if they understand the content are examples of review without calling it review. The questions could then be used in a game show format as another opportunity to revisit the content.

The E in CORE stands for *energize.* Everyone has natural cycles of alertness and those times when their ability to concentrate lags. By using quick energizing activities that stimulate people physically as well as mentally, we can help keep the entire class's energy level up.

Creative Training Techniques

For more than thirty years I've been applying what I call "Creative Training Techniques" (CTT) to all of the training that I've done. Simply put, CTT is thirty-six alternatives to lecture. These are techniques to help participants discover and "own" the content.

Adults bring experience to training programs. These experiences can be used to accelerate their learning and build their sense of confidence and self-esteem at the same time. We like to be acknowledged for what we know. We do not like being treated as though we are school children with only the teacher having any expertise. (As a matter of fact, we're learning that these techniques work for children, too!) Many of the ideas that I described in the CORE section of this chapter fall under the category of creative training techniques. Many additional techniques can be found on our website: *http://www.creativetrainingtech.com.*

IN SUMMARY

To sum it all up:

1. Training is a process, not an event.
2. The purpose of training is to deliver results.
3. When performance is the problem, training is only one possible solution.
4. Three people play the biggest roles in making sure that training gets results: the participant's manager, the participant, and the trainer.
5. Every program needs the CORE: closers, openers, review techniques, and energizers.
6. In training delivery we need to follow the 90/20/8 rule.
7. Creative Training Techniques are those techniques that allow us to honor the experience that adults bring to training. They include thirty-six alternatives to lecture.

I'm not sure that I'm a smart trainer, but as I've applied these principles over the last thirty years, I've certainly gotten smarter!

Recommended Reading

Arch, D. (1993). *Tricks for trainers* (Vols. I-II). Minneapolis, MN: Resources for Organizations, Inc.

Pike, B., & Arch, D. (1997). *Dealing with difficult participants: 127 practical strategies for minimizing resistance and maximizing results in your presentations.* San Francisco: Jossey-Bass/Pfeiffer.

Pike, R.W. (1994). *Creative training techniques handbook: Tips, tactics, and how-to's for delivering effective training* (2nd ed.). Minneapolis, MN: Lakewood.

Pike, B., & Busse, C. (1998). *101 games for trainers: A collection of the best activities from creative training techniques newsletter.* Amherst, MA: HRD Press.

Silberman, M., & Lawson, K. (1995). *101 ways to make training active.* San Francisco: Jossey-Bass/Pfeiffer.

Solem, L., & Pike, B. (1997). *50 creative training closers.* San Francisco: Jossey-Bass/Pfeiffer.

Ukens, L.L. (2000). *Energize your audience! 75 quick activities that get them started . . . and keep them going.* San Francisco: Jossey-Bass/Pfeiffer.

About the Author

Bob Pike *has developed and implemented training programs for business, industry, government, and the professions since 1969. He is founder and president of Creative Training Techniques International, Inc. He was named a Certified Speaking Professional (CSP) by the National Speakers Association. In August 1999, Pike received his CPAE (Council of Peers Award of Excellence) and was inducted into the Speakers Hall of Fame. He is past national board member of ASTD (formerly American Society for Training and Development) and has been one of the top-ranked presenters at their international conferences.*

Pike is a prolific author, having written or edited over twenty books, seminars, and training videos. He is founding editor of the popular Creative Training Techniques Newsletter *and author of the* Creative Training Techniques Handbook *with over 100,000 in print.*

CHAPTER TWENTY-ONE

Motivation in the Learning Environment

Larry Froman, Ph.D.
*Associate Professor and Director of Graduate Program
in Human Resource Development, Towson University*

Motivation in the learning environment is examined in the context of the changing workplace. Three major themes are discussed: The importance of creating a culture of learning that embraces the core values of employee development, shared learning, and intrinsic motivation; motivational theories and their relevance for training and development practitioners; and workforce diversity and globalization and their implications for the design of effective learning environments. Key issues discussed in this section concern the importance of recognizing and responding to individual differences in motivational patterns (that one size does not fit all in designing employee training programs). The chapter concludes with a discussion of how human resources in general, and training in particular, can best support the rapid pace of business globalization. Key themes of the new economy—flexibility, learning, and change—are discussed through the perspective of human resource development.

INTRODUCTION

Significant changes in the world of work have had important implications for the design and implementation of training programs. Two key forces of change are workforce diversity and globalization (Thayer, 1997). Both forces of change require a fundamental shift in mindset and orientation from *training to learning*. Thus, it is of substantive significance that the title of this chapter is "motivation in the learning environment" rather than "motivation in the training environment." Although the two concepts are inextricably linked, the concept of a *learning environment* goes beyond the training event per se and requires analysis and discussion of a broader range of organizational variables that can help trainers and other human resource professionals better understand and respond to the changing realities of their organizations.

This chapter examines various concepts of motivation in the context of a dynamic work environment and how these concepts can be applied to the forces of change impacting on employees and their organizations.

CREATING A CULTURE OF LEARNING

Organizations need to create a "culture of learning," not just an array of discrete training programs designed to help employees become more proficient in their jobs. Such cultures embrace not only the goal of skill development, but also a core set of values and attitudes that inspire and motivate employees and their managers to become *lifelong learners.* Lifelong learners are open to new ideas. They listen carefully and actively solicit opinions and ideas from others. They believe learning can be shared where anyone can learn from anyone. Lifelong learners also take risks; they are willing to push themselves out of comfort zones and engage in an honest assessment of successes and failures (Kotter, 1996).

Lifelong learners have what Kotter (1996) refers to as "a real sense of mission in their lives" and what Senge (1990) calls "personal mastery." Embedded in these concepts is an attitude toward *not only one's job but to life in general.* It means continually clarifying our values; what is really important to us as people first—and as employees of organizations second. To the extent that what motivates us in our personal lives is in alignment (at least to some extent) with what motivates us in our work lives, the opportunities for growth, job satisfaction, and enhanced performance become that much more possible.

The motivational concept most useful here is that of *intrinsic motivation* (Deci & Ryan, 1991). To be intrinsically motivated is to be focused on work that by its very content is felt to be important and meaningful by the individual. A person who is intrinsically motivated feels excited and challenged by his or her work. Moreover, the person feels relatively free from the pressures of externally driven rewards or contingencies. As such, work life is experienced with a greater sense of autonomy and self-regulated behavior. Put simply, work has intrinsic value when the *"why"* question can be answered with clarity and conviction. One example of a "why" question is: "Why do you do the work you do beyond doing it for the paycheck?" Some possible responses might be: "I do it because I find my work to be interesting, exciting, and challenging" or "I feel that I am contributing to society and that I'm making a difference in the lives of people," and so on. The fundamental issue from a motivational perspective is the issue of *control*. The individual employee is self-motivated and is less dependent on the traditional external rewards controlled by management.

From a practical perspective, training and development practitioners should consider the importance of intrinsic motivation as well as the more traditional external rewards and contingencies in assessing an organization's climate. Why might be it useful to assess an organization's climate from a training and development perspective? First, as noted by Wexley and Latham (1991), the environment may affect whether training can produce the intended behavioral impact on job performance. For example, if employees have negative attitudes about their jobs and organization, they are more likely to resist any kind of training given by the company, even if the training itself may be well-designed and effectively delivered. Some excellent programs will be doomed to failure if the employees are generally inclined to view such programs with skepticism, if not outright hostility. Environments such as these, characterized by mistrust, generally are associated with resistance to change. By identifying the problem areas within the organization through climate surveys, training and development practitioners can work with management to address employee concerns and consequently create a work environment more conducive to training objectives.

Cultures of learning provide an organizational context for employees to view training not just as means to some external reward or contingency, but as part of an ongoing process of lifelong learning and finding meaning and satisfaction in one's work.

MOTIVATION, LEARNING, AND CHANGE

As a consequence of the forces of change noted above, organizations are finding themselves in the midst of a revolution in organizing, managing, and developing people that will continue well into the 21st Century (Beer, 1997).

People As a Source of Competitive Advantage

A number of writers have addressed the importance of accessing and sharing knowledge throughout the organization as a foundation for establishing competitive advantage (Herling & Provo, 2000; Torraco, 2000; Ulrich, 1997). To be employed in the creation of value, knowledge must be applied to the organization's business operations. And, as noted by Herling and Provo, "Knowledge that has no value is reduced to mere information" (p. 3). Training and development practitioners, for example, might consider how well their training objectives align with their organization's need to create new markets, anticipate customer needs, and create innovative products. Within organizations that have diverse business units, the training and development function can promote *transfer of learning* and *sharing of best practices* to overcome some of the bureaucratic fragmentation that might stifle innovation and change.

The alignment of training with the organization's strategic objectives can be linked to a related concept—that of *core competencies* (Hamel & Prahalad, 1994). These competencies are critical to the organization's ability to gain competitive advantage in the global marketplace and reflect the organization's strategic view of the particular challenges it expects to confront in the near future and beyond. They represent the total pooling and integration of skill sets throughout the organization in ways that make the organization unique. The core competencies provide strategic advantage by contributing to perceived customer benefits, are difficult to imitate, and can be leveraged to a wide variety of markets (Herling & Provo, 2000).

A third concept related to leveraging human resources for competitive advantages is referred to as *knowledge management* (Torraco, 2000). Knowledge management can be defined in various ways, but the core idea is that it involves creating, capturing, and using knowledge to improve organizational performance. It is frequently associated with documenting and disseminating knowledge through venues such as a company-wide database.

As is the case with all important training and development initiatives, knowledge management is more likely to succeed in cultures of learning—cultures whose assumptions, values, and norms articulate, support, model, and reward learning throughout the organization. Ultimately, effective knowledge management depends on the willingness of people to share their ideas and expertise with others. And this *willingness* (that is, motivation) is strengthened in cultures that nurture trust along with a genuine commitment to the growth and development of the employees who work in the organization. There is a widely held belief among front-line workers, supervisors, and managers alike that the success of each individual can ultimately benefit the entire organization.

Motivation and Performance in Training

The concept of motivation is primarily concerned with what *energizes* human behavior, what directs such behavior, and how this behavior is sustained over time (Steers & Porter, 1991). Each of these components has relevance to our understanding of why people in organizations might differ from one another in their motivation to learn and participate in training programs. First, people have different internal drives or needs; arousal and energy levels vary. Second, individuals differ in their goal orientations; energy will be directed in different ways. Third, individuals differ in their perceptions and responses to environmental forces; the initial arousal levels may or may not be sustained.

The role of motivation in explaining job performance can also be applied to training and other learning environments. Several motivational theories have been found to be particularly relevant, and these will be discussed below.

Need for Achievement. McClelland believed that needs were learned or acquired by the kinds of events people experienced in their culture (Cherrington, 1991). These learned needs influence the way individuals perceive situations and motivate them to pursue a particular goal. One of these needs is the need for achievement. McClelland identified three characteristics of high need achievers.

1. High need achievers have a strong desire to assume personal responsibility for performing a task or finding a solution to a problem;
2. They tend to set moderately challenging goals and take calculated risks; and
3. They have a strong desire for performance feedback.

There are several implications of the above for human resource professionals and training practitioners. First, employees with high needs for achievement can be identified in training programs designed to help individuals understand their motivational patterns. Second, achievement motivation training can be part of an overall leadership development program designed to help the organization better prepare its managers for the entrepreneurial and technological challenges of the global economy. Research evidence has, in fact, supported the link between entrepreneurial success and high needs for achievement (Goldstein, 1993).

Social Learning Theory. Social learning theory has been embraced as a vehicle for learning new skills and changing employee behavior in organizations. For example, the theory has been applied to behavior modeling training programs designed to improve the interpersonal skills of first-line supervisors. Based on principles of cognitive information processing, practice, reinforcement, and feedback, these programs have been found to be among the most effective of all management training techniques (Wexley & Latham, 1991). Further research has shown that one reason for its effectiveness is that modeling can raise *self-efficacy*—a person's judgment about whether he or she can successfully learn knowledge and skills (Noe, 1999). Because modeling involves having employees successfully demonstrate skills to employees, trainees are likely to be motivated by the confidence and effectiveness of their successful peers.

Another important application of behavior modeling has been in the development of multimedia training programs (Noe, 1999). Using instructional video technology across a variety of content areas, such as listening skills, performance appraisal, teamwork, and problem solving, organizations have designed systematic training programs targeted to specific skill sets and job behaviors. In some of these programs, employees are given planning guides in which they describe a situation in which they expect to use the key behaviors and how they plan to use them. Techniques such as these can play a useful role in promoting better *transfer of training* from the program to the actual work setting.

Goal Setting Theory. Goal setting can affect performance on the job and in training programs in three ways. First, specific goals influence behavior by *more effectively directing energy and attention* than do generalized goals such as "do your best" (Robbins, 2001). That is, it focuses behavior in one particular direction. Second, given that a goal is accepted, people in work organizations, including trainees, tend to exert *effort in proportion to the difficulty/achievability level* (the extent to which the goal is perceived as challenging yet achievable) of the goal. Third, challenging goals lead to more *persistence* (that is, directed effort over time) than do easy goals (Cascio, 1998). These three dimensions, direction, effort, and persistence, have direct implications for training and development programs in organizations.

Practitioners should develop *SMART/C* learning objectives—objectives that are *specific, measurable, achievable, realistic,* and *timely.* Moreover, these objectives should also be *challenging,* as noted above. The influence of goal setting theory can be applied in ways that enable practitioners to monitor trainee progress throughout training by providing constructive feedback. Practitioners then can work with supervisors and managers in the actual job environment to promote transfer of training. That is, ultimately the effectiveness of any training program will need to be measured against the benchmarks of on-the-job performance behaviors and results. Goal setting theory, then, offers practitioners a useful set of guidelines for developing evaluation criteria to assess the effectiveness of training programs.

Reinforcement Theory. Reinforcement theory, based on the work of B.F. Skinner, emphasizes that people are motivated to perform or avoid certain behaviors because of past consequences that have resulted from those behaviors.

From a training perspective, trainers need to identify what outcomes learners find to be most positive (rewarding) and link those outcomes to the achievement of learning and performance objectives (Noe, 1999). In practice, however, it might be difficult to apply this principle, especially the specification prior to training of what will function as a reward (Cascio, 1998). For some trainees it might be praise from the trainer, for others perhaps a future promotion or salary increase or recognition from one's supervisor. Or, as discussed earlier, others might find their rewards through the intrinsic motivation derived from heightened feelings of self-determination and personal esteem. Given the complexity of human behavior, be it in the workplace or elsewhere, it is likely that, for many people, there are numerous sources from which rewards may originate.

Training and development practitioners should recognize two key principles: First, "one size does not fit all." People bring different values, needs, and goals to training and consequently will respond in different ways to organizational incentives. Second, notwithstanding these differences, as noted above, steps should be taken to work with supervisors to reinforce and support what is learned in training. Again, transfer of training should be a guiding principle.

APPLICATION TO WORKPLACE CHANGE

The last section of this chapter will focus on the forces of change impacting on organizations and their implications for motivation, learning, and training. Two key forces of change identified in the beginning of this chapter were workforce diversity and globalization, and it is these two issues that provide the focus here.

Workforce Diversity

Employees have different needs that can affect their attitude and response to training and development initiatives. Two application strategies can apply here. First, in order to maximize motivation, practitioners should use the needs assessment phase of program design to identify how their workforce is changing. Learning environments will undoubtedly be influenced by such changes. In terms of motivational strategies, the principle of *one size does not fit all,* discussed above in the context of reinforcement theory, has relevance for managing and developing a diverse workforce. People have different needs: some are motivated by money, some by a challenging job, some by a flexible work schedule, and some by the opportunity to learn new skills. Consequently, organizational incentives for training and development will have a differential impact based on these differences in need patterns.

A second application strategy focuses on the content and delivery of training. With respect to content, a centerpiece of most diversity programs is training (Robbins, 2001). For example, Robbins reports results from a recent survey indicating that among companies with diversity initiatives, 93 percent used training as part of their programs. These programs generally cover such topics as valuing individual differences, increasing cross-cultural understanding, and confronting stereotypes. Practitioners also need to consider how training is delivered and identify those methods that can better match the learning styles of participants. For example, persons from cultures that emphasize a strong *collectivist orientation* (Robbins, 2001) might learn better in groups, compared with those who prefer a more individualistic approach. Or some people might prefer visual modes of learning, whereas others might prefer a different medium for delivery of content.

Globalization

Closely related to the above discussion of workforce diversity is the fact that organizations are no longer constrained by national borders. That the world has become a global village is a reality of the new workplace, with far-reaching implications for human resource practitioners. The ever-expanding scope of global competition is forcing an ongoing re-examination of how human resource practices can best support the rapid pace of business globalization (Pucik, 1997).

How can training and development practitioners become partners in the globalization process? A key human resource issue, driven by globalization and related developments in technological change, is *employment security* in the new economy. Human resource practices in general, and training strategies in particular, must build new forms of security while embracing the new realities of globalization—flexibility, mobility, and change (Kanter, 1995). Training and development will continue to play a key role in preparing people for the new economy, particularly in areas of technology, change management, collaborative learning, and leadership.

As noted by Kanter (1995), "If security no longer comes from being employed, it must come from being employable" (p. 157). The new realities of globalization require a shift from traditional notions of job security to *employability security*— "the knowledge that today's work will enhance the person's value in terms of future opportunities" and that it "comes from the chance to accumulate human capital—skills and reputation—that can be invested in new opportunities as they arise. No matter what changes take place, persons whose pool of intellectual capital or experience is high are in a better position to find gainful employment— with the current company, with another company, or on their own" (p. 157).

Companies offering employability security invest in the development of their employees. They give them opportunities to develop their skills, encourage their involvement, and promote teamwork. They create *learning oriented* environments where work and learning are interdependent and highly integrated components of a person's job.

These companies create cultures of learning that understand the connection between *doing well* and *doing good.* People who work in these companies focus not just on the bottom line but also on the human pathways of growth and development that are critical for success in the new economy. This new economy requires a shift in our orientation and thinking about jobs, work, learning, and organizational life.

A core theme that will continue to resonate in the years ahead is the need to create and re-energize our organizations to be places that support the learning enterprise as a critical component of success in the global marketplace.

References

Beer, M. (1997). The transformation of the human resource function: Resolving the tension between a traditional administrative and a new strategic role. In D. Ulrich, M.R. Losey, & G. Lake (Eds.), *Tomorrow's HR management* (84–95). New York: John Wiley & Sons.

Cascio, W.F. (1998). *Applied psychology in human resource management.* Englewood Cliffs, NJ: Prentice Hall.

Cherrington, D.J. (1991). Need theories of motivation. In R.M. Steers & L.W. Porter (Eds.), *Motivation and work behavior* (31–44). New York: McGraw-Hill.

Deci, E.L., & Ryan, R.M. (1991). Intrinsic motivation and self-determination in human behavior. In R.M. Steers & L.W. Porter (Eds.), *Motivation and work behavior* (44–58). New York: McGraw-Hill.

Goldstein, I.L. (1993). *Training in organizations.* Pacific Grove, CA: Brooks/Cole.

Hamel, G., & Prahalad, C.K. (1994). *Competing for the future.* Boston: Harvard Business School Press.

Herling, R.W., & Provo, J. (2000). Knowledge, competence and expertise in organizations. *Advances in developing human resources, 5,* 1–7.

Kanter, R.M. (1995). Workplaces, careers, and employability security. In *World class* (145–173). New York: Simon & Schuster.

Kotter, J. (1996). Leadership and lifelong learning. *Leading change* (175–186). Boston: Harvard Business School Press.

Noe, R.A. (1999). *Employee training and development.* New York: McGraw-Hill.

Pucik, V. (1997). Human resources in the future: An obstacle or a champion of globalization. In D. Ulrich, M.R. Losey, & G. Lake (Eds.), *Tomorrow's HR management* (320). New York: John Wiley & Sons.

Robbins, S.P. (2001). *Organizational behavior.* Englewood Cliffs, NJ: Prentice Hall.

Senge, P.M. (1994). *The fifth discipline.* New York: Currency/Doubleday.

Steers, R.M., & Porter, L.W. (1991). The role of motivation in organizations. In R.M. Steers & L.W. Porter (Eds.), *Motivation and work behavior* (3–24). New York: McGraw-Hill.

Thayer, P.W. (1997). A rapidly changing world: Some implications for training systems in the year 2001 and beyond. In M.A. Quinones & A. Ehrenstein (Eds.), *Training for a rapidly changing workplace: Applications of psychological research* (15–30). Washington, DC: American Psychological Association.

Torraco, R.J. (2000). A theory of knowledge management. *Advances in Developing Human Resources, 5,* 38–62.

Ulrich, D. (1997). Human resources of the future: Conclusions and observations. In D. Ulrich, M.R. Losey, & G. Lake (Eds.), *Tomorrow's HR management* (84–95). New York: John Wiley & Sons.

Wexley, K.N., & Latham, G.P. (1991). *Developing and training human resources in organizations.* New York: HarperCollins.

About the Author

Larry Froman is an associate professor of psychology and director of the graduate program in human resource development at Towson University. He has served as the program's director since its inception in 1987. He teaches courses in organizational behavior, change in the workplace, industrial psychology, social psychology, and team building. He has published and presented papers at conferences dealing with such topics as motivation, collaborative learning, and educational leadership.

He also has served as a consultant to organizations in areas of workforce development, quality improvement, team building, and organizational change. Prior to joining the faculty at Towson University, he held several positions in government dealing with employment and training, mental health, and program evaluation. He received his B.A. in psychology from the City College of New York and M.A. and Ph.D. in social and organizational psychology from Wayne State University. He received additional training at Johns Hopkins University in public psychology.

PART FOUR

TRAINING AND
DEVELOPMENT METHODS

CHAPTER TWENTY-TWO

Facilitating Active Learning

Mel Silberman, Ph.D.
President, Active Training

ctive learning involves hearing, seeing, questioning, discussing, doing, and even teaching. Trainers who want to promote active learning need to include a wide variety of strategies to promote these six processes. In addition, they should be prepared to handle concerns effectively that may be expressed by participants who are not accustomed to learning in this way. Their own concerns about designing and facilitating active learning activities also must be addressed. This article contains numerous suggestions to handle these issues.

ACTIVE LEARNING

Training is a method to enhance human performance. Whenever a person's ability to perform a job is limited by a lack of knowledge or skill, it makes sense to bridge that gap by providing the required instruction.

Sounds simple enough? Not really. The problem begins with the notion that learning something you don't know already requires that another person (a trainer) or medium (a book, a computer) provides it. Let me explain.

One of my favorite exercises is to cover a wristwatch with the opposite hand and ask those who are observing: "What am I doing?" Immediately, someone will say: "You're covering your watch." I then request a synonym for the word *cover*. Typically, suggestions are given such as "hide," "obscure," or "block." With this opening, I quip that the next time *you* have something to cover with a person you are training, you might be hiding the information, obscuring it, or completely blocking it from view. That's because, at that moment, it's *your* information and *your* understanding of it. It does not belong to the *other* person. As you are covering the subject matter, the other person has to "uncover" what you are saying. This uncovering process only happens by virtue of the learners' own *activity*. Ultimately, you or a book or a computer cannot do the work for them.

Active learning occurs when the participants do "most of the work." If you neatly package the information or elegantly demonstrate the skills, you—not the participants—are doing "the work" for them. No one is suggesting that well-designed instruction is unnecessary. The key to effective training, however, is how the learning activities are designed so that the participants *acquire* knowledge and skill rather than merely *receive* it.

Learning is not an automatic consequence of pouring information into another person's head. It requires the learner's own mental involvement and doing. Lecturing and demonstrating, by themselves, will never lead to real, lasting learning. Only training that involves active learning will.

In order for people to learn something well, they must *hear* it, *see* it, *question* it, *discuss* it with their peers, and *do* it. They might even *teach* it to someone else in order to solidify their understanding of the information or skill. Facilitating active learning requires a variety of strategies that promote all six processes—*hearing, seeing, questioning, discussing, doing,* and *teaching.*

Let's consider more fully what these strategies might include.

Hearing

No one can learn anything really well by simply being told about it. But there are some things we can do as we explain material to people that will maximize understanding and retention.

- State your major points and conclusions first before you launch into the details to help participants organize their listening;
- Reduce the major points to headlines that act as verbal subheadings or memory aids;
- As much as possible, provide real-life examples of the ideas in the lecture; and
- If possible, create a comparison or analogy between your material and the knowledge or experience the participants already have.

Seeing

Studies have shown consistently that adding visuals to a training session results in greater retention. A picture may not be worth a thousand words, but it is several times more effective than words alone.

When teaching has both an audio and a visual dimension, the message is re-inforced by two systems of delivery. Also, some participants prefer one mode of delivery over the other. By using both, therefore, you have a greater chance of meeting the needs of several types of participants.

There are several "visuals" that aid learning:

- Words and graphics on flip charts;
- Slides or overheads;
- Handouts;
- Video;
- Live demonstrations;
- Props;
- Work exhibits;
- Real or simulated work environments;
- Cartoons; and
- Charts.

Questioning

Merely hearing something and seeing it is not enough to learn it. The adult brain does not function like an audio- or videotape recorder. Because of our vast store-house of old information, incoming information is being questioned continually. Our brain asks questions such as

- Have I heard or seen this information before? What does it remind me of?
- Where does this information fit? What can I do with it?
- Can I assume that this is the same idea I had yesterday or last month or last year?

The brain doesn't just receive information—it *processes* it. To process infor-mation effectively, it helps to carry out such reflection externally as well as inter-nally. If adult learners are invited to ask questions about what they are learning, their brains can do a better job of processing. However, just stopping every once in a while and asking: "Are there any questions?" is not sufficient. To prompt ques-tioning, you might do the following:

- Pair up participants and ask them to develop a question about what you are teaching them.
- Give participants an index card on which they write down a question. Collect them. Choose some to answer immediately and defer others to later on. Or shuffle the cards and give one to each participant that is not

his or her own. Invite the participants to answer the question they receive or to request that you answer it.

- Give participants a short document or chart and a highlighter pen. Ask them to read the material and highlight what they *don't* understand. Then, invite questions.

- Plant questions with some of the participants in the group.

- Provide a list of questions about the subject matter and ask the participants to select questions that interest them.

Discussing

Discussion also promotes the processing of information. There is a wide range of methods that can be used to obtain active participation in the discussion portions of a training session. If you use a few of them on a consistent basis, you will avoid the phenomenon of hearing from the same participants all the time. Here are some options.

Open Discussion. Ask a question and open it up to the entire group without any further structuring. If you have a very participative group and are worried that the discussion might be too lengthy, say beforehand: "I'd like to ask four or five participants to share. . . ." If you are worried that few people will volunteer, say: "How many of you can tell us. . . ?" instead of "Who can tell us. . . ?"

Subgroup Discussion. Form participants into subgroups of three or more to share and record information. This is one of the key methods for obtaining everyone's participation. You can assign people to subgroups randomly (for example, by counting off) or purposively (for example, by gender).

Partners. Form participants into pairs and instruct them to work on tasks or discuss key questions. Use partners when you want to involve everybody but do not have enough time for small-group discussion.

Go-Around. Go around the group and obtain short responses to key questions. Sentence stems (for example, "One thing that makes a manager effective . . .") are useful in conducting go-arounds. Invite participants to "pass" when they wish.

Calling on the Next Speaker. Ask participants to raise their hands when they want to share their views and request that the present speaker in the group call on the next speaker (rather than the trainer). Use calling on the next speaker when you are sure there is a lot of interest in the discussion/activity and you wish to promote participant interaction.

Panel. Invite a small number of participants to present their views in front of the entire group. Rotate panelists to increase participation. An informal panel can be created by asking for the views of a designated number of participants who remain in their seats.

Fishbowl. Ask a portion of the group to form a discussion circle and have the remaining participants form a listening circle around them. Use a fishbowl to help bring focus to large group discussions. Although time-consuming, this is the best method for combining the virtues of large and small group discussion.

Bear in mind that you can combine some of these methods of obtaining participation. For example, you might pose a question, form partners to discuss it, and then obtain whole group reaction through methods such as open discussion, call on the next speaker, and a panel. By inserting the partner exchange first, you will have more people ready to participate in the full group setting.

Doing

When participants are asked to do something with the learning material they have read, heard, questioned, and discussed, they are given the opportunity to really acquire knowledge and skill. Here are some tips to promote learning by doing:

- Ask participants to give examples of the concepts you are presenting;
- Have them recap the major points of a class session;
- Invite participants to create skits that demonstrate a skill you have taught them;
- Give participants a self-scoring test that assesses their knowledge and understanding;
- Provide real-life problems in which participants have to apply what they have learned in order to solve them;
- After providing step-by-step instruction to learn a skill, require participants to do the skill with prompting or job aids;
- Invite participants to perform a skill that they learned several hours previously to demonstrate to themselves that they can still do it; or
- Give participants an on-the-job assignment that requires them to extend the knowledge and skill they have acquired in the training.

Teaching

For many people, teaching something they have learned to someone else really helps to solidify what they have learned. Here are three ways to promote peer teaching.

Jigsaw Learning. Give different information to different participants. Ask them to study the material by themselves or with other participants who have received the same information. Then ask the participants to form small groups in which each participant is expert about different material. Each participant, in turn, teaches the material that he or she has studied to the other members of the group.

Peer Lessons. Divide a class into subgroups. Create as many subgroups as you have topics to be taught. Give each group some information, a concept, or a skill to teach others. Ask each group to design a way to present or teach its topic to the rest of the class. Advise them to avoid a lecture presentation and try to make the learning experience for participants as active as possible.

Peer Tutoring. Invite participants to teach a skill they have learned from you to someone else who has not attended the training session.

CONCERNS ABOUT ACTIVE LEARNING

Despite the wide range of methods I have presented to support an active approach to learning, many people are still apprehensive about it. If you share any of these frequently expressed concerns, I hope my responses are helpful.

Is active learning just a bunch of "fun and games"? No, it's not just fun, although learning can be fun and still be worthwhile. Actually, many active learning techniques present participants with unusual challenges that require much hard work.

Does active learning focus so much on activity for its own sake that participants don't reflect on what they are learning? This is a real concern. Much of the value of active learning activities comes from thinking about them when they are over and discussing their meaning with others. Don't overlook this fact.

Doesn't active learning require a lot of time? How can you cover course material using active learning methods? Isn't lecturing more efficient? There is no question that active learning takes more time than straight lecturing, but there are many ways to avoid a needless waste of time. Furthermore, even though a lecture can cover considerable ground, one has to question how much is really learned. Also remember the "coverage" trap. The more you try to cover, the more you may be hiding.

Can active learning methods spice up dry, uninteresting information? Absolutely! When the subject is interesting, it's easy to train. When it is dry, often the mere excitement of active learning methods catches up with participants and they become motivated to master even boring material.

When you use groups in active learning, how do you prevent the groups from wasting time and being unproductive? Groups can be unproductive when there has been little team building in the beginning of the class and when group work is not carefully structured from the outset. Participants become confused about what to do, organize themselves poorly, and get off task easily. Or they may do the work as quickly as possible, skimming the surface rather than digging into the material. There are several ways to teach participants how to learn in groups, such as assigning roles to group members, establishing group ground rules, practicing group skills, and so forth.

Doesn't it require more preparation and creativity to teach using active learning methods? Yes and no. Once you get the hang of it, the extra preparation and creativity will not feel like a burden. You will feel excited about your training, and this energy will transfer to your participants' learning. Until then, you should find that creating ideas for active learning can be challenging. At first, you will wonder how in the world you can teach certain topics actively! But then you'll get the hang of it.

I'm sold on active learning, but will my participants be? Generation Xers will buy into active learning enthusiastically. Because they have been "latchkey kids," many learned to be self-reliant. As a result, they are quite good at learning by their own doing. They also don't mind the fast pace of activity, having grown up in an MTV world. Of course, the less accustomed any participants are to active learning, the more uneasy they will be initially. They may be used to the trainer "doing all the work" while they sit back and believe that they have learned something and will retain it. Some participants will also complain that active learning is a "waste of time." Older workers, in particular, may prefer well-organized, efficient delivery of information or they may be anxious about learning by discovery and self-exploration. In the long run, they will benefit from active learning as much as anyone else. In the short run, they will be less anxious if you introduce active learning gradually. If you don't, you may get considerable resistance.

Recommended Reading

Bonwell, C., & Eison, J. (1991). *Active learning: Creating excitement in the classroom.* ASHE ERIC Higher Education Report No. 1. Washington, DC: The George Washington University.

Meyers, C., & Jones, T. (1993). *Promoting active learning.* San Francisco: Jossey-Bass.

Silberman, M. (1995). *101 ways to make training active.* San Francisco: Jossey-Bass/Pfeiffer.

Silberman, M. (1996). *Active learning: 101 strategies to teach any subject.* Needham Heights, MA: Allyn & Bacon.

Silberman, M. (1998). *Active training* (2nd ed.). San Francisco: Jossey-Bass/Pfeiffer.

About the Author

Mel Silberman is president of Active Training, a provider of training seminars for instructional designers, trainers, consultants, and facilitators. Dr. Silberman is also professor of adult and organizational development at Temple University and a best-selling author. His recent books include: 101 Ways to Make Meetings Active *(1999);* 101 Ways to Make Training Active *(1995);* Active Learning *(1996);* Active Training *(2nd ed.) (1998);* PeopleSmart *(2000). He is also editor of:* 20 Active Training Programs *(Vols. 1–3) (1992, 1994, 1997);* The Team and Organization Development Sourcebook *(1996–2001);* The Training and Performance Sourcebook *(1996–2001); and* The Consultant's Toolkit *(2000).*

Dr. Silberman has consulted for hundreds of corporate, governmental, educational, and human service organizations worldwide. He is a graduate of Brandeis University and holds an A.M. and a Ph.D. in educational psychology from the University of Chicago. A member of ASTD (formerly, American Society for Training and Development), the International Society for Performance Improvement, and the North American Simulation and Gaming Association, he is a frequent presenter at their national, regional, and chapter level conferences and meetings.

CHAPTER TWENTY-THREE

Transform the Person, Not the Behavior

The Traditional Concept of Training Is Wrong-Headed!

Robert Hargrove
Founder, Masterful Coaching, Inc.

The paradigm of learning that most trainers and corporate clients are familiar with is called *transactional learning,* which involves acquiring information. This is a fundamental misconception that prevents them from getting to the source of behavior, which involves breaking the grip and excelling beyond paradigms that keep people stuck in old patterns and prevent them from learning. To produce a true alteration in people's thinking and behavior requires that trainers take a different approach to learning, one that is based on producing a fundamental shift in thinking and attitude. This is called *transformational learning.*

INTRODUCTION

Picture the typical training session. The brilliantly put together PowerPoint® presentation is being flashed up on the screen. First come the bullet points about the latest business trends, then the "Ten Key Points" of you name it—innovative leadership, team collaboration, coaching. The trainer dressed in business "cashz" is creating a spin around each main point to drive home deeper insights. The participants' eyes dart from the screen to the spiral-bound course book containing a copy of each overhead.

GET BEYOND SUPERFICIAL INFOTAINMENT

It's my view that the popular conception of training is wrong-headed. Why? Ninety-five percent of all training is based on the assumption that great training depends on the trainer standing in front of the room and presenting principles, tips, and techniques to participants. The effectiveness is usually judged by how the trainer combines good, clear information with entertainment to produce understanding—without taking into account whether understanding results in changes in thinking or behavior. Other factors that are considered are how religiously the trainer sticks to the training manual and time schedule and, of course, the evaluations or "happy sheets" at the end.

The vast majority of trainers, no matter how sincere or well-intended, think and operate from the view that *what's missing* for leaders, managers, and professionals to alter their behavior is clear, well-presented information. This is a fundamental misconception that will, in almost every case, prevent you from getting to the source behavior, which in reality has to do with breaking the grip and excelling beyond paradigms that keep people stuck in old patterns and prevent them from learning.

Foster a Deeper Learning Cycle

The diagram on triple loop learning (Figure 23.1) below shows that it's people's *history* that shapes their *way of being* and it's their *mental models* that shape their *behavior*. That being the case, you don't change behavior by trying to change behavior. You change behavior by freeing people up from their history so they can develop a new way of being, as well as by altering the mental models so as to assist people in breaking the grip of action strategies that are no longer relevant. This approach is most powerful when done in the context of people committing to what I call an "ambitious aspiration" and their willingness to shift their way of being, thinking, and actions to realize it.

In coaching and training a CEO and a top management group of a wireless telecommunications company that we'll call Wireless Depot on leadership and teamwork, I discovered a written comment on the CEO's 360-degree feedback report under the area of "inspiring commitment." The comment read, "I have great one-on-one meetings with Bill [the CEO] where he shares his vision for the company. Then he goes to the meetings of the top management group and acts completely differently. He doesn't put out his vision. I put the vision out and then Bill abandons me and I get beaten up. He has great ideas, but he doesn't carry them on his shoulder. Why?"

I said to the CEO in a private coaching conversation before the team session, "What, if anything, in your history causes you to show up in the way that you have to the person who made this comment? What's the mindset that drives this

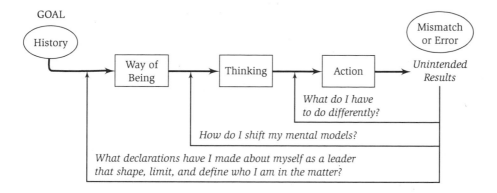

Figure 23.1. Triple Loop Learning

behavior?" The CEO explained that he had come from a top consumer product marketing firm (such as Proctor & Gamble) where senior managers were supposed to "be perfect," as well as "have all the answers" and "not make mistakes." He was only twelve months into his job at the Wireless Depot, and he felt insecure about his knowledge of the telecommunications business, especially its fast changing technology.

The CEO acknowledged that his commitment was to making a difference; yet what was showing up more loudly was his commitment to *looking good.* I asked him to write two sentences designed to produce an alteration in who he was being, as well as his underlying mental models and behavior: "I am committed to the possibility of. . . ." "What I am willing to give up is. . . ."

The first sentence that the CEO wrote was: "I am committed to the possibility of being a powerful leader who inspires commitment with his vision and acts with integrity." The second sentence was: "I am committed to giving up the need to look good, and doubting whether I make a difference." In the coming weeks, I continued to coach this CEO around his leadership declaration, and his behavior changed dramatically.

FROM TRANSFORMATIONAL TO TRANSACTIONAL LEARNING

As we can see from the example above, to produce a true alteration in people's thinking and behavior requires that trainers take a fundamentally different approach to learning. The paradigm of learning that most trainers and corporate clients are familiar with is called *transactional learning.* The participants (company) engage in a transaction where they pay the trainer a daily fee in exchange for *"infotainment"* or pouring a lot of information on top of people's heads. The notion behind this is that learning is the result of *acquiring information.*

Transactional learning is fine for teaching people subjects that require no more than acquiring information, such as how to invest in the stock market, grow roses, or use newly installed technology. It falls short, however, with what I consider the "big four" training topics: (1) leadership, (2) team skills, (3) sales, and (4) customer service. The reason is that these kinds of topics require an alteration in who people are and their mindsets, not just the information that they carry around in their heads.

The kind of learning necessary to produce a fundamental shift in thinking and attitude is called *transformational learning.* This is the kind of learning that is required to transform managers and technicians into leaders, a group of strong, talented individual egos into a real team, or telephone operators in a call center into consultative sales people. It has to do with shifting people's way of being or mindset.

Change the Rules of Engagement—From Speaking Better to Listening Differently

One of the first steps in becoming a masterful trainer is to fundamentally change the rules of engagement that shape, limit, and define how you interact with participants. As most trainers are wed to the transactional learning approach, their rules of engagement tend to center on their speaking: (1) Say something (inspiring) instructive; (2) provide examples; and (3) check for understanding. This may be a valid approach for the first fifteen minutes of a training session or if your goal is to increase understanding of basic principles; but if you want to have a deeper impact, the rules of engagement must be then radically altered.

Over the years I have used a transformational learning approach. I have found that the key to being effective with this approach is not to focus on how wonderful a speaker you are, but rather to learn to listen in a different way. In engaging participants, I always keep in mind Ralph Waldo Emerson's statement that "Everything you say reveals you." The smallest utterance participants make can reveal volumes about who they are and the underlying mindset and attitudes that drive their actions.

The rules of engagement I use start with

1. Make a *provocative statement* or *ask a provocative question* designed to make people think;

2. *Listen to what people say for clues that reveal who they are,* their mindsets and attitudes (especially for limiting beliefs and assumptions); and

3. *Reframe.* Here is how you are looking at yourself today. How do you need to see yourself differently? Here's how you are thinking about

leadership, teamwork, and so forth. Here's what you know about this. What do you need to learn?

Let's take an example. In giving leadership programs, I often start by making a provocative statement: "I have found that there are two kinds of people, 'chocolate' and 'vanilla.' The chocolate people have leadership potential due to the fact that they are oriented toward making a difference. Vanilla people are oriented toward security (survival) and tend to be risk averse." I immediately follow this with a very direct question that makes it possible for me to surface and challenge people's underlying beliefs and assumptions. "What kind of person are you? Chocolate or vanilla?" People will respond by arguing that they are chocolate, but will be unable to substantiate this with a recent example of where they took a risk. Others will respond that a leader can be both chocolate and vanilla, a sign that they probably are vacillating between taking a stand and the pressure to conform. Still others will claim that they are not really interested in leadership, to which I might respond, "Don't you want to make a difference?"

This dialogue can go on for two to three hours and is never just an intellectual exercise, pre-packaged leadership lesson that springs from a trainer's manual or daily program agenda. Rather, leadership lessons are generated in the context of the dialogue based on what people reveal to me about who they are, their mindsets and behaviors, and how they need to shift. If I am successful, the person to whom I am talking at the beginning of the conversation will not exist at the end of the conversation. A transformation will have occurred.

Creating the Cultural Clearing for Transformational Learning

As I mentioned earlier, a transformational learning approach works best when the individuals or groups we are working with have taken a stand for a strategic intent or goal and recognize that to reach it will require an alteration in who they are today, along with their mindset and behavior. As a result, I always make a committed attempt to structure any training programs I do around enabling people to accomplish something that they really need to accomplish (an ambitious aspiration), rather than just a typical training exercise.

There are a couple of other points that are very important to consider here for both the trainer and the human resource people or corporate universities that sponsor the training. The first point is that most trainers tend to adopt a transactional versus transformational learning approach because that is the approach that tends to be most welcome in the cultural clearing found in most organizations. I have found that, while training managers often espouse a sincere "commitment" to bring transformational learning into their company, they very quickly default to a higher level commitment, which is to "avoid disapproval" when things get hot.

The issue is that a transformational approach requires the trainer/coach to engage participants at a deeper level of intervention than merely presenting guiding ideas, methods, or techniques. Transformational learning often requires presenting information or asking questions that, while needed for growth and learning, are potentially embarrassing or threatening. Although the majority of participants will understand this approach, there are some participants for whom this might trigger "defensive routines" or negative reactions. The result is that the trainer will usually receive a message to pull in the horns. Often the response from most training managers is to collude with these defensive routines, in order to avoid the risk of disapproval. And the training becomes a watered-down version that is palpable to all. Professional HRD people must learn to stop colluding with the organization's defensive routines of participants and the enterprise.

HOW CAN TRAINING BE MORE IMPACTFUL?

If you want your training to be more impactful, it requires some self-reflection. First, you must look in the mirror and ask yourself whether you are committed to transformational or transactional learning. Second, whether it is a leadership course, a team-building program or whatever, each participant must be told about the nature of transformational learning and given a free and informed choice as to whether or not they want to participate. Third, HR managers and their sponsors must reflect on the extent to which they unwittingly collude with the defensive routines of participants and the organization and in so doing diminish the quality of the training effort.

HOW TO MAKE THE DIFFERENCE
YOU HAVE ALWAYS WANTED TO MAKE
Five Guidelines for Trainers

The following steps will set a context for training that has a much higher level of impact. At the same time, these few simple guidelines for trainers will support them in developing the skills and capabilities they need to succeed with transformational learning. First and foremost, if you are genuinely committed to making a difference, turn off the PowerPoint® projector, throw away the training manual, and engage people in a conversation through which your actual goal or intention is to produce a transformation. Again it starts with linking learning to people's goals and aspirations.

1. *Select a training topic that speaks to your highest aspirations and theirs.* I purposely chose leadership, creative collaboration, and masterful coaching as my lifetime training topics because it's a way for me to

make a difference in the world. I consciously and intentionally find ways to link these training topics to the highest goals and aspirations of the participants in my training sessions. This elicits from people a much higher willingness to transform who they are, that is, their thinking and behavior.

2. *Make new distinctions in a provocative way that allows people to see things differently.* I usually start by making some new distinctions that cause people to think differently. For example, if the topic is leadership, I might say: "Leadership does not arise from your position. It arises from taking a stand that a difference can be made in the absence of evidence or proof." Or if the topic is coaching, I might say: "Coaching is not about the answers; it's about empowering people to do their own thinking and discover their own answers." With just one or two distinctions like this (not a laundry list), I can engage people in a very impactful conversation that will: (1) Set a powerful context for the training; (2) get people to reveal their present mindset to me; and (3) allow me to diagnose where people need to make a shift.

3. *Listen "to" versus listen "for."* It is not only important to listen to what people are saying so as to be able to see whether they have understood what you have said about the subject, but it is also crucial to listen for the underlying beliefs, assumptions, and attitudes that will get in the way of them ever acting in a manner that is consistent with what you are saying. If I say in a training session, "Learning to lead when you are not in charge is key to collaboration," and a person responds by saying that their job as a manager is to keep everything under control, then I know that I need to work with that person on giving up the illusion of control.

4. *Reframe.* In listening "to" and listening "for," you are likely to discover the places where people or groups are thinking and operating from a frame of reference that is inconsistent with reaching their most important goals and priorities. The next step is reframing, which involves helping people to surface, test, and revise their beliefs and assumptions. There are four simple but powerful questions I use that are very effective for this: (1) Here is how you are looking at things now. How do you need to see things differently? (2) Here's how you are showing up as a leader today. How do you need to show up differently? (3) Here's how you are thinking today. How does your thinking need to change? and (4) Here is how you are acting in this situation. How do you need to act differently?

5. *Tips.* There's a time and place for everything. If, after reframing, I notice that people are not only clear about their goals but also have the right mindset that will shape, limit, and define their actions, I then

provide them with a practical tip or word of advice. In giving tips, I always respect the principle of free and informed choice: "Would you like a suggestion?" I also try to gear what I am saying to the personality of the individual and his or her particular set of preferences. A tip that will work well for one person won't necessarily work for the next.

CONCLUSION

I have focused in this article on coaching in training sessions. The triple loop learning and transformational approach I have written about here, however, lends itself equally well to one-on-one coaching and group coaching sessions.

Let me close with a quotation from a teacher I once had who told me, "Teach the student, not the subject." In order to do that, you need to discover the student's goals and aspirations, as well as what's missing that will make a difference. In most cases what's missing is not more information; it's breaking the grip and excelling beyond paradigms that limit people's creativity and effectiveness.

Recommended Reading

Argyris, C. (1993). *Knowledge for action: A guide for overcoming barriers to organizational change.* San Francisco: Jossey-Bass.

Argyris, C., Putman, R., & Smith, D.M. (1985). *Action science.* San Francisco: Jossey-Bass.

Goss, T. (1995). *The last word on power: Executive re-invention for leaders who must make the impossible happen.* New York: Currency/Doubleday.

About the Author

Robert Hargrove is the founder of Masterful Coaching, Inc., located in Brookline, Massachusetts. He has worked with more than thirty thousand people in transformational coaching programs that shift people's way of being, their thinking, and actions. He is the author of The eLeader *(2000),* Masterful Coaching, *and* The Masterful Coaching Fieldbook, *as well as* Mastering the Art of Creative Collaboration.

Hargrove is a sought-after, inspirational, and thought-provoking speaker. Program topics include lateral leadership, creating a strategy of pre-eminence, creating a collaborative organization, and masterful coaching with a transformational, results orientation. Hargrove is an executive coach and collaborative consultant to organizations in government, business, and education in the United States, Canada, and Europe. He has been the primary business guru or designer of many top executive leadership development programs, culture change efforts, and major breakthrough projects. His humanitarian interests include work with the United Nations Commission on Refugees and dispute resolution in South Africa. See www.MasterfulCoaching.com.

CHAPTER TWENTY-FOUR

Involve Your Learners; Enhance Your Training

Fran Rees
Rees & Associates

Adults come to training with a wealth of knowledge, experience, and real-world situations to which your topic can be applied. When you engage learners in discussions, group activities, and two-way communication, you increase the chances that your training will be lively, relevant, and appropriate for the audience. In this chapter, you will learn what the facilitation process is, how it benefits learning, when to use it, and how to apply it to your training programs. Your role as a trainer/facilitator will be explained, and a brief overview of facilitation skills will be presented.

INTRODUCTION

Experienced trainers use a variety of methods to enhance the quality of their training. One of these methods is facilitation process, which works wonders for both participants and instructor. Facilitation process engages learners and increases the chance that learning will occur. It makes your job as a trainer easier, more interesting, and more fun.

THE FACILITATION PROCESS

The facilitation process is a method of encouraging and structuring participation and communication during training to ensure and enhance learning. Sometimes referred to as *interactive learning,* facilitation process honors the experience and input of the learners as well as of the instructor. Facilitation occurs when the instructor gives learners a chance to talk and become involved in some way with the material. This process encourages learners to reflect on the subject matter, interact with the instructor and with one another, and consider how they might apply the learning.

Benefits of the Facilitation Process

There are many benefits to using the facilitation process in training. Facilitating puts you, the trainer, in touch with your learners—their issues, their questions, their ideas, and their responses to your topic. This connection allows you to adapt your training to better meet learners' needs and provides information to help you improve future training sessions.

Facilitation takes into account the way adults generally prefer to learn: They want to ask questions, discuss and apply the topic to real-world situations, and hear from their colleagues in the session. They resist being talked to for long periods of time without being given the chance to respond. In fact, few people listen attentively for long periods of time, no matter how interesting the subject. Facilitation keeps people engaged and alert. A learner's attention is less apt to wander when he or she is expected to contribute to the learning.

Facilitation makes it more likely that what is learned will be relevant to participants. Trainers cannot be expected to know the many ways learning can be applied, and learners are a great source for this. When participants are involved, they give clues to what they need to know. They often identify how the topic relates to their jobs. Thus, facilitation gives the trainer the chance to make his or her topic more appropriate to the learners.

Further, the facilitation process is an excellent way to build an atmosphere of trust. As a trainer, you show by your interest that you respect the perspectives of the learners, which increases their trust in you. Trust grows from repeated and affirming connections.

The facilitation process in training sessions, then, enhances learning in several ways: (1) It makes learning more relevant; (2) it holds learners' interest; (3) it uses a process that adults naturally prefer; (4) it capitalizes on what everybody, not just the instructor, knows; and (5) it builds trust between the instructor and learners.

When and How to Use the Facilitation Process

There are no formulas about when to use facilitation in training. Some general guidelines follow:

- Use facilitation alternatively with lecture to vary the delivery methods;

- Break up large amounts of material with facilitation, giving participants a chance to digest the subject;
- Plan facilitation after lunch or other times when participants may be tired or sleepy; and
- Involve participants in a facilitation activity before material is presented to increase their interest in the material.

Facilitation approaches may or may not be included in the training design. When they are, trainers can follow the script or vary the process as desired. If facilitation approaches are not designed into the training, or if the trainer designs his or her own program, the trainer must decide when to use facilitation. As a trainer, you can design in facilitation or you can spontaneously use it during the session. The facilitation process requires more time to conduct the training, but is well worth it. If you are new to training, it is best to plan ahead how you will use facilitation in your training. This gives you time to decide which activities would most improve the learning and how you will incorporate them. Spontaneous facilitation is not as easy as it looks!

Each facilitation activity should help achieve the session's learning objectives. Facilitation process can be used for the following:

- To stimulate thinking about a topic or skill;
- To assess learners' knowledge or ability levels;
- To give learners a chance to reflect on a topic or skill;
- To give learners a chance to apply a topic or skill to real-world situations; or
- To invite learners to augment or further develop a topic or skill.

Here are some examples of facilitation activities that support learning objectives:

- Discussion or an icebreaker to find out what participants already know about your topic;
- Open discussion of the topic at hand;
- Round robin comments (go around the room and ask each person to respond to a particular question or idea);
- Small group activities to apply or augment the topic;
- Small group presentations;
- "Buzz groups" (quickly formed small groups given a question to discuss);
- Skill practice;

- Group consensus activities;
- Individual or group research with results brought to others in the program; or
- Case studies given to participants to review and discuss that will require them to refer back to what has been presented.

New trainers should try different facilitation activities, observe what other trainers do, and use the many resources available to them, such as the ones listed at the end of this chapter.

YOUR ROLE IN THE FACILITATION PROCESS

To use facilitation successfully, you will be switching roles back and forth from presenter to facilitator during the training. When you are presenting, communication is one-way—from you to the learners. You are the expert, passing on information, demonstrating skills, and controlling the content of the session. *As a presenter, you express your ideas and opinions.* When facilitating, your role is to remain neutral, with the sole intent of drawing out responses, ideas, and questions. *As a facilitator you draw out the ideas and opinions of your learners.* During this time you ask questions, listen, and summarize, but should not take over. When asked questions by participants, you should refrain from giving too many answers. An excellent device is to throw the question back to the participants to see whether anyone else knows the answer before responding yourself.

The focus during facilitation is on the learners. This may be difficult for you as a trainer, especially if you have been selected for training because of your expertise in a given area and have not had any instruction or experience in facilitating groups. You may fall into the trap of attempting to convey your knowledge through presentations or demonstrations alone.

During facilitation, the atmosphere of trust and interest in the participants is key. Whether the learners have gotten it just right or not doesn't matter all the time. What matters is giving them the freedom to reflect on, question, and apply the learning. It is more important to let them work with and correct one another. Later, you, the instructor, can clarify misconceptions or supply more pertinent examples.

Skills You Need

Basic facilitation skills are required to use the facilitation process in an effective way. During facilitation you are asking, listening, summarizing, recording, referring back to comments made by participants, and structuring the involvement so that learning occurs. A few key skills are essential.

First, you must know how to formulate a good open-ended question. A well-formulated question jump starts discussion and keeps it focused on the learning. A stimulating question will elicit thoughtful responses and can be used to re-focus the group when it gets off track. An effective, open-ended question has some or all of the following characteristics:

- It invites multiple responses;
- It encourages thoughtful comments;
- It relates to the subject at hand;
- It draws on participants' experience and knowledge, while challenging them to expand their thinking; and
- It gives participants a chance to apply the learning.

For example, in a course on team leadership, you may ask, "What does a team need from its leader in order to function well as a team?" You can record ideas as they are presented, post the list, and refer to it later, if beneficial. You can note areas of disagreement and deal with them as the training moves along.

There is a simple secret to formulating good open-ended questions. Make sure your question begins with the word "How," "What," or "Where," and you will be off to a good start. Here are a few examples:

- "What are your reactions to what I have just said?"
- "How might this method be applied here?"
- "Where could this approach be used?"

To encourage even more responses to a question already asked, you can use statements such as

- "Tell us more about that" or
- "Say more about what happened."

Second, you must be able to record briefly and accurately people's comments so the group can see the material it has generated. This focuses the group on the topic at hand, lessens the likelihood of redundant comments, and gives you something to refer back to. Recording comments takes practice. Try to write large and legibly so that all can see. Keep your words to a minimum, while still capturing the thought. And, above all, do not change the meaning intended by the participant. When possible, use the participant's exact words (or some of them) and, if you are uncertain of the meaning, ask the participant whether you have accurately captured his or her thought. Post the thoughts and keep them for later use in the program.

Third, but probably foremost in importance, is to listen attentively to participants. This above all makes you a skilled facilitator. People will shut down if you interrupt, put words in their mouths, manipulate the meaning of their comments, or show in other ways that you really do not want to hear them.

Fourth, you need to remember some comments and refer back to them during the training program. This ties the facilitation into the material you have prepared. Referring back honors comments made by participants and reinforces the topic at the same time.

A fifth basic skill is summarizing. From time to time, it helps to summarize what has been said to keep participants focused and to keep you in charge of the learning. To further stimulate learners, you can ask someone else to summarize, if you feel confident that the person can do so. Summarizing gives you the chance to transition into the next subject or activity. Simply summarize by using words that lead you to the next topic. If a learner summarizes correctly, you can use his or her summary and move on.

The five basic skills mentioned above—asking open questions, listening, recording, referring back, and summarizing—will take you a long way in using the facilitation process in your training. These skills will be invaluable to your development as a trainer.

You can begin now to incorporate the facilitation process into your training programs. First, take a few opportunities to pause in your presentation and ask an open question. Remain neutral and listen, recording people's comments briefly on a flip chart. When comments wind down, briefly summarize and respond to what you heard, relating it back to your presentation. Another easy way to use facilitation is to divide the group into smaller groups of three or four people each and give them a short assignment. Ask them to discuss one or more questions in their group and write a few key points on a flip chart or white board. When you bring the groups back together, ask each small group to present its findings. Summarize and move on. This approach gives each person a chance to reflect on and apply what you are teaching. Once you become comfortable with simple facilitation approaches such as these, try new ones.

SUMMARY

The facilitation process is an effective way to add power and interest to your training. You do not have to be the only "teacher" in your sessions. Let your participants become involved discussing, applying, and enhancing the material. They undoubtedly will learn more this way, and you will be able to build trust and connect to your learners. Facilitation also will provide feedback you can use to improve both the content and delivery of your training. Over time, you may find yourself doing less and less lecturing and more and more interacting with your learners through the facilitation process.

Recommended Reading

Pike, R.W. (1994). *Creative training techniques handbook.* Minneapolis, MN: Lakewood.

Rees, F. (1998). *The facilitator excellence handbook.* San Francisco: Jossey-Bass/ Pfeiffer.

Silberman, M. (1998). *Active training* (2nd ed.). San Francisco: Jossey-Bass/Pfeiffer.

About the Author

Fran Rees consults to a variety of organizations in the areas of facilitative leadership, team performance, and diversity. An experienced facilitator and trainer, Rees is the owner of Rees & Associates and the author of four books on teams and facilitation, including How to Lead Work Teams *(1991),* Teamwork from Start to Finish *(1997), and* Facilitator Excellence *(1998). She has worked with a variety of industries and organizations, including computer manufacturing, health care, city and state governments, and biomedical technology. Her training design experience spans the areas of management development, teamwork, facilitation, workforce diversity, and training. In addition to training, she enjoys writing books and articles and facilitating groups to vision, set goals, and re-energize.*

CHAPTER TWENTY-FIVE

Training Games and Activities

Sivasailam "Thiagi" Thiagarajan, Ph.D.
President, Workshops by Thiagi, Inc.

Facilitating a training activity requires skills, knowledge, and attitudes that are different from those involved in presenting training content. Different types of training activities make use of our current understanding of the nature of human intelligence, as well as the laws of learning, to produce effective and enjoyable instruction. Principles of concurrent co-design provide an alternative to the steps of the traditional instructional systems design model for the development of training activities. Objective checklists help us select and adapt training games and activities. Debriefing discussions after a training activity are key for maximizing learning outcomes.

WHAT IS A GAME?

Let's begin with a basic definition of a "game." A game has four critical characteristics: *conflict, control, closure,* and *contrivance.*

Conflict refers to the fact that the players have a goal to achieve and different obstacles prevent them from achieving it. Very often, conflict is in the form of competition among players or teams, but the conflict also may stem from previous records, time limits, or the ingenuity of a computer "opponent."

Control refers to the rules of the game that specify how you take your turn, make your move, and receive the consequences. Some rules may be explicit, while others may be implicit.

Closure refers to the fact that the game has to come to an end. A special rule (the *termination rule*) specifies when and how the game ends. Termination rules may involve time limits, target scores, or elimination. They also determine who wins the game.

Contrivance refers to the built-in inefficiencies in a game. Obviously, there are more efficient methods for dropping a little white ball into a hole in the ground eighteen times than the rules of golf permit. This characteristic of contrivance is what makes people say, "After all, it was only a game."

A *training* game has a fifth characteristic that also begins with a "C": *competency*. This characteristic refers to the objective of a training game—to improve the players' level of competency in specific areas.

Effective Training Games

The five characteristics described above are the technical requirements for a game. They are not to be confused with desirable characteristics of an effective game.

Exhibit 25.1 is a ten-item evaluation checklist based on an analysis of outstanding training games nominated by experienced trainers and facilitators. Not all ten items in this checklist are relevant to all training games. For example, if a game does not involve a board or cards, then Item 5 does not apply. Depending on the training objective and the characteristics of participants, different items in this checklist may be more relevant than the others. You may use this checklist to select a suitable training game or activity. You also may use it to evaluate and improve your own games and activities.

WHAT IS AN ACTIVITY?

An *activity* is an experience in which a person participates. When used in the field of training, *activities* typically refer to observable, physical behaviors, rather than to covert, mental processes. According to this definition, all games are activities. However, some types of training activities are not games. Exhibit 25.2 presents brief definitions of forty types of training activities (including types of training games). This list is not complete, and the items are not mutually exclusive. The list simply presents a large number of active training strategies to expand your understanding of the concept.

USING GAMES AND ACTIVITIES

Frequently (and often justifiably), games and activities are considered to be "fluff" of insignificant instructional value—merely added to entice reluctant learners. However, research demonstrates that games and activities produce powerful training results—far beyond the limitation of training techniques.

Exhibit 25.1. Evaluation Checklist for Training Games

1. *Real-World Relevance.* Does the training game help participants learn skills and concepts that are applicable to the workplace? Do the roles in the training game relate to easily recognizable real-world counterparts?

2. *Appropriate Frame.* Is the basic structure of the training game appropriate for the instructional objectives, trainee characteristics, type of learning, and intended use?

3. *Flexible Format.* Does the training game permit easy modifications to suit local resources and constraints in terms of schedule, number and type of participants, and physical facilities?

4. *Participant Involvement.* Are all participants involved in the training game at all times?

5. *Effective Packaging.* If the game uses different components (such as game boards, cards, and dice), are they conveniently packaged in a box? Are the materials produced in an attractive and durable form?

6. *Effective Instructions.* Does the training game include clear and concise instructions? Do the rules avoid unnecessary and trivial items?

7. *Intellectual Stimulation.* Are the participants engaged in challenging tasks instead of trivial rote memory activities?

8. *Criterion Reference.* Does the scoring system reward achievement of the performance objectives rather than chance occurrences? Is the mastery of useful skills and knowledge obvious to the participants?

9. *User Friendliness.* Can a typical trainer use the game without having to spend too much time preparing the materials or learning the rules?

10. *Cost-Effectiveness.* Is the training game inexpensive? Can a cheaper alternative produce the same training outcomes?

Research on the nature of intelligence provides strong support for the use of games and activities for achieving training objectives. For example, Epstein (1993) presents the Cognitive Experiential Self Theory, which suggests that we have an experiential mind and a rational mind. According to Epstein, our *experiential* mind learns directly, thinks quickly, pays attention to the outcome, and forgets slowly. Our *rational* mind learns indirectly, thinks deliberately, pays attention to the process, and forgets rapidly. Epstein's contention is that we need both minds. Games and training activities appeal directly to the experiential mind. When combined with debriefing discussions, they provide a powerfully balanced approach to whole-brain training.

Exhibit 25.2. Training Activities

Action Learning involves a combination of action and reflection by a team solving complex strategic problems in a real-world organizational setting. Team members apply existing skills and knowledge and create new skills, knowledge, and insights through continuously reflecting on and questioning the problem definition, the collaborative behavior, and the ensuing results.

Board Games borrow structures and supplies from popular recreational games to create highly motivating training events. Board games typically use game cards and dice to encourage individuals and teams to demonstrate their mastery of concepts, principles, skills, and problem-solving strategies.

Case Studies involve a written account of a real or fictional situation surrounding a problem. Participants work individually and in teams to analyze, discuss, and recommend appropriate solutions and to critique each other's work. In some cases, the facilitator may recount the actual decisions implemented in the real-world situation on which the case was based.

Cash Games are a special type of simulation game that involves actual cash transactions. However, they are not gambling games, nor do they focus on accounting procedures or financial management. Instead, they explore interpersonal skills (such as negotiation) and concepts (such as cooperation). Why cash? Because it effectively simulates the real world and brings out natural behaviors and emotions in participants.

Classification Card Games involve pieces of information (such as facts, concepts, technical terms, definitions, principles, examples, quotations, and questions) printed on cards. These games borrow procedures from traditional games with playing cards and require players to classify and sequence pieces of information from the instructional content.

Closers are activities conducted near the end of a session. They are used for such purposes as reviewing main points, tying up loose ends, planning application activities, providing feedback, celebrating successful conclusions, and exchanging information for future contacts.

Coaching Activities involve an individual (the coach) supporting the learning or performance improvement of another (the coachee) through interactive questioning and support. The process usually includes the coach and the coachee establishing goals, then the coach observing the coachee, offering relevant feedback, suggesting suitable activities, and helping the coachee's professional and personal growth.

Computer Game Shells are a special type of framegame that is presented on a computer. The shells permit the loading of new content (usually questions) by the facilitator. The computer acts as a timekeeper and scorekeeper. These games can also be presented to large groups by projecting the display on large screens.

Consensus Decision-Making Activities involve a list of items (usually ten) to be arranged in order of priority. Participants complete the task individually and then reach consensus in groups. They compare their priority rankings with expert rankings. In the process, they learn more about factors that contribute to the priority value of the items and also factors that influence decision making and reaching consensus.

Corporate Adventure Learning involves physical activities and challenges (such as sailing, rafting, rappelling, rock climbing, exploring wilderness areas, and walking on rope bridges) in specially designed indoor or outdoor environments. Participants construct knowledge, skill, and value from their direct experiences through debriefing discussions.

Creativity Techniques provide a structure that enables participants to solve a problem or to utilize an opportunity in a creative fashion. These techniques are useful not only for learning new skills and knowledge but also for directly improving the performance of a team.

E-Mail Games are conducted through the Internet. They may involve the play of electronic versions of interactive training games or specially designed activities that permit asynchronous communication in which people receive and send messages at different times. Typical e-mail games exploit the ability of the Internet to overcome geographic distances and involve participants pooling their ideas and polling to select best ones.

Facilitated Activities help teams analyze problems, formulate goals, generate alternative solutions, and make decisions. Usually, a trained facilitator conducts these structured activities to help teams maximize their diverse talents and to arrive at collaborative solutions that are superior to individual solutions.

Framegames provide templates for instant creation of training games. The generic frameworks are deliberately designed to permit easy replacement of old content with new. You can use framegames to develop training activities that suit your needs rapidly.

Guided Learning Activities provide a special type of on-the-job training. New employees (or new members of a team) observe workplace processes using carefully designed checklists. Later, they perform job-related activities under the guidance of an experienced employee or team member and receive immediate feedback.

Icebreakers are activities conducted near the beginning of a session. They are used for achieving such purposes as previewing main points, orienting participants, introducing participants to one another, forming teams, establishing ground rules, setting goals, reducing initial anxieties, and stimulating self-disclosure.

Improv Games are activities adapted from improvisational theater. The actors do not use a script but create the dialogue and action as they perform. When used

Exhibit 25.2. (*cont.*)

as an interactive training technique, improv games facilitate the mastery of skills related to such areas as creativity, collaboration, communication, and change.

Instructional Puzzles challenge the participants' ingenuity and incorporate training content that is to be previewed, reviewed, tested, retaught, or enriched. Puzzles can be solved by individuals or by teams.

Interactive Lectures involve participants in the learning process while providing complete control to the instructor. These activities enable a quick and easy conversion of a typical lecture into an interactive experience. Different types of interactive lectures incorporate built-in quizzes, interspersed tasks, teamwork interludes, and participant control of the presentation.

Interactive Storytelling involves fictional narratives in a variety of forms. Participants may listen to a story and make appropriate decisions at critical junctures. They may also create and share stories that illustrate key concepts, steps, or principles from the instructional content.

Jolts lull participants into behaving in a comfortable way and deliver a powerful wake-up call. They force participants to re-examine their assumptions and revise their standard procedures. Jolts typically last for a few minutes but provide enough insights for a lengthy debriefing.

Magic Tricks incorporate a relevant magic trick as a part of a training session. Magic tricks provide metaphors or analogies for some important element of the training content. The tricks are also used as processes to be analyzed, reconstructed, learned, performed, or coached for training participants in appropriate procedures.

Matrix Games require participants to occupy boxes in a grid by demonstrating a specific skill or knowledge. The matrixes provide a structure for matching or classifying individual items or organizing and comparing a set of items. The first participant to occupy a given number of boxes in a straight line (horizontally, vertically, or diagonally) wins the game.

Metaphorical Simulation Games (MSGs) reflect real-world processes in an abstract, simplified fashion. MSGs are particularly useful to teach principles related to planning, generating ideas, testing alternatives, making decisions, utilizing resources, and working under time pressure.

Paper-and-Pencil Games require players to make their moves by writing or drawing something on paper. A typical game may involve players working on a small piece of paper or a large sheet of newsprint. Paper-and-pencil games may incorporate elements of role play, simulation, creativity technique, or quiz contest.

PC Simulations use playing cards to reflect real-world objects and processes. The rules of PC simulations typically encourage participants to discover principles of interpersonal interaction and inductive thinking.

Read.me Games combine the effective organization of well-written materials with the motivational impact of playful activities. Participants read a handout and play a game that uses team support to encourage recall and transfer of what they read.

Reflective Teamwork involves participants creating a product related to some aspect of teamwork. Teams then evaluate their characteristics and performance by using the product they created.

Role Plays involve participants assuming and acting out characters, personalities, and attitudes other than their own. These activities may be tightly or loosely structured and may involve a participant assuming multiple roles or reversed roles.

Simulation Games help participants experience an event close to the real experience—without experiencing the real event itself. Originally used in war games for training officers and soldiers, this strategy is currently used in business games for teaching complex concepts. Most simulations are based on models of reality. Computers are frequently used to translate complex models in such areas as space travel and urban planning into graphic representations.

Structured Group Discussions use a self-contained instructional format designed to help team members learn together. The activity is facilitated by a mediated system (such as an audiotape, a videotape, or a computer) that presents information, specifies a discussion topic, imposes time limits, and provides feedback in the form of model responses and checklists.

Structured Sharing represents a special type of framegame that facilitates mutual learning and teaching among the participants. Typical structured sharing activities create a context for a dialogue among participants based on their experiences, knowledge, and opinions.

Telephone Games use telephones and answering machines. They may involve the play of interactive training games over long distances. Typical telephone games may involve elements of role play and virtual teamwork.

Television Games borrow the structure of popular TV game shows to present the instructional content and to encourage participants to practice skills. They involve selected contestants and the "studio audience," who participate and learn vicariously. TV Games can be broadcast for distance learning, made available on videotapes, or presented live by using computer game shells and graphics.

Thought Experiments are internal role plays that involve guided visualization. Individual participants may mentally rehearse new patterns of behavior, ask Eleanor Roosevelt for advice, or hold a dialogue with their alter ego. These activities result in the learning of new knowledge and insights.

Training Devices involve physical activities performed on pieces of electrical and mechanical equipment. Participants solve a problem or meet a challenge with the device and relate the process to their workplace activities.

Exhibit 25.2. (cont.)

Video Vitamins enhance the instructional value of training videos. In a typical video vitamin, participants watch a videotape and then play one or more games that help review and apply the new concepts and skills.

Wall Games, frequently used with large groups by my colleague Steve Sugar, typically involve posters mounted on a wall (or on an easel) that require participants to write or draw. A typical wall game may present a vertical version of a board game, a matrix game, or an instructional puzzle. Participants may play these games individually or in teams.

Web-Based Games are interactive activities presented on the World Wide Web. A variety of games and simulations can be played either by individuals or by teams. Some Web-based games permit several people to interact with one another at the same time in chat rooms. Others require "asynchronous" interaction in which the exchange of information among participants is delayed by minutes, hours, or days.

Sternberg (1996) has demonstrated that a person with a low IQ can be highly creative and practical. According to this research, practical and creative intelligences are better predictors of job effectiveness than is analytical intelligence. Games and training activities directly contribute to the enhancement of practical and creative intelligences and ensure greater applications of newly learned skills and knowledge to the workplace.

Gardner (1999) has demonstrated that we have at least seven types of intelligence: linguistic, logical, kinesthetic, visual, musical, interpersonal, and intrapersonal. Traditional training caters almost exclusively to the first two. In contrast, games and activities tap into all seven and thus increase our learning potential.

Goleman (1998) has popularized the concept of emotional intelligence to emphasize the importance of self-awareness, impulse control, persistence, motivation, and empathy. The principles and procedures related to emotional intelligence are best learned by experiencing these factors and analyzing their impact. Games and activities are obvious strategies of choice for developing emotional intelligence.

Psychological support for the use of games and activities is not limited to recent research on the nature of intelligence. Exhibit 25.3 identifies seven "laws of learning" based on classic psychological studies conducted during the past century. Additional support and suggestions for the use of games and activities in mainstream training are provided.

Exhibit 25.3. Seven Laws of Learning

Here's a quick review of the seven laws of learning that have been consistently supported by psychological research during the past several decades. After a brief statement of each law is a discussion of ways to apply it to training games and activities.

Law of Reinforcement: Participants learn to repeat behaviors that are rewarded.

Make sure that training activities provide several opportunities for earning rewards. Require participants to make frequent decisions and responses. The scoring system rewards people for correct responses. During the first few rounds of the activity, reward even partially correct answers. Clearly associate the reward with the response. In addition to score points, have participant behaviors earn such social rewards as praise and recognition from team members and spectators.

Law of Emotional Learning: Events that are accompanied by intense emotions result in long-lasting learning.

Boredom is not conducive to learning. Training games, simulations, and role plays add an emotional element to learning, but make sure that emotions don't become too intense and interfere with learning. Also make sure that participants don't learn dysfunctional behaviors because of intense emotions. Debrief participants after emotional activities to analyze their feelings and learn from their reactions. You may want to conduct specially designed games to help participants unlearn undesirable behaviors acquired in the grip of powerful emotions.

Law of Active Learning: Active responding produces more effective learning than passive listening or reading.

Intersperse lectures and reading assignments with active learning episodes such as quizzes and puzzles. Provide participants with ample opportunities to respond by asking questions, encouraging them to ask questions, answering their questions, and questioning their answers.

Law of Practice and Feedback: Learners cannot master skills without repeated practice and relevant feedback.

Don't confuse understanding a procedure with ability to perform it. Invest ample time in conducting activities that provide repeated practice and feedback. Make sure that the training activities incorporate immediate and useful feedback from peers and experts. Use rating scales, checklists, and other devices to ensure that the feedback is objective and useful.

Law of Previous Experience: New learning should be linked to (and build upon) the experiences of the learner.

Exhibit 25.3. (*cont.*)

Check the entry level of the participants by using appropriate activities. Adults bring a variety of rich experiences to the training classroom. Design activities to ensure easy adjustments to fit different entry levels and to incorporate relevant experiences.

Law of Individual Differences: Different people learn in different ways.

Use training activities that accommodate a variety of learning styles. Make sure that participants can respond by writing, speaking, drawing, and acting out. Encourage and permit participants to learn individually, in pairs, and in teams. Through team learning activities, ensure that participants receive individual attention from their peers. Use a variety of scoring systems to encourage different learning styles.

Law of Relevance: Effective learning is relevant to the learner's life and work.

Use simulations and role plays to increase the link between the learning situation and the real world. Incorporate realistic problems and challenges from a variety of workplace situations. After a training activity, debrief the participants and discuss strategies for applying what they learned in the game to their real-world context. Require the participants to walk the talk and to demonstrate their ability to transfer abstract theory to concrete conditions.

DESIGNING GAMES AND ACTIVITIES

We can design training games and simulations, just like any other training material, by using the principles and procedures discussed in Chapter 16 on instructional design. However, in a series of interviews with creative designers of training games, I have discovered that the systematic instructional design process has not resulted in the most powerful training games and activities of the past decade. I personally do not use the instructional design model for designing games. Instead, I use a process that is more suited to the design of faster, cheaper, and better training materials that my clients and participants demand.

I call the game-design process *continuous concurrent co-design*. It is a *continuous* process because I never produce the "final" version of a training game or activity. The product is tweaked continuously to fit current training needs, resources, and constraints. It is a *concurrent* process because I mix up the design steps and arrange them in different sequences. It is a *co-design* process because I design training games with the active help of players. By designing while playing, everyone is both a designer and a player. The result is an organic co-creation. No one can figure out who contributed what to the final design. And no one cares about the recognition of individual contributions.

Concurrent co-design is not a procedure that you implement one step at a time. Instead, it is a set of design principles that you implement in any sequence. Here are some examples of these principles:

- *Don't analyze in isolation.* Do the learner analysis as you design and play the game. If your game does not match learners' needs, characteristics, and preferences, they will refuse to play or, better yet, come up with a superior set of rules.

- *Begin at the end.* Decide what type of learning is involved and select one or more game templates that have worked with similar goals in the past. Start playing the game, making up and altering the rules as you go.

- *Design and test together.* Play the game with real people as early in your design process as possible. The importance of using representative members of a target group is grossly exaggerated. I frequently test elements of a game with people riding in a crowded elevator or lining up at a ticket counter. An effective training game works with all types of players. Any necessary fine-tuning can be done quickly on the spot.

- *Manage paradoxes.* The heart of game design is the art of managing paradoxes. Make sure your game is fun to play *and* produces a serious training impact. Make sure that your game supports individual needs *and* forces individuals to take into account the needs of the team. Make sure your game rewards skills *and* has an element of chance to provide hope to the player who is left behind.

- *Ignore your objectives.* This is a major paradox for you to manage. Park the training objectives in the back of your mind. You will be surprised by the actual attitude change, skill acquisition, and knowledge mastery that result from the play of a game. Identify these outcomes and add them to your list of training objectives. And remember, your game does not have to teach everything. You can supplement it with debriefing discussions, reading assignments, and hands-on demonstrations.

- *Tinker.* Play with the rules, not within the rules. Don't begin with a complete set of rules. Instead, start with one or two basic rules and improvise the rest. Watch the rules emerge from the play—and from the players. Because every player has a different background, your game ends up with an eclectic flow.

- *Debrief players.* Find out what they enjoyed and what they disliked. Ask players for suggestions for improving the game. Play it again immediately to test new procedures.

- *Let go.* Don't be proprietary and insist that there is only one "correct" way to play your game. Apply an open-platform approach to your design. Encourage facilitators and players to alter your game. Minutes, days, or years later, when you least expect it, someone will share a brilliant twist to your game.

SELECTING AND ADAPTING TRAINING GAMES AND SIMULATIONS

The number of training games and activities has grown rapidly during the past decade. One of my graduate students recently counted 3,947 published icebreakers in books, magazines, and websites, and this number is continually increasing. Most publishers produce voluminous collections of training games and activities. The standard *Annual* published by Jossey-Bass/Pfeiffer (Biech, 2001) is currently in its thirtieth year. In the area of soft skills, you can select among 669 different training games and activities from this one source alone.

There are several reasons for the accelerating proliferation of training games, including increased demand from the newer generation of participants and facilitators, increased diversity among participants, greater demand for experiential and active training, and increased use of computers in training. Whatever the reason, you should have no difficulty locating games for any training objective and for any target population. However, you still have to review the available games and select the most suitable ones for your needs. The checklist presented in Exhibit 25.1 will assist you in this process. After you have selected the most suitable game, you have to adapt it to fit such factors as time, physical facilities, number of players, type of players, and type of facilitators. Such adaptation is best done with a group of facilitators and participants using the continuous concurrent co-design process described above.

FACILITATING TRAINING GAMES AND ACTIVITIES

The effectiveness of a training game depends to a large extent on the way it is conducted. Facilitating a game or an activity requires attitudes, skills, and knowledge that are different from those needed for making presentations.

Several years of reflective practice and objective observation have helped me identify the one constant factor in effective facilitation: Good facilitators keep changing their technique. Effective facilitators are flexible. They modify their process before they conduct an activity and while they conduct an activity. They continually change their strategy to better suit the goals, participant preferences, and group feedback.

To understand flexible facilitation, we should understand different dimensions of facilitation. My analysis suggests that seven dimensions can enhance or destroy a facilitated activity. The following rating scales identify these seven dimensions:

- *Interaction.* 1 = too competitive, 2 = competitive, 3 = neutral, 4 = cooperative, 5 = too cooperative
- *Pace.* 1 = too fast, 2 = fast, 3 = neutral, 4 = slow, 5 = too slow
- *Tone.* 1 = too playful, 2 = playful, 3 = neutral, 4 = serious, 5 = too serious
- *Duration.* 1 = too brief, 2 = brief, 3 = neutral, 4 = lengthy, 5 = too lengthy
- *Concern.* 1 = too much concern about individuals, 2 = concern about individuals, 3 = neutral, 4 = concern about the group, 5 = too much concern about the group
- *Control.* 1 = too loose, 2 = loose, 3 = neutral, 4 = tight, 5 = too tight
- *Privacy.* 1 = too intrusive, 2 = intrusive, 3 = neutral, 4 = protective of privacy, 5 = too protective of privacy

You already have the knowledge and skills required for flexible facilitation. What you need is an acceptance of the importance of balance. With some practice with real participants, you are well on your way to becoming a successful facilitator.

When an aspiring facilitator asks me, "Should I conduct the activity at a fast pace or a slow one?" I answer, "Yes." The appropriate location of an activity along the seven dimensions depends on several factors, including the number and types of participants as well as the structure and purpose of the activity. The secret of effective facilitation is to make these dimensions transparent. This is achieved by maintaining a balance between any of the two extremes. Unfortunately, "balance" resides in the perception of participants, rather than in outside reality. Thus, the balance along the cooperation-competition dimension may differ drastically between a group from an ashram in California and one from a brokerage firm in New York. Similarly, the balance in the privacy dimension may differ depending on the culture to which the participants belong.

The first step in balanced facilitation is to avoid the extreme positions on the rating scales. Beyond that, use a variety of common-sense tactics to move the activity along each dimension. Here are a few sample tactics:

Interaction

To increase competition, use a scoring system to reward effective performance. Periodically announce and compare scores of different teams. Reward the winning team with a valuable prize.

To increase cooperation, reduce the conflict among the participants and increase the conflict between participants and external constraints (for example, time limits). Use multiple criteria for determining winners: Reward individuals and teams for speed, quality, efficiency, fluency, creativity, novelty, and other such factors.

Pace

To speed up the pace, begin the activity promptly and get it rolling fast. Announce and implement intermediate time limits.

To slow down the pace, announce and implement minimum time requirements. If a participant or a team finishes the task before this time is up, insist on review and revision. Introduce a quality-control rule that punishes participants and teams for turning in sloppy ideas or products.

Tone

To increase seriousness, maintain a serious tone. Recognize and praise serious and thoughtful behaviors. Emphasize critical aspects of the game. Focus on negative consequences of flippant behaviors.

To increase playfulness, maintain a playful tone. Recognize and praise impulsive and playful behaviors. De-emphasize critical aspects of the game. Focus on the positive consequences of playful behaviors.

Duration

To lengthen the activity, add more factors and steps. Increase the number of participants. Repeat the activity with variations. Conduct a reflective debriefing.

To shorten the activity, reduce the number of factors and steps. Decrease the number of participants. Increase the amount of pre-work and follow-up activities.

Concern

To show more concern to individual needs, organize participants into teams of equal levels of competency. Encourage timid participants by providing them with additional information and responsibilities.

To pay more concern to group needs, identify dominant participants and give them additional roles (for example, keeping score or taking notes) to channel their excess energy. Have the team conduct periodic process checks to make sure that everyone's needs are met.

Control

To tighten the activity, begin with a detailed explanation of the rules. Stress the importance of adhering to these rules. Provide a printed copy of the rules for each participant. Frequently refer to these rules.

To loosen the activity, acknowledge that participants will be initially confused. Reassure them that it is not necessary to stick to the rules rigidly. Don't present all the rules in the beginning. Introduce the rules only if and when they are required.

Privacy

To increase the level of intrusion, make intimate self-disclosure statements and praise others for making such statements. Ask probing questions about personal feelings and emotions. Require everyone to respond to such questions.

To increase the protection of privacy, encourage personal choice of the level of self-disclosure. Avoid probing questions about personal feelings and emotions. Ask for anonymous written responses.

DEBRIEFING GAMES AND ACTIVITIES

The effectiveness of a training game depends not only on what happens during the activity but also on what happens *after* the activity. After the intensive play of a simulation game or a role play, conduct a debriefing discussion. This discussion helps your participants to reflect on the activity, relate their activities to the real world, discover useful insights, and share them with one another. Debriefing also helps you to wind down the activity, reduce negative reactions among participants, and increase learning insights.

A major dilemma in debriefing is maintaining a balance between structure and free flow. I suggest that you prepare several questions before the debriefing session. During actual debriefing, encourage and exploit spontaneous comments from participants. If the conversation degenerates into a stream-of-consciousness meandering, fall back on your prepared list of questions.

I use a six-phase model to structure debriefing questions. Here are some guidelines for each phase of this model.

Phase 1: How Do You Feel?

This phase gives the participants an opportunity to get strong feelings and emotions off their chests. It makes it easier for them to be more objective during the later phases.

Begin this phase with a broad question that invites the participants to get in touch with their feelings about the activity and its outcomes. Encourage them to share these feelings, listening actively to each other in a nonjudgmental fashion.

Phase 2: What Happened?

In this phase, collect data about what happened during the activity. Encourage participants to compare and contrast their recollections and to draw general conclusions during the next phase.

Begin this phase with a broad question that asks the participants to recall important events during the game. Create a chronological list of events. Ask questions about specific events.

Phase 3: What Did You Learn?

In this phase, encourage participants to generate and test different hypotheses. Ask participants to come up with principles based on what happened and discuss them.

Begin this phase by presenting a principle and asking participants for data that supports or rejects it. Then invite the participants to offer other principles based on their experience.

Phase 4: How Does This Relate to the Real World?

In this phase, discuss the relevance of the activity to participants' real-world experiences.

Begin this phase with a broad question about the relationship between the experience and events in the workplace. Suggest that the activity is a metaphor and ask the participants to offer real-world analogies.

Phase 5: What If. . . ?

In this phase, encourage participants to apply their insights to new contexts. Use alternative scenarios to speculate on how participants' behaviors would change.

Begin this phase with a changed scenario and ask participants to speculate on how it would have affected the process and the outcomes. Then invite participants to offer their own scenarios and discuss them.

Phase 6: What Next?

In this phase, ask participants to undertake action planning. Ask them to apply their insights from the activity to the real world.

Begin this phase by asking participants to suggest strategies for use in future rounds of the game. Then ask the participants how they would change their real-world behaviors as a result of the insights gained from the activity.

KEEP THE GAME GOING!

This chapter has provided introductory answers to the *what, why,* and *how* of training games and activities. Real understanding of the principles and mastery of the procedures related to games, however, comes only from serious play! You are now ready to embark on the experiential part of your learning regimen. In doing that, remember that true learning comes from playing *with* the rules of the game rather than playing *within* the rules of the game.

References

Biech, E. (Ed.). (2001). *The 2001 annual* (Vols. 1 & 2). San Francisco: Jossey-Bass/Pfeiffer.

Epstein, S. (1993). *You're smarter than you think.* New York: Simon & Schuster.

Gardner, H. (1999). *Intelligence reframed: Multiple intelligences for the 21st century.* New York: Basic Books.

Goleman, D. (1998). *Working with emotional intelligence.* New York: Bantam Books.

Sternberg, R.J. (1996). *Successful intelligence: How practical and creative intelligence determine success in life.* New York: Simon & Schuster.

Recommended Reading

Sugar, S. (1999). *Games that teach: Experiential activities for reinforcing learning.* San Francisco: Jossey-Bass/Pfeiffer.

Thiagarajan, S., & Parker, G. (1999). *Teamwork and teamplay: Games and activities for building and training teams.* San Francisco: Jossey-Bass/Pfeiffer.

Thiagarajan, S. (2000). *Interactive strategies for improving performance.* Bloomington, IN: Workshops by Thiagi, Inc.

Ukens, L.L. (1999). *All together now! A seriously fun collection of training games and activities.* San Francisco: Jossey-Bass/Pfeiffer.

About the Author

After losing numerous checkers games to his uncle, **Sivasailam "Thiagi" Thiagarajan** *designed his first game when he was seven years old. Interestingly, nobody has beaten Thiagi in this game. Since March 21, 1999, Thiagi has been conducting a study with a single experimental subject (himself) who is required to design one training game every day (including holidays) with the constraint that each day's game should be significantly different from the previous three days' games. At the time of writing this chapter, the study has yielded 371 training games, out of which seven have been sold to clients at exorbitant prices, sixty-one have been published, and the others have been stored on various hard drives. Thiagi currently has his own play pen called Workshops by Thiagi, Inc., whose corporate mission is to improve human performance effectively, efficiently, and enjoyably. He writes the monthly* Thiagi GameLetter, *published by Jossey-Bass/Pfeiffer.*

CHAPTER TWENTY-SIX

What Smart Trainers Know About Self-Directed Learning

George M. Piskurich
Principal, GMP Associates

Self-directed learning might be considered a design methodology or a learner attribute. However you look at it though, it is the foundation for interventions ranging from technology-based training to learning organizations. Smart trainers understand where and how learner self-direction affects their interventions. They prepare their learners to become more self-directed in knowledge sharing or individualized development environments and design their Web-based training in accordance with self-directed learning theory to make it as effective and easy to use as possible.

SELF-DIRECTED LEARNING

For starters, smart trainers know how to (or not to) define self-directed learning (SDL). This is not as simple as it might sound. At an annual international symposium on self-directed learning that is well into its second decade, the discussion concerning how to define SDL has been going on since the first meeting, with no consensus in sight.

However, if you take away a large measure of the philosophy, psychology, and some of the theory from the SDL process, you find that, for training purposes, the various definitions fall into two major camps: Self-directed learning as an *instructional design* and self-directed learning as an *attribute of learners*.

It doesn't matter which of these camps you fall into; in fact, smart trainers probably subscribe to both of them, as we will see. The issue as far as a definition is concerned is to realize that there is more to self-directed learning than your particular conceptualization; so when you're talking to others about it, they may or may not be hearing what you think you are saying (so what else is new?).

SDL As an Instructional Design

The instructional design camp is comprised mainly of those who view SDL as formalized self-instruction of one type or another. This includes everything from the long-out-of-favor mail-order correspondence course, advertisements for which were once found on matchbook covers, to the newest in Web-based degree granting college curricula, which don't advertise on matchbooks, although perhaps only because so few people smoke these days.

Surprisingly, these two examples are not extremes of the design concept of SDL, but simply steps on a technology continuum across which SDL functions. Whether the self-instruction comes in the mail or over the Web, the true extremes of the process are well-designed programs versus badly designed programs (that is, those programs that have a chance of being effective versus those that do not).

Smart trainers know that taking a classroom lecture and placing it on the Web does not create a self-instructional training program. Instead, its usual outcome is to bore trainees one at a time, rather than as a group. They also know that a poorly designed classroom program (that is, one that has not been based on proper analysis and does not contain good objectives, effective evaluation, and plenty of trainee activities) will not, through the magic of some piece of conversion software, become good self-instruction.

Very smart trainers realize that even the best classroom program will require a lot of modification to become effective self-instruction—and even more modification still if it is to take advantage of technologies such as CD-ROM or the Web.

Whether you are converting a classroom training program or developing a new learning process from scratch, you must follow a specific set of principles when trying to create self-instruction, the most important of which is that *there is no instructor.*

This may sound pretty obvious, but many trainers tend to forget this basic fact when designing self-instruction. Those four words mean much more than their simplicity might indicate. For example, if there is no instructor, who or what accomplishes those tasks that are the role of the instructor in the classroom?

One answer to this question is *well-written objectives,* which perform the instructor's role of telling the trainees what's most important—that is, what they need to learn. Another is the instructional designer who sets the instructional environment through the design, the sequence, and the general feel of the instruction—all instructor responsibilities in a stand-up program.

Having no instructor also means that there is no one to make up for lapses in the content or mistakes in the material, or simply to tell war stories. In all these cases, it is up to the designer to fulfill the instructor's role. The designer must make sure that the content is accurate, complete, and understandable and that those enlightening, learning-bridge developing, war stories (call them metaphors, simulations or whatever you like) are there when and where they are needed.

I could go on with this discussion of the differences between self-instructional and classroom designs and broaden it to include the presentation of graphics, video, and trainee interactions, but I hope I've made my point. Smart trainers know that there is a proper way to design self-instructional programs, and they make sure that those design parameters are followed for all their SDL, be it print, video, computer-based, or matchbook.

SDL As a Learner Attribute

The other camp of those defining self-directed learning, as we mentioned earlier, sees SDL as a learner attribute, not necessarily an instructional design. The word on their banner is "Choice," with a capital "C," which is where SDL often gets into trouble in a business environment.

The learner attribute camp contends that effective SDL is practiced by individuals who are self-directed, that is, they exhibit certain characteristics, such as achievement motivation, holistic thinking, and high life satisfaction, which make it important for them to have choices in their learning processes. A full list of these characteristics or behaviors (there is a lot of discussion as to how these attributes should be labeled) looks like the one in Exhibit 26.1.

Choice for these learners is not simply which day they need to learn something or how much time they spend on the learning, as in self-instruction, but how they might learn the content, how they'll evaluate their learning, and even what they really need to learn in the first place.

Now you might say, "Well, that's fine for education, but training is made of sterner stuff and can't allow that much learner control." I won't argue the point here, but I refer you to the definition of SDL as a learner attribute and to the list of attributes of self-directedness in Exhibit 26.1. Who would not want employees with these characteristics!

The interesting thing about self-direction and self-directed learning is that they are synergistic. With proper preparation, the more practice individuals have at SDL the more self-directed they are likely to become. Thus, characteristics, such as self-confidence and achievement motivation, and skills, such as goal setting and decision making, grow in individuals as they become comfortable

Exhibit 26.1. Attributes of Self-Directed Learners

• Self-confident	• Strong goal-setting skills
• Inner-directed	• Good decision maker
• Achievement motivated	• Accurate observer
• Reflective	• Effective listener
• Accommodating	• Strong reading skills
• Creative, holistic thinker	• Performs well on job
• More independent	• High life satisfaction
• Less dogmatic	• Does other learning projects
• High self-esteem	

with their ability to direct their own learning; in other words, they become more self-directed.

Notice that I prefaced the previous comment with the phrase *"with proper preparation."* This is another of those phrases that means a lot more than its brevity might indicate. Employees for the most part are not self-directed when it comes to their formal learning, be it education or training. They are used to being told what to learn, when, and how. This is basically because that is the way they were taught to learn, from their earliest classroom experiences through the mega-lecture halls of college campuses.

Strangely enough, this is not how they learn outside the formal learning environment. A number of studies have shown that 90 percent of all adults do at least one self-directed learning project a year outside of work. These projects can range from five to one hundred hours in length and might deal with anything from a hobby to a passing interest to a way to change one's life. The average adult engages in three to five of these projects each year, and all of them are self-directed!

To help your employees see how self-directed they really are, there are instruments available that estimate individual self-directedness. One of the most popular of these is the Self-Directed Learning Readiness Scale (SDLRS), developed by Lucy Guglielmino. She states that the instrument actually measures the individual's readiness to engage in self-directed learning activities should the opportunity present itself, which is perfect for an organization seeking to increase employee self-directedness. The SDLRS has been validated in a number of industries and cross culturally as well. It is the source instrument for the list of self-directed attributes given earlier in this chapter.

PREPARATION FOR SDL

Breaking the employees' dependence on others to decide their learning needs in the work environment through the realization that they are already capable of doing it themselves is one of the cornerstones of preparing employees for self-direction. Other cornerstones include providing support and encouragement for the newly self-directed learner (often a supervisor's role), providing chances for small self-directed learning successes for the employees (instead of giving them a full-blown system and adopting the "sink or swim" philosophy that is often prevalent in technology-based training [TBT] interventions), and facilitating a self-directed environment (usually a job for managers and management in general). Some methods for establishing and nurturing the SDL environment in an organization include

- Giving permission to engage in self-direction by supplying the opportunity and the time;
- Providing learning resources for the self-directed learner to utilize;
- Training supervisors to be learning coaches who encourage and provide feedback;
- Rewarding self-directed successes;
- Establishing learning groups;
- Reducing the new self-directed learner's fear of failure;
- Supporting the outcomes of self-directed learning on performance measuring tools and systems;
- Training supervisors to model self-direction in their own work;
- Allowing self-directed learners time for reflection; and
- Training supervisors to look for and utilize informal learning possibilities.

Much of the preparation process can be initiated through a series of classes designed for this purpose. This may seem a bit of an oxymoron—using classrooms to teach self-direction—but remember that employees are comfortable with classes and, for the most part, uncomfortable with the idea of self-direction. If you are going to change this mindset, begin with something that is familiar and work from there.

You should plan classes for both managers and individual contributors, as each has a different role to play in the search for self-direction. The best systems combine both audiences in the basic class and then give the managers special training on creating and facilitating the SDL environment. Using instruments like the SDLRS early in this process is also an effective way to enhance self-directed learning preparation.

This preparation process brings up one of the areas where the concepts of the two camps overlap. If one must be self-directed to take advantage of self-directed learning possibilities, or as the designer camp calls it "self-instruction," then you had better prepare your employees to be self-directed before embarking on any self-instruction, such as computer-based training (CBT) or Web-based training.

Lack of proper preparation to enhance participant self-direction is why so many self-instructional, technology-based training interventions fail. Just giving employees the chance to learn, to use desktop deliveries, or to slide in CD-ROMS does not necessarily mean they will take advantage of it. Employees need to be, and must be, prepared to become self-directed learners if your technology-based training initiative or your knowledge management intervention is to have any chance of succeeding.

Which brings up still another aspect of self-direction for organizations. If you've read Senge's (1990) work on the learning organization, you may have noticed a number of similarities between his concepts and those of self-direction. In a nutshell, for the learning organization to function, its members must be self-directed—or at least exhibit many self-directed attributes.

Self-direction is also a key issue in the knowledge management interventions that are at the heart of organizational learning processes. Most of these interventions require the sharing of knowledge in one form or another, from one person to another. Without a certain amount of self-direction on the part of the employees, the chances of this happening are rather slim.

Finally, self-direction is a baseline requirement for individualized development. Many organizations now speak of the new contract with employees—not lifelong employment, but lifelong *development*. Such a process cannot be handled simply by previous career development methodologies such as career paths and succession planning.

The burden of deciding what development is needed and how it will occur must be on the employee. Supervisors have neither the time nor expertise to take the lead in this process. Rather, they must become coaches to self-directed employees who are creating a structure for their own individualized development.

SUMMARY

So what do smart trainers know about self-directed learning?

- They know that it is a design methodology that requires the utilization of appropriate design techniques if it is to be effective for learners;
- They know that it is an attribute of the employee/learner that needs to be nourished if a variety of organizational interventions are to be successful;

- They know that it is the foundation for individualized development;
- They know that it is a key issue in the creation of a learning organization and a basic aspect of organizational learning/knowledge management; and
- They know that they, and their organization, probably need to know more about SDL if they are to function effectively.

Reference

Senge, P.M. (1990). *The fifth discipline.* New York: Currency-Doubleday.

Recommended Reading

Hammond, M., & Collins, R. (1991). *Self-directed learning: Critical practice.* New York: Nichols/GP Publishing.

Hatcher, T.G. (1997, February). The ins and outs of self-directed learning. *Training & Development,* 35–39.

Hiemstra, R., & Sisco, B. (1990). *Individualizing instruction.* San Francisco: Jossey-Bass.

Knowles, M.K. (1980, May). How do you get people to be self-directed learners? *Training & Development,* 96–99.

Long, H. (1990). Changing concepts of self-direction in learning. In H. Long and Associates, *Advances in research and practice in self-directed learning.* Tulsa, OK: University of Oklahoma Press.

Piskurich, G. (1991, September). Ensure quality and quality training through self-directed learning. *Training & Development,* 45–48.

Piskurich, G. (1993). *Self-directed learning: A practical guide to design, development, and implementation.* San Francisco: Jossey-Bass.

Piskurich, G. (1994, March). Developing self-directed learning. *Training & Development,* 31–36.

Solomon, C.M. (1997, March). When training doesn't translate. *Workforce,* 40–44.

Warr, P., & Bunce, D. (1995). Trainee characteristics and the outcomes of open learning. *Personnel Psychology, 48,* 347–375.

About the Author

George M. Piskurich is presently consulting in instructional design and technology based training implementation. He has been in the training profession in various positions and industry settings for over twenty years. His areas of special interest include self-directed learning, performance improvement, customer service, and management/supervisory development. He has presented at over thirty conferences and symposia, including the International Self-Directed Learning Symposium and the ISPI and ASTD international conferences, speaking on topics ranging from mentoring systems to interactive distance learning to telecommuting.

Piskurich has authored books on learning technology, self-directed learning, instructional design, and telecommuting; edited three books on instructional technology; and written extensively in his areas of interest for a number of periodicals. He is currently working on a book on human performance improvement. He has served in a number of capacities for ASTD and ISPI on both local and national levels. Currently residing in Macon, Georgia, he can be reached by e-mail at GMP1@Compuserve.com.

CHAPTER TWENTY-SEVEN

Guaranteed Results with Multimedia and Online Training

Kevin E. Kruse
Principal, Kenexa, Inc.

Organizations are embracing technology-based training initiatives in record numbers. While classroom-based training will never (and should not) go away, the benefits of online learning are extremely compelling. They include a reduction in costs associated with student travel, a reduction in time spent away from the job, reduced learning times for equivalent material, and increased student retention rates. When working with learning technologies or creating a new self-paced training program, there are four key factors that will influence the success of the project: (1) Choosing the right technology (CD-ROM and Web technologies have unique strengths and weaknesses); (2) designing effective instruction (retention is optimized if the training is sequenced properly and highly interactive); (3) managing the project lifecycle (keeping the project on-time and on-budget can be realized by using the process of analysis, design, development, implementation, and evaluation); and (4) measuring the results (evaluating current project success and obtaining support for new initiatives).

INTRODUCTION

The pace of change in the world of technology has truly become breathless. People now talk about Internet years the same way they talk about dog years—at least seven to one. As always, such changes bring both challenges and exciting opportunities. The application of technology for learning is now a core component of most organizations' strategy for developing human talent.

Looking just at online learning as a category, in 1997 total expenditures on Web-based training (WBT) were estimated at $197 million, while spending on WBT in the year 2003 is now projected to be $11 billion, representing over a 100 percent annual growth rate (press release, International Data Corporation, 1998).

This chapter is intended to provide you with a crash course in the design, development, and management of technology-based training programs that will achieve measurable results for your organization. This chapter is *not* about the specific tasks related to scripting, creating media, or programming. Rather, it provides the fundamental principles behind quality instruction, project management, vendor relations, and program evaluation—in other words, all the elements necessary to manage or produce an interactive learning project successfully.

WHAT IS TECHNOLOGY-BASED TRAINING?

Technology-based training can be a confusing topic, in part because of the alphabet soup of acronyms, technology related buzzwords, overlapping definitions, and variety of delivery options. Today, what most people really mean when they use the term technology-based training (and its multiple synonyms) is multimedia CD-ROM and Web-based training. Training products that take these forms are the particular focus of this chapter.

Technology-based training (TBT) is really nothing more than using technology to deliver training and educational materials. Technology-based training is the all-inclusive term for training delivered by a number of means. In the past, these have included the use of mainframe computers, floppy diskettes, multimedia CD-ROMs, and interactive video disks. Most recently, Internet and intranet delivery have become preferred delivery options.

Understanding what is and what is not TBT can be confusing due to the number of different terms that exist to define the same thing. Some people prefer the word learning to training (as in "dogs are trained, people learn") and use technology-based *learning* (TBL) instead of technology-based training (TBT). In business, where most companies have training, not learning, departments, the term technology-based training is most frequently encountered.

Other commonly used terms include computer-based training (CBT), computer-based learning (CBL), computer-based instruction (CBI), computer-based education (CBE), Web-based training (WBT), Internet-based training (IBT), intranet-based training (also IBT), browser-based training (BBT), online learning, and a number of others. Some of these, such as Web-based training, can be seen as specific subsections of TBT, while others, notably computer-based training, are less specific. Other confusion arises from technical definitions that differ from their popular use. For example, the terms CBT, CBI, and CBL are sometimes used generically to refer to all types of TBT but are generally used to describe older disk-based training.

A term beginning with the word "computer" frequently, but not always, refers to interactive tutorials that are distributed on floppy diskettes. The term "multimedia training" is usually used to describe training delivered via CD-ROM. This rule of thumb is complicated by the fact that advances in Internet technology make it possible for network-based training to now deliver audio and video elements as well.

Distance learning, another commonly used term, accurately describes many types of TBT, but it is used most often to describe interactive satellite video-conferences and the use of the Internet/intranet for live instructors to facilitate a training class.

To further complicate matters, some theorists divide TBT into three distinct branches: CAI, CMI, and CSLR. The first, computer-aided instruction, encompasses the portion of a given TBT product that provides the instruction, such as the tutorials, simulations, and exercises. The second, computer-managed instruction, refers to the testing, record keeping, and study guidance functions of a TBT product. The last term, computer-supported learning resources, describes the communication, database, and performance support aspects of TBT. While these distinctions can prove useful in academic research and discussion, it is enough for most of us to know that they exist and that they all refer to parts of the greater whole, technology-based training.

ADVANTAGES AND DISADVANTAGES OF TBT

The vast movement toward TBT is clearly motivated by the many benefits it offers. However much TBT is praised and innovated, computers will never completely eliminate human instructors and other forms of educational delivery. It is important to know exactly what TBT advantages exist and when these outweigh the limitations of the medium.

Technology-based training, like no other training form, promises to provide a single experience that accommodates the three distinct learning styles of auditory learners, visual learners, and kinesthetic learners. Other unique opportunities created by the advent and development of TBT are more efficient training of a globally dispersed audience and reduced publishing and distribution costs as Web-based training becomes a standard.

Technology-based training also offers individualized instruction, which print media cannot provide—and that instructor-led courses allow clumsily and at great cost. In conjunction with assessing knowledge and skill gaps, TBT can target specific needs. And by using learning style tests, TBT can even locate and target individual learning preferences.

Additionally, TBT is self-paced. Advanced learners are allowed to speed through or bypass instruction that is redundant, while novices slow their own progress through content, eliminating frustration with themselves, their fellow learners, and the course.

In these ways, TBT is inclusive of a maximum number of participants with a maximum range of learning styles, preferences, and needs.

Advantages to the Organization/Trainer

Some of the most outstanding advantages to the *trainer* or *company* are listed below:

- *Reduced overall cost* is the single most influential factor in adopting TBT. The elimination of costs associated with student travel, lodging, meals, meeting room rentals, and instructors' salaries are directly quantifiable. The reduction of time spent away from the job by student-employees, also known as the "opportunity" costs, may be the greatest savings;

- *Learning times are reduced* an average of 40 to 60 percent as compared to classroom-based instruction, as found by Hall (1997, p. 108);

- *Increased retention and application of information* to the job increases an average of 25 percent over traditional methods, according to an independent study by Fletcher (1991);

- *Consistent delivery* of content is possible with technology-based training, whereas content is often diluted by filtering through various instructors; and

- *Proof of completion and certification,* essential elements of training initiatives, can be automated.

Advantages to the Learner

Along with the increased retention, reduced learning time, and other aforementioned benefits to students, particular advantages of TBT include

- *On-demand availability* allows students to complete training conveniently at off-hours or from home, and closer to the time and place of need;

- *Self-pacing* for slow or quick learners reduces stress and increases satisfaction; and

- *Interactivity* engages users and forces them to become active participants in the learning process.

Disadvantages to the Trainer/Organization

Technology-based training is not, however, the be all and end all of every training need. It does have limitations, among them

- *Up-front investment* required of a TBT solution is larger due to development costs. Initial budgets and cash flow will need to be weighed against the benefits; and
- *Technology issues* that play a factor include whether the existing technology infrastructure can support the bandwidth and media requirements of the TBT.

Disadvantages to the Learner

The ways in which TBT may not excel over other training include

- *Learner techno-phobia* or unfamiliarity with the interface may impede access to the content;
- *Portability* of TBT has improved with the proliferation of Internet connections and notebook computers, but it does not compare with the portability and ease of use of print media; and
- *Reduced social and cultural* interaction potentially eliminates peer-to-peer learning and can negatively impact employee engagement and retention.

WHEN TO USE WBT OR CD-ROM

A question often asked by training managers is, "Should we do our new program on CD-ROM or the Web?" The major advantage of CD-ROM delivery is its ability to deliver high quality audio and video content, and the major advantage of online learning is the ease of updating the content. Exhibit 27.1 shows a simple decision grid to help answer this question. It assumes that students have the technology to access either type of delivery.

The horizontal access plots the need for video and audio, while the vertical access plots the likelihood of changes to the content. If you think your content will change more than once a year, consider that a frequent update. When determining the need for video and audio, think carefully about the true value it brings to your program. While talking head narrators are nice to have, using text and graphics instead probably won't change the learning outcomes. However, if you are training people to use certain behaviors (for example, selling skills, coaching, or interviewing), then the ability to view video clips of model behaviors in realistic scenarios is beneficial.

Exhibit 27.1. Decision Grid for CD-ROM vs. WBT

	No	Yes
Frequent Updates	*Frequent Updates/ No Multimedia* Use WBT	*Frequent Updates/ Need Multimedia* Hybrid CD-Web solution or high-bandwidth WBT.
Infrequent Updates	*Stable Content/ No Multimedia* Either CD-ROM or WBT is acceptable; costs associated with WBT probably lower	*Stable Content/ Needs Multimedia* Use CD-ROM

Audio and Video Needed for Instructional Purposes?

INSTRUCTIONAL DESIGN IS MORE IMPORTANT THAN TECHNOLOGY

The most profound statement uttered in the training community over the last ten years was the simple declaration in 1998 by M. David Merrill that "information is not instruction" (Zemke, 1998). Although Merrill, professor of instructional technology at Utah State University, was reacting to the inadequacies of many Web-based training programs, his statement reflects that it has always been too easy to become enamored with the "technology" portion of technology-based training—at the expense of proper design and learning outcomes.

In the early days of disk-based computer-based training (CBT), there was a rush to pour content into electronic tutorials. At the time, computers could only display black and white text. Audio, video, and graphics were years away. A few innovative designers made the most of the limited media and created engaging simulations, quizzes, and even games. But this was the exception to the rule, and most early programs were nothing more than books on a computer. Learners were forced to read the text on the screen passively, often clicking the "Enter" button or space bar to move on. Eyestrain and boredom, rather than improved learning and performance, often were the end results. These types of programs, derisively known as page-turners, tainted the image of CBT for many years.

With the advent of interactive video disks and multimedia CD-ROMs, design-ers gained the ability to add graphics, animation, audio, and video. Today's CD-ROM training programs often use creative themes and production elements that make them look more like the latest blockbuster movie or Nintendo® video game. These bells and whistles can keep students engaged, but many of these programs lack implementation of sound principles of instructional design. Fre-quently, development budgets are consumed by dramatic themes and Hollywood production values, leaving few resources to spend on instructional activities. The result is an audience who has been entertained—but who has not acquired new skills or knowledge.

Most early Web-based training programs were nothing more than online doc-uments. Trainers created electronic versions of traditional printed student man-uals, articles, tip sheets, and reference guides. While valuable and accessible resources, these conversions to the Web cannot be considered true training pro-grams. The rush to the Web without consideration given to instructional design led to Merrill's passionate defense of a scientific approach to learning. In his 1998 interview with Ron Zemke, Merrill put it simply, "If you don't provide ade-quate practice, if you don't have an adequate knowledge structure, if you don't provide adequate guidance, people don't learn" (Zemke, 1998, p. 36). To guar-antee the effectiveness of any training program, remember that, while technol-ogy will always change, the way adults learn will not.

Adult Learning Theory

Malcolm Knowles is widely regarded as the father of adult learning. In 1970 he released his seminal work, *The Modern Practice of Adult Education: Andragogy vs. Pedagogy.* Pedagogy, defined as the art and science of teaching, has its ori-gin in Greek and traditionally has applied to the teaching of children. Knowles' book clearly drew a new distinction between classic methods of pedagogic in-struction and adult learning principles.

His theories of adult learning are complex, but Knowles' conclusions can be summarized into four main points:

1. Adults need to know *why* they are learning something. They should be told how it effects them directly.

2. Adults have a repository of *lifetime experiences* that should be tapped as a resource for ongoing learning. Similarly, adult learners bring vari-ous levels of prior exposure to any topic, and that fact should be acknowledged.

3. Adults use a *hands-on,* problem-solving approach to learning. Rote memorization of facts and figures should be avoided.

4. Adults want to *apply* new knowledge and skills immediately. Retention decreases if the learning is applied only at some future point in time.

The Science of Instructional Systems Design

Just as Malcolm Knowles is widely regarded as the father of adult learning theory, Robert Gagne is considered to be the foremost researcher and contributor to the systematic approach to instructional design and training. Gagne and his followers are known as behaviorists, and their focus is on the outcomes—or behaviors—that result from training.

Gagne's book, *The Conditions of Learning,* first published in 1965, identified the mental conditions for learning. Gagne created a nine-step process called the Events of Instruction, which correlate to and address the conditions of learning (Gagne & Medsker, 1996). Table 27.1 shows these instructional events in the left column and the associated mental processes in the right column.

1. Gain Attention. In order for any learning to take place, you must first capture the attention of the student. A multimedia program that begins with an animated title screen sequence accompanied by sound effects or music startles the senses with auditory or visual stimuli. An even better way to capture students' attention is to start each lesson with a thought-provoking question or interesting fact.

2. Inform Learners of Objectives. Early in each lesson, students should encounter a list of learning objectives. This initiates the internal process of expectancy and helps motivate the learner to complete the lesson. These objectives should form the basis for assessment and possible certification as well.

Table 27.1. Events of Instruction

Instructional Event	Internal Process
1. Gain attention	Stimuli activation of receptors
2. Inform learners of objectives	Creation of level of expectation for learning
3. Stimulate recall of prior learning	Retrieval and activation of short-term memory
4. Present the content	Selective perception of content
5. Provide "learning guidance"	Semantic encoding for storage in long-term memory
6. Elicit performance (practice)	Response to questions to enhance encoding and verification
7. Provide feedback	Reinforcement and assessment of correct performance
8. Assess performance	Retrieval and reinforcement of content as final evaluation
9. Enhance retention and transfer to the job	Retrieval and generalization of learned skill to new situation

Adapted from Gagne and Medsker, 1996.

3. Stimulate Recall of Prior Learning. Associating new information with prior knowledge can facilitate the learning process. It is easier for learners to encode and store information in long-term memory when there are links to personal experience and knowledge.

4. Present the Content. This event of instruction is where the new content is actually presented to the learner. Content should be chunked and organized meaningfully and typically is explained and then demonstrated.

5. Provide "Learning Guidance." To help learners encode information for long-term storage, additional guidance should be provided along with the presentation of new content. Guidance strategies include the use of examples, non-examples, case studies, graphical representations, mnemonics, and analogies.

6. Elicit Performance (Practice). In this event of instruction, the learner is required to practice the new skill or behavior. Eliciting performance provides an opportunity for learners to confirm their correct understanding, and the repetition further increases the likelihood of retention.

7. Provide Feedback. As learners practice new behavior, it is important to provide specific and immediate feedback on their performance. Unlike questions in a post-test, exercises within tutorials should be used for comprehension and encoding purposes, not for formal scoring. Additional guidance and answers provided at this stage are called formative feedback.

8. Assess Performance. Upon completing instructional modules, students should be given the opportunity (or be required) to take a post-test or final assessment. This assessment should be completed without the ability to receive additional coaching, feedback, or hints. Mastery of material, or certification, is typically granted after achieving a certain score or percentage correct (typically 80 to 90 percent).

9. Enhance Retention and Transfer to the Job. Effective training programs have a "performance" focus, incorporating design and media that facilitate retention and transfer to the job. Creating electronic or online job aids, references, templates, and wizards are other ways of aiding performance.

Applying Gagne's nine-step model to any training program is the single best way to ensure an effective learning program. A multimedia program that is filled with glitz or that provides unlimited access to Web-based documents is no substitute for sound instructional design. Although those types of programs might entertain or be valuable as references, they will not maximize the effectiveness of information processing—and learning will not occur.

MILESTONES IN MANAGING THE DEVELOPMENT PROCESS

Today's technology-based training programs require careful organization and communication among a team of experts. Team members typically include a project manager, instructional designer, writer, subject-matter expert, graphic artist, audio and video producer, narrators, actors, programmers, and quality control experts. Although many interactive training producers wear many hats, most projects still require careful coordination for a positive outcome.

Successful project management starts with clearly defined project milestones that include client reviews and approvals at each point. Recommended project milestones are detailed below.

Project Kick-Off

The kick-off meeting gathers all key team members from the client and the vendor for a face-to-face review of the major project parameters. Typically, the proposal is reviewed, schedules are confirmed, and individual roles and lines of communication are clarified. If available, source materials and technical specifications are turned over to the vendor at this time.

Analysis, Design Document, and Rapid Prototype

The vendor conducts a thorough needs analysis or reviews the client's analysis if one has been completed ahead of time. This step culminates in a high-level design document that reviews audience demographics; details technical specifications; provides a detailed content outline; and describes strategies for interactivity, navigation, testing, and tracking. Along with the design document, the vendor supplies a rapid prototype that is reviewed with the same technology that will be available to the students. The prototype shows the interface, structure, and performance of the software. The client carefully reviews the design document and prototype and provides written feedback to the vendor. After the vendor makes requested changes, approval is granted to continue.

Script or Storyboard

Sometimes called a "detailed design document," in this step the vendor's instructional designers produce detailed scripts or storyboards. This document describes the details of every screen, including text, audio narration, video, and a description or sketch of graphics. Notes on each screen provide direction to the programmer and client about special navigation or other options. The client reviews these documents carefully and provides written feedback to the vendor. Revisions are made and approved before proceeding.

Development

After final script approval, development begins on all media. Artists create graphics and illustrations while audio narration and video are recorded, edited, and digitized. When these media items are complete, programmers produce the final program. A thorough round of quality control uncovers any software bugs or other problems.

Pilot Test or Formative Evaluation

At this stage, the program is tested with members from the actual student population. This pilot test is completed with three to ten individuals in an environment that is identical to the one the actual students will use. This pilot test is designed both to uncover any technical glitches or bugs and to confirm that the instructional program is sound and achieving its objectives. Based on the results of this test, bugs are fixed and final adjustments are made to the content.

Delivery

To prepare for delivery, a final round of quality control is conducted on the master CD-ROM or actual website location where the program is held. After thorough testing, the vendor produces any necessary CD-ROM labels, jewel case packaging, or quick reference user instructions. CD-ROMs are duplicated and distributed or the Web-based training program is uploaded to the server and opened for access.

Evaluation

Finally, the vendor and client work closely to evaluate the results of the program. Ideal evaluations include all four levels of the classic Kirkpatrick model (Kirkpatrick, 1998) of evaluation, which includes

- *Level 1: Reaction*—Students evaluate the training after completing the program. This type of evaluation is sometimes called "smile sheets" or "happy sheets" because, in their simplest form, they measure how much students liked the learning experience. However, in advanced forms, students can be queried about the ability of the course to maintain their interest, the ease of interface and navigation, and the perceived value of the content to the workplace.

- *Level 2: Learning*—This level measures whether students actually learned the knowledge, skills, or attitudes that the program was designed to teach. Most often this is shown through pre-test and post-test results.

- *Level 3: Behavior*—This provides a measure of whether or not newly acquired skills are retained and transferred to the job. Typically, this measurement is conducted three to six months after the training. The students, or their managers, can use behavioral scorecards to indicate whether or not certain skills and knowledge are being used.

- *Level 4: Results*—Now the trainer evaluates the business impact of the training. In other words, did the training lead to an increase in positive customer service evaluations, or a reduction in material defects, or a reduction in calls to the help desk?

CALCULATING FINANCIAL RETURNS OF TBT

The Kirkpatrick model described above is an excellent methodology for evaluating the success of training initiatives. However, the model can be taken a step further with the addition of evaluating the *financial* return of the training. This is especially critical for *technology*-based training because this form of training often requires a large up-front investment in either equipment or training development. Using financial metrics is both a good way to "sell" a project proposal internally— when you need to acquire funding, for example—as well as a way to show the tremendous value training initiatives are yielding for the organization.

Measuring Costs and Returns

Your first step in any kind of financial analysis will be to determine the true and complete costs of the program. For technology-based training, remember to include development costs, the cost of the students' time to complete the training (that is, their salary and benefits incurred during the course completion time), and delivery costs associated with online access or duplication of CD-ROMs or other materials.

The second step is to determine the revenue either saved or earned as a result of the training intervention. This step naturally builds upon the Kirkpatrick Level 4 evaluation described above. For example, if the training

- Increased sales by 5 percent, what is the dollar amount of that increase?
- Improved quality on an assembly line, what is the dollar amount of the savings from bad parts and product returns?
- Improved customer satisfaction scores, what is the dollar value of each "saved" customer or repeat sale?

These revenue increases aren't often quantified by organizations, so it may take some sleuthing and extrapolating on your part to come up with usable numbers. But it will be well worth it when it comes time to share the results with senior executives.

Once you have your basic measurements, there are four simple calculations you can use when building a business case: Total cost savings, break-even analysis, cost/benefit ratio, and return on investment. Each measurement is detailed below.

Calculating Cost Savings over Traditional Delivery

The most basic and frequently used analysis is a simple comparison of how much money technology-based training will save over more traditional instructor-led workshops. Exhibit 27.2 shows the formula and an example of this calculation.

Conducting a Break-Even Analysis

The total savings number in the analysis above does not tell the whole story. Because technology-based training is more expensive to create initially than instructor-led training, the payback often doesn't begin until year two or three. Using a break-even analysis will identify at what exact point in time the program begins to "save" money. The value of this measurement is usually in terms of the number of students one must train in order to reach break-even. To put break-even analysis simply, it answers the question: "How many students will we have to train in order for our up-front investment in technology-based training to begin to pay off?"

Exhibit 27.3 shows the three-step formula for calculating the break-even point, along with sample data. Note that, in this analysis, the calculated cost to deliver the training to each student factors in both standard delivery costs and administration and maintenance costs. The final break-even is 263 students in the example and is another indicator that the investment in TBT is a wise one, as there are eight hundred total students to be trained. If fewer than 263 students were to be trained in the three-year period, instructor-led training would make more sense from a financial perspective.

Cost/Benefit Ratio

The cost/benefit ratio is a simple calculation that depicts the total financial return for each dollar invested in the training program. The example in Exhibit 27.4 is based on a fictitious case of a Web-based quality training program that cost $54,000 to develop and deliver and which saved $430,000 in the first year due to a reduction in defective widgets.

Return on Investment (ROI)

The return-on-investment analysis, commonly called ROI, is one of the more popularly used financial measures. It simply states the return on the training investment in terms of a percentage. The example in Exhibit 27.5 is based on a fictitious case of a Web-based sales training program that cost $425,000 to develop and deliver and which increased sales by $975,000 in the first year.

RESOURCES ON THE WORLD WIDE WEB

The field of technology-based training is fast evolving and puts all of us in the mode of continuous learning. The Internet is the single best place to obtain up-

Exhibit 27.2. Formula to Calculate Cost Savings

Total Cost Savings of TBT
Formula:

Instructor-Led Costs – Technology Training Costs = Total Cost Savings

$1,091,648 – $500,600 = $591,048

Total Savings = $591,048

Exhibit 27.3. Sample Break-Even Analysis for TBT

Step 1. Per-Student Delivery Cost of Tech-Based Training (TBT)
= Total TBT Delivery Costs / Total Number of Students
Step 2. Per-Student Delivery Cost of Instructor-Led Training (ILT)
= Total ILT Delivery Costs / Total Number of Students
Step 3. Break-Even Point = Total TBT Design & Dev. Costs – Total ILT Design
& Dev. Costs/Per-Student ILT Costs – Per-Student TBT Costs

Step 1. ($134,400 + $16,200) / 800 students = $188.25 per student
Step 2. ($1,026,920 + $5,168) / 800 students = $1,290.11 per student
Step 3. $350,000 – $60,000 / $ 1,290 – $188 = $290,000 / $1,102 = 263

Break-Even Point = 263 Students Trained

Exhibit 27.4. Sample Cost/Benefit Analysis

Cost/Benefit Ratio

Financial Benefits / Total Cost of Training = Cost/Benefit Ratio

$430,000 / $54,000 = 7.96

Cost/Benefit Ratio = 7.96

Exhibit 27.5. Sample ROI Calculation

Return-on-Investment (ROI) Ratio

(Total Benefits – Total Costs) / Total Costs x 100 = ROI

($975,000 – $425,000) / $425,000 x 100 = 129%

ROI = 129%

to-date, detailed information on multimedia and online learning, and the sites below are industry leaders.

Technology-Based Training Supersite: *www.TBTSuperSite.com* (vast amount of information, including articles, presentations, news, tools, templates, and glossary of terms);

Brandon Hall Resources: *www.brandonhall.com* (sponsored by industry guru Brandon Hall, this site reviews the latest trends and offers many industry reports); and

Masie Center: *www.masie.com* (a wealth of presentations, articles, and research reports from Elliot Masie's international think tank, dedicated to exploring the intersection of learning and technology).

References

Fletcher, J.D. (1991, Spring). *Multimedia Review,* 33–42.

Gagne, R.M., & Medsker, K.L. (1996). *The conditions of learning: Training applications.* Orlando, FL: Harcourt Brace.

Hall, B. (1997). *Web-based training cookbook.* New York: John Wiley & Sons.

Kirkpatrick, D.L. (1998). *Evaluating training programs: The four levels* (2nd ed.). San Francisco: Berrett-Koehler.

Knowles, M. (1970). *The modern practice of adult education: Andragogy versus pedagogy.* New York: Wadsworth.

Zemke, R. (1998, June). Wake up! (and reclaim instructional design). *Training,* 36–42.

Recommended Reading

Cooper, A. (1995). *About face: The essentials of user interface design.* Foster, CA: IDG Books.

Dick, W., & Carey, L. (2000). *The systematic design of instruction* (5th ed.). Reading, MA: Addison-Wesley.

Gagne, R., Briggs, L., & Wager, W. (1992). *Principles of instructional design.* New York: Wadsworth.

Kruse, K., & Keil, J. (1999). *Technology-based training: The art and science of design, development and delivery.* San Francisco: Jossey-Bass.

Reynolds, A., & Iwinski, T. (1996). *Multimedia training: Developing technology-based systems.* New York: McGraw-Hill.

About the Author

Kevin E. Kruse *is a senior executive with Kenexa, Inc., a leading provider of both off-the-shelf and customized online learning programs. His interactive training work has won awards from ASTD (formerly, American Society for Training and Development), the International Society for Performance Improvement, and Brandon Hall Resources. Kruse is also the author of* Technology-Based Training: The Art and Science of Design, Development, and Delivery, *and pens a monthly column, Web Rules, for ASTD. To receive three free chapters from Kruse's book, visit* www.TBTSuperSite.com. *Contact Kruse directly at* kevin.kruse@kenexa.com.

CHAPTER TWENTY-EIGHT

Applications of Communication Technology in Training and Education

Zane L. Berge, Ph.D.

Director, Training Systems Graduate Program,
University of Maryland Baltimore County

T his chapter describes how communication technology is applied to education and explores how it is a catalyst for changing how we teach and learn. This changing technology-rich environment causes instructors to re-evaluate how they teach, how training is delivered, and what is expected of learners. In fact, the changes in society, brought about in large part by technology, demand that teaching and learning change also.

INTRODUCTION

E-mail CD-ROM Multimedia fiber optics Computer Simulations Computer Lab/ Classroom WWW-based Resources Super Audio CD Audio DVD MP3 MPEG-2 digital TV digital samplers digital video recorders (TiVo, RelayTV) Internet pay-per-view CD-R (recordable) CD-RW (rewritable) recordable DVD high-definition TV (HDTV) interactive television cable modem digital cable network computer Internet browser Intranet Internet 2 digital darkroom virtual reality integrated services digital network (ISDN) video-on-demand flat-screen TV cellular phones digital phones smart phones WebTV digital nonlinear editing speech recognition software Microsoft Windows CE Internet broadcasting video dial tone digital audio tape (DAT) digital audio broadcasting (DAB) digital audio radio services (DARS) direct broadcast satellite (DBS) Sony mini-disc digital video, or versatile, disc (DVD) DIVX (alternative to DVD) digital compact cassette (DCC) personal digital assistant (PDA) paging and messaging products satellite phones multimedia V-chip virtual reality modeling language (VRML) on-line chat Windows 98 desktop video production (Avid) desktop publishing desktop audio production video game systems (PlayStation) digital photography audio and video streaming

Never before have so many new communication and information technologies been introduced in so short a time as during the past decade. Any list of "new" communication technologies is outdated by the time it is printed—seemingly in the time it takes to *read* the list! Clearly, telecommunication and computer systems are combining to bring people an overwhelming number of products, services, and applications. In fact, the merging of technologies seems likely to increase in the future, with satellite, cable, and telephone companies all wanting a larger part in what had started as more or less three separate industries. The same technologies that are used for games, videos, and home shopping can also be used for training, educational and informational services.

COMMUNICATION TECHNOLOGY

Communication technology involves audio, video, text, and graphics. These channels are converging on the desktop—and it is becoming harder for users to separate (tele)communication technology from computer systems. Computer-mediated communication (CMC) is the name given to a large set of functions in which computers are used to support human communication. For our purposes here in exploring training and educational applications, four common threads can be seen in the computer and communication use of information systems users. Computer-mediated communication is defined along four dimensions: *computer conferencing, informatics, computer-based instruction* (Santoro, 1995), and *publication.*

Computer Conferencing. *Conferencing* involves direct human-human communication, with the computer acting simply as a transaction router or providing simple storage and retrieval functions. This category includes such functions as electronic mail, interactive messaging, and group conference support systems such as mailing lists (for example, Listserv, Listproc, Majordomo), newsgroups, and bulletin board systems.

Informatics. The computer has a more active role in *informatics,* compared to conferencing, as the repository or maintainer of organized information. The information is generated by humans making contributions, and humans are the end users of this information after retrieval from the systems. Part of the current explosion of interest in the Internet/World Wide Web is a result of the rapid growth of accessible informatics resources, including library catalogs, interactive remote databases, and program/data archive sites.

Computer-Based Instruction. Here the computer is programmed to take a more active role toward the human user, rather than the computer passively carrying out commands. In *computer-based instruction,* the computer (through programming) is structuring and managing what content can be presented to the learner, how that information can be presented to the learner, and the possible choices available to the human user in responding to this information.

Publication. One of the most powerful uses of communication/computer system technologies for education is when learners *publish their own work.* In a way, it can be thought of as the opposite of informatics. With informatics, a student using technology retrieves information that other people, who are often thought to be more expert than themselves, have stored on the Internet or at a remote site to which the student has access. Technology is allowing students to more easily publish their own work to a broad audience. This increased size and changed composition of the audience often increases the motivation and effort of the student when producing the assigned project.

TRAINING AND EDUCATIONAL APPLICATIONS

Some of the ways that we can conceptualize training and communication technology to support learning (Frayer, 1997; Kozma & Johnston, 1991) include providing: (1) an asynchronous/synchronous communication; (2) a virtual space for interpersonal interaction, social networking, changing roles and dimensions of students, instructors, curriculum and institution; and (3) a technological environment combining telecommunication systems and computer networks to solve problems of access, quality, and productivity (Berge, 1997b).

Asynchronous/Synchronous Communication

Asynchronous communication allows time independence and permits twenty-four-hour access to other people and resources. It may be more convenient for students who also want to meet work, family, and other responsibilities. Such communication promotes self-paced learning and allows time to compose responses. On the other hand, real-time or synchronous communication means course document(s) or assignments can be modified by more than one person simultaneously. Real-time discussions and brainstorming can occur, given that this communication channel shares some flexibility with the spoken word. Designers of synchronous, technologically mediated training should note that this characteristic cancels the advantages of time independence.

Virtual Space for Interpersonal Interaction

Technologically mediated training can foster learning that is collaborative and that uses peer review/support activities and projects. To the extent that this collaboration occurs online, students and instructors become part of a virtual community of learners. This community is often characterized as multi-cultural and international. The role of the student is more that of a lifelong, self-directed learner who takes more responsibility for his or her own learning than has been the case in a traditional classroom. The role of instructor as facilitator and co-learner fosters a multiple perspective. Technology permits work on messy, but authentic, often interdisciplinary problem solving. It allows mentoring and apprentice models to be used that often open doors to planned events (personal networking) and to unplanned interactions (serendipity)—both course and non-course related.

Solutions to Problems of Access, Quality, and Productivity

The creation of a technological environment combining telecommunication systems and computer networks helps in solving problems of access, quality, and productivity. Students' progress, assessment, and records can more easily be kept. Technology-enhanced learning can foster independence and greatly reduce accessibility issues, while sensitivity to various learning styles and individual learner needs may be more easily accomplished. Currently, most CMC is text-based, but this will change in the next several years to include audio, music, graphics, and video, which will allow representations in multiple modes (for example, 3-D and auditory help students to visualize hard-to-see processes and events). These environments allow for fast modification of document content in areas in which information becomes outdated quickly, organization of materials, and collection of assignments. In general, technology provides access to the world's people and resources. Such practice in using technological tools is useful during training and later on the job. Experts' reasoning can be explicitly modeled, while the drudgery from computation and writing tasks can be removed.

CATALYST FOR CHANGE

Computing and communication systems are serving as catalysts for new media, such as hypermedia and the World Wide Web. These new media are creating and enabling new channels of access for learners and ways of teaching and learning that have not been possible—or at least not been effective—in the past. As Chris Dede (1995) stated:

> "What does the evolution of new media mean for distance educators? A medium
> is in part a channel for conveying content; new media like the Internet mean

that we can readily reach wider, more diverse audiences. Just as important, however, is that a medium is a representational container enabling new types of messages (e.g., sometimes a picture is worth a thousand words). Since the process of thinking is based on representations such as language and imagery, the process of learning is strongly shaped by the types of instructional messages we can exchange with students."

The use of computers, telecommunications, and other emerging technologies is allowing educators to fulfill age-old desires, such as being able to individualize instruction more easily. "We can create simulations through which students can discover important relationships and construct new knowledge. We can even put the reins into the hands of students and watch as these tools take them to destinations they envision" (Peck & Dorricott, 1994, p. 14).

From an organizational perspective, for companies, universities, and other organizations to remain competitive, viable, and profitable, the marketplace will not allow "business as usual" as an option. So while it is possible to improve significantly much of the training and education that is done by using a learner-centered, collaborative, social, constructivist approach, demand from students and recent, increased competition also is causing changes.

TECHNOLOGICALLY MEDIATED LEARNING

Ordinarily, what matters most is not the technology per se, but how it is used, not so much what happens in the moments when the student is using the technology, but more how those uses promote larger improvements in the fabric of the student's education (Berge, 1998).

The power of technology in teaching and learning is in its use of models different from the traditional approach to training, which has in the past usually involved a "stand and deliver," in-person presentation by an instructor to students located in the same physical space. Technology used in training and education promotes a learner-centered approach with the emphasis on a learning environment that is collaborative, authentic, and interactive (Berge, 1997a).

Collaborative Learning Environment

A collaborative learning environment has several key characteristics. First, there is a sharing of knowledge among instructors and students. Although it is recognized that instructors have a wealth of knowledge about content, in a collaborative classroom the knowledge, experiences, language, and culture of the students are valued and brought into the learning situation. Implicit in this is a shared authority among instructors and students.

A second element in a collaborative environment involves students being able to participate in setting specific goals for themselves within the framework of what is being taught. There are options for projects and other learning activities that capture different students' interests and learning goals. Collaboration, by definition, involves people working together. Within the collaborative learning environment, the above elements suggest a sharing of authority that, when implemented, means the instructor is often a learner, and learners are just as often teaching.

Authentic Learning Activities

The essence of inquiry is a student being personally challenged by being faced with a problem to solve, a project to complete, or a dilemma to resolve. Joyce and Weil (1996) remind us that this challenge causes the inquiry to be personally meaningful for the student. Through individual or group investigation, curiosity leads to explicit formulation of the topic being investigated and the process that will be used for solving the problem or project. Both the process and the tentative solutions are studied, reflected on, and thereby improved.

Interactive

From the learner's perspective, there are at least three types of interaction involved in the process of school (guided or formal) learning. These are interaction with the content, interaction with the instructor and other students (Moore, 1989), and interaction with the institution. Although this chapter is not focused on how the institution promotes learning, it is an important aspect of interaction, mainly through structuring and supporting the learning situation.

Generally, when a student and instructor have the opportunity to meet face-to-face in real time, the impetus is for the instructor to talk to students, rather than give a mediated presentation (Bates, 1984). There are many reasons for this, perhaps one of the more significant being that often students request feedback on specific points (Howard, 1987). The same thing appears to be true in technologically mediated communications. Perhaps a significant factor in determining whether a learning objective should be practiced by the learner alone using recorded media (text, video, and so forth), in a small peer group, or in real-time with an instructor is how much feedback and guidance are needed by the student from a more learned person. These decisions affect the choice of media (Bates, 1991).

CONCLUSION

The union of telecommunication technologies and computer networks has given us new tools to support teaching and learning. Taken together, these tools can be applied in training and education to create learning environments that have been impossible, or at least not worth the effort, previously. One significant result of this changing, technology-rich, learning environment is that instructors are re-evaluating how they teach, how training is delivered, and what is expected of learners. Similarly, learners are taking more responsibility for their learning. Both of these changes seem necessary and good.

References

Bates, A.W. (1984). *The role of technology in distance education.* New York: St Martin's Press.

Bates, A.W. (1991). Third generation distance education: The challenge of new technology. *Research in Distance Education, 3*(2), 10–15.

Berge, Z.L. (1997a). Characteristics of online teaching in post-secondary, formal education. *Educational Technology, 37*(3), 35–47.

Berge, Z.L. (1997b). Computer conferencing and the on-line classroom. *The International Journal of Educational Telecommunications (IJET), 3*(1), 3–21.

Berge, Z.L. (1998). Technology and changing roles in education. In Z.L. Berge & M.P. Collins (Eds.), *Wired together: Computer-mediated communication in K-12: Volume 1. Perspectives and instructional design* (1–13). Cresskill, NJ: Hampton Press.

Dede, C. (1995, July). The transformation of distance education to distributed learning. [Online.] *http://www.gsu.edu/ ~ wwwitr/docs/distlearn/index.html.*

Frayer, D.A. (1997, April). *Education uses of information technology.* Presentation to AAHE TLTR Information technology conference, Massachusetts. Copy at: *http://www.anu.edu.au/CEDAM/euit.html.*

Howard, D.C. (1987). Designing learner feedback in distance education. *The American Journal of Distance Education, 1*(3), 24–40.

Joyce, B., & Weil, M. (1996). *Models of teaching* (5th ed.). Boston: Allyn and Bacon.

Kozma, R.B., & Johnston, J. (1991). The technological revolution comes to the classroom. *Change, 23*(1), 10–23.

Moore, M.G. (1989). Three types of interaction. *The American Journal of Distance Education, 3*(2), 1–6.

Peck, K., & Dorricott, D. (1994). Why use technology? *Educational Leadership, 51*(7), 11–14.

Santoro, G.M. (1995). What is computer-mediated communication? In Z.L. Berge & M.P. Collins (Eds.), *Computer-mediated communication and the online classroom: Volume 1. Overview and perspectives* (11–28). Cresskill, NJ: Hampton Press.

Recommended Reading

Berge, Z.L. (1995). Facilitating computer conferencing: Recommendations from the field. *Educational Technology, 35*(1), 22–30.

Berge, Z.L., & Collins, M.P. (Eds.). (1995). *Computer-mediated communication and the online classroom* (Vols. 1–3). Cresskill, NJ: Hampton Press.

Berge, Z.L., & Collins, M.P. (Eds.). (1998). *Wired together: Computer-mediated communication in K-12* (Vols. 1–4). Cresskill, NJ: Hampton Press.

Schreiber, D.A., & Berge, Z.L. (Eds.). (1998). *Distance training: How innovative organizations are using technology to maximize learning and meet business objectives.* San Francisco: Jossey-Bass.

About the Author

Zane L. Berge is currently director of training systems in the Instructional Systems Development Graduate Program at the University of Maryland System, UMBC Campus. His scholarship in the field of computer-mediated communication and distance education includes numerous articles, chapters, workshops, and presentations. He is the co-editor of a three-volume set, Computer-Mediated Communication and the Online Classroom, *that encompasses higher and distance education, and a four-volume set,* Wired Together: Computer-Mediated Communication in the K-12 Classroom. *More recently, he co-edited* Distance Training *(1998). Berge's newest book is* Sustaining Distance Training *(Jossey-Bass, 2000). He consults internationally in distance education and can be contacted at* berge@umbc.edu.

PART FIVE

EMPLOYEE AND ORGANIZATIONAL DEVELOPMENT

CHAPTER TWENTY-NINE

Diversity: The Right Competitive Strategy for a Changing World

Julie O'Mara
President, O'Mara and Associates

Diversity is an increasingly important business strategy that is evolving to meet the needs of a workplace with the challenges and opportunities of changing values, changing demographics, and globalization. Presented here is a rationale for managing diverse environments in three overlapping sectors, within the workforce, markets, and organizational structures. In this chapter, the competencies required for effective trainers/facilitators are outlined in the following four major areas: self-knowledge, leadership, subject-matter expertise, and facilitation skills. A comprehensive list of diversity resources and tools is made available.

LEVERAGING DIVERSITY

As our world continues to change at an ever-quickening pace, leveraging diversity is both the right thing and the smart thing to do.

What do we mean by leveraging diversity? Diversity involves more than recognizing individual differences. According to Roosevelt Thomas (1996), it is a collective mixture of similarities and differences. Managing diversity is proactively addressing the challenges and opportunities brought about because of the diversity of people, business goals, and strategies in the world of work.

327

WHAT SMART TRAINERS KNOW

Managing diversity requires trainer/facilitator competencies that are unique to the field of training in some significant ways. An effective trainer/facilitator must have at least an intermediate degree of skill in the following four major areas (O'Mara, 1994):

1. *Self-Knowledge:* Recognizing personal values, biases, assumptions, and stereotypes in the workplace and how those may affect others.
2. *Leadership:* Taking responsibility for championing diversity by articulating the goals of the organization's diversity effort.
3. *Subject-Matter Expertise:* Knowing the issues and goals of diversity and influencing others to achieve success in the organization.
4. *Facilitation Skills:* Knowing how to communicate and to facilitate the exchange of ideas in a sensitive, organized, effective manner.

Gaining Self-Knowledge

Diversity training is challenging because it engages our emotions as well as our intellect. If you have not come to grips with your own biases, you will find it nigh impossible to help anyone else deal with theirs. Diversity requires facilitating the learning of others in this sensitive arena.

Facilitating diversity demands that you become aware of your own internal reactions to differences and that you confront personal prejudice, bias, and the impact of privilege. Because we have grown up with assumptions and personal points of view, we find it difficult to see the world from someone else's perspective or to understand that someone else might interpret the same situation differently. We tend to filter out views that are not part of our own personal frames of reference. These filters are our prejudices and biases.

This mindset is called *ethnocentricity,* and we all have it to some degree. The journey away from ethnocentricity requires a concentrated effort to move beyond a natural way of being and thinking to embrace what feels unnatural and unsafe until we can develop a reliable personal response system that encounters ambiguity with curiosity rather than with defensiveness.

For example, most of us have difficulty with the concept of white privilege. In the context of diversity, *privilege* is unearned advantage. Examples of privilege: If someone is white, he or she is not presumed to have received a job because of skin color. Because someone is white, he or she isn't being tailed by security officers in an upscale shop. Because someone is heterosexual, he or she can put a picture of a partner on his or her desk without being concerned about what people will say. Because someone can hear, he or she is presumed to be able to interact with clients. Most persons have difficulty acknowledging this type of privilege because these privileges are taken for granted. Privilege applies to any dominant group holding power and opportunity.

We get to know our own prejudices and biases by

- Interacting with others;
- Engaging those different from ourselves in dialogue;
- Asking for feedback;
- Talking about race, gender, age, disabilities, and other diversity dimensions; and
- Reading and attending workshops.

It is a lifelong process.

Providing Leadership

Promoting diversity requires steadfast champions. It is important that the diversity message be consistent and continuous across levels, functions, and businesses. The skilled trainer/facilitator

- Understands the nature of the organization's business and how to integrate diversity into goals and performance management;
- Understands that managers are important to implementing diversity, but that everyone is responsible for leveraging diversity;
- Understands and communicates the business imperatives for leveraging diversity in formal and informal ways and seeks market opportunities for diversity at every level of the organization;
- Encourages a range of ideas and perspectives and knows that there is more than one way to do things;
- Acknowledges others for supporting diversity and demonstrates cultural sensitivity; and
- Communicates effectively with people from different cultures and acts without bias.

Another important area of leadership is taking risks and challenging the norm. Conflicts can surface because of resistance to accepting differences. It is important to bring conflicts out in the open in a firm and timely way and to work with the person or group to address the issues. Containing rumors and gossip about promotions and proactively announcing promotions and communicating qualifications are keys to effective conflict management.

A diversity leader is an ally who stands up for the rights of others. Effective change results when a Christian stands up for a Jew or a white person is an ally to a black person. Developing, mentoring, and coaching others are more challenging roles taken by diversity leaders. Facilitators/trainers empower managers to become mentors. They are change agents who anticipate what is needed in the work environment and take initiative.

Developing Subject-Matter Expertise

What Is Diversity? The diversity facilitator must have some core fundamental knowledge. An increasingly important business process, diversity is a collective mixture of similarities and differences (Thomas, 1996). In their book, *Workforce America,* Loden and Rosner (1991) distinguish some dimensions of diversity, such as ethnicity, age, gender, and sexual orientation, as *primary* dimensions and educational background, income, and marital status as *secondary* dimensions.

From an objective point of view, the vast array of physical and cultural differences constitutes the spectrum of human diversity. From a subjective point of view, diversity is "otherness," those human qualities that are different from our own and outside the groups to which we belong, yet present in other indi-

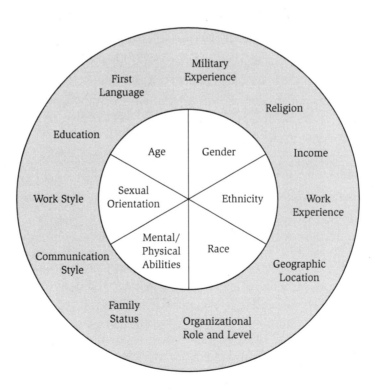

Figure 29.1. Primary and Secondary Levels of Diversity

viduals and groups. Thus, diversity is "a mixture of people with different group identities within the same social system" (Nkomo & Cox, 1996, p. 339).

Managers and human resource professionals agree that the workforce is becoming more heterogeneous than ever before and that business is becoming more global. Demographics tell us that today's workforce has more women, ethnicities, lifestyles, people with disabilities, and differences at work across generations. In addition, multinational corporations abound, with greater numbers of employees engaged internationally. In the domestic arena, managing diversity refers to voluntary and proactive initiatives undertaken to value the collective similarities and differences of people and to use those differences to gain a competitive business advantage. In the international arena, diversity means cultural competence, that is, mastering the art of cross-cultural relationships to interact successfully abroad.

A recent, emergent diversity paradigm connects diversity not only to different identities, but also to the varied perspectives and approaches to work that members of different identity groups bring to the workplace. Managing diversity is about learning to use these work perspectives and approaches as a source of individual and organizational effectiveness. It is leveraging differences to unleash the powerful benefits of a diverse workforce.

The Most Effective Approach. To succeed, we must implement and integrate diversity within three overlapping areas: our workforce, our marketplace, and our organizational structures (see Figure 29.2). In the working world, these three are engaged in developing within employees the skills, attitudes, and competencies that will establish a corporate identity that communicates cultural effectiveness. They help bring into being an organization ready to meet the diverse needs of customers and markets domestically and worldwide. Within organizational structures, they are seeking to produce an environment in which business platforms, geography, divisions, and departments can interact systematically and seamlessly.

By focusing on diversity, we are overcoming barriers and adopting open attitudes, communication, and behavior that make us stronger in all three areas. We embrace the fact that a diverse workforce gives us greater insight into the needs of our customers and communities and that removing structural barriers improves our ability to work together more effectively as employees. The three components are intertwined, and they all should be taken into account simultaneously if we want to maximize our ability to leverage diversity (O'Mara, 1999).

The Difference Between AA/EEO and Diversity. Managing diversity requires making a distinction between compliance issues, such as Equal Employment Opportunity (EEO), Affirmative Action (AA), or sexual harassment, and high performance management. Equal Employment Opportunity and AA refer to

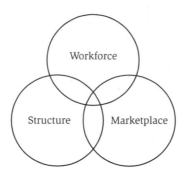

Figure 29.2. Three Areas of Business Diversity
Copyright ©1996 O'Mara and Associates.

government-initiated and compliance-based programs, while managing diversity differs significantly in that it is comprised of voluntary strategic initiatives.

In a recent study, researchers found that women and minorities hired under a scenario of proactive diversity management were viewed as more qualified than affirmative action hires (Gilbert & Stead, 1999). While the authors make it clear that the time has not yet come to relax policies and procedures that ensure unbiased treatment of women and minorities, the study does point to the value of a diversity management environment: "When the effect of positive perceptions of women and minority hires is coupled with the competitive advantage of including their perspectives, an enlightened management will support diversity management as both appropriate and integral to corporate success" (p. 255).

The Business Imperatives for Managing Diversity. To promote diversity initiatives successfully, the business reasons for diversity must be clearly understood, embraced, and communicated at all levels in the organization (see Figure 29.3). Today's organizations serve myriad cultures, ethnicities, and lifestyles.

As we go about connecting new technologies with new customers, diversity provides a distinct market advantage. It brings relevant knowledge and perspectives to strengthen our personal relationships with diverse customers. Not only does diversity bring "niche" or insider information to customer service, but it also brings important, different, and competitive information about how to do work. Research demonstrates that diverse teams outperform homogeneous teams for tasks that demand creativity, innovation, problem-solving ability, and flexibility in changing work conditions (Early & Mosakowski, 2000; McLeod, Lobel, & Cox, 1996; Peterson & Nemeth, 1996).

Competition for a skilled worker in today's market is intense. Attracting and retaining the best employees are two of the most compelling reasons for diversity management. The workforce is diverse. When employers fail to focus on a

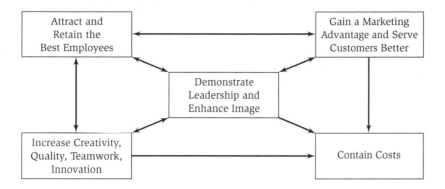

Figure 29.3. Business Diversity Imperatives

climate that recognizes and values differences, they will not attract and retain the best workers.

Last and most important, an organization that embraces diversity demonstrates a willingness to provide the leadership to help its workforce change, grow, and prosper in an increasingly competitive and complex business environment. Diversity makes use of all of an organization's creative potential and skills to grow business and minimize risk. Diversity leadership is focused on broadly based, long-term, strategically focused initiatives and makes sure that diversity is seen as a strategic change management process designed to meet business goals. The corporate climate then becomes inviting, inspiring, and energetic.

Utilizing Effective Facilitation Skills

The competent facilitator knows how to exchange ideas and learnings effectively. Preparation includes learning to know the audience and understanding how to facilitate based on the audience needs. He or she plans for and provides appropriate material, facilities, supplies, equipment, and other aids to create an optimal learning environment.

A positive attitude toward the subject matter is a vital dimension of delivery, as is speaking clearly and concisely with a variety of inflections, not in a monotone. The delivery is supported with appropriate nonverbal communication techniques—eye contact, natural gestures, and reinforcing language. The agenda, concepts, purposes, procedures, transitions, and summaries of the training sessions must be explained clearly.

The competent facilitator is a competent questioner, using open-ended questions to develop participation and to explore the knowledge, attitudes, and awareness levels of participants. He or she gives correct and concise answers in a nondefensive manner and uses the class as a resource by referring questions back to the participants. He or she listens carefully and respectfully to participants' statements, questions, and comments.

Classroom control is an important skill of diversity facilitators because emotions sometimes run high. He or she handles hostile, withdrawn, domineering, or otherwise difficult participants in an effective manner. Group learnings are focused and reinforced using summarizing, clarifying, and restating skills. The skilled facilitator makes certain that the class stays on topic, achieves closure when possible, and manages time effectively.

The skilled facilitator is willing to challenge participants and organizational norms and practices. Employee resistance to diversity often stems from not understanding the business rationale for moving ahead with diversity management and how it will affect the productivity and viability of a department and the organization. Sometimes belief in the melting pot (people should adapt and become one big, happy family) or ignorance about culture and its potential as an effective tool for empowering employees contributes to resistance. The challenge is to frame concepts and discussions to avoid pitting people and groups against each other and to help participants to identify what they stand to lose or gain if the status quo remains. The facilitator is willing to assist participants to examine their behaviors, attitudes, and values and to guide them to develop new, more accepting attitudes and beliefs.

Skilled facilitators seek to exemplify valuing diversity by consistently demonstrating a commitment to understanding and respecting differences, a sensitivity to the many cultures in their communities, an avoidance of conduct that puts a group at a disadvantage, and a commitment to operate within the work and community environments to deepen and broaden mutual understanding about diversity issues. How to manage diversity issues continues to be researched extensively by social scientists. Many theories exist about social identity in diverse settings as a basis for understanding how organizations can secure harmonious and cooperative relations among departments or divisions. The topic of managing diversity within large organizations is an important one in the research at present (Special Forum, 2000). Interest and expertise will continue to grow because diversity is an inescapable reality. (See the listing of diversity resources in Exhibit 29.1.) The positive results gained from managing diversity effectively will not only enhance organizational performance, but, more importantly, enhance the quality of human experience.

Exhibit 29.1. Listing of Diversity Resources

101 Actions You Can Take To Value and Manage Diversity
This is a 24-page, bound booklet of practical, useful diversity actions.
Cost 1–5 $10, over 6 quoted, O'Mara & Associates; 510/582–7744;
www.omaraassoc.com.

Blue-Eyed
This 90-minute video, featuring Jane Elliott, the Riceville, Iowa, teacher known
for the "Blue-Eyed/Brown-Eyed" exercise, can follow her *A Class Divided* or
Eye of the Storm videos or stand alone. Purchase: $295, California Newsreel;
800/621–6196.

Bridging Cultural Barriers: Managing Ethnic Diversity in the Workplace
This video for managers is narrated by Sondra Thiederman, Ph.D. It will be
of help to managers who are managing persons from different cultural
groups—especially those recently immigrated. Purchase: $695, Barr Media.

Building a House for Diversity: How a Fable About a Giraffe and an Elephant
Offers New Strategies for Today's Workforce
Roosevelt Thomas, Jr. (1999), New York: AMACOM.

Competing Through Managing Diversity with Roosevelt Thomas
Roosevelt Thomas is author of the landmark diversity book, *Beyond Race and
Gender,* director of the American Institute for Managing Diversity at Morehouse
College in Atlanta, and recipient of the Distinguished Contribution to the
Profession Award from the American Society for Training and Development.
In this video, he gives his views on valuing and managing diversity. Lease/
Purchase: $1,495, American Media Incorporated; 800/262–2557; ami@
ammedia.com.

Discovering Diversity Profile® Exploring Differences in the Workplace
Carlson Learning Company. To order, call O'Mara and Associates,
510/582–7744 or fax 510/582–4826.

Diverse Teams at Work©
Based on the work of Lee Gardenswartz and Anita Rowe, this video addresses
the issues of diversity and teamwork. One week rental: $225, corVISION
MEDIA; 800/537–3130; www.corvision.com

Diversity Activities and Training Designs
This manual by Julie O'Mara includes thirty-six diversity activities, nine lecturettes, and twenty-five training designs—complete with reproducible checklists, charts, and master overheads! Pages 9–11. Cost: $159.00, O'Mara &
Associates; 510/582–7744; www.omaraassoc.com.

The Diversity Factor
Various issues. Published by Elsie Y. Cross. For subscription information, call
201/833–0011 or fax 201/833–4184.

Exhibit 29.1. (cont.)

The Diversity Game™ and The Global Diversity Game™
  Designed to raise awareness of diversity so employees become better able to communicate and interact with fellow employees from different cultures. Cost: $395 (discounts available), Quality Educational Development, Inc.; 800/724–2215.

DIVERSOPHY®: Understanding the Human Race
  Designed to be used by managers and trainers whose objective is to improve the management of diversity in their organization. Cost: $199, ODT Inc.; 800/736–1293; www.diversophy.com.

Homophobia in the Workplace
  Brian McNaught, author of three books and two videos on sexual orientation, describes the major issues of homophobia in this 58-minute video. Cost: $29.95, TRB Productions; 508/487–3700; www.TRB.com.

Managing Diversity
  As an overview on diversity, this 22-minute video uses actors and diversity consultants to convey messages about diversity. Purchase: $845, CRM Films; 800/421–0833.

No Potential Lost®
  The key concept of this three-disc CD-ROM series is that diversity, relationships, and cultural dynamics impact on performance-related energy and need to be consciously managed to increase personal, interpersonal, and organizational effectiveness. Corporate: $895 per disc, Griggs Productions; 415/668–4200; www.griggs.com.

A Peacock in the Land of Penguins
  Based on the book by Barbara "BJ" Hateley and Warren Schmidt, this 10-minute animated video focuses on the advantages and disadvantages of fitting in. Purchase: $495, CRM Films; 800/421–0833; www.crmfilms.com.

Talking 9 to 5: Women and Men in the Workplace
  Based on Deborah Tannen's research and book, *Talking from 9 to 5,* this video shows how men and women can communicate better in the workplace by learning to understand and respect each other's conversational styles. Purchase: $695, ChartHouse International; 800/328–3789; www.charthouse.com.

True Colors
  ABC News Prime Time Live anchor, Diane Sawyer, explores skin color prejudice in America with the help of two friends virtually identical in all respects but one—John is white, Glen is black. Cost: $325 (includes discussion guide), corVISION MEDIA; 800/537–3130.

References

Early, C.P., & Mosakowski, E. (2000). Creating hybrid team cultures: An empirical test of transnational team functioning. *Academy of Management Journal, 43,* 26–49.

Gilbert, J.A., & Stead, B.A. (1999, June). Stigmatization revisited: Does diversity management make a difference in applicant success? *Group & Organization Management, 24*(2), 239–256.

Loden, M., & Rosner, J. (1991). *Workforce America: Managing employee diversity as a vital resource* (18–22). Homewood, IL: Irwin.

McLeod, P.L., Lobel, S.A., & Cox, T.H. (1996). Ethic diversity and creativity in small groups. *Small Group Research, 27,* 248–264.

Nkomo, S.M., & Cox, T. (1996). Diverse identities in organizations. In S.R. Clegg, C. Hardy, & W.R. Nord (Eds.), *Handbook of organizational studies* (338–356). London: Sage.

O'Mara, J. (1994). *Diversity activities and training designs.* San Francisco: Jossey-Bass/Pfeiffer.

O'Mara, J. (1999). Expanding the scope of diversity programs: A new model. In E. Biech (Ed.), *The 1999 annual: Volume 1, training* (13–18). San Francisco: Jossey-Bass/Pfeiffer.

Peterson, R.S., & Nemeth, C.J. (1996). Focus versus flexibility: Majority and minority influence can both improve performance. *Personality and Social Psychology Bulletin, 22,* 14–23.

Special forum on organizational identity and identification. (2000). *Academy of Management Review, 25,* (1).

Thomas, R., Jr. (1996). *Redefining diversity.* New York: AMACOM.

Recommended Reading

Baytos, L.M. (1995). *Designing and implementing successful diversity programs.* Englewood Cliffs, NJ: Prentice Hall.

Carr-Ruffino, N. (1996). *Managing diversity: People skills for a multicultural workplace.* Cincinnati, OH: Thompson Executive Press.

Cox, T. (1993). *Cultural diversity in organizations.* San Francisco: Berrett-Koehler.

Cross, E.Y., Katz, J.H., Miller, F.A., & Seashore, E.W. (1994). *The promise of diversity: Over 40 voices discuss strategies for elimination of discrimination in organizations.* New York: Irwin.

Gardenswartz, L., & Rowe, A. (1994). *Diverse teams at work: Capitalizing on the power of diversity.* Chicago: Irwin.

Hateley, B., & Schmidt, W.H. (1995). *A peacock in the land of penguins: A tale of diversity and discovery.* San Francisco: Berrett-Koehler.

Hayles, R., & Russell, A.M. (1997). *The diversity directive: Why some initiatives fail & what to do about it.* Chicago: Irwin.

Hubbard, E.E. (1997). *Measuring diversity results.* Petaluma, CA: Global Insights.

Jamieson, D., & O'Mara, J. (1991). *Managing workforce 2000: Gaining the diversity advantage.* San Francisco: Jossey-Bass.

Loden, M. (1996). *Implementing diversity.* Chicago: Irwin.

Thiederman, S. (1991). *Bridging cultural barriers for corporate success: How to manage the multicultural work force.* Lexington, MA: D.C. Heath and Company.

Trompenaars, F. (1993). *Riding the waves of culture: Understanding cultural diversity in business.* London: The Economist Books.

Wellington, S.W. (1998). *Advancing women in business—The catalyst guide: Best practices from the corporate leaders.* San Francisco: Jossey-Bass.

Zemke, R., Raines, C., & Filipczak, B. (2000). *Generations at work: Managing the clash of veterans, boomers, Xers, and nexters in your workplace.* New York: AMACOM.

About the Author

*Since 1972, **Julie O'Mara** has been president of O'Mara and Associates, an organization development consulting firm specializing in leadership and the process of managing diversity. A former national president of ASTD (formerly, American Society for Training and Development), she also teaches at John F. Kennedy University. She serves on the board of directors of World Trust, a nonprofit organization that works to attain social, economic, and educational sustainable transformation. O'Mara is a partner with Performance Champions and is a consultant to e-memes.com, Inc., an Internet start-up company in the e-performance arena.*

She is co-author of the best-seller, Managing Workforce 2000: Gaining the Diversity Advantage, *and author of* Diversity Activities and Training Designs, *a manual of activities, lecturettes, and guidelines for effective diversity training.*

CHAPTER THIRTY

Learning to Lead

James M. Kouzes
Chairman Emeritus, tompeters!company

Barry Z. Posner
Dean and Professor of Leadership,
Santa Clara University, Leavey School of Business

Even with all the exuberance about the "new" economy, a few fundamentals still govern the design of effective leadership development programs. It's principles before prescriptions. These principles are that (1) leadership is a relationship, (2) leadership is everyone's business, (3) leadership is a set of skills and abilities, and (4) leadership development is self-development. Also keep in mind that training isn't the only way. People learn to lead through trial and error and by observing others far more effectively than by sitting in a classroom or at a computer—even if they are connected to the hottest new online technologies. Smart trainers integrate all three modes of learning, as well as pre- and post-training activities, into their programs—inside the classroom and out. With these principles in mind, prescriptions become more focused and more powerful elements of design.

PRINCIPLES BEFORE PRESCRIPTIONS

We religiously apply a golden rule to the design of leadership development programs: *Principles before prescriptions.* Before we talk about how to do something, we need to understand what we believe about leadership and whether or not there's evidence that these beliefs are true.

In our research on leadership, spanning over twenty years and involving well over 100,000 leaders, we've discovered a few principles that stand the test of time and science. Regardless of content, learning activity, or setting, these critical few principles inform all our designs:

- Leadership is a relationship;
- Leadership is everyone's business;
- Leadership is a set of skills and abilities; and
- Leadership development is self-development.

Leadership Is a Relationship

Leadership is a relationship between those who aspire to lead and those who choose to follow. Sometimes the relationship is one-to-many. Sometimes it's one-to-one. But regardless of whether the number is one or one thousand, leadership is a relationship.

Evidence abounds for this point of view. For instance, in examining the critical variables for success in the top three jobs in large organizations, Jodi Taylor and her colleagues at the Center for Creative Leadership (CCL) found that the number one success factor is "relationships with subordinates" (personal communication, April 1998).

We were intrigued to find that even in this nanosecond world of e-everything, opinion is consistent with the facts. In an online survey, the techno-hip readers of *FAST COMPANY* magazine were asked to indicate, among other things, "Which is more essential to business success five years from now—skills in using the Internet, or social skills?" ("Where are we," 1999, p. 306). Seventy-two percent selected social skills compared to 28 percent for Internet skills. Even when Internet literati complete a poll online, they realize that it's not the web of technology that matters the most, it's the web of people.

Similar results were found in a study by Public Allies, a nonprofit dedicated to creating young leaders who can strengthen their communities. Public Allies sought the opinions of eighteen-to-thirty-year-olds on the subject of leadership. Among the items was a question about the qualities that were important in a good leader (Public Allies, 1998). Topping the list for this age group is "Being able to see a situation from someone else's point of view." In second place was "Getting along well with other people." Young and old alike agree that success in leadership, success in business, and success in life has been, is now, and will be a function of how well we work and play together.

Leadership Is Everyone's Business

Myth associates leadership with superior position. It assumes that leadership starts with a capital "L" and that when you're on top you're automatically a leader. But leadership isn't a place or a position; it's a process. It involves skills and abilities that are useful whether one is in the executive suite or on the front line, on Wall Street or Main Street.

A recent study of leadership development by a distinguished training association is a case in point. While its aims were noble and of the highest integrity, the study really wasn't about leadership development at all. As we pointed out to the sponsors and to the lead researcher, the study was really about executive development.

The study didn't look at leadership development on the front lines, among young people in schools, or in the volunteer sector. It looked only at what was being done for middle to upper managers in large corporations. While the cases were undeniably exemplary best practices, they were by no means representative of the breadth and depth of leadership development. The point is that leadership development is something that's done in schools with young people, in communities with activists, and in corporations with front-line employees. Leadership development is not synonymous with executive development.

In nearly two decades of research, we've been fortunate to hear or read the stories of over 7,500 ordinary people who have led others to get extraordinary things done. There are millions more. If there's one singular lesson about leadership from all of the cases we have gathered, it's that leadership is everyone's business.

We must broaden our concept of leadership to include those on the front lines as well as those in the executive suites. The secret of high-performing organizations is that everyone within them knows that leadership at all levels is expected and rewarded and that individuals everywhere are responsible for making extraordinary things happen.

Leadership Is a Set of Skills and Abilities

The most pernicious leadership myth of all is that leadership is destiny, reserved for only a very few of us. The myth is perpetuated daily whenever anyone asks, "Are leaders born or made?" Leadership is certainly not a gene, and it's most definitely not something mystical and ethereal that cannot be understood by ordinary people.

Sure, *all* leaders *are* born. So are athletes, scholars, artists, accountants, sales people, and trainers; you name it. But then what? It's pure myth that only a lucky few can ever decipher the leadership code, and of all the leadership myths, this one has done more harm to the development of people and more to slow the growth of countries and companies than any other.

Interestingly, no one has ever asked us, "Can management be taught? Are managers born or made?" These questions are always raised about leadership and leaders, never about management and managers. It is a curious phenomenon. Why is management viewed as a set of skills and abilities and leadership seen as a set of innate personality characteristics? People have simply assumed that management can be taught and, on the basis of that assumption, have established hundreds of business schools and thousands of management courses. In the process, schools and companies have educated hundreds of thousands of managers and spent billions of dollars doing so. Certainly some of those managers are better and some are worse than others are, but, in general, we've raised the caliber of managers by assuming that people can learn the attitudes, skills, and knowledge associated with good management practice.

Leadership Development Is Self-Development

Human beings are toolmakers. We are developers of technology and techniques that enable us to do our work more productively and live our lives more happily. Engineers, for example, have their software and computers. Golfers have their clubs and balls. Painters have their brushes and canvas. What, then, are the instruments of a leader?

The leader's primary instrument is the self. That's really all we have to work with. It's not going to be the code written by some brilliant programmer, the smart chip inside the personal digital assistant, or the phrase turning of a clever speechwriter that makes us better leaders. It's what we do with our selves that's going to make the difference. The extent to which leaders become masters of their craft is the extent to which they learn to play themselves. Leadership development is self-development.

We often ask participants in our workshops to think about a leader from history whom they wish they could have over for dinner and conversation. "If you really had this chance," we inquire, "what questions would you ask this person?" Invariably, the questions people would ask are variations on a few themes: "What made you believe that you could do this?" "What kept you from giving up?" "How did you get the courage to continue?" "What did you do when you were discouraged or afraid?"

The quest for leadership is first an inner quest to discover who we are. Through self-development comes the confidence needed to lead. Self-confidence is really awareness of and faith in our own powers. These powers become clear and strong only as we work to identify and develop them.

HOW WE LEARN TO LEAD, OR TO DO ANYTHING FOR THAT MATTER

So how do you become the best leader possible? To find the answer to that question, we asked the people in our study to tell us how they learned to lead. From our analysis of thousands of responses, three major opportunities for learning to lead emerge. In order of importance, they are

- Trial and error,
- Observation of others, and
- Education.

Other studies support these conclusions. The Center for Creative Leadership interviewed successful executives to find what career events they considered to be important to their development and clustered their results into these categories (McCall, Lombardo, & Morrison, 1988):

- Job assignments that the executives had had;
- Other people with whom they had come into contact;
- Hardships that they had endured; and
- Miscellaneous, including formal training.

At the Honeywell Corporation, senior executives wanted to improve the ways they developed their managers. As a part of this project, Honeywell undertook a six-year research program to determine how managers learn to manage (Zemke, 1985). The Honeywell study resulted in these categories:

- Job experiences and assignments;
- Relationships; and
- Formal training and education.

While neither of these studies asked exclusively about leadership, as we did, the results are so similar that, whether we're talking about managing or leading, experience is by far the most important opportunity for learning to lead. Other people rank a close second in importance. Formal education and training are also significant contributors.

Trial and Error: Learning on the Move

There's no suitable substitute for learning by doing. Whether it's facilitating your team's meetings, leading a special task force, heading your favorite charity's fundraising drive, or chairing your professional association's annual conference, the more chances you have to serve in leadership roles, the more likely it is that you'll develop the skills to lead—and the more likely that you'll learn those important leadership lessons that come only from the failures and successes of live action.

Not every kind of experience, however, supports individual development. *Challenge* is crucial to learning and career enhancement. (For a discussion of the role of challenge in executive development, see Berlew & Hall, 1996; Bray

& Howard, 1983; Magierson & Kakabadse, 1984; Morrison & Brantner, 1992; Wick, 1989). Boring, routine jobs do not help you improve your skills and abilities. They don't help you move forward in your career. You must stretch. You must take opportunities to test yourself against new and difficult tasks. Experience can indeed be the best teacher—if it contains the element of personal challenge.

Observing People: Learning from Others

Other people are essential sources of guidance. We all remember the parent we looked to for advice and support; the special teacher who filled us with curiosity for our favorite subject; the neighbor who always let us watch, even take part in, the tinkering in the garage; the coach who believed that we had promise and inspired us to give our best; the counselor who gave us valuable feedback about our behavior and its impact; the master artisan who instructed us in the fundamentals and nuances of a craft; or the first manager who taught us the ropes to skip and the hoops to jump.

Cynthia D. McCauley (1986), of the Center for Creative Leadership, found that of all the potential relationships at work, the three most important are

- Mentors,
- Immediate supervisors/managers, and
- Peers. (pp. 9–14)

Mentors are particularly valuable as informal sponsors and coaches (see especially Clawson, 1980, pp. 44–165; Gibbons, 1986; Kantner, 1977; Kram, 1985; Levinson, 1978). They help us learn how to navigate the system; they make important introductions; and they point us in the right direction.

Managers are obviously important to our careers. They can help us to advance or can slow our progress. Managers serve as extremely important sources of performance feedback and modeling. The best ones are those who challenge us, who trust us, who are willing to spend time with us, and who are consistent in their behavior.

Peers are valuable sources of information, because they can tell us what is happening in other parts of the organization. Trusted peers also can serve as advisors and counselors, giving us feedback on our personal style and helping us to test out alternative ways of dealing with problems.

Education and Training: Learning Through Life

Formal leadership education and training represent a third way we learn to lead. *Training* magazine found that corporations spend over $50 billion dollars each year for employee education. Leadership training is the second most common type of training, after employee orientation, offered by 75 percent of companies (Industry Report, 1999). Unfortunately, formal training still does not reach the majority of U.S. employees, and thus does not play as significant a role in leadership development as it could. While the majority of large organizations provide formal training, only 16 percent of the labor force receive formal training from their companies (Carnevale & Carnevale, 1994; Training Jumps, 1994).

Although less important as a source of learning than either experience or other people, formal training and education can be of greater importance in developing your skills as an executive and leader than you might assume. Training is a high leverage way of improving your chances of success. "Research shows," reports the American Society for Training and Development (ASTD), "that learning on the job accounted for more than half of the productivity increases in the United States between 1929 and 1989. Additional research shows that people who are trained formally in the workplace have a 30 percent higher productivity rate after one year than people who are not formally trained" (Carnevale, 1990, p. 11; also see, Denison, 1974, 1976, 1980, 1985, 1988).

TWELVE TIPS FOR PRACTITIONERS

Given the ways we learn to lead and the fundamental principles that inform our leadership development efforts, here are twelve tips for creating the best possible learning experiences for leaders in your organization.

1. Stress Interpersonal Skills. Trust and personal credibility form the foundation of leadership. They should, therefore, form the foundation of leadership development. Successful leaders must be able to build and sustain trusting relationships with a highly diverse group of people. Intensive training in interpersonal skills is fundamental to every successful leadership development effort.

2. Provide Feedback. Who really decides whether someone is an exemplary leader? It's the constituents, whether they're immediate managers, direct reports, peers, customers, or other colleagues. One of the most valuable ways to build trust and to assist the leader in getting a rounded view is to provide 360-degree feedback. It's one of the single most valuable things we can do in providing leaders with a realistic agenda for development.

3. Focus on the Future. There's a footnote to our emphasis on the interpersonal. In our research, we consistently find that being forward-looking is the one attribute that differentiates leaders from other credible people. Constituents want their leaders to have a vision of the future, to know where they're headed. In leadership development, it's not unreasonable to suggest that 20 to 25 percent of the time should be devoted to thinking externally, to looking five to ten years down the road, to learning how to build consensus about shared aspirations.

4. Train in Person. With the proliferation of online learning and other electronic courseware, we feel compelled to remind everyone that there's no such thing as virtual trust. You can't build trust and, therefore, leadership abilities over the Internet. Sure, we can all learn a lot of www.stuff over the Net. We can exchange information; we can maintain the relationships we've established; and maybe someday, when the bandwidth is broad enough, we can even do some wonderful interactive exercises and role plays. But the very idea that somehow we can learn to lead without ever interacting with other people is laughable. Leadership is a relationship between human beings, and if we're going to successfully develop leaders we have to get them in the same room together, live.

5. Be Inclusive. Don't offer leadership development only to managers. Offer it to everyone. And we mean *everyone.* We've worked with organizations that have provided the same leadership training to the entire population—to individual contributors on the front lines as well as managers at senior levels. They know that value-added is intelligence-added; leadership can come from anywhere and must come from everywhere.

6. Look Outside for Talent. When we've asked people to identify leadership role models, approximately 40 percent of respondents nominate family members. This is especially true of young people. So tap into the rich resources of your community, and bring in lots of different leaders from lots of different settings. Invite the coach of the local university's women's soccer team to talk about how she builds teamwork while also letting the stars shoot. Ask the local teacher-of-the-year to talk about how he stimulates learning and growth. Give a local community activist the chance to take learners on a tour of a blighted neighborhood and speak about how she's organizing the residents to fight crime, drug abuse, and city hall.

7. Plan and Offer Challenging Career Assignments. Because experience is the most common, and most available, developmental opportunity, work projects should offer potential leaders broader and broader responsibility and challenge. For example, we can significantly influence someone's growth by offering the chance to switch from line to staff and vice versa; to change job content, status, or location; to take on assignments dealing with the implementation of radical change; to start something from scratch; or to fix a troubled operation, to name a few. Project teams and task forces can add to a prospective leader's abilities to work with diverse groups inside and outside the company. In developing leaders, don't hesitate to offer new assignments within the first two years, if not sooner. Today's younger workforce is very impatient. They're looking for challenges early and often.

8. Encourage Participation in Outside Opportunities. The job is not the only place to learn leadership. While it may be the main source of training for product-specific and customer-specific information, the same is not true for leadership. In developing leadership abilities, don't neglect the people, places, and activities that bring joy outside of the workplace. Remember that there are lots of opportunities to develop, practice, and sharpen leadership skills and talents. You might find just the spot in voluntary organizations, civic activities, churches, synagogues, temples, clubs, professional associations, or parent-teacher associations.

9. Encourage Initiative. Leaders don't wait to "get fixed." They don't wait for others to tell them what they need to do to improve. Encourage your leaders and prospective leaders to get clarity about their strengths and weaknesses. Make sure they ask for feedback from people they know. Ask human resource professionals or other colleagues to recommend any useful diagnostic questionnaires. Everyone who wants to lead must have a plan for his or her own development and take charge of executing it.

10. Create Time to Reflect. Even the most venturesome developmental experiences—whether they're challenging projects or rigorous simulations—will not help people grow if they don't take the time to reflect on what they've learned from life's trials and errors. When we do recall, in vivid detail, the people, the places, the events, the struggles, the victories—the very smell and texture of the action—we discover lasting lessons about how to lead others more effectively. We find embedded in experience the grains of truth about ourselves, others, our organizations, and life itself. Unexamined experiences do not produce the rich insights that come with reflection and analysis.

11. Create Space to Explore the Self. While working well with others is the critical success factor for leaders, ironically, perhaps, that success comes only to those who have deep knowledge of self. Dizzying rates of change can be very disorienting. It's easy to lose one's way when markets gyrate wildly and technology spins a World Wide Web. The only way to stay on course is to have an inner compass that is true.

In all of our leadership development programs, we include many opportunities for people to reflect on, clarify, and test their personal values. Personal credibility is earned when we do what we say we will do, and that can only happen when we're convinced of what we want to say. As Max DePree, former chairman of Herman-Miller, puts it, "To become a leader, one need always connect one's voice and one's touch. . . . But there is, of course, a prior task. Finding one's voice in the first place" (DePree, 1992, pp. 3 & 5).

12. Coach. A recent study by the HayGroup, comparing *Fortune* magazine's "Most Admired Companies" to peer companies in the same industry, found that the most admired companies offered twice as much coaching in their leadership development initiatives as did their peers (Stark, n.d.). As professional trainers and educators, it's humbling to realize that our training efforts are not the critical differentiator between average and top-of-the-class. Yet, we all know that it's really what happens after training and on the job that makes the real difference. We can inspire the desire for learning, but someone else has to nurture it continuously. Coaching is critical to that process.

STAGE THREE LEADERSHIP

Several years back Jim and Donna Kouzes attended a retrospective of Richard Diebenkorn's work with their artist friend, Jim LaSalandra. Toward the end of the gallery walk, LaSalandra made this observation: "There are really three periods in an artist's life. In the first, we paint exterior landscapes. In the second, we paint interior landscapes. In the third period, we paint ourselves. That's when you begin to have your own unique style." This is the most important art appreciation lesson we've ever received. It applies equally to the appreciation of the art of leadership.

When first learning to lead, we paint what we see outside of ourselves—the exterior landscape. We read biographies and autobiographies about famous leaders. We read trade books by experienced executives and dedicated scholars. We attend speeches by decorated military officers. We buy tapes by motivational speakers, and we participate in training programs with skilled facilitators.

We do all this to master the fundamentals, the tools, and the techniques. We're clumsy at first, failing more than succeeding, but soon we can give a speech with ease, conduct a meeting with grace, and praise an employee with style. It's an absolutely essential period. An aspiring leader can no more skip the fundamentals than can an aspiring painter.

Then it happens. Somewhere along the way we notice how that last speech sounded mechanically rote, how that last meeting was a boring routine, and how that last encounter felt terribly sad and empty. We awaken to the frightening thought that the words aren't ours, that the vocabulary is someone else's, that the technique is right out of the text, but not straight from the heart.

This is a truly terrifying moment. We've invested so much time and energy in learning to do all the right things, and we suddenly see that they're no longer serving us well. They seem hollow. We feel like phonies. We stare into the darkness of our inner territory, and we begin to wonder what lies inside.

For aspiring leaders, this awakening initiates a period of intense exploration. A period of mixing and testing new ingredients. A period of invention. A period of going beyond technique, beyond training, beyond copying what the masters do, beyond taking the advice of others. And if you surrender to it, after exhausting experimentation and often painful suffering, there emerges from all those abstract strokes on the canvas an expression of self that is truly your own.

Most leadership development is stuck at stage one. It's mostly about painting exterior landscapes. It's mostly about copying other people's styles. It's mostly about trying to mimic the great leaders.

To become truly great at developing leaders, we must move beyond stage one. We must find our own true voices. That's the leadership development challenge we all face. We must get past asking others to paint what's out there and, instead, invite them to paint what's inside. When they can do that, eventually they'll be introduced to the leader within.

References

Berlew, D.E., & Hall, D.T. (1996). The socialization of managers: Effect of expectations on performance. *Administrative Science Quarterly, 11*, 207–223.

Bray, D.W., & Howard, A. (1983). The AT&T longitudinal studies of managers. In K.W. Shaie (Ed.), *Longitudinal studies of adult psychological development.* New York: Guilford Press.

Carnevale, A.P. (1990). Put quality to work: Train America's workforce. *Training & Development, 11.*

Carnevale, A.P., & Carnevale, E.S. (1994, May). Growth patterns in workplace training. *Training Development*, S22-S28.

Clawson, J.G. (1980). Mentoring in managerial careers. In C.B. Derr (Ed.), *Work, family and the career.* New York: Praeger.

Denison, E. (1974,1976,1980,1985,1988). *Accounting for United States economic growth 1929–1969.* Washington, DC: The Brookings Institution.

DePree, M. (1992). *Leadership jazz.* New York: Currency-Doubleday.

Gibbons, T.C. (1986). *Revisiting the question of born vs. made: Toward a theory of development of transformational leaders.* Unpublished doctoral dissertation. Santa Barbara, CA: The Fielding Institute.

Industry Report 1999. (1999, October). *Training*, 37–81.

Kanter, R.M. (1977). *Men and women of the corporation.* New York: Basic Books.

Kram, K.E. (1985). *Mentoring at work: Developmental relationships in organizational life.* Glenview, IL: Scott, Foresman.

Levinson, D.J. (1978). *The seasons of a man's life.* New York: Knopf.

Magierson, C., & Kakabadse, A. (1984). *How American chief executives succeed.* New York: American Management Association.

McCall, M.W., Lombardo, M.M., & Morrison, A.M. (1988). *The lessons of experience: How successful executives develop on the job.* Lexington, MA: Lexington Books.

McCauley, C.D. (1986). *Developmental experiences in managerial work: A literature review.* (Technical Report No. 26.). Greensboro, NC: Center for Creative Leadership.

Morrison, R.F., & Brantner, T.M. (1992). What enhances or inhibits learning a new job? A basic career issue. *Journal of Applied Psychology, 77*, 926–940.

Public Allies. (1998). *New leadership for a new century.* Washington, DC: Author.

Stark, M.J. (n.d.). *Leading the pack: The leadership profile of the world's most admired companies.* [Slide Presentation]. Toronto: HayGroup.

Training jumps 45% since 1983 as companies restructure. (1994, June). *People Trends,* 11.

Where are we on the Web? (1999, October). *FAST COMPANY.*

Wick, C.W. (1989). How people develop. An in-depth look. *HR Report, 6*(7), 1–3.

Zemke, R. (1985, August). The Honeywell studies: How managers learn to manage. *Training,* 46–51.

About the Authors

James M. Kouzes and *Barry Z. Posner* are the authors of The Leadership Challenge: How to Keep Getting Extraordinary Things Done in Organizations *(1995). With over one million copies in print, the book has been published in eleven languages, was a selection of the Macmillan Executive Book Club and the Fortune Book Club, and won the 1989 James A. Hamilton Hospital Administrators' Book Award and the 1995–96 Critics' Choice Award. Kouzes and Posner have also written* Credibility: How Leaders Gain It and Lose It, Why People Demand It *(1993), chosen by* Industry Week *as one of the five best management books of 1993;* Encouraging the Heart *(1999); and* The Leadership Challenge Planner *(1999). They developed the widely used and highly acclaimed* Leadership Practices Inventory *(LPI), a 360-degree questionnaire assessing leadership behavior (1988–1999). Their work also is featured in several instructional videos available from CRM Learning.*

Kouzes is chairman emeritus of tompeters!company, a professional services firm that develops leaders at all levels. He is also an executive fellow at the Center for Innovation and Entrepreneurship at The Leavey School of Business, Santa Clara University. Not only is he a highly regarded leadership scholar, but in September 1993, the Wall Street Journal *cited him as one of the twelve most requested non-university executive education providers to U.S. companies.*

Posner is dean of The Leavey School of Business and professor of leadership at Santa Clara University, where he has received numerous teaching and innovation awards. An internationally renowned scholar and educator, Posner has published more than one hundred research and practitioner-focused articles and is on the editorial review boards for the Journal of Management Inquiry, Journal of Management Education, *and* Journal of Business Ethics. *Having consulted with a wide variety of public and private sector organizations around the globe, he currently sits on the boards of directors for three companies and is a frequently requested conference keynoter.*

CHAPTER THIRTY-ONE

Approach Team Training One Step at a Time

Lorraine L. Ukens
Principal, Team-ing With Success

Increasingly, organizations have turned to work teams as a basic tool for keeping up with competition. Demographic projections indicate that organizations will have to continue doing more with less for quite some time, as fewer people enter the workforce. In order to make the most effective use of teamwork as a competitive tool, it is important to understand a few basics. A team is a small number of people with complementary skills who are committed to a common purpose, set of performance goals, and approach for which they hold themselves mutually accountable (Katzenbach & Smith, 1993). However, groups do not become teams simply because someone calls them one. The question often confronted is: How does a traditionally run organization, in which the individual is the primary unit, change into a team-oriented one?

INTRODUCTION

First, it is important to remember that a team's performance includes *both* individual and collective results. A major objective in team development is to create an environment that will simultaneously result in team cohesiveness and harmony between the team and organizational goals and expectations. In addition, team development efforts should help work-group members build upon their strengths and take better advantage of opportunities. To this end, a training program that takes a comprehensive, systematic, action-based approach can help an organization build and maintain effective work teams.

TRAINING EFFORTS

Training can play a key role in the development of the team concept. It is a critical component of a team's success or failure. However, team training often has been viewed merely as an effort to make people feel good about each other, and the emphasis traditionally was placed on reducing tensions or building relationships between members. Although important, relationship building is only one of several things that effective teams need. Equally important is task completion, that is, results. Teams must learn to use individual talents to the best advantage and to interact effectively with other elements of the organization (Huszczo, 1996).

Team-building efforts should concentrate on how team members relate to one another *and* on how work is completed. Thus, task and process should receive equal attention. Through the process of team building, a team will analyze and build a better understanding of the dynamics that exist among team members and the impact these dynamics have on task accomplishment. Team members can then use this understanding to work together toward greater team effectiveness and growth.

Team effectiveness, however, can be an ambiguous concept, because the definition of "effectiveness" can change with the task at hand and with the characteristics of individual team members. From an ideal perspective, an effective team is one that is efficient, productive, and cohesive. A primary purpose of team training, therefore, is to help a work group learn to examine itself continually so that it can keep functioning successfully.

Individuals who work together as a team need to learn new, more effective ways of solving problems, planning, making decisions, coordinating, integrating resources, sharing information, and dealing with conflict situations that arise. The major tasks facing a new team are basically the same as for a team that has been together for a while. Team members must (1) build a relationship, (2) establish a facilitative emotional climate, (3) work out methods to set goals, develop a collaborative effort, solve problems, make decisions, ensure completion of tasks, establish open communication, and (4) provide an appropriate support system that will let people feel accepted and yet keep issues open for discussion and disagreement.

Although team training is important, many organizations rush to provide it without taking the time to make sure it will be effective. Certain measures should be taken to help prevent your team-building approach from failing (Huszczo, 1996):

- Assess individual team needs before starting training;
- Do not confuse team building with teamwork;
- Use a systematic model to plan team development activities;
- Do not assume that teams are basically all alike;
- Send team members to team training collectively rather than individually;
- Hold teams accountable for following through and using their training;
- Treat team building as a process rather than simply a program;
- Do not rely on training alone to develop effective teams;
- Set ground rules for expected behaviors at the beginning of the training session; and
- Help the team leader take a major role during training.

Some basic principles can help in designing training sessions that will make a difference. These include conducting a systematic team assessment prior to training; designing opportunities for diagnosis, planning, experimentation, discussion, and reinforcement; clarifying objectives and ground rules at the beginning of the session; utilizing experiential-based learning that allows for the active participation of all team members; and providing the opportunity for action planning that transfers to the job.

NEEDS ASSESSMENT

Too many companies plunge into the use of teams without recognizing that learning to work in a high-involvement workplace requires more than just technical skills. The move into teamwork should be accompanied by the realization that certain conditions reveal a need for teams to work on their ability to function effectively. William Dyer (1977), in his early studies on team building, identified typical symptoms that might signal the need for team training. These include

- Loss of production or output;
- Increased number of complaints within the staff;

- Conflicts or hostility among staff members;

- Confusion about assignments or unclear roles;

- Decisions that are misunderstood or not carried through properly;

- Apathy or lack of interest or involvement among staff members;

- Ineffective staff meetings or low participation in group decisions;

- Start-up of a new group that needs to develop quickly into a team;

- High dependency on or negative reactions to the manager; and

- Complaints from customers (internal or external) and the quality of service.

When the diagnosis indicates that a work group is no longer functioning productively, a team-development program is advisable to help improve performance. Another situation requiring team building occurs when a new department is formed or when units merge to form a new working group that will function over a long period of time.

Two common pitfalls to team building include the failure to assess team needs appropriately and the assumption that all teams are alike. Therefore, it is critical to look closely at each team to discover what areas should be targeted for improvement. This information will guide the design and implementation of your program. It also will assist you in determining whether or not team effectiveness actually improved after training by providing baseline data against which to compare future measurements.

Various methods should be used for gathering data. For example, standardized surveys and questionnaires are a good way to monitor changes between pre- and post-training measures. Dyer (1977) suggested that such areas as goals and procedures, leadership, communication, trust and conflict resolution, problem solving and decision making, group dynamics, and growth and development be explored when assessing team performance. Based on these topics, team members can be given comprehensive surveys, combining both scaled ratings (see Exhibit 31.1) and open-ended queries (see Exhibit 31.2) to provide a more complete picture of how individuals perceive the team to be functioning.

Or teams can be assessed on specific content areas that are indicated as ineffective. Some of the other widely used assessment techniques include direct observation, general feedback from supervisory personnel, and personal interviews. Where appropriate, hard data (for example, quality statistics, production effectiveness, and overtime reports) also may be used. Work group output measures can provide a more thorough understanding of the problems facing the team and the impact of those difficulties on the whole organization. Documents also may be a source of information from which needs can be inferred. Although records represent conditions but not necessarily the underlying cause

Exhibit 31.1. Sample Scaled Rating Questionnaire

Instructions: Circle the number that indicates your rating of your team's current level of functioning in each of the following areas.

Goals and Procedures

Confusing goals; group uninvolved/ indifferent; no set guidelines or procedures	1	2	3	4	5	6	7	Clear, specific goals; planned together and shared by all; set guidelines and procedures

Leadership

Needs not met; dependence on one individual	1	2	3	4	5	6	7	Met by various members as needs arise

Communication

Limited exchange; passive listening; little/ no feedback	1	2	3	4	5	6	7	Free exchange; active listening; specific feedback

Trust and Conflict Resolution

Distrust; self-contained; fear of criticism; conflicts ignored or unresolved	1	2	3	4	5	6	7	High trust; self-disclosure; no fear of reprisal; conflicts resolved constructively

Problem Solving and Decision Making

Assumptions; decisions not made or made by few; uncommitted	1	2	3	4	5	6	7	Careful diagnosis; consensus sought; decisions supported

Group Dynamics

Disassociation; hostility; some dominate, others passive	1	2	3	4	5	6	7	High cohesion; empathy; all participate actively

Growth and Development

Rigid roles; no change, growth, or risk; creativity discouraged	1	2	3	4	5	6	7	Flexibility; change, growth, and risk; creativity encouraged

---

Exhibit 31.2. Sample Open-Ended Questionnaire

Teamwork Questionnaire

1. What are the main objectives of the team as a whole?

2. What is the purpose of your job?

3. What measurement methods let you know that you *personally* have been effective in accomplishing your purpose? How timely is this feedback?

4. What measurement methods let you know that the *team* has been effective in accomplishing its purpose? How timely is this feedback?

5. What one thing hinders you most from doing an effective job? How does it hinder you and why?

6. What changes would you recommend to make your work team more effective?

---

of problems, they can help pinpoint trouble spots worth investigating or support other evidence.

TRAINING MODEL

A major flaw that occurs frequently is confusing *team building* with *teamwork.* Individual team members can obtain the basic knowledge of team skills and group dynamics through a general course on teamwork concepts. However, actual team building occurs through the interplay of working together on the concepts as an intact team. For example, a company that sends one or two workers from each of its separate divisions for "team" training is not incorporating a "team-building" philosophy. For teams to become cohesive, each team member must move from an individual perspective, recognizing his or her own contribution, to a team perspective. Team-building efforts, then, allow the team to assess and improve itself continuously. Real development is never completed.

For effective team building to occur, team members should spend time during their developmental activities actually negotiating with one another, discussing issues, establishing team goals, identifying the roles each member should play, and establishing or reviewing procedures that the team will use to become more effective. Therefore, it is suggested that the training techniques include structured experiential activities, feedback from group discussion, and an examination of the team's actual work experiences. The experiential learning process helps transfer the skills practiced in the classroom to on-the-job application.

It is recommended that a team training program take a three-step approach, as shown in Figure 31.1 (Ukens, 1994):

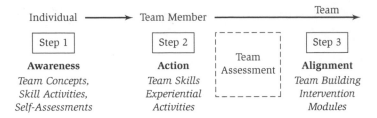

Figure 31.1. Team-ing With Success Training Model™

1. Individuals gain an *awareness* of general team concepts through structured activities and of their individual strengths/weaknesses through the use of self-assessment tools. This is where the individual begins to see his or her own role in the team process.

2. Groups of individuals put team skills into *action* by participating in experiential learning activities that allow individual members to practice their roles as team players.

3. Team-building workshops are conducted on an ongoing basis to promote *alignment* of the team process, based on an individual team's particular need for improvement.

In this model, group members initially need to explore basic concepts that underlie the foundation of teamwork. This constitutes the awareness stage and should not be confused with actual team building. Step 1 helps in identifying the strengths and weaknesses that are the critical building blocks for the team's actual performance. Step 2 allows the individual team members to practice the skill concepts in a hands-on learning experience. In Step 3, actual team building occurs, where an intact work team engages in the process of continual self-examination so that it may be aware of conditions that keep it functioning successfully. Alignment of the team process is fundamental to maintaining effective teamwork. This fine-tuning of the team's performance is a continuous process (Ukens, 1996).

DESIGNING TEAM TRAINING SESSIONS

As mentioned previously, it is important to remember that team training should be tailored to meet the specific needs of the target team as shown by the needs assessment. However, certain guidelines for the general design of the sessions can help make team training more effective. These include

- Hold training sessions off-site to minimize job distractions;
- Include all aspects of diagnosis, discussion, planning, experimentation, and reinforcement;
- Realize the importance of "experience" and let team members become actively involved in the learning process, rather than lecture to them;
- Address both relationship-building skills (for example, communication or conflict management) and task-oriented skills (for example, goal setting or problem solving);
- Provide ample opportunities for skills practice; and
- Allow team leaders to facilitate discussions, rather than an external facilitator.

Research shows that shorter training sessions, spread across time, result in more long-term retention than do concentrated multiple day programs. Most important, however, is the fact that, for training to really work, the insights gained must be translated into actions.

Experiential Learning

Because experiential learning provides participants with a structured activity that contributes to content (task) and process (relationship) objectives, it is an ideal vehicle for the examination of team skills. Also referred to as hands-on or action-based learning, experiential learning emphasizes what participants do rather than what they are told by the trainer. Learning occurs when a person engages in some activity, looks back on it critically, abstracts some useful insight, then puts the result to work through changes in behavior. It means that the outcomes of the activity are analyzed in relation to the appropriate learning objectives planned into the design. The analysis becomes the foundation for action planning that transfers the skills to on-the-job application.

The use of experiential learning activities has many advantages, especially in regard to teams. It presents the opportunity for holistic understanding by forming an integrated big picture, rather than a fragmented one. The activities themselves allow conditions to be varied to meet the needs of each group. Active involvement of all participants is encouraged through the structure of the activities. Therefore, all members of a team have an opportunity to interact with one another and explore the dynamics of the group. Experiential learning also fosters team empowerment. Peer learning promotes group dynamics, and personal responsibility is emphasized because team members are involved in self-directed evaluation.

In this situation, individuals are provided a "safe" environment in which to explore and practice team skills. This ability to practice gives team members a chance to work on their performance without worrying about actual results. They can experiment, learn from the experience, make corrections, and try again. They can try out new roles, take different positions, and do things that they might not be able to do in real-life situations. But the practice sessions parallel the real world. Analogies drawn from the experiences can be applied to a variety of situations: competition, realistic goal setting, effective communication processes, resolving differences, demands of limited resources, time pressure of deadlines, and so forth. Discussing *what* and *why* things occurred provides insight into how individuals interact during the group process. This knowledge becomes the catalyst that enables the team to analyze its current state and plan action steps to improve its effectiveness.

EVALUATION

It is important to remember that behavioral changes occur gradually over a period of time. It may take as much as six months or even one year for such changes to become internalized. To monitor progress, the surveys and questionnaires used in the assessment stage (for example, Exhibits 31.1 and 31.2) can be retaken to determine differences between pre- and post-intervention at approximately three months, then again at six months and one year. These results can be combined with personal observations and a formal follow-up meeting with each team to analyze the effectiveness of training. Once again, hard data (statistics, production, reports, and so forth) may be used to show performance improvement.

Follow-up must become an integral part of the process in order to determine whether further interventions are necessary. It is important to implement an *ongoing* team-building training program to support continuous improvement.

ORGANIZATIONAL SUPPORT

Although training can play a significant role in moving teams toward greater effectiveness, it is important to remember that team building does take time. It is a process, not just a one-time activity. Continuous improvement requires a commitment to learning. Providing development opportunities sends a message that management supports teamwork; but it is not a strong message unless other corporate functions are connected to it (Parker, 1990). The organization itself must sustain team-development procedures and build necessary changes into its basic structure. Without top management's support, teams cannot move forward with their efforts.

Team members should undergo cross-training within and across teams to help them master a variety of roles in day-to-day activities. This will increase their ability to become flexible and respond quickly to urgent customer needs. Team leaders can continue the "learn by doing" approach by integrating the training with the overall job responsibilities so that the normal performance of the job becomes another mode of training.

If the team process is to succeed, managers must train their work teams on how to use skills, provide them with opportunities to take risks and learn from experience, and celebrate *team* accomplishments. Rewards, recognition, and compensation should focus on combined efforts in addition to personal achievement so that there is an incentive to work together as a team, rather than merely pursue individual interests.

Most importantly, organizations must model the team concept. This can be accomplished by involving employees on an ongoing basis and promoting collaborative leadership. The policies, environment, and support systems of the organization must sustain a spirit of teamwork. For example, open communication and information systems provide ready access to information that empowers teams to move toward more effective work. A team becomes a unified, cohesive group of people only insofar as it can obtain the resources and support to do its job.

References

Dyer, W.G. (1977). *Team building: Issues and alternatives.* Reading, MA: Addison-Wesley.

Huszczo, G.E. (1990, February). Training for team building. *Training & Development,* 37–42.

Huszczo, G.E. (1996). *Tools for team excellence: Getting your team into high gear and keeping it there.* Palo Alto, CA: Davies-Black.

Katzenbach, J.R., & Smith, D.K. (1993, March/April). The discipline of teams. *Harvard Business Review,* 111–120.

Parker, G.M. (1990). *Team players and teamwork.* San Francisco: Jossey-Bass.

Solomon, C.M. (1993). Simulation training builds teams through experience. *Personnel Journal, 72,* 100–108.

Ukens, L.L. (1994, May). *Team-ing with success: A training approach.* Poster session, ASTD Conference, Anaheim, California.

Ukens, L.L. (1996). *Pump them up! 35 workshops to build stronger teams.* King of Prussia, PA: HRDQ.

Recommended Reading

Fisher, K., Rayner, S., Belgard, W., & Belgard/Risher/Rayner Team. (1995). *Tips for teams: A ready reference for solving common team problems.* New York: McGraw-Hill.

Larson, C.E., & LaFasto, F. (1989). *Teamwork: What must go right/what can go wrong.* London: Sage.

Noe, R.A. (1999). *Employee training and development.* Boston: Irwin/McGraw-Hill.

Robbins, D. (1993, December). The dark side of team building. *Training & Development, 47,* 17–21.

Ukens, L.L. (1997). *Working together: 55 team games.* San Francisco: Jossey-Bass/Pfeiffer.

Ukens, L.L. (1999). *All together now! A seriously fun collection of interactive training games and activities.* San Francisco: Jossey-Bass/Pfeiffer.

Zenger, J.II., Musselwhite, E., Hurson, K., & Perrin, C. (1994). *Leading teams: Mastering the new role.* Homewood, IL: Irwin Professional.

About the Author

Lorraine L. Ukens *is the owner of Team-ing With Success, which specializes in team building and experiential learning. Her business experience has been applied in designing, facilitating, and evaluating programs in a variety of areas. She has teamed with private companies, nonprofit organizations, and government agencies in helping them achieve higher levels of success. Her degree in human resource development is from Towson University (Maryland), where she is currently an adjunct faculty member. Ukens served as president of the Maryland Chapter ASTD from 1999–2000. She is included in* Who's Who of American Women 2000–2001.

*Ukens is the author of training activity resources that make learning interactive and fun. These include books (*Getting Together, Working Together, All Together Now!, Energize Your Audience, Pump Them Up, SkillBuilders: 50 Customer Service Activities*), consensus activities (*Adventure in the Amazon, Arctic Expedition, Stranded in the Himalayas*), and a game (*Common Currency: The Cooperative-Competition Game*). Visit her website at* www.team-ing.com.

CHAPTER THIRTY-TWO

Strategic Employee Development Planning

Robert O. Brinkerhoff, Ph.D.

Professor, Counseling Psychology, Western Michigan University

Nicholas A. Andreadis, M.D.

Assistant Professor, Counseling Psychology, Western Michigan University

S trategically aligned employee development should not be considered a perk offered to reward good performance and loyalty, nor simply a means to enable personal choice and registration in a cafeteria of organization-sponsored training programs. On the contrary, it can be an essential ingredient of an organization's competitive advantage. Despite this business imperative, many organizations have yet to systematically employ the methods and tools that are available to assist managers and employees in creating and implementing individual development plans that can lead to real business impact and value. This chapter reviews the problems most commonly associated with individual development planning and provides recommendations for overcoming them. Seven principal purposes for employee development are described, as well as the three most important drivers of employee development: An organization's competitive environment, annual business goals that are linked to individual performance improvement needs, and each employee's personal career aspirations. Finally, a three-step method for instituting employee development in any size organization is presented, along with specific recommendations for implementation.

INTRODUCTION

This chapter provides trainers with conceptual guidance and application suggestions for designing and implementing strategic employee development planning systems, methods, and tools. Employee development (which for purposes of brevity we abbreviate with the acronym ED) refers to a systematic process by which an organization builds plans to develop its workforce for the general purposes of helping employees advance in the organization and/or their careers. Employee development includes all of the education and training that organizations might invest in their employees, such as training employees to perform effectively in their current jobs, orienting employees to the workplace, developing them for advanced positions or programs, and building organizational capability for future success.

In this chapter, we define ED to mean "individual development planning"— the system an organization operates to build overall workforce capability and help individual employees identify the learning outcomes and activities that will help them most to achieve their career goals. Typically, ED planning is done on an annual cycle and includes assessment of the employee's current proficiencies, identification of specific learning objectives, a plan for participating in one or more learning activities, and a timeline for implementation of the plan, including measures to gauge success.

Our focus in this chapter is strategic, as the title indicates. When we describe employee development as being strategic, we mean that it is linked to a plan to achieve a set of future-oriented goals or objectives that provides the maximum possible value both to the individual and to the organization.

PROBLEMS WITH TYPICAL ED SYSTEMS

Employee development efforts are frequently viewed with a great degree of skepticism and pessimism in most organizations—and often with good reason. Far worse than their simply being held in low regard is the fact that most ED systems are not effective; they do not provide the value they should, either to the people who participate in them or to the organizations that sponsor them. Our experience and research have uncovered several common issues and problems with most ED systems. We list them here and later in this chapter provide our suggestions to remedy each.

Lack of Management Support. Most ED systems require the employee's manager to provide assessment feedback, authorize resources, and otherwise support the employee's development. A manager's participation is necessary to allocate resources, to interpret organizational needs, and to assist employees in assessing their current capabilities. In our experience, managers in typical organizations view ED as an administrative burden rather than as a useful performance improvement and planning tool, and thus they give it only the most cursory attention. When the managers do not fully and thoughtfully participate in the development of the plan, it will not be seen as important and is unlikely to be implemented.

Lack of Accountability. If organizations do not hold both managers and employees accountable for thorough and thoughtful development planning, then the overall plan will languish. In many organizations, there is virtually no accountability for adhering to the ED requirements and no consequence for failure to participate. Senior managers must provide the appropriate incentives and consequences to ensure responsible participation by managers and employees.

Perception That Development Is a Perk. All too often, the expenditure of time and money for development is considered a perk or reward for hard work and loyalty, rather than a strategic investment in the employee. Training that is available through the ED system is often considered something that the organization is willing to "give away" to employees. When ED is seen as simply a means to distribute an employee benefit, both managers and employees are less likely to take the effort seriously and the entire training and development initiative loses organizational credibility.

Training "Wish Lists" Instead of Business-Linked Competency Development. When asked, most people would say that they have a long list of training courses they would like to take to enhance their "toolkit." Some are valuable, whereas others will have little immediate applicability to work being done today or in the future. In the absence of a clear business need for training and development, managers and employees often will select training programs that seem nominally appropriate and valuable on the surface, but their relationship to work processes and organizational impact is tangential at best.

Focus on Competency Gaps Versus Performance Improvement Needs. In organizations that have subscribed to the popular competency movement, it is not unusual to find that there are long "laundry lists" of competencies (skill definitions) that have been defined for each job position in the organization, sometimes delineating dozens of competencies for each job. These competency lists often serve as the basis for the ED assessment, wherein employees are rated on each specific competency. The competency gaps, where one's current capabilities are most discrepant from gold-standard levels, become the highest priority targets for development. Although this approach is seemingly "scientific" and attractive in its simplicity, the largest gaps may not be the best targets for development. Needs for development should be driven by the demands of the business context as it is projected to exist when the developed skills will become available for deployment. It is fully possible, for example, that an employee should develop a skill that is already rated as "adequate," because the particular business needs in that employee's work area will require an extraordinary degree of capability in the near future.

Exclusive Focus on Near-Term Goals. Every organization is under pressure to meet the obligations that confront it on a daily basis. This often leads to a form of myopia that prevents the identification of capabilities needed for future growth and competitiveness. Without an adequate, well-developed process that provides the time and space for managers and employees to plan against a thoughtful projection of the future, organizations become trapped in being especially good at tasks that are needed for today, but may be obsolete tomorrow.

Unfocused and "Scattershot" Development Targets. Employee development systems in most organizations are not designed to be strategic. Typically, development targets are driven by individual interests or by a manager's idiosyncratic perceptions of useful skills required for the future. Because neither of these viewpoints is likely to be based on a systematic reflection and analysis of strategic business needs, the resultant development needs are diffuse, highly variable in scope and quality of definition, and not integrated with an informed business analysis. As a result, senior managers have little reason to believe that investment in this wide array of development needs will lead to a significant payoff in business performance or vital organizational capability.

SEVEN KEY PURPOSES FOR DEVELOPMENT PLANNING

A comprehensive and effective ED system should be more than just an employee benefit or a means to enroll people in a menu of training opportunities provided by a company. We identify seven key purposes for ED that balance the needs of the organization and its employees. The seven are listed in no particular order, as their relative importance will vary according to the needs of an organization. A growing organization, for instance, might need an ED system to focus on filling emerging leadership positions, while an organization that is having difficulty recruiting and retaining talented people might want the system to focus on meeting employee aspirations for personal and career growth.

1. Build Organizational Capability for Future Success. The rapid pace of change in global market conditions, technology, demographics, and other similar variables almost certainly will demand new competencies and capabilities. Successful organizations will be those with readiness to perform effectively in new situations. Clearly, ED systems need to look beyond skills required for today's workplace and focus on a longer horizon. Employee development can be seen, to some extent, as a form of "insurance" that employees will possess the knowledge and skills to best leverage the opportunities that the future will surely present.

2. Develop "Bench Strength" for Succession Planning. Ideally, an organization will have a back-up person ready to replace each person in a key role, should the current person suddenly depart. In this respect, a major purpose of ED is to build the capability of the organization to move people quickly and comfortably into vacant or new positions, with the assurance that the new inductee is indeed capable of performing at the same level of competence as the person being replaced, if not more capably. An effective ED system provides the training and education that prepares people for these new roles.

3. Improve Performance. Emerging business needs and organizational challenges inevitably require improved performance from employees. Providing learning and development that are focused on critical performance improvement needs is one of the methods by which managers continuously improve organizational effectiveness. A good ED system will generate substantial opportunity for performance improvement and serve to remedy deficient performance.

4. Satisfy Individual Needs for Growth and Feeling "Invested In." Employee morale is known to be an important part of an overall effective organization. Organizations have many means by which they can show their concern for the personal health and welfare of their employees. Systematic, effective, and constructive ED sends a message that each employee's learning and growth are important and that the organization is willing to invest in its people.

5. Enhance Recruiting and Retention. More than ever, employees expect that their employer will provide them with growth opportunities. People in today's turbulent workplace know that a corporate downsizing, reorganization, merger, or acquisition is only as far away as tomorrow's morning news. In the face of this uncertainty, employees are compelled to upgrade their skills and knowledge continuously so that they are ready to move to a new job if and when the opportunity is provided or circumstances dictate that they must. It is not uncommon for recruits to inquire about developmental opportunities, and opportunities for development may sometimes be a key factor in choosing an employer.

6. Stimulate Individual Development Planning and Career Growth. A good ED system will not only provide opportunities for employees to learn skills that will make them promotable (or attractive to new employers), but will systematically help employees define career opportunities, assess career choices, and clarify career paths and milestones to help them plan their advancement. Career growth not only benefits each individual, but it is also a key component of successful recruiting, retention, and succession planning. By providing learning linked to career growth, organizations increase the likelihood that employees will remain satisfied and that competent people will be available to fill new openings, reducing the costs of external recruitment and selection.

7. Provide a Basis for Planning and Allocating Development Resources. By "rolling up" development needs of all employees, an organization is able to project the capabilities and resources it will have to provide learning to meet these needs. There is a bewildering array of learning opportunities available through community colleges, private vendor workshops, online instructional programs, mentoring programs, and action-learning activities. A key challenge for the ED function is to plan, coordinate, and manage the learning opportunities so that resources are readily available to meet learning needs.

BALANCING INDIVIDUAL AND ORGANIZATIONAL NEEDS

Organizations must be structured and managed to obtain the best performance from people, while at the same time nurturing the health and well-being of employees. People are not consumable supplies, but are a unique individual capacity, capable of nearly infinite development and ongoing renewal. We know that people, to remain effective in employment roles, must be healthy in the other roles of their lives, as parents, caretakers, and social and spiritual entities. On the other hand, to remain competitive, organizations must continuously leverage the very best performance from their employees. To represent the need for this balance, we refer to the need for ED to balance the "give" and the "get" needs depicted graphically in Figure 32.1.

The "give" portion of the oval represents what the organization provides each employee within a nurturing environment that promotes healthy growth, learning, and opportunity for advancement. The "get" portion of the oval represents the need for the organization to obtain the best performance from its people.

When the give and get forces are out of balance, the organization is at risk. If the organization expects people to work too hard for too long, they burn out, become less effective over time, and eventually perform well below their capa-

Figure 32.1. Balancing Individual and Organizational Behavior

bility. If the organization is too generous, too undemanding, too lax and laissez faire, people will likewise perform below their capability.

At any given time, needs for give and get will vary—from work unit to work unit, from individual to individual, and from one business scenario to another. Almost always, needs for "give" and "get" will be to some extent in conflict. Managers are the focal point for this conflict, and they must continuously and effectively balance the task versus people conflicts inherent in their role. A good ED system provides managers with a simple but effective means to help them strike the optimum balance.

DISENTANGLING DEVELOPMENT PLANNING FROM PERFORMANCE REVIEW

Most organizations implement some sort of formal performance appraisal and review progress at least annually. Performance reviews are intended primarily to result in ratings (judgments) of an employee's performance to aid in decisions about whether to retain, promote, or place the employee on the "fast track."

Employee development and performance review have fundamentally different purposes. The purpose of performance review is to render summative judgments about employee performance that will guide future employment status. The purpose of ED is to guide future learning to provide the greatest possible opportunity for employees to succeed. In preparing for a performance review, employees will adopt a "selling" mentality, presenting their capabilities in the most positive, even exaggerated manner. In a development review, the purpose is to win learning resources; thus, the proper stance is to underestimate one's capabilities.

When ED and performance review are not seen as independent in the eyes of employees and managers, each purpose will subvert the other and weaken both systems. Performance review and development planning should be separated, both in purpose and in schedule, so that the processes occur as far apart on the calendar as possible.

THE KEY EMPLOYEE DEVELOPMENT PLAN DRIVERS

Three interdependent drivers influence the processes and outcomes of individual development planning. They are listed below and shown in Figure 32.2.

1. The future "marketplace" or competitive environment;
2. Current business goals; and
3. Each individual's career and development goals.

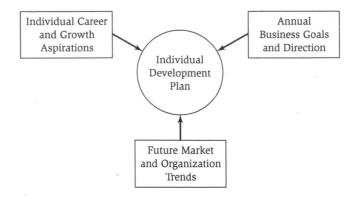

Figure 32.2. Drivers of Employee Development Plans

The relative influence of each driver should vary from time to time, depending on the specific dynamics of the organization, each employee, and the environment in which each must perform. We describe each of the three drivers separately and then describe a process that integrates them into individual development planning.

Driver 1: The Future Marketplace and Competitive Environment

In the midst of unprecedented levels of economic growth and employment, organizations are faced with a new and significant dilemma: How to ensure that they have the requisite human capabilities to perform effectively in the future. The most significant threat to continuing growth is the relative lack of motivated, trained, and focused talent. Strategic human capability planning is as important to an organization's success as financial and capital planning. Effective human capability planning starts from the outside in, such that leaders of an organization peer into the future and develop a picture of the likely marketplace and competitive environment. Human resource leaders can then analyze these (one or more) scenarios to anticipate what competencies (knowledge, skills, and personal attributes) the organization will require to implement its strategy in the future marketplace.

Driver 2: Current Business Plans and Goals

Business goals and issues inevitably entail various needs for improved performance. In turn, improved performance needs may drive the need to improve employee capability. Development planning is a powerful tool for focusing learning on immediate performance improvement needs that are in turn linked to pressing business goals and issues. When development planning focuses on performance improvement needs, several benefits are realized. First, managers are more likely to support development when it is keyed to business goals and objectives for which they are accountable. Second, improving employee capability in areas of key business improvement needs helps the organization perform more effectively, which benefits the organization, of course, and also highlights the role of training and development as a vital business contributor. Finally, employees who demonstrably help the business succeed are better positioned for career success and promotion.

Driver 3. Each Individual's Career and Personal Development Goals

The relative influence of this driver on strategic employee development has increased significantly over the last decade. A rash of corporate downsizing and outsourcing has created an unfortunate legacy of distrust and abandoned loyalties. One constructive result of these disruptions is that individuals are assuming more responsibility for their careers and their employability. It is not uncommon nor unwise these days for individuals to develop a personal training and development plan. With or without the support of their organizations, they are determined to add valuable knowledge and skills to their personal "toolkit." In this sort of environment, employees increasingly expect—and deserve—employee development systems that will help them chart a course and develop the competencies for future success.

BUSINESS LINKED EMPLOYEE DEVELOPMENT

In the preceding paragraphs, we have described the changing nature of ED and its critical role in building and sustaining personal and organizational performance. In this section we present a three-step employee development process that integrates the concepts and principles and provides organizations with useful guidance for getting started. The underlying principle of the three-step process is that successful strategic employee development is best done when managers and employees collaborate at all stages of the process. Employee development planning done in this manner aligns the strategic planning and goal-setting processes with employee career growth and learning objectives. Joint planning promotes cohesion and interdependence among participants and helps establish a more mature and productive professional relationship. Continuous dialogue is an essential ingredient for this form of ED planning, with each round of discussion sharpening the focus of training and development and improving the likelihood that organizational and personal resources will be used efficiently. For a more detailed description of and tools for this process, see Brinkerhoff & Messinger (1999).

Step One: Aligning Goals

Following development and communication of the organization's business goals, managers develop individual performance goals that are linked to these business goals. Simultaneously and independently, each employee defines his or her personal performance improvement and career aspiration goals. What follows is a dialogue between manager and employee, wherein they compare and discuss one another's statements and ultimately arrive at agreed on goals that align the needs of both the organization and the individual.

Step Two: Setting Development Targets

Once organizational and individual goals are aligned, the manager and employee jointly identify the key skills and knowledge necessary for achievement of business-linked performance goals and personal career growth goals. Next, the manager and employee agree on the few most important competency development needs that will best serve both the employee and the organization. It is our experience that trying to develop more than three or four new skills per year diffuses energy and attention and produces a diminishing return on time and money.

Step Three: Planning a Learning Strategy

During this final step, the employee prepares a detailed plan that identifies (1) the specific development targets, (2) the learning methods to be employed for each target, and (3) the measures by which the acquisition and application of learning will be assessed. Often at this point, the employee receives assistance from the training and development function (many use online resource systems), as there may be a number of options for learning and professional assistance can be very helpful. The employee and manager then review the plan together, revise it if necessary, and ultimately commit to its implementation.

BENEFITS OF STRATEGIC EMPLOYEE DEVELOPMENT

Most training and development professionals intuitively believe that investing time, money, and energy in the process of strategic employee development is worthwhile. We hope that the information presented in this chapter strengthens and fortifies that commitment. In addition to the stated benefits that accrue when employees and managers communicate effectively about goals of mutual and individual interest, other good things happen when ED is done strategically. These include

- A partnership among training and development professionals, employees, and line managers;

- Greater clarity and agreement among employees and their managers as to business direction, goals, and priorities;
- The ability of employees to articulate with precision the business goals of the organization and the value added for the business from their attendance at training programs;
- Training results that can be measured in terms of actual business performance;
- Line managers who are willing to spend time and money on training because they are confident in their investment;
- The surprising fact that frequently less money is spent on training, but with the probability that the return on the training investment is greater; and
- Training and development units that achieve credibility within the organization.

References

Brinkerhoff, R.O., & Messinger, R.C. (1999). *Strategic employee development: Manager's guide.* San Francisco: Jossey-Bass/Pfeiffer.

Recommended Reading

Brethower, D., Smalley, K., & Alexander, L. (Eds.). (1998). *Performance based instruction: Linking training to business results.* San Francisco: Jossey-Bass.

Brinkerhoff, R.O. (1994). *The learning alliance: Systems thinking in human resource development.* San Francisco: Jossey-Bass.

Brinkerhoff, R.O., & Messinger, R.C. (1999). *Strategic employee development.* San Francisco: Jossey-Bass/Pfeiffer.

Nadler, L., & Nadler, Z. (1994). *Designing training programs: The critical events model.* Houston, TX: Gulf.

Tobin, D.R. (1997). *The knowledge-enabled organization: Moving from "training" to "learning" to meet business goals.* New York: AMACOM.

About the Authors

Robert O. Brinkerhoff is an internationally recognized expert on training and organizational effectiveness and evaluation, with thirty-four years of experience starting as a training officer in the U.S. Navy in 1966. A well-known author of ten books on training effectiveness and measurement, he has been a keynote speaker at dozens of major conferences and institutes. Many corporations have adopted Brinkerhoff's training impact, measurement, and effectiveness principles and methods to help their organizations achieve demonstrable business results from training. He has broad research, speaking, facilitation, and consulting experience in the United States, Russia, Europe, Australia, Saudi Arabia, and South Africa. Brinkerhoff is professor of counseling psychology at Western Michigan University, where he coordinates a graduate program in human resources development.

Nicholas A. Andreadis is assistant professor of counseling psychology at Western Michigan University in Kalamazoo, Michigan, where he provides leadership to graduate programs in human resources development. Prior to joining Western Michigan University, he served as senior consultant for TSI Consulting Partners, Inc., and vice president, global leadership development, for Pharmacia and Upjohn Inc. He consults with for-profit and not-for-profit organizations on issues of leadership and organizational development. Dr. Andreadis has contributed to the literature of clinical medicine and science. He received a B.A. from Kent State University and an M.D. from Creighton University and is board certified in internal medicine and cardiovascular diseases.

CHAPTER THIRTY-THREE

Self-Directed New Employee Orientation

Jean Barbazette
President, The Training Clinic

One of the significant trends in new employee orientation (NEO) is the increasing number of organizations that conduct orientation over a period of time. These organizations see orientation as a process, not a one-meeting event. Another significant new trend is to use a variety of self-directed orientation delivery methods. Many of these self-directed methods are particularly attractive to new employees in their twenties and thirties. Eight specific techniques are recommended in this chapter, and four checklists are given to make the redesign of new employee orientation easier for the smart trainer.

ORIENTATION TRENDS

The Training Clinic has been conducting new employee orientation (NEO) benchmarking research since 1985. One of the significant trends that we have seen is the increasing number of organizations that conduct orientation over a period of time, thus treating orientation as a process, not a one-meeting event. Techniques that promote NEO as a process include

- Sending information to new employees prior to the first day of work;
- Ordering materials and preparing the new employee's work space;

- Spreading out information over the first weeks and months of work, providing information closest to the time it is needed or about to be used so that it is relevant and will be remembered; and

- Partnering with new employees and allowing employees to take the initiative to orient themselves.

This last technique is the focus of this chapter. Smart trainers are using a variety of self-directed delivery methods to make NEO more effective and more productive and to give a better first impression of the organization to the employee. Many of these techniques are particularly attractive to new employees in their twenties and thirties.

BENEFITS OF SELF-DIRECTED ORIENTATION

How new employees will act on the job depends on how they are treated during the new employee orientation period. If employees are taught to be passive during orientation and all information is provided or "spoon fed" to them, the message is that the way work is conducted at this organization is to wait for someone or something to come to you.

On the other hand, if employees are required to take some initiative during the NEO process, then they are more likely to be proactive and take the initiative during the course of the job. The organization that tells new employees, "Your first job here is to figure out who we are, what we do, and how you can fit in and make a contribution" is likely to have a new employee who is willing to take the initiative in completing job tasks.

HOW TO SET UP A SELF-DIRECTED ORIENTATION

Smart trainers use one or all of the following delivery methods to design or redesign NEO as a more self-directed process:

1. *Identify the types of employees who would benefit from a self-directed orientation.* Employees who are not allowed much initiative in carrying out normal job responsibilities may not be good candidates for this type of orientation. The selection process may require the development of alternative materials for a self-directed NEO, while keeping other more directed processes for employees who require closer supervision.

2. *Identify what information is appropriate to give to the employee prior to the first day of work.* The more information that can be provided, the easier it will be for the new employee to take the initiative. Information

about the organization and what it does would be helpful, along with other resources. (See Exhibit 33.1 for a list of potential materials that can be sent prior to the employee's first day.)

3. *Prepare for new employees to take the initiative by conducting several planning activities before the first day.* A suggested checklist of preparation activities is provided in Exhibit 33.2. Many of these activities will give new employees a quick start and the ability to take the initiative.

4. *Identify the format of the information.* Some printed materials may exist already, such as an annual report, union contract, newsletter, benefit plan information, and employee handbook. Other information may be available on the organization's intranet or web page. Information that changes periodically can be stored more easily in an electronic format; examples of this type of dynamic information are organization charts and the company's products or services. This allows the new employee access to correct information that is always up-to-date.

5. *Provide materials (hard copy or electronic) and a guide for the new employee to access and use them.* Make a list of questions for each resource so that the new employee can find value while exploring the

---

Exhibit 33.1. List of Materials to Send to an Employee Before the First Day

---

❑ Maps
❑ Parking areas, sticker or pass
❑ Where and when to report
❑ Supervisor's name and location
❑ To whom to report the first day
❑ Employee handbook
❑ Benefit plan information
❑ Company newsletter
❑ Annual report
❑ Uniform ordering information
❑ Dress code information
❑ Relocation kit
❑ Confirm position, title, and salary
❑ Copy of job description
❑ Length of probationary period
❑ Organization chart for employee's area
❑ Information about collective bargaining organization that may represent the employee

---

Exhibit 33.2. Checklist of Activities to Be Completed Before the First Day

- ❑ Welcome letter sent confirming reporting time, date, and place
- ❑ Internal memo to co-workers announcing new employee's arrival date and duties
- ❑ Prepare work area/desk; remove signs of previous employee
- ❑ Paint office or clean carpet if needed
- ❑ Order supplies
- ❑ Assemble materials (see Exhibits 33.3 and 33.4)
- ❑ Order name plate
- ❑ Order business cards
- ❑ If moving, send relocation kit
- ❑ Order telephone cards and other credit cards
- ❑ Install telephone (or complete change order)
- ❑ Select a buddy
- ❑ Plan a meaningful first work assignment
- ❑ Prepare job standards
- ❑ Arrange for lunch with appropriate person on first day
- ❑ Schedule training
- ❑ Review other checklists

resources that are provided. For example, when sending the employee handbook, prepare a list of questions about work practices and rules that can be looked up and answered in various parts of the handbook. When sending benefits information, provide a list of decisions to be made and the due date to file appropriate forms to announce the employee's choices for benefits. (See Exhibit 33.3 for a suggested list of written materials.)

6. *Identify and list resource people and how to reach them.* Tell how to reach the appropriate people by telephone and e-mail so that these people can answer questions not answered by resource materials. Also identify the type of information each resource person can provide.

7. *Identify resource people with whom the new employee will interact as a regular part of the job.* Instruct the new employee to introduce himself or herself to these employees, set an appointment for an interview, and then interview them. The purpose of the interview is to get off to a good start with co-workers, to clarify expectations, and to set an appropriate tone for future situations when the two will be working together. (See Exhibit 33.4 for a sample list of questions.)

8. *Have a method to account for the new employee's progress.* For example, the new employee could periodically complete a checklist and

Exhibit 33.3. Written Materials to Give to a New Employee

- ❑ Annual report
- ❑ Benefits information
- ❑ Company history
- ❑ Car pool information
- ❑ Credit union information
- ❑ Employee assistance program
- ❑ Employee handbook
- ❑ Facility maps
- ❑ Job description
- ❑ List of key people
- ❑ Newsletter
- ❑ Operations manual
- ❑ Organization charts
- ❑ Pay schedule
- ❑ Retirement plan
- ❑ Safety and emergency procedures
- ❑ Sample forms (expense account, accident reporting, performance appraisal)
- ❑ Social clubs
- ❑ Telephone directory; telephone equipment operation manual
- ❑ Training program schedule
- ❑ Tuition reimbursement plan
- ❑ Union contract
- ❑ Vacation and holiday policy

Exhibit 33.4. Sample Interview Questions for Self-Directed Orientation

The following are typical questions asked in an interview by a new employee of a co-worker, an "internal customer," or a supervisor. This format has been most successful in orienting a staff or professional person who will have many contacts throughout the organization.

1. What is the main purpose of your job?

2. Describe the occasions when we might be working together.

3. When we work together, what will you expect from me?

4. When we work together, what can I expect from you?

5. What past problems have occurred when you have worked with someone from my department, and how can similar problems be avoided in the future?

discuss progress with a buddy, supervisor, manager, or human resources representative. Provide a series of milestone events to be reached with a due date for each activity or assignment.

Finally, be sure to customize these ideas and suggestions to make NEO more self-directed. You only have one opportunity to make a good first impression.

Recommended Reading

Barbazette, J. (1993). Make new employee orientation a success. In *The 1993 annual: Developing human resources.* San Francisco: Jossey-Bass/Pfeiffer.

Barbazette, J. (1999). *Employee orientation.* In D.G. Langdon, K.S. Whiteside, & M.M. McKenna (Eds.), *Intervention resource guide: 50 performance improvement tools* (pp. 149–157). San Francisco: Jossey-Bass/Pfeiffer.

Barbazette, J. (2001). *Successful new employee orientation* (2nd ed.). San Francisco: Jossey-Bass/Pfeiffer.

Barbazette, J., & Barbazette, R. (1990). *New employee orientation slide series and organizer.* Seal Beach, CA: The Training Clinic.

Barksdale, K., & Rutter, M. (1999). *Corporate view: Orientation.* Cincinnati, OH: SouthWestern.

France, D.R., & Jarvis, R.L. (1996, October). Quick starts for new employees. *Training & Development,* 47–50.

George, M., & Miller, K. (1995, July). Assimilating new employees. *Training & Development,* 49–50.

Holton, E. (1998). *The ultimate new employee survival guide.* Lawrenceville, NJ: Peterson's.

Jenking, J. (1990, February). Self-directed workforce promotes safety. *Human Resources,* 54–56.

Klein, C.S., & Taylor, J. (1994, May). Employee orientation is an ongoing process at the DuPont Merck Pharmaceutical Co. *Personnel Journal,* 67.

Rossett, A., & Brechlin, J. (1991, April). Orienting new employees. *Training,* 45–50.

About the Author

Jean Barbazette is president of The Training Clinic, Seal Beach, California, a training consulting firm she founded in 1977. Her company conducts needs assessments, designs training programs, and specializes in new employee orientation, train-the-trainer, and enhancing the quality of training and instruction for major national and international clients.

Her best-selling book, Successful New Employee Orientation, *was nominated by* Human Resource Executive Magazine *as the product/book of the year for 1994.*

The Society for Human Resource Management (SHRM) gave the book an "honorable mention" in its 1994 competition for book of the year. Barbazette was cited as an authority on orientation on the front page of the Wall Street Journal *on October 13, 1998. This article was later reprinted in the San Francisco* Chronicle. *The Training Clinic has trained over 130,000 trainers since its first public workshop in 1983.*

CHAPTER THIRTY-FOUR

Mentoring to a "T"

Beverly Kaye, Ph.D.
President, Career Systems International, Inc.

Marilyn Greist
Senior Associate/Director of Client Services,
Career Systems International, Inc.

Training, timing, talking, testing, truth-telling, tending, tinkering—all words that begin with "T" and all words that underlie successful mentoring processes. In the best of all worlds, mentors and protégés find one another. Trying to duplicate a process that happens naturally is very difficult. When left to their own devices, people form relationships that work. When we practitioners intervene, we need to be aware that the process will, in fact, work differently! This chapter covers all of the principles of mentoring. It was written to help trainers who have the task of designing mentoring programs on their plates!

MENTORING—TO A "T"

Whether a mentoring process is assigned, or involves self-selected pairs, or happens within a group setting, there are some basic principles that will help to improve its effectiveness, including training, timing, talking, testing, truth-telling, tending, and tinkering.

Training

It is particularly important that mentors and mentees understand their roles and responsibilities, that they understand what success will look like and how they both will be held accountable for results. So the very first step for the practitioner (and the first T) is *training.*

A mentor's role is to promote intentional learning. That includes developing people's capabilities through instructing, coaching, modeling, and advising, as well as by providing stretching experiences.

There are several common myths about mentor programs:

- All mentors are good communicators;
- Mentors control the next career stop;
- Mentors have the latest scoop on what's happening in the organization;
- The mentor's role is to keep the protégé's manager up-to-date on the relationship; and
- A mentor is a mentor for life.

Conversely:

- All protégés are high potential and know it;
- All mentees are good learners;
- All mentees have career development plans that are well-thought-out and realistic;
- All mentees want to advance in the organization as quickly as possible; and
- The mentee's role is to sit at the feet of the mentor, catching pearls of wisdom dropped by the master and evolving into a clone.

The roles a mentor might play during the relationship will, at various times, include being a storyteller, teacher, guide, advisor, friend, counselor, challenger, coach, catalyst, consultant, role model, and advocate. A mentor's role is to promote intentional and deliberate learning, and the practitioner needs to ensure that this happens.

Initial training should include assessment of the mentor's ability to assume the above roles. For some, it will come naturally. For others, remedial coaching will be in order.

For all their obvious advantages, formal and successful mentoring programs are not easy to establish. Here are actual questions often asked by mentees:

- Will I feel comfortable?
- Who starts these meetings?
- Does my mentor really want to mentor me?
- Do I initiate contact or does the mentor?
- When we get together, what do we talk about?
- Will he or she think I'm prying?

- Am I being too personal if I ask questions about his or her career?
- Will I be too much of a burden if I call her or him frequently, and just how frequently is "frequently"?
- How much does my mentor really know?
- What if we don't really "click"?

Mentors, of course, have their own set of questions:

- Who am I to give this person advice?
- What should I be telling him or her about this organization?
- Am I saying too much or too little?
- What do I get out of this?
- How much time will it really take?
- What if we don't really "click"?

It is essential that the practitioner see to it that both "partners" in the mentoring relationship have the chance to think about their expectations. This enables them to begin testing how realistic those expectations are in light of the developing relationships.

Timing—There Isn't Any

"I have no time for mentoring" is a common response from senior managers when approached to participate in a mentoring process. One reason for their reluctance is the old paradigm of mentoring and how they view the process. It used to be that mentors were paired with protégés who stuck close, followed their mentor around with a bucket to catch their pearls of wisdom, sat at their feet during meetings and watched, listened, and acted like a sponge. There was a very real hierarchy and paternalism to the process, and the mentor felt responsible to the protégé for moving his or her career forward—for years to come.

But mentoring has many faces, and it doesn't require a major time commitment. When designing a mentoring process for your organization, you can decide how large or small the commitment should be. With a group mentoring process (one-on-group instead of one-on-one), a mentor may meet with the group once a month for a few hours or less.

In reciprocal mentoring the onus is on the individual to drive the mentoring process upward, downward, and across hierarchies. Some of these mentoring relationships may last a week, some months, and some years. But despite the process selected, the design and architecture of the mentoring approach should not be burdensome to either the protégé or the mentor in regard to their time commitments.

Talking About What? Specifically?

There is no substitute for personal advice, assistance, and support from someone who knows the ropes and is in a position to help others move across the organization. One of the keys to crafting successful mentoring processes is to suggest that individuals always approach others with a clear idea of what they hope to get from them. This can include information, support, more visibility, feedback, or connections. Without a clear sense of purpose, you will find that mentees often make mistakes like these:

- *Asking for too much:* "Can you tell me all about the field of. . . ?" This is an overwhelming question and can alienate the recipient, requiring too much time to answer. Because this request is so vague, the mentor has no clear reference point from which to start.
- *Missing opportunities.* If you are not specific, you might not recognize a connection if you fall over it.
- *Wasting everybody's time.* Without a specific agenda and desired outcome, conversations may miss the mark, go on forever, and leave both parties frustrated and reluctant to repeat the connection.

So get them to talk, but ask them to talk to their mentors with a goal in mind, such as

- "I want help with gaining more visibility and exposure in my company."
- "I want help to do my current job better, faster, or more efficiently."
- "I want help with building skills and competencies for the future."
- "I want to have someone in my corner who will support me emotionally by listening to my frustrations, fears, successes, and so on."

In other words, mentees must know what they want and be able to articulate it before entering into a mentoring relationship, regardless of the nature of the process.

In order to help them answer the "What do I want" question, it may be necessary to introduce a career development process that contains specific assessments for the end user so they can find answers for themselves. Then they can be more specific.

Testing

Practitioners might advise that individuals look for mentors who have successfully performed substantial overt career planning of their own, have experienced overcoming obstacles, and have had acknowledged successes in moving toward career goals. Such an individual can help test the validity of the developmental action plan designed by a mentee. The mentor may suggest alternative actions and present ideas for working around obstacles. In addition, mentors can teach the inner workings of the informal system, share information generated from the informal system, and advise on ways to best use that system.

Also, warn mentees to test the waters. When seeking mentorship, it's important to test the odds of clicking with a mentor. Mentees should ask themselves whether they will have enough in common and whether the mentor is in an area of the company they'd love to learn about. Also, it is vital for mentees to consider what they might give back to their mentors. If employees seek their own mentors, ask them their motives for seeking out specific individuals. Even in processes that are self-managed, some testing is needed to keep the learning goals of the process pure.

Truth-Telling

There is no substitute for the truth when delivering feedback. Leaders who are mentors often require some training in this area. Feedback is not synonymous with criticism. It is a powerful talent-building tool. Instead of just pointing out weaknesses and mistakes, a good mentor shows protégés how they can do it better. Telling one's own stories is key. Mentors should share more than just how to do things the right way. Their failures or how they did it wrong can create a forum for discussing and analyzing the realities of the organization.

Mentors should tell their real-life stories. Personal scenarios, anecdotes, and case histories can offer valuable, often unforgettable insights. Mentors who share their experiences can establish great rapport with protégés. The more the practitioner can help them do this, the better!

Tending

One of the chief reasons that formal, structured, one-to-one, "matched-pair" mentoring programs fail is that meetings between mentor and mentee just don't happen often enough. The commitment to a certain number of in-person meetings may sound like a good idea at first, but with the extreme mobility of today's workforce and the multi-national nature of leadership responsibilities, practitioners may want to suggest a more flexible approach.

The measure of success at the end of the mentoring process is whether the protégé has grown, tackled something new, or is able to achieve a stated goal. The road taken by each mentoring pair may be different and involve in-person meetings, phone calls, e-mail, voice mail, and any other kind of contact you can design. If a mentor puts too much emphasis on *quantity* of contacts, the burden will feel greater and will shift from "How well am I doing?" to "How often am I mentoring this person?"

But there are times during the life of the relationship when one must take the temperature of its effectiveness. Like any growth, this process requires tending. If mentor and mentee are not meeting, you must find out why. Is it time, distance, personality clashes, lack of understanding of roles, or what?

So we recommend that you build a "customer service satisfaction survey" into your process at strategic points in order to catch problems early on. You will have to develop solutions as an ongoing function of guiding the program.

Tinkering

Fine-tuning will go on forever. And the key to getting it right—eventually—is to be open to new ways of looking at learning relationships. Tinker with the process. Try something new for an intact work team or cohort group. It has been said that the definition of insanity is doing the same thing in the same way over and over and over again . . . yet expecting a different result!

Here are three different ways to view mentoring. Each works in a different way. None is exclusive of the other, and all three may co-exist within the organization at the same time. One size does not fit all.

Matching Mentor/Mentee Pairs. Typically the mentor/protégé relationship is an informal one, adopted by two individuals who are simply drawn to one another. However, many organizations have formalized the system, generally by asking for volunteers to form a pool of mentors and matching them with individuals who are either new to the organization or who have been identified as high potential/high performers whom the organization wants to groom for leadership. In this case, it is generally the mentor's responsibility to provide information and make suggestions to his or her protégé concerning the skills, knowledge, experience, training, and other developmental requirements an individual would need in order to qualify for the senior management level. Matched pairs are often quite successful. Sometimes, however, the chemistry is not there and just never materializes. So keep an eye on your pairings.

Mentoring in Groups. Groups have become popular because many formal one-on-one mentoring programs have trouble tapping into the subtle, but essential, personal chemistry found in successful informal mentor relationships. And few organizational reward systems support the one-on-one process. Also, one-on-one relationships sometimes narrow the opportunities for employees whose development requires diverse networks—including peer support. Groups are especially helpful when mentor talent is tight!

This approach expands the idea of mentor/mentee development to groups of employees led by organizational veterans who are networked together so that nontraditional learning occurs. Mentee groups meet with their mentor once a month for several hours. The agenda is set by the group, and the mentees' managers are included in the learning process at the very beginning as additional support for the mentees. Much of what takes place in these groups will evolve naturally from the group and the members' particular needs.

Reciprocal Mentoring. A third model (and perhaps a new model for practitioners to consider) suggests that every individual in an organization be taught how to find mentors for himself or herself and, in return, how to mentor others. This model suggests that varied relationships are required to give individuals all the information and support required for success. It also suggests that a reciprocal learning network will boost individual capability and organizational capacity. Here, the relationship is nonhierarchical (anyone can learn from anyone else) and fluid (mentoring can occur in sound bites!).

One value of this model for learners is in the great variety of individuals from whom to learn. With exposure to different styles (in an intentional way) employees can choose what best fits their needs. Practitioners should encourage the idea of reciprocity by structuring forums and events where all employees can offer up their (mentoring) wisdom and simultaneously apprentice with those from whom they need to learn.

SUMMARY

Mentoring programs can be the strongest career development and retention programs your company has to offer its people. Planning and careful attention to individual needs are essential. Learning that mentoring has more than one face is critical to building programs that work in your own organizational culture. Remember the Ts: training, timing, talking, testing, truth-telling, tending, and tinkering. You'll have mentoring down to a "T."

Recommended Reading

Bell, C.R. (1996). *Managers as mentors.* San Francisco: Berrett-Koehler.

Caruso, R.E. (1992). *Mentoring and the business environment.* Brookfield, VT: Dartmouth Publishing.

Coley, D.B. (1996, July). Mentoring two by two. *Training & Development, 7,* 46–48.

Fritts, P.J. (1998). *The new managerial mentor: Becoming a leader to build communities of purpose.* Palo Alto, CA: Davies-Black.

Gunn, E. (1995, August). Mentoring: The democratic version. *Training,* 64–67.

Huang, C.A., & Lynch, J. (1995). *Mentoring: The Tao of giving and receiving wisdom.* New York: Harper.

Jeruchim, J., & Shapiro, P. (1992). *Women, mentors and success.* New York: Fawcett Columbine.

Jossi, F. (1997, August). Mentoring in changing times. *Training,* 50–54.

Kaye, B. (1997). *Up is not the only way.* Palo Alto, CA: Davies-Black.

Kaye, B., & Bernstein, B. (1986, November). Teacher, tutor, colleague, coach. *Personnel Journal.*

Kaye, B., & Bernstein, B. (1998). *MentWorking™—Building relationships for the 21st century.* Scranton, PA: Career Systems International.

Kaye, B., & Jacobson, B. (1995, April). Mentoring: A group guide. *Training & Development, 4,* 22–27.

Kaye, B., & Jacobson, B. (1996a, August). Mentoring: A new model for building learning organizations. *OD Practitioner,* 35–44.

Kaye, B., & Jacobson, B. (1996b, August). Reframing mentoring. *Training & Development, 8,* 44–47.

Kaye, B., & Jacobson, B. (1998). *Learning group guide: A collaborative development process.* Scranton, PA: Career Systems International.

Kaye, B., & Scheef, D. (1997, November 23–29). Shared brain power. *National Business Employment Weekly,* 11–12.

Kram, K.E. (1988). *Mentoring relationships at work.* Lanham, MD: University Press of America.

Kram, K.E. (1985). *Mentoring at work: Developmental relationships in organizational life.* Glenview, IL: Scott, Foresman.

Murray, M., & Owen, M. (1991). *Beyond the myths and magic of mentoring.* San Francisco: Jossey-Bass.

Peddy, S. (1998). *The art of mentoring: Lead, follow and get out of the way.* Houston, TX: Bullion Books.

Robinson, S. (1990, May). Mentoring has merit in formal and informal formats. *Training Directors' Forum Newsletter,* 6.

Scandura, T. (1992). Mentorship and career mobility: An empirical investigation. *Journal of Organizational Behavior, 13,* 169–174.

Wickman, F., & Sjodin, T. (1996). *Mentoring: A success guide for mentors and protégés.* New York: McGraw-Hill.

Zeldin, M., & Lee, S. (Eds.). (1995). *Touching the future.* Los Angeles: Rhea Hirsch School of Education, Hebrew Union College.

Zey, M.G. (1984). *The mentor connection.* Homewood, IL: Dow Jones-Irwin.

About the Authors

Dr. Beverly Kaye is president of Career Systems International and Beverly Kaye & Associates, Inc. Her cutting-edge management and career development programs are used by leading Fortune 500 corporations. Kaye is the author of Up Is Not the

Only Way *(Davies–Black, 1997) and co-author of* Love 'Em or Lose 'Em: Getting Good People to Stay *(Berrett-Koehler, 1999). Kaye has received many honors and awards, including the National Career Development Award of the American Society for Training and Development (ASTD). Most recently she received the Best Practice Award from ASTD for her work with a global client, Dow Corning.*

Marilyn Greist *is a senior associate/director of client services for Career Systems International, Inc., A Beverly Kaye & Associates company, and is devoted to improving the quality of individual work lives through training in career self-reliance, managing for development, and talent management. She has co-authored articles on mentoring and career development. Greist has been a keynote speaker for many professional conferences and a guest lecturer at the University of New Haven. She has delivered keynote addresses in the areas of career development and talent retention to management and leadership audiences of Fortune 500 companies.*

CHAPTER THIRTY-FIVE

The Critical Importance of Rewards and Recognition in the 21st Century

Barbara A. Glanz, CSP
President, Barbara Glanz Communications, Inc.

inally, managers are beginning to recognize the critical importance of rewards and recognition in such vital areas as employee retention, productivity, and morale. In the past decade, so much time has been spent on systems and processes that many organizations have forgotten or simply given lip service to their most important asset—their people. With the extremely tight job market today, finding and keeping good people is perhaps management's most important task. Study after study has confirmed that, more than money, employees cite intangible or "soft" aspects of corporate culture as having the strongest influence on their commitment. Rewards—more formal, often annual, costly kinds of positive reinforcement—have been the mainstay and, in some cases, the token concession from management. However, in the new workplace, frequent, creative, personal, and informal recognition will make the critical difference between employee commitment and abdication.

INTRODUCTION

In the changing environment of the 21st Century, one of the most important tasks of management is to hire, motivate, and retain good employees. In the past, workers expected to stay at one job for long periods of time, so loyalty was often a matter of habit. Today, according to a study by Walker Information and the Hudson Institute (Walker Information, 1999), only three in ten employees feel an obligation to stay with their current employer. Thus, in an extremely tight job market, motivating and retaining good employees has become critical to an organization's success.

THE RESEARCH

Research has shown again and again that money is not the highest motivator, yet management continues to grasp onto this solution because of its simplicity and impersonal nature: "All we have to do to keep good employees is to offer them more money and benefits. Certainly, we don't have to spend time getting to know them. Just raise their pay regularly, pat them on the head now and then, and give out a plaque and a parking space to the employee of the year, and they'll be happy!"

In the past, many organizations have used timeworn, boring, impersonal, and extremely exclusive formal rewards as tokens of appreciation. In the future, it will be essential to find ways to reward and recognize employees that are frequent, personal, creative, and fun. Certainly, some formal rewards (high cost) are important; however, it is the little, daily acts of appreciation that employees have been found to value most.

In 1946, 1988, and again in 1995, a study (Kovach, 1995) was done on what employees want from their jobs. Employees were asked to rank ten motivators from high to low, and then their supervisors and managers were asked to rank order what they *thought* their employees would say. Amazingly, the results were the same each year! Managers guessed that their employees would want (1) good wages, (2) job security, and (3) promotion and growth in the organization. The employees, on the other hand, ranked "interesting work," "full appreciation," and "a feeling of being in on things" as their top three motivators.

It is interesting how little managers really understand their employees' needs, as well as how little control they have over the top three things they thought their employees wanted. When you consider the top three employee motivators, however, it is amazing how simple they are, *and* they cost little or no money. Each of these employee motivators is based on a personal relationship with management.

As many as 25 percent of good employees who quit left due to lack of recognition, according to a survey of executives by Robert Half International, Inc. (Van Warner, 1994). How often do managers recognize outstanding performance with nonmonetary rewards? Never, say more than one-third of the workers surveyed in a 1995 study, People and Their Jobs: What's Real, What's Rhetoric? by

Kepner-Tregoe. Almost 20 percent of the managers agreed with this perception. Another 37 percent of both groups agreed that individuals receive recognition only once per year. Respondents included 611 managers and 905 workers.

In the study by Walker Information and the Hudson Institute (Walker Information, 1999), researchers found that, more than money, employees cite intangible or "soft" aspects of corporate culture as having a strong influence on their commitment. This, in turn, was shown to translate into a higher likelihood of positive work behaviors and performance. In fact, the second-ranked most important factor in their work life was "care and concern for employees." Interestingly, only four in ten of the employees surveyed believe that their organization shows genuine concern for its employees.

The Gallup Organization found that 69 percent of employees say nonmonetary forms of recognition provide the best motivation, according to their 1998 nationwide survey of U.S. workers (Jasniowski, 2000). The survey builds on an earlier Gallup study that confirmed that loyal, engaged employees tend to generate high-performance business outcomes as measured by sales, improved productivity, enhanced employee retention, and bottom-line profitability.

"Just as the accumulation of small improvements can make a dramatic, lasting change in the organization's products or services, the repeated, numerous small occasions of taking note of the contributions of individuals and teams can create a different company."

Patrick Townshend and Joan Gebhart
The Quality Process: Little Things Mean a Lot

DEFINITIONS

Generally, *rewards* are defined as those formal acts of appreciation that cost money. *Recognition,* on the other hand, can be defined as "treating someone as a worthwhile human being." Acts of recognition or appreciation are often spontaneous and have little or no cost. Unfortunately, many organizations spend a great deal of time and money on formal rewards that affirm only a few select people and neglect completely the more simple, day-to-day forms of recognition that employees crave.

Rather than differentiating between terms, the Tennant Company of Minneapolis, Minnesota, has outlined three dimensions of recognition, as shown in Exhibit 35.1.

Exhibit 35.1. Three Dimensions of Recognition

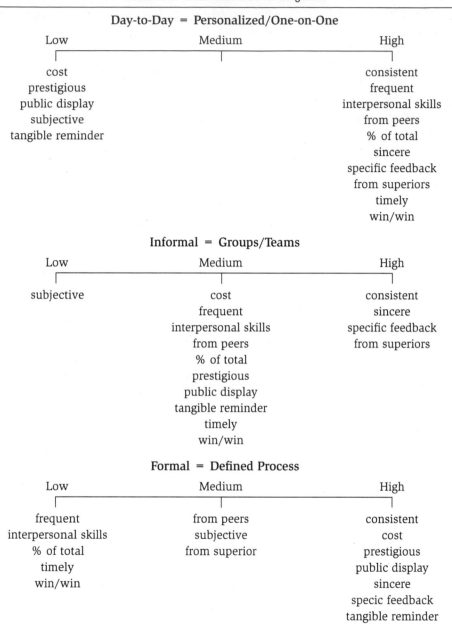

Day-to-Day = Personalized/One-on-One

Low	Medium	High
cost		consistent
prestigious		frequent
public display		interpersonal skills
subjective		from peers
tangible reminder		% of total
		sincere
		specific feedback
		from superiors
		timely
		win/win

Informal = Groups/Teams

Low	Medium	High
subjective	cost	consistent
	frequent	sincere
	interpersonal skills	specific feedback
	from peers	from superiors
	% of total	
	prestigious	
	public display	
	tangible reminder	
	timely	
	win/win	

Formal = Defined Process

Low	Medium	High
frequent	from peers	consistent
interpersonal skills	subjective	cost
% of total	from superior	prestigious
timely		public display
win/win		sincere
		specic feedback
		tangible reminder

1. From this model, which is the kind of recognition that best corresponds with your personal preference?
2. Which kind of recognition best corresonds with your organization's climate?

Day-to-Day = Personalized, One-on-One
Informal = Groups/Teams
Formal = Defined Process

These dimensions take into account the changing nature of today's workplace to a more team-oriented environment and also offer a clear way to achieve balance in the recognition process. In the past, organizations have focused almost exclusively on formal rewards and recognition, while today's employees are demanding much more informal, day-to-day appreciation based on a caring relationship with one's manager.

PRINCIPLES OF RECOGNITION
Frequent

Recognition in the 21st Century must be frequent in order to keep employees motivated. Ceremonies once a quarter or once a year are not enough. Too often we hear from employees, "When I do something wrong, it only takes minutes for me to be called on the carpet, but our awards ceremony only happens once a year." Every supervisor or manager should dedicate a portion of his or her day to recognizing employees who are doing a good job. Remember that one of the top three things employees want is full appreciation for the work they've done.

Keep a supply of praise notes, stickers, candy treats, and coupons in your office and do something to appreciate one of your employees *every day*. It is important to be sincere and specific in your affirmation (not randomly walking around saying, "You're doing a great job"). However, as Ken Blanchard (Blanchard & Johnson, 1981) has said, you can always catch someone doing something right if you are looking for it.

Creative, Caring, and Fun

No matter how serious our work, our workplaces should be places of joy and caring. After all, we are spending most of our lives there, so we need to commit to making the atmosphere as fulfilling and meaningful as possible. As managers begin to recognize and appreciate employees on a day-to-day basis, this spirit will become a part of the culture and meaningful relationships of respect will develop. Employees will feel much more committed to an organization and co-workers who care for them.

One of the delightful aspects of day-to-day and informal appreciation is the creativity and fun that can result. The Christian Management Association has adopted a process that they call "Hoopla!" to demonstrate to employees how highly they are valued. They say, "The time and resources you spend on 'Hoopla!' are directly proportional to the morale and spirit of your staff." Take the Hoopla! Rating Test in Exhibit 35.2 to see how your organization is doing.

Exhibit 35.2. Hoopla! Rating Test

Here's a test. Answer "yes" or "no" to each statement below regarding your organization's "Hoopla" culture. (If you're in a larger organization, you may prefer to rate your department.) Check "Y" for Yes or "N" for No for each question.

Y   N

❏   ❏   1. In the last thirty days, our team has celebrated the achievement of a key goal or target with a fun or humorous ceremony, coffee break, or event.

❏   ❏   2. Supervisors are encouraged to honor team members on their individual employment anniversary dates.

❏   ❏   3. In the last ninety days, we have had a spontaneous party, food break, or brief "stress reliever" event that was not on the staff calendar.

❏   ❏   4. In the last twelve months, our team has enjoyed an off-site event (such as a picnic, day at the ballpark, etc.) during office hours.

❏   ❏   5. Our dress code includes year-round "business casual" clothes at least one day a week.

❏   ❏   6. We have a specific budget for staff fun, events, parties, etc.

❏   ❏   7. Planning fun events for the staff (formal and informal, scheduled and spontaneous) is on someone's job description—and this person knows it!

❏   ❏   8. We have a written statement of core values that includes our beliefs on the importance of celebrations, valuing people and their accomplishments, and just plain enjoying work and life!

❏   ❏   9. In the last twelve months, we have invested at least $100 per team member on fun.

❏   ❏   10. When interviewing prospective team members, it's not uncommon to hear, "Your staff tells me it's fun to work at your organization."

Rate your organization by the number of "yes" responses:

8 to 10   Congratulations! Team members are highly valued!
6 to 7   Sounds fun. Moving in the right direction.
4 to 5   Better do a Hoopla audit before it's too late.
1 to 3   It may be too late, but try a "Snack Alert" at 3 p.m. today and empower a Hoopla Team immediately.

If you need starters, here are just a few:

• Do breakfast followed by a bucket of golf balls at a driving range;

- Schedule a staff meeting and when everyone's assembled, go out for ice cream cones;
- Give team members $5 each to buy a "stress reliever" toy for their desks or cubicles;
- Provide free soft drinks and pretzels every Friday afternoon;
- Hold an Academy Awards ceremony for the best staff team "home video" on "How We Deal with Stress."
- Install a putting green in the conference room and hold daily "best out of ten balls" tournaments.

You get the idea.
Have fun!

Source: Pearson, 1999. Used with permission.

It is also important to be creative in the ways you recognize employees, because doing the same things over and over becomes meaningless after a time. Certainly each organization should have highly prized formal awards that become a part of the company tradition. However, in the day-to-day and informal dimensions of recognition, it becomes important to try new things and surprise employees. At least once a quarter, a supervisor or manager should try something new and different. This will delight employees and keep the workplace fresh and innovative.

After I had spoken to a large manufacturing company, one of the managers approached me and said, "Barbara, I have the lowest performing team in the whole company. Never once have they met their goals. But you've got me thinking." Nine months later he called me, his voice bursting with pride and enthusiasm. He said, "Barbara, I must tell you what I did. After you were here, I thought and thought and finally called my team together. I said to them, 'Any of you who meet your goals this quarter, I'm going to call your mothers.'" He continued, "It was unbelievable. Every single one of them met his or her goals for the first time ever!" And he went on to share that it was one of the nicest things he had ever done. He told me that some of the mothers even cried when he called! Think about the creativity of this idea. I don't care how old we are, it would feel wonderful to have someone call our mother, spouse, or significant other to tell him or her what a great job we are doing.

The final section of this chapter includes many other easily implemented, creative ideas for employee recognition.

Personal

For recognition to have real meaning, it must be personal. Ask your employees what they would like. Each of us appreciates praise in a different way. Make it your job to find out the passion of each of your employees and then keep a file noting this information. What is it that they love? What excites them? What are their hobbies/collections/talents? Do your homework. Information can be gathered from the employees themselves, from family, and from former managers regarding their likes, dislikes, hobbies, and personal interests for extra clues as to how to appreciate them in tangible, meaningful, personal ways. Then use your own creativity to make the recognition special.

When I was working with a large state government several years ago, one of their major concerns was how to reward their employees and still stay within financial limitations. The management assumption was that the state workers would only feel rewarded with things that cost money. I asked them whether they would be willing to poll the workers to determine what they would like as rewards and recognition. The managers agreed, and when the results came in two requests had overwhelmingly occurred:

1. That they could spend one hour in their commissioner's office, just watching what he or she did—a feeling of "being in on things."
2. To change jobs with someone in the state for half a day.

The amazing thing was that neither of these requests cost any out-of-pocket money, and they were relatively easy to implement. In fact, within two weeks, various departments of the state government had begun to implement them as rewards for extraordinary service to citizens.

SELECTING APPROPRIATE REWARDS AND RECOGNITION

Let your creative juices flow and get out of your mental locks as you begin to think in a different way about personalizing rewards and recognition. Unfortunately, most formal reward programs provide awards that employees do not want or value. The Employee Needs and Wants Recognition Index (ENRI) is a tool that Ford uses to rank rewards. As reported in BI Performance Services' *Spotlight on Performance* newsletter, which used the index to review more than four thousand different items selected for service recognition awards, 70 percent or more of employees do not want any of the selections that they're offered! This points to the startling conclusion that, because the importance of daily and informal recognition lies in honoring the individual employee, it is *critical* that managers and supervisors find ways to personalize their appreciation so that the employee will feel cared for and valued.

The Tennant Company has devised a checklist to determine both personal perceptions of recognition and perceptions of the organizational recognition climate (see Exhibit 35.3). Employees can begin by looking at their personal preferences about recognition and then look at their perceptions of the organizational recognition climate (shown in Exhibit 35.4).

Use these surveys and, after respondents have finished, have them go back to Exhibit 35.1 and determine the kind of recognition that best corresponds with their personal preference continuum. Next, have them look at what kind of recognition best corresponds with the organization's climate. What Tennant found was that they were out of alignment. The employees wanted much more day-to-day and informal feedback, while the organization was focused on formal recognition or rewards. Currently, they are working on finding a better balance between the different levels of recognition, based on employees' personal preferences.

Another powerful exercise is to have employees in work groups brainstorm specific things they would like in each of the three areas of recognition. This exercise helps managers and supervisors better know what their workers value and what, in turn, will impact morale, retention, and productivity. Volunteers from different areas of the company may be selected to form a recognition team to help carry out the informal and formal suggestions. However, the real key in today's workplace, according to the research, is the behavior of each individual manager and supervisor in giving continuous, day-to-day feedback. Let's look at some creative ideas in this category.

"Simple observation suggests that most of us are trinket freaks if they represent a genuine thanks for a genuine assist."

Tom Peters
Thriving on Chaos

Day-to-Day and Informal Recognition Ideas

Here are some ideas for managers to try:

- Give the employees personal, tangible reminders of your appreciation, such as stress toys, silly mugs ("We can't spell success without U"), hats (a crown for being the king/queen of positive affirmation), quotation plaques ("The difference between ordinary and extraordinary is that little EXTRA!").

Exhibit 35.3. Personal Perceptions on Recognition

1. For each sentence, place a check mark in the column that best represents its importance to you.

Personally, I feel recognition should:	Low	Medium	High
1. Be *consistent*	____	____	____
2. Be high *cost*	____	____	____
3. Be *frequent*	____	____	____
4. Require a high level of *interpersonal skills*	____	____	____
5. Come from *peers*	____	____	____
6. Recognize a large *percentage*	____	____	____
7. Be *prestigious*	____	____	____
8. Have a *public display*	____	____	____
9. Be *sincere*	____	____	____
10. Be given with *specific feedback*	____	____	____
11. Be *subjective*	____	____	____
12. Come from *superiors*	____	____	____
13. Include a *tangible reminder*	____	____	____
14. Occur in a *timely* way	____	____	____
15. Foster a *win/win* atmosphere	____	____	____

2. Based on your above preferences, write the attribute item under the appropriate heading below. (List the attributes you checked as low under the *low* heading, as well as the medium under the *medium* heading, and so forth for the high.)

Low	Medium	High

Exhibit 35.4. Organizational Recognition Climate

1. For each sentence, place a check mark in the column that best represents the climate within your organization.

In my organization, recognition generally:	Low	Medium	High
1. Is *consistent*	___	___	___
2. Is high *cost*	___	___	___
3. Is *frequent*	___	___	___
4. Requires a high level of *interpersonal skills*	___	___	___
5. Comes from *peers*	___	___	___
6. Recognizes a large *percentage*	___	___	___
7. Is *prestigious*	___	___	___
8. Has a *public display*	___	___	___
9. Is *sincere*	___	___	___
10. Is given with *specific feedback*	___	___	___
11. Is *subjective*	___	___	___
12. Comes from *superiors*	___	___	___
13. Includes a *tangible reminder*	___	___	___
14. Occurs in a *timely* way	___	___	___
15. Fosters a *win/win* atmosphere	___	___	___

2. Based on your above preferences, write the attribute item under the appropriate heading below. (List the attributes you checked as low under the *low* heading, as well as the medium under the *medium* heading, and so forth for the high.)

Low   Medium   High

- Call the employee's mother, spouse, or significant others when he or she has done a great job.

- Use candy bars. One of my clients was going to be shorthanded the next day at work, so on the way to the office, she stopped and bought several boxes of Nestles' "Crunch" bars. When the other employees arrived, in each of their in-boxes was a candy bar with a note saying, "Thanks in advance for helping out in the 'CRUNCH'!" She says it was one of the best days they ever had. Go to the store and look at candy names: Payday, $100,000 Bar, Extra, Snickers, Zero, Lifesavers, Bar None, Skor, and so on. Then find ways to use them to recognize individual or group effort.

- Send a family book to the employee's home as a thank you to the family when he or she has been spending a lot of energy at work.

- Tennant has a "Positive Feedback Day" when employees are met at the door with giveaways. Another organization has the senior management team meet employees in the parking lot to shake their hands and thank them for being a part of the organization.

- Wash the car of an employee who has done an outstanding job that day.

- Invite an employee to lunch or breakfast and let him or her bring a spouse or significant other.

- Send flowers. One person I know sends himself flowers when he's done a great job and no one's noticed. That way, all day long, people come into his office and say, "Oh, how lucky you are! Who sent you those beautiful flowers?" He says he gets all the attention he needs to refill his emotional bank account!

- Give a subscription to a hobby magazine.

- Allow him or her to "shadow" someone else in the company for a half day.

- Allow flex time so the employee can participate in outside professional or personal activities.

- Write short notes of praise that can be posted on a small bulletin board.

- Give a coupon for an extra thirty minutes for lunch on the day of his or her choice.

- Send a T-shirt or something with a company logo to the employee's family.

- Choose a company executive to give a one-hour speech to the organization of the employee's choice.

- Name a place in the building after the person. Hallways can be marked by road signs with employees' names.
- Make a donation to a favorite charity in the person's name.
- Take out an advertisement in the local paper and include his or her picture and name.
- Give the person coupons for an hour of your time doing anything he or she chooses.
- Name an item in the company cafeteria after the person.
- Serve him or her coffee each morning for a week.
- Keep a "prize box" of fun items, perhaps from the dollar store. When employees have done something special, let them choose something from the box.
- Have "recess" for thirty minutes at least once a week.
- Give someone an opportunity to choose a class or training session on any topic.
- Send a bunch of balloons.
- Present a coupon for a family dinner out.
- Walk to the employee's desk and say "Thank you" in person.
- Invite employees and their families to your home.

FINAL GUIDELINES

As you re-examine your own behavior in giving recognition in the 21st Century, consider the following guidelines:

1. Does it fit with the values of the organization? Are you recognizing and rewarding those behaviors that exemplify the beliefs and values to which your organization is committed?

2. Are there opportunities for *everyone* in the organization to be recognized, not just the stars?

3. Is it ongoing and continually changing?

4. Are people enjoying the kinds of recognition you are using?

5. Is it personal, sincere, and caring—focused on showing the individual how much you value him or her?

6. Is there a built-in accountability check for each supervisor and manager in the organization?

References

BI Performance Services. (n.d.). *Spotlight on performance, 11*(5).

Blanchard, K., & Johnson, S. (1981). *The one minute manager.* New York: Berkley Books.

Jasniowski, R. (2000). Bring out the best in people and keep them! *Innovative Leader, 9*(2), 9.

Kovach, K.A. (1995). Employee motivation: Addressing a crucial factor in your organization's performance. *Employment Relations Today, 22*(2).

Pearson, J. (1999, November/December). Hoopla. *Christian Management Report.*

Tennant Company. (1989). Tennant Company recognition workshop, Minneapolis, MN.

Van Warner, R. (1994, September 26). A little praise goes a long way in keeping employees on the job. *Nation's Restaurant News, 19.*

Walker Information. (1999). 1999 n*ational employee relationships report benchmark.* Indianapolis, IN: Author.

Recommended Reading

Canfield, J., & Hansen, M. (1999). *A third helping of chicken soup for the soul.* Deerfield Beach, FL: Health Communications, Inc.

Conari Press. (Eds.). (1992). *Random acts of kindness.* Berkeley, CA: Author.

Garfield, C. (1992). *Second to none: How our smartest companies put people first.* Burr Ridge, IL: Irwin Professional.

Glanz, B.A. (1993). *The creative communicator—399 tools to communicate commitment without boring people to death!* New York: McGraw-Hill.

Goodman, J. (1995). *Laffirmations—1001 ways to add humor to your life and work.* Deerfield Beach, FL: Health Communications, Inc.

Hyde, C.R. (1999). *Pay it forward.* New York: Simon & Schuster.

Kaye, B., & Jordan-Evans, S. (1999). *Love 'em or lose 'em: Getting good people to stay.* San Francisco: Berrett Koehler.

Lundin, S.C., Paul, H., & Christensen, J. (2000). *FISH! A remarkable way to boost morale and improve results.* New York: Hyperion.

Nelson, B. (1994). *1001 ways to reward employees.* New York: Workman.

Nelson, B. (1997). *1001 ways to energize employees.* New York: Workman.

About the Author

Barbara A. Glanz works with organizations that want to improve morale and with people who want to rediscover the joy in their work and in their lives. She is an internationally known author, speaker, and consultant with a master's degree in adult education who specializes in three areas: regenerating spirit in the workplace and in the home, building customer and employee loyalty, and creative communication. She is the author of CARE Packages for the Home—Dozens of Ways to Regenerate Spirit Where You Live, CARE Packages for the Workplace—Dozens of Little Things You Can Do to Regenerate Spirit at Work, The Creative Communicator—399 Ways to Make Your Business Communications Meaningful & Inspiring, *and* Building Customer Loyalty. *Glanz has spoken on four continents and in forty-seven states to associations, government agencies, and companies both large and small. She lives and breathes her personal motto, "Spreading Contagious Enthusiasm." Her website is* www.barbaraglanz.com.

CONTRIBUTORS

NICHOLAS A. ANDREADIS, M.D.
Counseling Psychology
CECP Department, Sangren Hall
Western Michigan University
1903 West Michigan Avenue
Kalamazoo, MI 49008–5201
   616–387–3504
   nicholas.andreadis@wmich.edu

JEAN BARBAZETTE
President
The Training Clinic
645 Seabreeze Drive
Seal Beach, CA 90740
   562–430–2484
   800–937–4698
   562–430–9603 (fax)
   jean@thetrainingclinic.com

ZANE L. BERGE, PH.D.
Director
Training Systems Graduate Programs
UMBC
1000 Hilltop Circle
Baltimore, MD 21250
   410–455–2306
   berge@umbc.edu

ROBERT O. BRINKERHOFF, PH.D.
Professor
Counseling Psychology
Western Michigan University
1903 West Michigan Avenue
Kalamazoo, MI 49008–5201
   616–387–3881
   robert.brinkerhoff@wmich.edu

MARY L. BROAD, ED.D.
Principal Consultant
Performance Excellence
3709 Williams Lane
Chevy Chase, MD 20815-4951
  301-657-8638
  marybroad@earthlink.net

JAY A. CONGER, PH.D.
Professor
London Business School
Bridge Hall 204
Center for Effective Organizations
University of Southern California
Los Angeles, CA 90089
  213-740-4318
  jconger@marshall.usc.edu

MAXINE ARNOLD DALTON, PH.D.
Director
Global Leadership
Center for Creative Leadership
POB 26300
Greensboro, NC 27438-6300
  336-286-4406
  daltonm@leaders.ccl.org

LARRY FROMAN, PH.D.
Director
Graduate Program in Human
Resource Development
Department of Psychology
Towson University
8000 York Road
Towson, MD 21252
  410-704-2678
  lfroman@towson.edu

BARBARA A. GLANZ, CSP
President
Barbara Glanz Communications, Inc.
4047 Howard Avenue
Western Springs, IL 60558
  708-246-8594
  708-246-5123 (fax)
  bglanz@barbaraglanz.com

MARILYN GREIST
Director of Client Services
Career Systems International
578 Cleveland Avenue
Bridgeport, CT 06604
  203-368-6096
  marilyn.greist@csibka.com

JUDITH A. HALE, PH.D.
Hale Associates
1202N 75th Street PMB 333
Downers Grove, IL 60516
  630-427-1304
  haleassocia@aol.com

ROBERT HARGROVE
Founder
Masterful Coaching, Inc.
1689 Beacon Street, Suite 1
Brookline, MA 02445
  617-739-3300
  robert.hargrove@rhargrove.com

BEVERLY KAYE, PH.D.
President
Career Systems International, Inc.
3545 Alana Drive
Sherman Oaks, CA 91403-4708
  818-995-6454
  beverly.kaye@csibka.com

DONALD L. KIRKPATRICK, PH.D.
Professor Emeritus
University of Wisconsin
1920 Hawthorne Drive
Elm Grove, WI 53122
   262-784-8348
   262-784-7994 (fax)

JAMES M. KOUZES
Chairman Emeritus
tompeters!company
1784 Patio Drive
San Jose, CA 95125-5550
   408-978-1809
   jim@kousesposner.com

KEVIN E. KRUSE
Principal
Kenexa, Inc.
87 Nelson Drive
Churchville, PA 18966
   215-354-9095
   kevin.kruse@kenexa.com

GARY P. LATHAM, PH.D.
Secretary of State Professor of
Organization Behavior
Joseph L. Rotman School of
Management
University of Toronto
105 St. George Street
Toronto, Ontario
Canada M5S 3E6
   416-978-4916
   latham@mgmt.utoronto.ca

KAREN LAWSON, ED.D.
President
Lawson Consulting Group
1365 Gwynedale Way
Lansdale, PA 19446-5366
   215-368-9465
   klawson@lawsoncg.com

SETH N. LEIBLER, ED.D.
President and CEO
The Center for Effective Performance
2300 Peachford Road, Suite 2000
Atlanta, GA 30338
   770-458-4080
   sleibler@cepworldwide.com

RICHARD LEPSINGER
Managing Vice President
Right Manus
100 Prospect Street, South Tower
Stamford, CT 06901
   203-316-9613
   rick.lepsinger@right.com

ANTOINETTE LUCIA
Managing Vice President
Right Manus
100 Prospect Street, South Tower
Stamford, CT 06901
   203-316-9612
   toni.lucia@right.com

DEBORAH L. MACKENZIE
Ph.D. Candidate
Joseph L. Rotman School
of Management
University of Toronto
105 St. George Street
Toronto, Ontario
Canada M5S 3E6
   416-978-7019
   mackenzie@rotman.utoronto.ca

MICHAEL J. MARQUARDT, PH.D.
President
Global Learning Associates
1688 Moorings Drive
Reston, VA 20190
   703-437-0260
   mjmq@aol.com

PATRICIA A. MCLAGAN
Principal
McLagan International, Inc.
3008 P Street NW
Washington, DC 20007
   202–944–3992
   patmclagan@cs.com

JULIE O'MARA
President
O'Mara and Associates
5979 Greenridge Road
Castro Valley, CA 94552
   510–582–7744
   510–582–4826 (fax)
   julie@omaraassoc.com

ANN W. PARKMAN
Executive Vice President
The Center for Effective Performance
2300 Peachford Road, Suite 2000
Atlanta, GA 30338
   770–458–4080
   aparkman@cepworldwide.com

JACK J. PHILLIPS, PH.D.
President
The Jack Phillips Center for
Research and Assessment
A FranklinCovey Company
12276 Old Highway 280
Chelsea, AL 35043
   205–678–9700
   roipro@wwisp.com

PATRICIA PULLIAM PHILLIPS
Chairman and CEO
The Chelsea Group
350 Crossbrook Drive
Chelsea, AL 35043
   thechelseagroup@aol.com

BOB PIKE, CSP, CPAE
Chairman and CEO
The Bob Pike Group
7620 West 78th Street
Minneapolis, MN 55439
   612–829–0260
   bpike@bobpikegroup.com

GEORGE M. PISKURICH
Principal
GMP Associates
102 Fenwood Court
Chapel Hill, NC 27516
   919–968–0878
   gmp1@compuserve.com

BARRY Z. POSNER
Dean and Professor of Leadership
Santa Clara University
Leavey School of Business
500 El Camino Real
Santa Clara, CA 95053–0410
   408–554–4634
   bposner@sco.edu

FRAN REES
Rees & Associates
4341 West Dublin Street
Chandler, AZ 85226
   602–961–9885
   480–961–9924 (fax)
   firees@uswest.net

DANA GAINES ROBINSON
President
Partners in Change, Inc.
2547 Washington Road #720
Pittsburgh, PA 15241–2557
   412–854–5750
   412–854–5801 (fax)
   drobinson@partners-in-change.
   com

JAMES C. ROBINSON
Chairman
Partners in Change, Inc.
2547 Washington Road #720
Pittsburgh, PA 15241–2557
    412–854–5750
    412–854–5801 (fax)
    jrobinson@partners-in-change.
    com

ALLISON ROSSETT, PH.D.
Professor
Educational Technology
San Diego State University
5500 Campanile Drive
San Diego, CA 92182
    619–594–6088
    619–594–6376 (fax)
    arossett@mail.sdsu.edu

WILLIAM J. ROTHWELL, PH.D.
Professor
Human Resource Development
The Pennsylvania State University
605C Keller Building
State College, PA 16802
    814–863–2581
    wjr9@psu.edu

EDGAR H. SCHEIN, PH.D.
Sloan Fellows Professor of Management Emeritus and Senior Lecturer
MIT Sloan School of Management
One Parkway Terrace
Cambridge, MA 02138
    617–497–7515
    scheine@mit.edu

MEL SILBERMAN, PH.D.
President
Active Training
26 Linden Lane
Princeton, NJ 08540–3828
    609–924–8157
    mel@activetraining.com

LINDA BYARS SWINDLING, ESQ.
The Peacemaker
2713 Scarborough Lane
Carrollton, TX 75006
    972–416–3652
    linda@lindaswindling.com

SIVASAILAN "THIAGI" THIAGARAJAN, PH.D.
President
Workshops by Thiagi, Inc.
4423 East Trailridge Road
Bloomington, IN 47408–9633
    812–332–1478
    thiagi@thiagi.com

CATHERINE TOBIAS
Lieutenant Commander
U.S. Coast Guard
4801 Fairmont Avenue, #406
Bethesda, MD 20814
    301-656-3348
    njseoul@email.com

LORRAINE L. UKENS
Principal
Team-ing With Success
4302 Starview Court
Glen Arm, MD 21057–9745
    410–592–6050
    410–592–8263 (fax)
    ukens@team-ing.com

KAREN VANKAMPEN
Director, Performance Consulting
The Center for Effective Performance
2300 Peachford Road, Suite 2000
Atlanta, GA 30338
770-458-4080
kvankampen@cepworldwide.com

JOE WILLMORE
President
Willmore Consulting Group
5007 Mignonette Court
Annandale, VA 22003
703-855-4634
willmore@juno.com

RON ZEMKE
President
Performance Research Associates
821 Marquette Avenue, Suite 1820
Minneapolis, MN 55402-2999
612-338-8523
pra@socksoff.com

SUSAN ZEMKE
Senior Consultant
Linkage, Inc.
8301 Golden Valley Road, Suite 270
Golden Valley, MN 55427
763-797-5226
763-797-5848 (fax)
szemke@linkage-inc.com

ABOUT THE EDITOR

Lorraine L. Ukens is the owner of Team-ing With Success, which specializes in team building and experiential learning. Her wide range of business experience has been applied in designing, facilitating, and evaluating programs in a variety of areas. An adjunct faculty member at Towson University in Maryland, Ukens is the author of several training books and games, including Getting Together: Icebreakers and Energizers, Working Together: 55 Team Games, All Together Now! A Seriously Fun Collection of Interactive Training Games and Activities, *and* Energize Your Audience: 75 Quick Activities That Get Them Started. . .and Keep Them Going. *She received her M.S. degree in human resource development from Towson University and is an active member of ASTD (formerly American Society for Training and Development).*

Name Index

A

Abernathy, D. J., 36
Alexander, L., 373
Allerton, H. E., 36
Andreadis, N. A., 363, 374
Arch, D., 237
Argyris, C., 105, 266
Arvey, R. D., 184
Atwater, L. E., 184

B

Baldwin, T. T., 162, 164, 173, 174
Bandura, A., 183
Barbazette, J., 375, 380–381
Barksdale, K., 380
Barron, T., 36
Bartol, K. M., 184
Bassi, L. J., 4, 12, 15, 20
Bates, A. W., 321, 322
Baytos, L. M., 337
Beard, M., 191, 196
Beatty, R. W., 183
Beckschi, P., 229
Beer, M., 240, 245
Belgard, W., 361
Bell, C. R., 388
Bellman, G., 15, 20
Benjamin, B., 53

Benson, G., 4, 12
Berge, Z. L., 316, 318, 320, 322, 323
Berlew, D. E., 343, 349
Bernardin, H. J., 183
Bernstein, B., 389
Biech, E., 69, 286, 291
Birnbaum, D., 184
Blanchard, K., 395, 404
Blank, W. E., 204, 208
Block, P., 12, 166, 173, 233
Bonwell, C., 257
Boothman, T., 162, 165, 174
Bowen, D., 184
Boyatzis, A., 193, 196
Brache, A. P., 106, 161, 162, 174
Braden, R., 194, 196
Branch, R., 192, 199
Brantner, T. M., 344, 350
Bray, D. W., 343–344, 349
Brechlin, J., 380
Brethower, D. M., 80, 373
Briggs, K. C., 204, 208
Briggs, L., 314
Brinkerhoff, R. O., 162, 165, 174, 363, 371, 373–374
Broad, M. L., 5, 12, 140, 157, 160, 162, 174, 175
Broadbent, B., 192, 196

Subject Index